A Hundred Years of
Family Welfare

A study of The Family Welfare Association
(formerly Charity Organisation Society)
1869–1969

By the same author

YOUTH AND LEISURE
VOLUNTARY SOCIETIES AND SOCIAL POLICY

MICHAEL JOSEPH BOOKS ON LIVE ISSUES

Series Editors: H. L. Beales, O. R. McGregor

A Hundred Years of Family Welfare

A Study of The Family Welfare Association
(Formerly Charity Organisation Society)
1869–1969

MADELINE ROOFF

LONDON
MICHAEL JOSEPH

First published in Great Britain by

MICHAEL JOSEPH LTD
52 Bedford Square
London, W.C.1
1972

Set and printed in Great Britain by
Unwin Brothers Limited at the Gresham Press, Woking,
in Imprint type, eleven-point leaded, and bound by
James Burn at Esher, Surrey

To the memory of
James and Mary Ann Rooff

Contents

A*

List of Diagrams

List of Tables

* Photostat of original

Acknowledgements

I gratefully acknowledge the grant from the Nuffield Foundation (Small Grants Scheme in the Social Sciences) which enabled me to prepare material for the publication of this book.

I am much indebted to the Goldsmiths Library, University of London, and to the library of The National Institute for Social Work Training for allowing me to have some F.W.A. documents on long loan, and to the librarian of the Greater London Council for giving me access to the Archives.

I could not have carried through the task of examining the material amassed by the Family Welfare Association in the course of one hundred years without the co-operation of the F.W.A. itself. Mr Astbury was the first secretary to welcome the plan for a history and to give me free access to all documents. After his retirement he enabled me to complete the biographical section by answering questions about his early life; Mr Durham and Mr Burt in turn gave me full support, the latter reading the entire manuscript before his resignation.

From time to time I have had valuable help in collecting documentary evidence and I should like to thank Miss Millard, Miss Chambers, Miss Tracy and Dr Cynthia White. The latter also drew Diagram 6 and made some interesting suggestions, particularly for the section on the volunteers. I owe a special debt to Miss Flynn and to Miss Lonsdale who, at different periods, helped me to discover minute books and other material stacked on dusty shelves or in dark cupboards of the basement.

I was fortunate in being able to discuss policy with some of the older members of the F.W.A. and I am especially grateful to Miss Crosse and Miss Hugh-Smith who followed up interviews by sending most useful notes. It would be difficult to mention all the family caseworkers who helped me by discussion and by correspondence but I would particularly like to thank Miss Renall, Miss H. Morris and Mrs Torr who saw the changeover from C.O.S. to F.W.A., and Miss Luce who went on from wide experience with the Association to work for International Social Service. I have been much helped by several members of the Association who left for other spheres of work, particularly Mrs Enid Balint (formerly Eichholz), Mrs Pincus and Miss Boselli.

Of those who were involved in the changes since the Cunliffe Report I am indebted to Miss Daniel, casework consultant, and Mr Ford who gave generously of their time and kept me up to date with recent developments. Miss Daniel also read and commented upon the section on casework in its first draft. Mrs Welldon of Area IV followed up a very helpful interview by sending information and comments. Mrs Ann Hawkins, C.A.B. Officer, also gave unstinting help, reading the relevant section of the manuscript and arranging for her colleague, Mrs Heathcote, to prepare some C.A.B. statistics and diagrams. All the Central officers were most co-operative and I should like to thank Miss Twentyman, National Casework Secretary, and Miss Collins, Honorary Pensions Secretary, for so readily answering my questions. I owe a special debt to the late Mr Blunden, Assistant Honorary Treasurer, who discussed the financial aspects of the study and prepared the interesting Table 6. He and Mr Burt were particularly helpful in throwing light on recent administration.

My contact with members of Social Science Departments of Universities gave me opportunities to discuss the education and training of students and related questions. I was fortunate in the early stages of the study to have interviews with Dr Gertrude Willoughby, Miss Muriel Cuncliffe and Dame Eileen Younghusband. Dame Eileen continued to give me encouragement from time to time and put me greatly in her debt by reading a substantial portion of the manuscript.

Others who gave generously of their time to read and comment upon sections of the manuscript included the late Professor Charles Loch Mowat, who also lent me some family papers relating to Loch and Pringle, Mrs Barbara Shenfield, Mr R. Huws Jones, Miss Robina Addis, and Mrs Margaret Godfrey. Professor Ilersic kindly checked some of the graphs and diagrams. I found the various comments and criticisms challenging and stimulating but I accept full responsibility for the use I have made of the material and for the views expressed.

Finally, I am glad to be able to pay tribute to my friends who, since my retirement from Bedford College, have done so much to support me in the last stages of collating the material and writing the book. In particular I acknowledge most gratefully the help of Miss Dorothy Trollope, who read and commented on each section of typescript as it was received, and of Miss Margaret Pugh, who gave me hospitality during an extremely difficult period and also read some sections of the manuscript. I should like, too, to record the intelligent help I received from Miss J. Mills who deciphered my handwriting and typed the first draft of the manuscript.

MADELINE ROOFF

The author also thanks the following for permission to quote from their publications: George Allen & Unwin, Ltd., for material from *Voluntary Action* by Lord Beveridge, *The Social Servant in the Making* by Elizabeth Macadam, *In a World I Never Made* by Barbara Wootton; G. Bell & Sons, Ltd., for material from *The Social Worker* by C. R. Attlee; Constable & Co. Ltd., for material from *My Life* by George Lansbury; J. M. Dent & Sons, Ltd., for material from *Men, Movements and Myself* by Lord Snell; The Fabian Society, for material from *The Case against the Charity Organisation Society*, Fabian Tract No. 158, by Mrs Townshend; The Greater London Council, for material from The Report of the L.C.C. P.A.C. of December, 1932; Harvard University Press, Belknap Press, for material from *English Philanthropy* by David Owen; Her Majesty's Stationery Office, for material from *Problems of Social Policy* by R. M. Titmuss; The London School of Economics and Political Science, for material from *My Apprenticeship* by Beatrice Webb; Macmillan & Co. Ltd., for material from *The Strength of the People* by Helen Bosanquet; Methuen & Co. Ltd., for material from *The Charity Organisation Society* by C. L. Mowatt; The Metropolitan Visiting and Relief Association, for material from *Social Work of the London Churches* by J. C. Pringle; John Murray, Ltd., for material from *Social Work in London* by Helen Bosanquet; The

National Institute for Social Work Training, Bedford Square Press, for material from *Welfare in the Community* by E. M. Goldberg; Routledge and Kegan Paul, Ltd., for material from *The West Indian comes to England* edited by S. K. Ruck, *Social Casework* by Noel Timms.

Summary of the Functions of the Family Welfare Association in the Centenary Year

To provide a family casework service in order to assist persons in distress towards a solution of family difficulties.

To help those who are unable to take advantage of the resources provided by the community and who are in difficulties, either through their own or Society's limitations, and to assist them to take their place as useful citizens.

To initiate and conduct research in social problems particularly affecting family life.

To undertake pioneer work in the field of social service and, where necessary, to initiate new services.

To provide practical training in family casework for students from Universities and other specialised training organisations.

To maintain a Citizens Advice Bureau service in Central London.

To provide an Information Service to advise about the status, work and resources of charitable organisations.

The Association acts as agent for other voluntary societies and administers several Trust Funds.

Charities Digest, 1969

Introduction

There is today considerable public interest in problems of family welfare, reflected in B.B.C. radio and television programmes and in many articles, both serious and popular, in the Press. Less widely known is the 'Social Work in Action'* of a pioneer Association which has recently celebrated a hundred years of family social work.

In the following study of the development of the Family Welfare Association I have tried to show not only what the Association did, and how they did it, but what conceptions, philosophical, economic and social, underlay the structure. I have also tried to show how the social, political and economic changes of the century influenced the attitudes and methods of the Association and how two world wars affected its development in the modern era.

For nearly three-quarters of its history the Association was influenced by the beliefs and attitudes current at the time of its foundation. These were made explicit in the principles and practice of its outstanding Secretary, C. S. Loch. Loch was the representative of 'the widely diffused beliefs of the educated classes of the Victorian era'. For this reason I have given a prominent place to the biography of Loch (Chapter 2).

A federation of District Committees was characteristic of the structure of the Association from its foundation, and as family social work was done by the Districts and as variation between the Districts has been one of the interesting features of development within the Association, a considerable section of the study is devoted to the Districts.

* The title of a popular radio serial broadcast.

Family casework has been an integral part of the Association's work and I have given examples throughout the study. I have also selected some for separate consideration to illustrate the Association's changing attitude to this part of its function—to see what problems it thought 'typical' at various periods and how family social workers saw their role (Chapter 13 and Appendix).

For much of the time family social work was done by voluntary workers; until the 1950s it was the volunteers who manned the committees and carried out the duties of Honorary Treasurer, etc., even after salaried secretaries had been appointed in all the Districts. It was the voluntary workers who for many years practised the principles of charity accepted by the Association. Today we are again noting the contribution to be made by volunteers to community service. I have, therefore, made a special study of the volunteers* (Chapter 14).

The Association prided itself on its administration. Its forms and procedures became models for development in other agencies, both public and private. Its records and documents were scrupulously kept. Recent changes in administration pointed the way to developments which should be of general interest in the field of family social service. Much of the administrative material is contained in the study of 'Central' and of the Districts but the subject has special features which are discussed separately (Chapter 11).

Some parts of the Association's work are given detailed consideration, for example, those which have made a substantial contribution to the social services in this country. The outstanding example is the pioneer work of the Standing Medical Committee and the practice of the District Committees in relating health and social conditions (Chapters 4, 5, 8 and 10). Another pioneer venture with far-reaching consequences is described under 'Education and Training' (Chapter 12). Various projects and special services include the Advisory Services (Citizens Advice Bureaux and Family Discussion Bureau), Problem Families, The Family: Patients or Clients, The West Indian Comes to England and The Family Centre (Chapter 10).

Earlier histories of the Family Welfare Association have ended

---

* A sample of one in five of all the annual reports of 'Central' and of the Districts was examined, supplemented by reference to the Association's journals. Notices were read of volunteers who had resigned or who had died after very long service.

with the resignation of Charles Loch and the outbreak of the First World War. I have therefore examined the documentary evidence since the First World War with special care, particularly to see whether the generally held view that the period 1918–39 was one of stagnation was justified (Chapters 7 and 8).

The Second World War and the post-war social and economic changes ushered in a new era and established new conceptions of public and private responsibility. The changes already at work within the Society were now openly recognised. In 1946 the Association acquired a new name,* more in keeping with established practice and with the new social theory (Chapter 9).

I have also given a special section to criticisms of the Charity Organisation Society since the hostility aroused in the pioneer period had considerable influence on the early history of the Association (Chapter 16).

Some reflections on the contribution of the Association during a century of family social work will be found in the Conclusion.

---

* The Charity Organisation Society was renamed Family Welfare Association in 1946.

Part I

THE PIONEER PERIOD

CHAPTER ONE

Foundations

1. *Influence of Ideas and Events*

The Family Welfare Association, formerly the Charity Organisation Society, celebrated its Centenary in 1969. Although mainly a London Society, its early influence spread rapidly to wider fields. It forged close links with existing kindred societies, and helped to establish other similar organisations in many parts of the British Isles. Its principles and practice, transplanted overseas,* particularly to North America and Australia, took root and spread vigorously, to be brought back later to give new life to the country of origin. Few societies have inspired such devotion; few have roused such bitter hostility.

Its history covers a hundred years of vital change in the economic, social and political life of Great Britain. Since the Society was concerned with family welfare its ability to adjust to changing needs has been a condition of its development. One of the paradoxes of its history is the tenacity with which it held to an out-dated social theory while its family social workers showed awareness of the changing environment, and identified and met new needs. The history of the F.W.A. is characterised by contrasts and apparent contradictions, which can only be understood in relation to the interplay of ideas and events at various periods of its development.

When the Charity Organisation Society was founded in 1869, in spite of some recent disquiet,† the country was in an optimistic mood. There had been a long period free from war; the export trade was expanding rapidly; in general, industries at home were

---

* For an interesting study of these developments, see Kathleen Woodroofe's *From Charity to Social Work*.

† E.g. the effect of the American Civil War on the Lancashire cotton industry and the increasing cost of relief to 'paupers'.

flourishing; population was increasing; London had become the financial centre of Europe and agriculture benefited from the general prosperity; the new railways encouraged wider distribution of food and other goods. Real wages had risen, and many of the artisans shared the greater security which membership of Friendly Societies and Trade Unions had brought. Political reform had widened the franchise to include a proportion of urban workers. It was the age of 'Progress'.

It was widely assumed by philanthropists that social distress was on its way out, to be finally overcome 'by strengthening the moral fibre of the nation'. Old age, sickness or unemployment could be provided for by sufficient forethought in times of prosperity. Unforeseeable distress could be met by charity; destitution must be dealt with by a reformed Poor Law.

Few had sufficient knowledge or imagination to appreciate the plight of those who lived a precarious existence on a low and uncertain weekly wage. (Seasonal trades or casual work left little margin for union or thrift club payments.) Unemployment, sickness or accident might plunge them and their families into dire poverty. There was no provision for social security, apart from the dreaded Poor Law.* Such families were particularly vulnerable in parts of London where the new Metropolitan Railway and the widening of roads left them homeless.† No one yet knew the full extent of poverty, for the first volume of Booth's great survey was not published until 1892.

Yet few could ignore the beggars of the London streets: parents with ragged, barefoot children, cripples and others exhibiting their sores for alms, importunate crossing sweepers who were not above using threats, or tramps who were said to converge on London as the wealthy came into residence. In the mid-nineteenth century, Henry Mayhew had given a vivid account of the street beggars, the thieves and the prostitutes, as well as of the many street sellers, in his four volumes *London Labour and the London*

* Outdoor relief was seldom available for the able-bodied unemployed; others received insufficient for basic needs. Although there was some improvement after the passage of the Metropolitan Poor Act, 1867, in infirmaries and asylums in London, workhouses were so repellent that only the desperate sought admission.

† In this connection the Charity Organisation Society was to investigate the possibility of sending displaced Londoners to the industrial North where the cotton trade seemed to offer better openings (see pp 71 and 85).

Poor.* A collection of social facts was contained in the reports of the Royal Commissions of the eighteenth and nineteenth centuries† and these were widely quoted in serious journals. There was also a large reading public for the 'novels with a purpose' of Mrs Gaskell, Charlotte Brontë, Benjamin Disraeli and Charles Dickens. The Christian Socialist writers, F. D. Maurice and Charles Kingsley aroused considerable interest as they gave practical illustration of the relation between faith and works.

Although, as Engels[1] noted with some bitterness, 'the happier classes' lived in a separate territory, preserved from contact with the workers' quarters, there were signs of a developing social conscience. Later observers preferred to describe it as a sense of guilt. There were some who were moved to take action by fear: for them there was little to distinguish the very poor from the rogues and criminals—'the dangerous classes'. Many motives led men and women to take part in a wide variety of charitable work.

Philanthropists were upheld by the optimism of economists and political theorists. As Alfred Marshall said later, in evidence to the Royal Commission on the Aged Poor, 'I regard all this problem of poverty as a mere passing evil in the progress of man upwards'.[2]

To assist such upward progress the pioneers of the Charity Organisation Society saw two urgent needs: that self-respecting families who were struggling to keep themselves from destitution should be helped and encouraged, and that charities should be organised and co-ordinated, so that the best use could be made of available resources. Conversely, begging should be repressed and indiscriminate almsgiving strongly discouraged. Parallel with such constructive and preventive activities by charity should go a reformed Poor Law administration which would give adequate assistance, instead of the miserable pittance which barely kept the destitute from starvation.‡

In the nineteenth century the C.O.S. was essentially an upper

---

* Earlier still, in 1797, F. M. Eden had published *The State of the Poor*.

† The C.O.S., under Loch, appreciated the value of 'Blue Books' as it built up its fine collection of Parliamentary Papers. F. A. Hayeck has recently questioned whether the nineteenth century Reports of Royal Commissions were not biased (cf. 'Capitalism and the Historian').

‡ From time to time Coroners' Courts were reporting deaths from starvation, even though outdoor relief had been given.

middle class foundation—with eminent men from the medical, legal and business worlds prepared to give considerable service in time and money to put the new organisation on a sound basis. Its appeal was sufficiently in line with the traditional development of philanthropy to attract many of the well-to-do leisured class to give voluntary service. In many London parishes it had the strong support of the clergy. The appeal was also attractive in new ways, since the Society claimed to be in line with the scientific spirit of the age. On the one hand men were invited to enter upon a crusade for the betterment of society; on the other, they were encouraged to take part in a movement to make benevolence scientific. They were to be pioneers of a new philanthropy. The C.O.S. could also make its appeal to the practical members of the middle class who were aware of some of the evils arising from poverty. Charity, properly administered, was not only benevolent, it was an insurance for the well-being of the community.

Another of the social problems of special concern to charitable persons was the apparent widening of the gulf between rich and poor. Sir Charles Trevelyan, a staunch supporter of the C.O.S., was asking how 'to close this gulf and to bring back the rich into such close relations with the poor as cannot fail to have a civilising and healing influence, and to knit all classes together in the bonds of mutual help and goodwill'.[3] He saw the Charity Organisation Society, with its system of 'personal visitation' as helping the middle and upper classes to understand 'the real evil and danger of the existing state of things', through being brought into close contact with the poor. The class structure as such was not questioned.

Amongst the outstanding evils and dangers, as Trevelyan and his fellow members saw them, were the increasing number of paupers[*][4] and beggars. The 'unemployed poor' raised problems so great that the pioneers felt bound to exclude them from their schemes.[†] 'Poverty' was not the immediate concern of the C.O.S.; 'pauperisation' was. The Society was actively hostile not only to 'the lax administration of the Poor Law', but also to the indiscrimi-

* In fact, the rate of pauperism in London was declining: the absolute numbers were increasing with the growth of population.

† A proposal to find employment for labourers and to reform the rough and criminal classes by getting them to work on waste lands was included in one of the earlier plans—but was dropped as being impracticable.

nate doles of many charitable bodies; both, they held, 'pauperised' the recipient of relief.

Londoners could appreciate the emphasis of the C.O.S. on the 'repression of mendicity'. There was also considerable sympathy from those reared on Samuel Smiles with the C.O.S. insistence on self-help.* 'Character' was the spring-board for sound charitable effort. Above all, the C.O.S. was able to make a strong case for the need to bring some order into the numerous overlapping charities. Few societies knew what the others were doing, or who was being helped. Some applicants might be 'going the rounds', while others, 'the deserving', went unassisted. The declared aim of the C.O.S. was so to organise charity that the condition of the poor would be permanently improved: worthy families in temporary distress would be assisted to become independent, self-respecting citizens. The Society firmly believed, and frequently asserted, that their methods of enquiry and assistance went to the root of the problem: they were dealing with *causes*, not with symptoms. So far as they went, their investigation was thorough. Unfortunately, their analysis did not go far enough.†[5] The widely accepted postulates of the existing urban industrial society remained unchallenged.

The persistence with which the Charity Organisation Society held to its original social theory can only be understood in relation to the age in which it was founded: an age when the new economic and social forces of a growing urban industrial society were imperfectly recognised and often misunderstood. The theories of the Classical Economists and of the Individualists were widely accepted in the 1860s. The ideas of Bentham, J. S. Mill and Malthus had strongly influenced thought in the nineteenth century.‡[6] The severity of the Protestant ethic underlay the work of many philanthropists while the warmth of Evangelicalism guided the practice of many others. At the same time scepticism was widespread amongst the intellectuals. Darwin's *Origin of Species*, 1859, and the publication of *Essays and Reviews*, 1860,

* Samuel Smiles's *Self Help* was first published in 1859 and ran into many editions.

† They were not alone in this. As Clapham has pointed out, when Henry Fawcett wrote, in 1871, *Pauperism and its Causes*, unemployment was ignored as a cause.

‡ C. S. Loch put the influence of F. D. Maurice and of J. S. Mill high on the list of thinkers who helped shape the Society.

had led to questioning in many traditional strongholds. While Herbert Spencer taught a new dogmatic sociology, the 'social scientists' were rousing considerable public interest in practical issues. The Social Science Association was a comparative newcomer (1857–86); its discussions and *Transactions* did not reach the high level of its models,* but they gave the opportunity for a more widespread consideration of social questions.

In 1868 two outstanding questions were considered, in papers at the Society of Arts, which helped to precipitate the Charity Organisation Society. These were *How to Deal with the Unemployed Poor of London and with its Roughs and Criminal Classes*, by Henry Solly,[7] and *Charities of London and Some Errors of their Administration*, by Dr Hawksley.† Both writers were founder-members of the C.O.S. Henry Solly, at that time a unitarian minister, acted for a few months as the first honorary secretary (he was an engaging and energetic philanthropist with wide interests, particularly in Working Men's Clubs).‡ There were other pioneer philanthropists who, about the same time, submitted plans and brought considerable practical experience to the cause of 'improving the condition of the poor in London'. Among these was G. M. Hicks who drew up one of the early schemes outlining the structure and function of a new society similar to that ultimately accepted. He was already experienced as an Almoner of the Society for the Relief of Distress and became one of the first Honorary Secretaries of the C.O.S. Another distinguished S.R.D. Almoner whose work and writing had considerable influence on the early counsels of the founder members was Edward Denison, § who gave his name to the later headquarters of the Society.

The Charity Organisation Society was the product of the interplay of ideas and practice whose sources were so varied that later writers had some difficulty in deciding who were the founder-

* I.e. the British Association and the Royal Statistical Society, which were well-established.

† Dr Hawksley, a physician and writer on various social questions, read his paper to the Association for the Prevention of Pauperism and Crime in December 1868.

‡ Solly's writings, in addition to the paper mentioned in the text, included *The Destitute Poor*, 1868; *Working Men*, 1870; *These Eighty Years*, 1893.

§ Edward Denison, 1840–70, was the son of the Bishop of Salisbury and nephew of the Speaker of the House of Commons. His work in Stepney, his enquiries on the Continent, and his letters and articles gave inspiration to the founders. Pringle referred to him as 'Our Patron Saint'.

FOUNDATIONS   29

members.* Lord Lichfield, who was invited to lead the new
organisation, did much to save it from being wrecked by the
multiplicity of schemes put forward at the various preliminary
meetings. On 29th April, 1869, the new Society's function was
finally limited to 'Organising Charitable Relief and Repressing
Mendicity', which gave it its first title. The following year a short
title, 'The Charity Organisation Society', was agreed upon.†

The C.O.S. was by no means the first in the field of family
social work, although it was to make a special contribution.
Liverpool had set up its Central Relief Society in 1863 under the
influence of the pioneer, William Rathbone.[8] The Jewish Board
of Guardians had been founded in 1859.[9] Many 'Visiting Societies'
had a long history of social work with families; the Metropolitan
Visiting and Relief Association was established in 1843.‡[10] Earlier
still, Thomas Bernard had founded The Society for Bettering the
Conditions and Increasing the Comfort of the Poor.§ Evangelicals,
attached to churches of many denominations, had engaged in a
variety of charitable work which pointed the way to family social
work.[12] Scotland had been famous for the work of Thomas
Chalmers in Glasgow, 1819–23, while Edinburgh had established
its own scheme. Germany, too, had its 'Elberfeld Scheme', in
1857, which had much in common with Chalmers' system and
became well known in England.

It is questionable how far the C.O.S. pioneers based their
principles and practice directly on any one of these. Loch, for
example, was to doubt the immediate influence of Chalmers on

* When C. B. P. Bosanquet, the first appointed Secretary, wrote a pamphlet,
in 1874, entitled *The History and Mode of Operation of the Charity Organisation
Society*, he was challenged by Thomas Hawksley. This account, in turn, was
objected to by W. M. Wilkinson and G. M. Hicks in 1875. A reasoned discussion of the various papers was published by E. C. Price in the Charity
Organisation *Review* (Oct.–Nov. 1892). See Chapter I (2) following.

† On 9th April, 1870, it was resolved to adopt the short title. The longer
descriptive title was retained for more formal purposes until 1910, when it was
changed to 'The Society for Organising Charity and Improving the Condition
of the Poor'. The C.O.S. became 'The Family Welfare Association' in 1946.

‡ Its full title was 'The Association for Promoting the Relief of Destitution
in the Metropolis, and for Improving the Condition of the Poor, by means of
Parochial and District Visiting under the superintendence and direction of the
Bishops and Clergy, through the Agency of Unpaid Visitors, and without
reference to religious persuasion'.

§ Thomas Bernard, in 1796, had called upon philanthropists 'to make
inquiry into all that concerns the poor and the promotion of their happiness a
science'.

Society for Organising Charitable Relief and Repressing Mendicity.

Central Office—15, BUCKINGHAM STREET, STRAND, W.C.

PRESIDENT—THE LORD BISHOP OF LONDON.
CHAIRMAN OF EXECUTIVE COUNCIL—THE EARL OF LICHFIELD.

N.B.—No applications for Relief can be received at the Central Office.

ROUGH SKETCH OF PROPOSED PLAN.

A CHARITY OFFICE is intended to be established, where practicable, near to each Poor-Law Relieving Office throughout the Metropolis, under the management of the Committee of Charity of each Parish or District ; and a Charity Agent will be appointed, who will be in direct communication with the Relieving Officer, the Local Charities, the Police, the Clergy and Ministers, and the District Visitors. Every case, on presentation of a Ticket (as below), will be carefully inquired into, and referred to the appropriate channels of relief, or otherwise properly dealt with.

Confirmed Beggars and Vagrants will be sent to the Poor-Law Guardians, or prosecuted before the Magistrate, as circumstances demand.

The Charity Agent will thus be to his Committee what the Poor-Law Relieving Officer is to the Board of Guardians, and will be specially charged to compile and keep up such a Register of cases relieved by the several Charities as devised by this Society, and recommended by the Poor-Law Minute of 20th Nov., 1869; the Register to be accessible to all persons interested in the efficient Relief of the Poor, whether through legal or voluntary agencies.

With respect to the expenses of organisation in the poorest Districts, the Council hopes to be enabled to supplement local efforts made for the purpose either out of its own general funds or through the liberality of the richer Districts in Union with it.

The Public are, therefore, earnestly requested not, under any circumstances, to give direct relief to applicants in the streets, but to offer them the Tickets provided by the District Committees. For street-begging cases, a few of these Tickets should always be carried by each member of a household.

District Tickets given to persons not resident in the District named on the Ticket will, by arrangement with the several Committees, be recognised and attended to at the Office of the District in which such persons reside.

Apart, however, from the use of the machinery above, the personal services of a large number of willing Agents, acting through existing Societies, or in direct communication with the several District Committees, so as to ensure a complete visitation of the Poor in the Metropolis, must be secured for the complete organisation of Relief contemplated by the Society.

The Plan and Rules of the Committees, as now adopted in several Districts, with other information, may be had at the Central Office of the Society.

Subscriptions and Donations towards the expenses of the necessary General Organisation may be paid to the Society's Bankers, Messrs. COUTTS & Co., Strand ; or at the Office, 15 Buckingham Street, W.C.

C. B. P. BOSANQUET,
ALSAGER HAY HILL, } *Hon. Secs.*
GEORGE M. HICKS,

C. J. RIBTON-TURNER, *Organising Secretary (pro. tem.)*

COMMITTEE	COMMITTEE
FOR ORGANISING CHARITABLE RELIEF AND REPRESSING MENDICITY.	FOR ORGANISING CHARITABLE RELIEF AND REPRESSING MENDICITY.
This Ticket to be presented at	This Ticket to be presented at
Where the case will be carefully inquired into and properly dealt with.	Where the case will be carefully inquired into and properly dealt with.
Hours, 10 to 12, and 4 to 5, Sundays excepted.	Hours, 10 to 12, and 4 to 5, Sundays excepted.

N.B.—Mr. RIBTON-TURNER will at all times be happy to give the benefit of his experience to the representatives of any Committees, established or in course of formation, on the Plan of the Society.

TABLE I

the early development of the C.O.S.* but such ideas were certainly 'in the air' in mid-Victorian England. Some organisations were more immediately involved; for example the system of mendicity tickets and local subscriptions, introduced by the Reverend Martyn Hart in Blackheath, was incorporated in early C.O.S. practice. The Society studied the loan scheme of the Jewish Board of Guardians and adopted it as a valuable method in helping families to preserve their independence. Visitors of the Society for the Relief of Distress worked closely with the C.O.S. District Committees, and new C.O.S. volunteers were often sent round with an S.R.D. almoner to gain experience.

The C.O.S. distinguished itself as a propagandist body from the outset. It enlisted the support of many eminent public men and received the backing of a number of journalists.† The Archbishop of Canterbury and the Bishop of London, Cardinal Manning, Gladstone, Sir Charles Trevelyan, Ruskin and Octavia Hill were among its early supporters.‡ *The Times* and a number of journals were ready to publish letters and articles and meetings were widely reported. Lord Lichfield, who became the first Chairman, met the expenses of the Society's headquarters in Buckingham Street, Adelphi, and seconded his private secretary, Ribton-Turner, to furnish it and to get it started.§ This remained the Central Office until 1905 when the Society moved to its quarters at Denison House, Vauxhall Bridge Road.

In 1870, C. B. P. Bosanquet, a barrister and landowner, halfbrother to the philosopher Bernard, became the first paid Secretary, with Ribton-Turner as organising secretary. They undertook, with tremendous energy, the task summed up by Lord Lichfield

* It should be noted that C. B. P. Bosanquet was steeped in Chalmers' work, as his own work *London: Its Growth, Charitable Agencies, and Wants*, 1868, testified. The C.O.S. also, in 1870, issued a list of recommended books which included Chalmers' *Christian and Civil Economy of Large Towns*, and lectures issued by the Chalmers Association, together with a biography of Chalmers.

† Joseph Dare was one such journalist who submitted an early plan or 'prospectus' for consideration.

‡ Ruskin gave considerable financial help at a time of crisis in the Society's affairs.

§ Ribton-Turner was one of the four honorary secretaries who served the Society during the first year (with the aid of two successive paid assistants, both of whom proved unsatisfactory). The others were G. M. Hicks, Hay-Hill and C. B. Bosanquet. Salaries for a Secretary and an Organising Secretary were introduced in the second year.

as, 'the plan for organising charitable relief through district committees co-operating with the Poor Law. . . . On this alone there was work enough for any society. We all agreed that such a society, once established, would soon obtain sufficient influence to deal with many of the urgent questions affecting the condition of the poorer classes of London'.[13]

Within a year the C.O.S. had opened District Offices in some twelve Poor Law Districts; by 1872 there were thirty-six offices. St Marylebone, the first to be established, with Lord Lichfield as Chairman, and with strong local support, was able to achieve a considerable measure of organisation. It had amongst its members Octavia Hill, already well known in the field of housing, and some of her band of helpers, experienced in practising the ideas of charity which were later to be developed as casework. Many others were not so successful in winning the confidence of the local charitable societies or of enlisting the co-operation of Poor Law officials. Loch was later to reflect that District Committees had been set up too hastily, a few of them doing such indifferent work as to discredit the Society.* The C.O.S. certainly aroused considerable hostility in some quarters, both on account of its methods of investigation and of its social theory. It became, under C. S. Loch, one of the most criticised, as well as one of the most admired, of English charitable organisations.†

The Society had considerable success in bringing together in a coherent scheme, methods of charitable work which it systematically documented and publicised. By the time Bosanquet resigned in 1875,‡ the District Committee system had been firmly established: so had the administrative pattern of the Districts' relationship with Central on the one hand and with the statutory and voluntary bodies in their own areas on the other.

It remained for Bosanquet's successor to work out more fully the principles and practice which were to guide the Society into the twentieth century. Loch's tenure of office was so long and distinguished that later writers have even referred to him as 'the Founder of the C.O.S.'[14] As his secretaryship coincided with the

* Lord Lichfield gave up the Chairmanship of the Society because he disagreed with the policy of covering London rapidly with District Offices. He remained as Chairman of St Marylebone District Committee.

† See Chapter 16.

‡ He left to administer his estate in Northumberland.

years of the Society's greatest influence we must look in some detail at his life and character.

2. Summary of Preliminary Meetings and of Early Papers

1. Several preliminary meetings were held in 1868 at which papers were read—especially that of Mr Solly and Dr Hawksley—resulting in the formation of an 'Association for the Prevention of Pauperism and Crime'. Its objects were wide-ranging, including practical measures such as the Use of Waste Land.

2. Conferences of Charities called—not as widely attended as was hoped, e.g. for one in February 1869, 1,251 invitations were issued, 378 cards of admission applied for. After a meeting in March, when prospectuses were sent out, there were only two responses from Charities.

3. *February 1869.* Lord Lichfield was persuaded to join 'if large objects' (including 'Waste Land Scheme') were abandoned.

4. *March 9th.* Decision to create a separate society,* Lord Lichfield and others guaranteeing funds for three years. Members of the Association formed the nucleus of the new Society.

5. *March 18th.* (Lord Lichfield in the Chair), Hawksley, Solly and Wilkinson present. Resolution to merge Council and Executive Committee in an Executive Council with full powers to carry out the objects of the Association, and to restrict the Society to secure Mutual Co-operation between the various Charities. (Move to Buckingham Street at about this time.)

6. *April 29th.* Approval of Change of Name to 'Society for Organising Charitable Relief and Repressing Mendicity'.

* Some confusion arose as the last recorded entry in the Minute Book of the Association for the Prevention of Pauperism and Crime was that of the change of name. But two more short meetings under the old title were recorded in the new Minute Book, the first dealing with irregularities by its only paid officer and the second recording the appointment of an Hon. Treasurer. Captain F. A. Maxse was in the Chair on 25th April, 1869, when the first Hon. Treasurer (General Cavanagh) was appointed. H. Solly had been Secretary for the early foundation meetings. He resigned as Secretary on 1st March, 1869, but remained a member of the Committee. Ribton-Turner became Assistant Hon. Secretary 18th March, 1869, and Organising Secretary in December 1869. C. B. P. Bosanquet joined as Hon. Secretary in April 1870 and was appointed Secretary in July 1870.

B

7. *May 13th.* Date on which Wilkinson's plan and prospectus adopted with few alterations. (He had acknowledged his debt to Hawksley and others.)

A volume, lately re-discovered, in the F.W.A. Library, entitled *Origins of the C.O.S.*, contained seven papers whose dates, titles and authors are listed below. Three of the writers claimed to be the pioneer founder, namely Thomas Hawksley, W. M. Wilkinson and G. M. Hicks. The volume also has newspaper cuttings of a later date, particularly an interesting letter from Henry Solly to *The Times* in September 1897 (when he was 84). Solly writes: 'So many men eminent for their philanthropy and position were concerned in the genesis and development of the great and useful society above named' (the C.O.S.). He then adds several more names to those of the three claimants above and draws special attention to the journalist, Mr Dare. Solly refers to the History of the London C.O.S. drawn up by Mr Price and published in the 94th number of the *Charity Organisation Review* (October and November 1892). With the exception of the insufficient acknowledgment given to Mr Dare he considers this a full and perfectly accurate résumé of all that took place.

The seven papers are as follows:

1. Hawksley, Thomas. 'The Charities of London and some Errors of their Administration: with suggestions for an Improved System of Relief', 1869.

2. Bosanquet, C. B. P. 'The History and Mode of Operation of the Charity Organisation Society', 1874.

3. Hawksley, Thomas. 'Objections to "The History" of the Society published by the Authority of Council', 1874.

4. Wilkinson, W. M. 'A Contribution towards the History of the origin of the Charity Organisation Society', 1875.

5. Hicks, G. M. 'A Contribution towards the History of the Origin of the Charity Organisation Society, with Suggestions on the Reports, Balance Sheets and Audit of Accounts', 1875.

6. 'Philanthropic Tailoring and Historical Cobbling', 1875.

7. 'The C.O.S. Its Objects and Modes of Operation', 7th ed. 1875.

CHAPTER TWO

Charles Stewart Loch

Secretary, Charity Organisation Society, 1875–1914

When C. S. Loch died in 1923 a *Times* notice read, 'He made the C.O.S.; he was the C.O.S.'[1] This would seem to be an exaggeration when we know that the Charity Organisation Society had been in existence for six years, with its main structure already established, when Loch was appointed in 1875. There was, however, a large element of truth in the claim. His appointment was looked upon as a 'victory for the broader party . . . upon him mainly fell the responsible task of giving it a shape and a direction'.[2] Loch himself was in no doubt about his role. Within a short time he is writing in his diary: 'a policy is wanted in the society'; he analyses the weaknesses, and lists the requirements, with the forceful comment: 'these things are what I must get and I must get them in this order'.[3] Before the century ended, Loch had become identified with the C.O.S. and the Society was a well-known social institution. As *The Times* reported, in the same obituary notice, 'Loch of the C.O.S. was a household word among workers for the poor and public administrators'.

After a serious illness in 1913 Loch was no longer able to take a direct part, but his influence continued to pervade the Society. In the 1930s a distinguished speaker from the Vienna School of Social Work was proclaiming: 'his ideas are as up-to-date and useful now as when he uttered them'.[4]

This was no isolated sentiment. Generations of students were introduced to the C.O.S. *Handbook** with its special section on 'Principles and Methods of Charity' by C. S. Loch. In the

---

* The *Handbook* appeared under various titles between 1882 and the late 1930s, viz *How to Help Cases of Distress* and *The Prevention and Relief of Distress*. Its later title was *Guide to the Social Services*.

thirty-fifth edition of 1936 the editors announced that although the chapter had lost none of its intrinsic value the phrasing was sometimes puzzling to students. They added: 'The Society hopes to have this classical document modernised but not bowdlerised in time for the thirty-sixth edition'. About the same time Loch's successor prepared 'A memorandum of Reasons adduced by Members of the Charity Organisation Society to Make the Writings of the late Charles Stewart Loch more available to Students than they are at present.'* Pringle reported that pressure had come from both sides of the Atlantic for republication of Loch's works.

To understand the development of the C.O.S. it is necessary to understand C. S. Loch. What kind of a person was he? What circumstances brought him forward as the avowed leader of a new charity organisation? The main events of his life are well documented.†

The Lochs came of a professional family in Edinburgh and Charles Stewart was in due course to be sent to school in Scotland.‡ His father, at first in the service of the East India Company, became Judge of the High Court on its creation in 1862. Charles Stewart was born in 1849 in Bengal but, as his mother died at his birth, he was brought up in England by friends of the family. He was never robust and his intermittent bouts of asthma hampered him more than was generally known.§ It was the cause of his late graduation from Oxford with results which did not reflect his real ability. Oxford had, however, contributed very largely to his development. He went up to Balliol in 1869, the year of the foundation of the Society with which he was later to be identified. Jowett became Master the following year but T. H. Green, his tutor, seems to have had the more immediate influence. A large part was also played by his friends, all of them destined to make their mark in academic or public life. They included

* I am indebted to the late Professor Charles Loch Mowat for the loan of a number of papers in the possession of his family, of which this memorandum was one.

† E.g. in the study of the Charity Organisation Society 1869–1913 by his grandson, C. L. Mowat, who had access to family papers. I have found Loch's own writings, particularly his *Diary*, a valuable source.

‡ He went with his brother to Glenalmond, Perthshire.

§ His *Diary* later reveals how much he felt this handicap, e.g. an entry on 13th September, 1880: 'It is hard to substitute intensity of will for physical strength.'

Bernard Bosanquet,* A. C. Bradley, A. L. Smith and F. H. Peters, whose sister, Sophia Emma, he was to marry. After some hesitation, Loch decided against entering the Church. He could not join the Indian Civil Service, on medical grounds. He might read for the Bar.† Meanwhile he accepted a post as Clerk to the Royal College of Surgeons.

In his spare time in the evenings, Loch did social work in Islington. In 1874 we find him a member of the Executive Committee of the Islington District of the C.O.S. In the following year he was an Honorary Secretary. Later, in 1875, he was invited to apply for the post of Secretary of the Charity Organisation Society on the resignation of C. B. P. Bosanquet, half-brother to his Oxford friend, Bernard. He was then twenty-six and 'taken aback' at the offer of such responsible work.[5] However, in spite of his youth,‡ he was appointed in November and began his long life of strenuous service for the Society. Like other thoughtful men and women of his class, he kept a 'commonplace book'§ in which he noted his ideas, or discussions with friends. Often he sketched in his plans for the Society or wrote of his frustrations when development fell short of his ideals. His most joyous entries were the accounts of his holidays. His first entry was dated 14th September, 1876; his last, 5th November, 1888.‖ We have, therefore, a valuable record of his reflections for the important early years of his work for the C.O.S.

Loch's published books were the product of his mature years, though many of the ideas had been noted earlier. His first, *Charity Organisation*, 1890, ran into several editions. It was based on a

* Bosanquet later married Helen Dendy and they became close friends of the Lochs at Oxshott where they were neighbours.

† He did in fact try to do this during the early years of his secretaryship with the C.O.S. but found it impossible to keep it up, with the pressure of other work.

‡ Mary Richmond recalled, in a memoir written in 1923, 'The only thing that had made the Council hesitate to appoint him was his comparative youth but they reflected that this "was a defect he was likely to outgrow" .'

§ This is usually referred to as his *Diary*, but, although entries were dated, there were sometimes long gaps between. Some entries were pages long, reading more like a memorandum relating to his work, or an essay on a philosophical question; they are written in a 'sort of exercise book'.

‖ A typed copy, probably made by his successor, J. C. Pringle, now in the University of London Library, is wrongly dated 1875–92. The last entry is as stated above—the entry for 1892 is probably a letter written on holiday which the editor decided to add. I am indebted to the late C. L. Mowat for this answer to my query.

lecture given the year before at the Congrés International d'Assistance and was intended for readers from other countries, those 'not specially acquainted with English Life and Thought'.* His best known work was a long contribution on 'Charity' in the 10th edition of the *Encyclopaedia Britannica*, which was to form the core of his second main publication, *Charity and Social Life*, 1910. This was more broadly based than his earlier work, following 'the growth of the conception of charity', to use the author's own words. As late as 1938 the C.O.S. thought it worth re-publication and it appeared under the title *Three Thousand Years of Social Service*. He had, in 1904, edited 'Short studies in social practice by various authors' under the title *Methods of Social Advance*. When he died, in 1923, his friends brought together a selection of his papers and addresses, published with a foreword by the editor, Arthur Clay, with the high-sounding title *A Great Ideal and Its Champion*.

He was a prolific writer and many of his lectures, addresses to conferences and special articles are to be found in the Society's journals and reports. For example, the important statement of his ideas on 'The Development of Charity Organisation' made in June 1903, was published in the *Charity Organisation Review* in the following February. A number of papers on special topics were issued as *Occasional Papers*. His many letters to the Press were an essential part of his vigorous campaigns on social questions. He also contributed to the *Economic Journal*. He often broke into his precious leisure to make sure that his material was accurate and thoroughly prepared. 'It is hard', he writes, 'to keep this ocean of work and business from dashing round and up and over one',†[6] yet he found time to write poetry. Near the end of his life he collected his poems 'for friends who would care to know me better'; *Things Within* was published in 1922.

Loch's active participation in the social problems of his day made him something of a public figure. He served on several important Royal Commissions: that on The Aged Poor, 1893–95; on The Feeble Minded, 1904–08; and, above all, on the important Royal Commission on The Poor Laws, 1905–09. He had been

---

* The 3rd edition, 1905, quoted a review in the *Manchester Guardian* which is of interest for its reference to the need for 'an exposition of the true principles of Charity . . . in spite of the change which has come over public opinion'.

† Characteristically, he resolved on this occasion to get up earlier so that he could have more time for his chosen reading and music.

awarded the Guy Medal of the Royal Statistical Society in 1899 and was a member of the International Statistical Institute. He was Tooke Professor of Economic Science and Statistics at King's College, London, 1904–08, and Dunkin Trust Lecturer at Manchester College, Oxford, in 1896 and 1902. He shared with W. H. Beveridge and others, courses of lectures at the School of Sociology in London. He had also acquired a reputation overseas and we find him participating in a conference on 'Charities' in the United States in the mid-90s, and in the Congrés International d'Assistance in Paris in 1899. These connections were welcomed by the Society as a valuable C.O.S. contribution to the development of social work. In later years the C.O.S. (F.W.A.) was in turn to benefit from the vigour of these overseas societies and schools of social work whose casework had by then outstripped that of the London Society.

In 1900, when Loch had completed twenty-five years as Secretary of the Charity Organisation Society, he was presented with his portrait, painted by John Sargent. So much was subscribed that a second portrait by Sargent was presented to the Council. It was hung in Denison House, the headquarters of the Family Welfare Association.

Academic recognition of Loch's work was given in the early twentieth century when he received honorary degrees from the Universities of St Andrews and Oxford.* At the end of his service with the C.O.S. a knighthood was conferred on him.† These facts tell us much of Loch's public life and something of him as a person, but to a later generation Loch has seemed a shadowy figure.[7] To know him better we need to see him in his leisure hours as he and his family enjoy a wide range of activities, serious and gay. We must look into his diary as he records some of his deeper feelings and tries out his ideas. Only so can we penetrate further and begin to know something of his character and personality, and to understand better why he thought and behaved as he did, until he became identified with the Charity Organisation Society.

* St Andrews with the LL.D.; Oxford with the D.C.L., both in 1905. A memorial tablet was put in the ante-chapel at Balliol in 1925 which read 'To Sir Charles Stewart Loch, D.C.L., once a Commoner of the College, for thirty-nine years secretary of the Charity Organisation Society, and all his life a servant and interpreter of Charity, unquenchable in spirit and in life, this memorial is dedicated by his followers and friends 1849–1923'.

† In 1915. He was then too ill to receive it in person.

Loch's view of life owed much to his family background, professional, middle class, cultured. He was himself talented in several fields. He had studied under Ruskin, and at one time thought of becoming an artist. We have already noted his love of poetry. His own poems ranged from the deeply serious to the light-hearted and gay; one of the lighter ones was written for Miranda Hill's *Rumpelstiltskin*, a play for children performed in Loch's home. This is a delightful reminder of the relationship between the Lochs and Hills, the most famous member of which was Octavia, the pioneer of housing reform. Octavia had a long and close friendship with Loch and was a staunch supporter of the C.O.S.*[8] His grandson shows us something of Loch at leisure:

> . . . His letters and sketch books from abroad were adorned with delicate little sketches and watercolours . . . his letters full of precise observation of flowers, birds, fossils and lively descriptions of scenery and of fellow-travellers. At home he was a keen gardener, and a lover of walking. He was fond of music and had a fine singing voice.[9]

His son-in-law also refers to Loch's joy in country walking and recalls an incident when he joined 'a gang of University men' who constructed the *Ruskin Road* from Ferry Hinksey to Botley.†[10] Another glimpse of Loch's home life is given by his daughter who recalled the Sunday lay sermons which her father gave her and her brother: Loch preferred this unconventional method to Church attendance. Reading was another of Loch's great pleasures. His diary overflows with references to books he has enjoyed. From time to time an entry gives us a delightful period piece as Loch reads aloud, and he and Sophie discuss what has been read,‡ or they both visit Octavia Hill where Loch found reading to Octavia and listening to her stories 'delightful'.[11]

Gradually Loch devoted more of his leisure to reading Blue Books, etc. He records sadly in 1884 that the books read, other than professional ones, had been few. He then gives a wide-ranging

---

* We are told that her death in 1912 was a great grief to him. Loch himself wrote 'To many who knew her the death of Miss Octavia Hill is like the withdrawal of a light in the path of their daily life'. See also Chapter 14 below.

† Loch took part in this venture in 1874 when he went up to Oxford during his employment in London.

‡ E.g. *Diary* entry 12th November, 1877. 'We have just finished reading *Henry IV* . . . .'

list which would put most modern readers to shame. It was fortunate that his wife shared so many of his interests, including his work. She had learned something of social conditions for some two years before her marriage, as secretary to Octavia Hill. Her father, Edward Peters, was also an active voluntary worker for the C.O.S. It was to Sophie that Loch declared his determination to make some drastic changes in the C.O.S.[12]

Although Loch tackled his arduous task with skill and apparent self-confidence we know from his diary that he suffered considerable strain. There is no doubt that Loch found a valuable outlet for some of the frustration of his work in the jottings in his commonplace book. He had too much self-discipline to let it appear in his relations with his colleagues. It may account, in part, for the one recorded outburst in public debate when he was accused of making a personal attack on Canon Barnett.[13] Early in his career he was writing 'What can I do to make my life more joyful, less anxious, to act up to my resolutions without worry or strain?'[14] Two years later he notes: 'the end—the improvement of man, must rest not on any systematic practical charity, but on influencing the mind of men—and this has put me out of heart with my work'. He even wondered whether he had chosen the right sphere of work—'But, however this may be, I cannot now withdraw or take up any other line.'[15] Holidays meant a great deal to him. An early entry reads 'a ten days' holiday—the necessity for which I hardly knew to be so great as I felt it to be when the strain of anxiety and thought was first taken from me'.[16] Yet even on holiday we find him welcoming colleagues to consider further plans for the Society. Or he enjoys a long discussion with his brother-in-law, Frank, on a philosophical question.

The hidden frustrations of Loch's apparently successful career were largely the result of the clash between his Idealism and the practical demands of his exacting work. Early in his career he is noting that while 'Chalmers' principle' must be kept 'steadily in view' the immediate needs of the C.O.S. for funds demanded other action.* It is difficult to assess how far Chalmers' social

* This first reference to Chalmers in Loch's *Diary* is dated 20th September, 1876 (in the F.W.A. M/s) whereas D. Owen gives the date as 17th September, 1876. I cannot find any entry on either of those dates which go as far as Owen's conclusion: 'To reconstruct the C.O.S. on the Chalmers pattern and to infuse it with this particular brand of social idealism was Loch's conscious purpose.' (D. Owen, *English Philanthropy*, p. 225.)

B*

theory influenced Loch's thinking. Thomas Chalmers (1780–1847), a Presbyterian divine, a writer and a man of action, had introduced a system of parochial charity in Glasgow (1819–23). It was much publicised and it influenced experiments in Germany (particularly in Elberfeld) and in America. In England there was a revival of interest in his work at the end of the nineteenth century,[17] and Loch gives an account of Chalmers' teaching due place in a long article on 'Charity' in the 10th edition of *Encyclopaedia Britannica* of 1902–03. But, as Loch pointed out, there had been many contributors to the ideas and practices of charity in the late eighteenth and the nineteenth centuries: there had also been a parallel interest in the Poor Law and all the chief problems of local administration. However, Loch's summary of the main features of Chalmers' social theory reveals how much he had in common with Chalmers' views on 'society as a growing self-supporting organism' which 'had within it, as between family and family, neighbour and neighbour, master and employee, endless links of sympathy and self-support. Poverty is not an absolute, but a relative term'.[18] Loch, commenting later on Chalmers' teaching, adds 'In the development of the theory of charitable relief on the economic side this has been a main factor'.[19] Later still, addressing a C.O.S. Winter Conference, he speaks of Chalmers as 'a Father in Charity Organisation'. But he points out that the early efforts to introduce a scheme on 'quasi-Elberfeld' lines in London was thought by the C.O.S. not to be appropriate.[20]

But if Loch reflected particularly on Chalmers' teaching 'on the economic side', his whole outlook on the broader issues of charity organisation is infused with the Idealist philosophy.

To understand the strength of his Idealism we must look at the philosophy taught in the Oxford of his day, particularly that of T. H. Green. Loch's son-in-law noted that he was 'profoundly influenced by Green's character and philosophy and the two men remained intimate for life'.[*21] Although Loch himself makes no reference to this in his diary we have other evidence that Green's life and teaching had considerable influence.†[22] Loch was constantly emphasising the need to relate theory and practice. It is

* David Owen makes only passing reference to T. H. Green, seeing Chalmers as the more influential (*English Philanthrophy*, p. 225).

† See *Jowett* by Geoffrey Faber, p. 356, for an interesting reference to Green's 'enthusiasm' and 'magnetic influence'.

significant that T. H. Green had combined philosophy with an active participation in social reform.*

It was generally thought that Loch's great contribution to the development of the Charity Organisation Society was his ability to combine idealism with sound administration. Probably Canon Barnett's suggestion that the C.O.S. was out of touch with reality did as much as any part of his criticism to kindle Loch's rage.† Perhaps Loch's debt to the 'self-conscious Idealist School' can best be summed up in his address, 'The Development of Charity Organisation':[23]

> If I were asked why I joined the Society I should answer that through its work and growth I hoped that some day there would be formed a large association of persons drawn from all churches and all classes who, disagreeing in much, would find in charity a common purpose and a new unity. That, it seemed to me, was 'worth anything'. Such an organisation, I thought, could do more than Parliament, or preaching or books, or pamphleteering; these indeed, without the other, seemed likely to effect but small results. But such an organisation might bring to bear on the removal and prevention of evils a combined force that would far exceed in weight and influence any yet existing. It could make legislation effective, could see that it was enforced. Apart from all legislative interference and with the use of means and influences more far-reaching it could renew and discipline the life of the people by a nobler, more devoted, more scientific religious charity. It could turn to account all that newer knowledge would bring to the help of charity. It could eventually provide out of all classes and sects a great army of friendly and, by degrees, well-trained workers. It could help us to realise in society the religion of charity without the sectarianism of religion. It would open a new path for the exercise of personal

---

* He was closely involved in temperance reform and took an active part in the civic politics of Oxford. He had been Assistant Commissioner to a Royal Commission on education and a co-founder of a High School for Oxford boys for which he gave both time and money.[22]

† Loch also thought that Barnett was attacking the very foundation of the Society when he denounced it as 'out of sympathy with the forces which are shaping the times'. He rose fiercely to its defence. See *Canon Barnett* by his wife, p. 65 *ff*. See also K. Woodroofe, *From Charity to Social Work* for an interesting reference to Loch's reaction to criticism.

influence—influence with the Churches, the Guardians, the Friendly Societies, the residents of a district and 'the common people'. Differing in much many might unite in this. . . . The C.O.S. was to be (a peace-making, unifying body . . .) a large offer to those who give their time and thought to the Society's service (at all levels) . . . that men and women should spend their lives in a splendid cause.

It is characteristic of Loch that he should immediately consider the practical implications of the larger objective—the 'Church of Charity' as he liked to call it. The rest of his address is concerned with the steps to be taken to reconsider, re-state and re-organise the Society's work.

Like Green, Loch believed passionately that men should be left free 'to make themselves better'. Action by their fellows or by the State should do nothing to hinder this. The removal of obstacles and the maintenance of certain conditions for the exercise of self-determination were necessary for the common good. Rights were inherent in men both as individuals and as members of society. The family, a vital part of the 'society of societies', also had inherent rights and duties.

Loch also thought, with T. H. Green, that the provision of basic services such as education and sanitation should be a statutory obligation. He was scornful of the 'feeble philanthropists' who so often overlooked the need to abolish filthy dwellings and brutal conditions.[24] He gave a forceful account of the crowded, stunted, penurious lives of the large mass of low paid, unskilled workers.[25] He could not, however, accept State provision for the feeding of schoolchildren or for pensions for the aged. These seemed to him to violate the rights and the duties inherent in families to make such provision and so maintain their role and their self-respect. If circumstances overwhelmed them and their own efforts were insufficient to meet a crisis, then here was the opportunity for the exercise of the goodwill of neighbours and friends, of all classes and sects. Charity would be the unifying force and provide the common purpose. It demanded understanding and compassion. It recognised and respected the right of those in need to participate in their own 'rehabilitation'.

Loch firmly believed that the giving of indiscriminate alms was not only an affront to self-respect, but an abuse of privilege.

Charity, rightly interpreted, meant help directly related to need. It meant the personal concern of the giver for the receiver. It meant, too, patience in the search for the nature and extent of the need. This required knowledge as well as 'the suffering with those to whom the loving act is done'.[26] The first entry in his diary shows both his practical and idealist approach: 'physical expedients must be resorted to for the cure of much mental agony. In the same way the affliction of body or estate requires other healing as well as that of money or food or physic'.[27] Although Loch does not use the actual phrases current amongst social workers today, he comes close to them in his discussions of the true meaning of charity. He sees the implications of 'rehabilitation' in his references to self-help. Like modern caseworkers he stresses the importance of relationships, both between members of a family and between the social worker and the person in need of help. To read Loch's books and articles is to be impressed by the way his ideas anticipate much of the later discussion on casework. His language is less psychological but his underlying thought is very close.

It was fundamental to all Loch's work that moral purpose should be the basis of social life. He agreed absolutely with his friend, Bernard Bosanquet, that 'the ultimate end of Society and the State, as of the individual, is the realisation of the best life'.*[28] How came it then that a modern sociologist could accuse Loch and the C.O.S. of doing great harm and perverting the moral content of society?[29] The answer is to be found in the interpretation of what are the best conditions for the realisation of the good life and what are the chief hindrances. Loch, like many of his contemporaries, had accepted the teaching of the classical economists. He shows in his *Encyclopaedia Britannica* article[30] how much he distrusts the new socialism which in his view aimed at 'recasting society itself on a new economic plan'. He saw that 'Socialism indeed offers the people a new state of social security . . . a final stage in which none shall want because all shall be supported by society or be dependent on it industrially'. But for Loch and his fellow workers in the Charity Organisation Society 'this position seems to exclude the ethical element in life and to treat the people primarily or chiefly as human animals. It seems also to exclude the motives for energy and endeavour that come from self-maintenance'. He believed that charity properly conceived

* Bosanquet's book, first published in 1899, was dedicated to C. S. Loch.

had none of these dangers. 'It has sought to transform the world by the transformation of the will and the inward life in the individual and in society. It would intensify the spirit and feeling of membership in society and would aim at improving social conditions, as science makes clear what the lines of reform should be.'

Loch also points to what has since been one of the chief claims of voluntary societies, 'it has initiated many improvements afterwards taken up by public authorities'. He instances prison reform, industrial schools, child protection, housing, etc., and notes that charity has been 'a friendly ally' in many other reforms. 'But charity and socialism . . . imply ultimately two quite different theories of social life. The one would reform society industrially, the other would develop it and allow it to develop.' Citizenship for Loch, as for T. H. Green, meant Christian citizenship. Although, like many of his contemporaries, Loch questioned the traditional forms of Christianity, his religious attitude to life was unmistakable.* Like most of his generation, too, he believed in progress and in man's inherent ability to overcome obstacles. 'The strength of the people' was no idle phrase.† It expressed an essential part of the Individualist, Idealist philosophy.

The argument reached an acute form in the analysis of poverty and the proper roles of charity and the Poor Law. The C.O.S. claimed that in seeking to help the poor they were concerned with the causes of poverty. Their analysis of causes, however, was severely limited. It started, and often ended, with the individual and his family. The C.O.S. admitted that there were occasional economic reasons for excessive unemployment, but they argued that crises could be anticipated and generally provided for by care and forethought: thrift was one of the great virtues of the Victorian era. Exceptional misfortune should be met through the goodwill, friendship and neighbourly service of the charitable. The C.O.S. workers asked the question, 'what has brought John or Mary to this condition?' They looked for the answer in the response of the individual and his family to their circumstances, particularly the efforts made already to preserve their independence and self-

* Early in his career we find him looking critically at the District Committee Visitors and considering whether some paid visitors could be appointed. He writes 'to get the right men a religious basis must be found'.

† It was used as the title of Helen Bosanquet's book on social economics, published in 1903.

respect. Yet Loch was acutely aware of the difficulties under which many of the poor were living; he urged the Districts not to restrict their efforts to 'case-work' but to include in their larger objects the attack on evil conditions such as over-crowding and 'bad dwellings'.*[32]

Yet even while Loch recognised the misery and the struggles of many of the poor he still remained convinced that in the long run freedom in industrial and social life were essential to man's full development. Meanwhile, those who could be helped must be helped constructively. Moral failure was more difficult to deal with. The most promising approach seemed to be preventive action within the family, to remove hindrances to responsible behaviour. The support of those who had struggled in the past and who might be helped to regain their self-confidence and self-respect for the future was the most hopeful line of advance. The C.O.S. must be selective. It was right to concentrate action on 'the helpable'.

Pauperism was the real enemy of the people. It went beyond poverty of possessions. It was the habitual reliance on others, due to want of foresight and self-control. Those who gave indiscriminate alms or who condoned a lax administration of the Poor Law were hastening the degradation. The argument went further: not only were the individual and his family degraded but the process of democracy was retarded. The State needed independent citizens. 'It cannot afford to have any outcast or excluded classes. . . . It cannot be content with the chronic indigence and social feebleness of any great mass of citizens—with paupers, who are paupers indeed, whether they be classified as such in public returns or are the habitual recipients of the casual bounty of the rich and of charitable institutes.'[33]

Loch is careful to point out that in the practical application of charity organisation the problem 'is not whether the person is "deserving" or "undeserving" but whether, granted the facts, the distress can be stayed and self-support attained'.[34] But since, in practice, character was one of the essential facts in the assessment it is not surprising that many failed to appreciate the difference. It was common practice in Loch's day to draw a distinction between 'the deserving' and 'the undeserving'. The *Goschen*

* E.g. the efforts of the C.O.S. to tackle some of the 'Bad Areas' in a constructive way. See p. 87 *ff*.

Minute had done so in 1869. It is more surprising to find the same distinction appearing in a Fabian Tract, as late as 1894, where it was argued that if the Poor Law was to be humanised 'the first step . . . must be the adoption of a radically different treatment for the deserving and the undeserving'.[35] The whole Tract might have been written by C. S. Loch himself.

A further influence which shaped Loch's thinking was the new scientific approach to many current questions. We know from his diary that Darwin's *Origin of Species* was of considerable interest to him.[36] He admires Darwin's slow, patient accumulation of knowledge and asks whether it was not right 'to be a naturalist in social matters'. Loch felt acutely his own lack of knowledge of the manual working classes. He writes, a year after his appointment, 'At every step I appear baulked by want of personal knowledge. Semi-theoretical writing leads to very definite, but . . . also to very false conclusions'.[37] In 1886 Beatrice Webb is noting:

> Met at C.B.s (i.e. Charles Booth's) office Mr Loch, secretary of C.O.S. Enthusiastic for accurate knowledge of the conditions of the poor.[38]

Loch's *Encyclopaedia Britannica* article draws attention to the new approach in the field of charity: 'the springs of charity lie in sympathy and religion and, one would now add, in science'.[39] 'Scientific Charity' became one of the gibes used by the opponents of the C.O.S. Beatrice Webb was later to sum up this aspect of C.O.S. work as she saw it 'in the years of my apprenticeship' (1883–87) . . . 'there arose, among the more enlightened philanthropists, a reactionary movement—a movement more potent in deterrence than the arguments of ratiocinating philosophers or the protests of cross-bench politicians, because it was based on the study of fact, and took the form of an alternative scheme for grappling, then and there, with poverty. . . . The C.O.S. appeared to me as an honest though short-circuited attempt to apply the scientific method of observation and experiment, reasoning and verification, to the task of delivering the poor from their miseries by the personal service and pecuniary assistance tendered by their leisured and wealthy fellow-citizens'.[40]

One result of this method was the Society's readiness to contribute evidence whenever public enquiries on a variety of social questions were undertaken. The C.O.S. also set up its own special committees, many of them modelled on official enquiries, with minutes of evidence and reports very like Blue Books.* Under Loch's guidance the Society built up a valuable library. It was the necessary foundation of 'Scientific Charity', based on knowledge and research. The reference library reached a total of some 2,000 volumes in Loch's day and held a wide range of books and journals on economic and social questions. It also had an excellent collection of Parliamentary Papers.†

The conduct of C. S. Loch and his associates has sometimes been denounced as hypocritical. This judgement, in my view, fails to take account of the thought and opinions of their time. Beatrice Webb, who knew Loch personally, never made this accusation. Writing later, she recalls Loch and other 'leading spirits of the Charity Organisation Society' and sums them up as 'distinguished for moral fervour and intellectual integrity'.[41] Considering the ferocity of Beatrice Webb's hostility to the basic social theory of the Society she writes with singular detachment in later years:

> From the standpoint of the mid-Victorian time spirit there was no gainsaying the worth of the three principles upon which this much-praised and much-abused organisation was avowedly based: patient and persistent personal service on the part of the well-to-do; an acceptance of personal responsibility for the ulterior consequences alike to the individual recipient and to others who might be indirectly affected, of charitable assistance; and finally, as the only way of carrying out this service and fulfilling this responsibility, the application of the scientific method to each separate case of a damaged body or a lost soul; so that the assistance given should be based on a correct forecast of what would actually happen, as a result of the gift, to the character and circumstances of the individual recipient and to the destitute class to which he belonged.[42]

As we look back on Loch's long years of service with the C.O.S. we may note three small incidents which throw some light on his

---

* See a lively account of these 'semi-official' reports in C. L. Mowat, *The Charity Organisation Society*, p. 7.

† These books and Parliamentary Papers were given, in the mid-1960s, on permanent loan to the University of London Goldsmiths Library. Journals went to the National Institute for Social Work Training.

personality and on the C.O.S. itself. Not long after his appointment Loch is considering the urgent need for economy if the Society is to remain solvent. One of his suggestions is to call a private meeting of working members to invite them 'to meet the debt at once by contributions from members'. He adds 'self to give £100'.[43]

After his retirement the Council passed a resolution[44] in which they expressed their 'great indebtedness to him . . . not only for his administrative ability and unsparing devotion to the work of the Society, but also for his power of inspiring and encouraging others, his fertility in suggesting fresh lines of action, his valuable public services . . . his untiring energy in upholding principles, combined with a warmth of feeling and grace of manner which has endeared him to all who came in contact with him . . .'. The Council also expressed 'a strong wish that Dr Loch will accept from the Society a pension of not less than £250 as a slight recognition of his past services'. Loch replied thanking them for the offer of an annuity but added 'I do not feel that I can accept it'. The reason he offers for his refusal is characteristic; he would have accepted it gratefully had there been any need, but he was quite comfortably provided for.

The last illustration was reported by his successor, J. C. Pringle.[45] 'When offered a permanent building for the C.O.S. Sir Charles Loch refused it, preferring to be a tenant.' (This was in spite of the recurrent difficulties of the Society in raising funds.) Again, the reason given by Loch reflects something of his character: 'The possession of a building', he declared, 'would be a temptation to perpetuate our particular guess at a solution after it had outlived its usefulness.'

This third example illustrates a little-known aspect of his character. He is most often remembered today for his tenacity in holding to 'an outworn social theory' which became repugnant to later generations. Loch's diary bears witness to his constant examination of the principles and practice of the C.O.S. in the light of changing needs. Apart from his tenacity in holding to the Idealist philosophy, he was far-sighted and amongst the least rigid and most tolerant of men.

Loch seems to have combined many apparently contradictory qualities. He was forceful, even dominating, and yet had true humility. He was tolerant and without bitterness, and yet capable of fierce denunciation of those who attacked the Society. He had grace and charm and a great capacity for friendship, yet he offended many. He was at once an idealist and a realist. He excelled as an administrator, not hesitating to retrench and reduce staff if necessary, yet he preserved his humanity.*[46] 'The work of the Society, both inside the office among the staff, and outside among the volunteers, proceeded with extraordinary cheerfulness and zeal.'[47] He was a man of vision, imagination and compassion, yet he advocated a policy widely denounced as harsh and repellent. He had 'an eye for the proportion of things,†[48] was flexible and enlightened, yet held to a social theory which, to a later generation, and to an increasing number of his own contemporaries, seemed reactionary and obstructive.

Loch sought to replace the chaotic, indiscriminate charity of his day by planned giving which would use available resources responsibly. He formulated schemes which would prevent over-lapping. He failed in his main purpose, but some of his ideas are being put forward today. Loch is remembered widely for his opposition to the introduction of statutory old age pensions and the feeding of schoolchildren: to a later generation this attitude has become totally discredited. But his opposition stemmed from his belief that the universality of such measures would ignore personal needs, and remove the responsibility of the family for each of its members. His attitude was combined with the emphasis he placed on the duty, whether through charity or the Poor Law, to discover the full extent of the need and to relieve adequately: a pension of five shillings was a miserable dole, unrelated to individual need. Finally, we should note that Loch foresaw, and regretted, the fragmentation of the social services. He emphasised that public and voluntary social services must be family-centred.

It seems to have been extraordinarily difficult for later generations to strike a fair critical balance on Charles Stewart Loch and his work. He was so closely identified with the C.O.S. that many of its mistakes and shortcomings were attributed to him, although, in many instances, he was their sternest critic. It was perhaps a

* A much-quoted saying in his *Diary*, 'that for good charity organisation was wanted the heart of a Dickens and the head and will of a Bismark' was not, in fact, his own, but the recorded words of a colleague, A. H. Hill. Loch uses it as an opportunity for reflection, particularly on the 'marvellous observation and quick but not always true sympathy' of Dickens. It would be misleading to infer that Loch was inclined to be ruthless (c.f. K. Woodroofe, opus cit).

† Loch's own comment on Bagehot as he analysed his *Physics and Politics*.

great disservice to his memory that his successor was so great an admirer. Loch's ideas were conserved and perpetuated when he himself might have shown a more lively response to a changing world.

Loch's chief misfortune was to have been grounded in the classical economy and individualist philosophy so widely accepted when the C.O.S. was founded. It was soon to be outdated. It marked the end of an era.

CHAPTER THREE

Structure of the Society:
Relation between Structure, Organisation and
Function

1. The Poor Law and the C.O.S.

The structure of the C.O.S. reflects the very close relation which was envisaged between the Society and the Poor Law.

The C.O.S., from its foundation, consisted of a federation of District Committees with a representative Central Council. One of the Provisional Rules presented to the Council in June 1869 ran 'That the district of the Committee should be defined and be, so far as possible, co-terminous with the Poor Law District.'[1] District offices were rapidly opened, twelve in the first year, rising fast to some forty offices by the time C. S. Loch became Secretary in 1875. The pattern was preserved. In 1900 when Fulham and Hammersmith were separated, after twenty-nine years as a combined district, the annual report announced 'There were now two Boards of Guardians, therefore the Committee felt there should be two C.O.S. offices.'

The Society was founded some months before the issue of the famous *Goschen Minute*.[2] It was generally believed that the President of the Poor Law Board had written his *Minute* in close consultation with members of the Society. When the *Minute* was out of print the C.O.S. published it as an *Occasional Paper*[3] because 'it is of so much importance'. The *Goschen Minute* poses the question: 'How far is it possible to mark out the separate limits of the Poor Law and of Charity respectively and how is it possible to secure joint action between the two?' The practical issues arising are then considered and it is suggested that appropriate charitable action might be taken in spheres where relief was legally prohibited. As long as the Poor Law remained on the Statute Book the C.O.S.

continued to consider urgent applications for assistance where Poor Law Guardians (later Public Assistance Officers) had no power to relieve. These include redeeming tools or clothes from pawn, purchasing tools, purchasing clothes (Guardians might do this only in cases of urgent necessity), paying the cost of conveyance to any part of the United Kingdom and paying rent or lodging. C.O.S. case papers were heavily weighted with these items, particularly in the recurrent periods of great distress.

There is no doubt that the Poor Law Board, in 1869, favoured close co-operation in several directions between the Guardians and voluntary organisations. They suggested, for example, mutual exchange of information: 'There should be every opportunity for every agency, official or private, engaged in relieving the poor to know fully and accurately the details of the work performed by all similarly engaged.' In fact, it was the C.O.S., not the Boards of Guardians, which later established a system for the mutual registration of assistance.* The *Goschen Minute* had suggested that once the means of communication was established the charities might agree to observe certain regulations '. . . not indiscriminately, or as an inflexible rule, but as a general practice'. Co-operation would also include interchange whereby the voluntary agencies would apply to the relieving officer on behalf of destitute persons whom they found in need, while the relieving officer in turn would put an applicant not actually destitute in touch with an appropriate charity. This form of co-operation was to prove more acceptable than mutual registration.

The Board was bound to point out that such schemes were optional. Schemes could be authorised but not forced upon 'any Union which may be less disposed to co-operate'. C.O.S. Districts soon discovered that Guardians varied considerably in their attitude in different parts of the Metropolitan area. In some cases co-operation was very close: for example, in Kensington and Lambeth where every Poor Law Guardian (and in Kensington overseers too) was *ex officio* a member of the C.O.S. Committee.[4] In St George's, Hanover Square, five C.O.S. Committee members were elected to the Board; three were already there. In other parts of London, however, Districts were reporting year after year that

* See page 83.

there was no co-operation.* There was even hostility. In Islington Loch reports 'There is no co-operation with the Guardians. The Poor Law returns show that out-relief is lavishly given; and so long as the present policy of the Board prevails, closer co-operation with them is impossible. I have strongly urged the Committee, either directly or indirectly, to secure for the next election nominees who will pledge themselves to a reform.'[5]

St Marylebone, the first of the C.O.S. District Offices to be established, had the experience of Octavia Hill to guide it in working out special schemes of co-operation.[6] Where knowledge of individuals, such as 'a poor sick person' or an 'infirm person', showed that each could be helped to stay in her own home instead of being sent to the workhouse, this was arranged by mutual consent. The first Marylebone report stated 'the scope of the operation of the Society is as wide as that of the Poor Law . . . It aims by a more gracious instrumentality to make an impression upon that vast and increasing mass of pauperism . . . which has become a burden and a reproach to the civilisation of the age.'

On the whole, the division of labour or 'sphere of influence' principle was closely observed throughout the Districts. It was rare for the C.O.S. to help 'chronic cases' or to supplement relief. There were exceptions, for example when it was shown that a family had applied for relief temporarily, in an unforeseen crisis, but that timely help would take the family 'off the Poor Law' and make them self-supporting again. One most unusual case was reported where the Guardians and the C.O.S. agreed upon joint action on behalf of 'a very respectable old woman'. The Guardians allowed 4s. weekly and the C.O.S. raised the rest from 'private persons' to provide a pension sufficient to keep her out of the workhouse. This seemed to be contrary to the oft-quoted rule 'no supplementation of Poor Relief'. It was argued in extenuation that 'it cost the rates much more to keep people in the workhouse than in their own homes'.† As a general rule the C.O.S. continued for

---

* That the difficulties persisted is well illustrated at the turn of the century in Chelsea.[7] Chelsea had an active C.O.S. District Committee with a Chairman who was also a Borough Councillor and a J.P., while its Vice-Chairman was a doctor. The Committee failed, however, to win the co-operation of the Guardians until one of its members was elected to the Board.

† Later generations were to appreciate the same point in relation to children in 'Homes' and children boarded out with foster parents or 'subsidised' in their own homes.

many years to advocate 'no supplementation' together with separate treatment for the 'helpable' and 'worthy' poor and strict administration of the Poor Law for paupers. This meant, in fact, the application of the 'workhouse test' and a great reduction in outdoor relief, if not, indeed, its elimination. Some C.O.S. members were asking, 'Would not the creation of The Common Poor Fund lessen the responsibility of the poorer unions, with the consequent loss of incentive to careful administration?' They had considerable success in St George's in the East and in Whitechapel, where the District Committees and the Poor Law Officers were in complete agreement. Perhaps nowhere was the C.O.S. so bitterly hated. Canon Barnett,* an ardent supporter of the C.O.S., was to change his mind on this issue in the 1880s. Pauperism might be reduced: some families might be helped by careful charitable effort; but the vast mass of poverty remained.

2. *Repression of Mendicity and Organisation of Charity*

There were other influences besides that of the Poor Law which helped to shape the policy of the first District Committees. In the early years the C.O.S. was much concerned with the prevention of begging and the detection of impostors. The District agents, usually the only paid members of staff, spent much of their time 'patrolling the neighbourhood' and tracing and reporting to the police men and women who were 'preying upon public generosity'. Regular reports were made to subscribers of successful prosecutions instituted by the C.O.S. Some Districts gave detailed and lively stories of attempted fraud and imposture thwarted by their vigilance. These often took a greater share of available space in the annual reports than the more prosaic 'case histories' of the widow provided with a mangle, or the workman enabled to get his tools out of pawn, or the costermonger helped to re-stock his barrow. Not all Districts lent themselves to this kind of publicity.† It was to cause C. S. Loch much concern that so much effort went into the detection of impostors and so little into the broader issues of the organisation of charity. Soon after his appointment he was

* He was Vicar of St Jude's and a great supporter of Toynbee Hall and had a very thorough knowledge of East End conditions.
† E.g. Marylebone in the early years was one of several Districts which avoided such appeals to subscribers.

wondering how he could replace one of his own colleagues at Central who was 'altogether too detective'. Closely linked with inquiry and detection in the first few years of District work was the attempt to deal with vagrants. One District, Fulham, published a list of signs 'used by the fraternity to chalk on gateposts and doors': e.g. a cross within a circle meant 'religious but good on the whole'. Subscribers were reminded that if a tramp were genuinely hungry he could get bread at the District Office 'to be then and there eaten'.

As the years passed less prominence was given to reports on vagrants and impostors, and the account of court proceedings was omitted. But the C.O.S. never quite lived down its early reputation. Islington reported, in 1883, 'The C.O.S. loses no opportunity of insisting that the repression of mendicity and the prosecution of impostors are matters subsidiary to the organisation of charity and *not* of primary importance.'[8] This message had often to be repeated over the years. In the same way some committees had been happy to tell their subscribers how often they had turned away the unworthy: 'some forty per cent of the applicants for charitable relief were not entitled to such consideration on the part of the public'.[9] Later reports gave more prominence to the proportion assisted. The need for thorough investigation was still upheld: it was necessary to satisfy subscribers that the C.O.S. was making the best use of charitable contributions. But another purpose was receiving greater emphasis in the more enlightened Districts. Full enquiry was necessary 'so that the true nature of the need might be discovered and adequate help given'.

3. *Practice in the Districts: Nature of Early Social Work*

Some of the District Reports give details of how they carried out their work. Fulham and Hammersmith's First Annual Report, 1872, throws light on current practice:

> The statement of any applicant for relief who comes to the office with or without a ticket* is taken down by the Agent who, after a thorough investigation of the case, makes a written report of it; this having been entered in a book (for future

---

* Tickets were furnished gratuitiously to all householders on application to the office . . . to be given to Mendicants in lieu of money. (See plan p. 30 above.)

reference) is then submitted to the sub-committees, who hold their meetings every Wednesday evening, when the case is disposed of. The applicant is then informed of the decision. Any applicant in a starving condition is immediately supplied with bread. The general meeting, consisting of all the members, meet on the first Wednesday of every month, at 5 p.m. for the general business of the Committee and for dealing with the more important cases referred to them by the Sub-Committee.

It is a little surprising, after this, to find the Committee declaring their readiness 'to investigate both the character and the prospects of every applicant, with a view to show how he may best be benefitted permanently'—adding 'the proper investigation of character and circumstances is a work which requires considerable care and considerable experience'. Self-confidence was not wanting in these early C.O.S. District Committees.

Some modification of the procedure was introduced when certain members of the Committee decided to take part in 'personal visiting'.* This was reported from Islington in 1876–77 where, hitherto, the agent had collected the facts which were scrutinised by the Honorary Secretary and then submitted to the Committee to be scrutinished again.† Another modification was the arrangement by which the applicant could see the Honorary Secretary if he wished. It was implied that there was some merit in the fact that applicants were not obliged to see the Secretary. By 1882 this same Committee reconsidered its work and decided that there was need for 'a higher ideal of how each case should be treated, so that an investigation which would have been regarded as sufficient in the early days of the Society, was considered as superficial and inadequate at this time'.

As early as 1874 the Central Council had instructed the Organising Secretary and the District Committee Visitors 'to visit all the offices of the Society . . . and examine into the sufficiency of their system of investigation'. A digest of the report was considered by Council and 'much valuable information was thus obtained'. It was published in *The Reporter* (III. 276). C. S. Loch was much concerned to raise the general standard of work in the

* This was, in fact, suggested by C.O.S. 'Central'.
† 'Scrutinised' was the term twice used to report the procedure.

Districts and one of his suggestions, adopted by the Council in 1881* was the regular visiting of Districts, *seriatim*, the report to be discussed by Council. This became part of the accepted administrative structure of the C.O.S. until the 1960s. It no doubt helped to pass on ideas and to keep up standards. It was also bound to raise some misgivings and some friction. On the whole it worked well. In 1882 one such report was made by Loch on Islington, the District where he himself had had his first experience of the C.O.S. He noted that: '. . . the investigation appeared to be discriminating and careful; and the decisions were based on a true conception of what is meant by adequate relief . . . I found at Islington a precision in the requests for information which betokened thoughtful work.' After discussing finances and other related matters Loch goes on to consider the C.O.S. position in the District and his comment is worth noting. He speaks of the difficulty of getting the co-operation of those who are content 'to *alleviate* distress; the District Committee is pledged to look into the causes in each case, and to endeavour to remove them—to attempt a cure. Were the Committee to adopt a lower standard of work, and conform to the views of the charitable workers in the District, they could obtain co-operation from the clergy and laity, the Guardians, and other bodies'.

The resolution of 1881 which led the Society to work out the method of systematic visiting of District Offices was also memorable for another innovation which later became common practice. One section read: 'That, in the interest of the Society, wherever necessary, Committees should be immediately strengthened—if possible, by voluntary help; if not, by well-paid officers—according to the special circumstances of each District.'[10] Hackney and Poplar, two of the poorest areas, had the first paid secretaries in the year 1882–83. Islington's first secretary, a woman, was appointed in 1886–87.† Salaries were paid from central funds and secretaries could be moved around from District to District.

The C.O.S. had intended that charity organisation should come first in its activities. It was much concerned about the lack of

* Loch had thought out this idea and written of it in his Diary before submitting it for discussion by a special conference of Honorary Secretaries and delegates in February 1880.

† A few years later she married a member of the Executive Committee and, as Mrs Blyth, gave long years of voluntary service to the C.O.S. and other charitable agencies. See Chapter 14.

success in the Districts and as early as 1872 set up a Special Committee to report.[11] One of the recommendations adopted by the Council in November, 1872, is akin to Chalmers' scheme, but it was not followed up. In the 1880s Loch was writing in his diary: 'We want a set of combiners rather than investigation apparatus— a friendly society rather than a committee of the formal kind. But many of our Honorary Secretaries have no talent for 'combination': dealing with cases and writing letters for relief are easier'.[12]

By this time the C.O.S. had accepted the inevitable: it set out in some detail the various ways of 'dealing with cases' and gave a more 'individual' interpretation of charity organisation: 'Charity Organisation is a development of the functions of each person or institution engaged in charity, so that they may combine for mutual help and act up to a higher standard'.[13] The Society recognised that 'for the progress of charity organisation the Council has to rely mainly on the development of the District Committees'.[14] Part II of the *Objects and Methods of the Charity Organisation Society*[15] set out the responsibility of District Committees 'to Improve the Condition of the Poor' as follows:

ON THE PART OF DISTRICT COMMITTEES (1883–84)

1. By careful inquiry regarding all applications for assistance (whether they be referred to the District Offices or apply of their own accord), in order to ascertain how and by whom they should be helped, and to test the truth of their statements.

2. By applying to each case, susceptible of permanent benefit, and suitable for assistance by charity rather than by the Poor Law, such remedies as are likely to make the applicant self-dependent.

3. By obtaining the various kinds of help required from those interested in the applicants, from their relatives, from charitable institutions, and from private persons.

4. By making loans, on security, but without interest.

5. By making grants, when the help required cannot be obtained from other quarters.

6. By endeavouring to procure pensions from charities and from private persons for chronic cases in which there has been evidence of good character, of thrift and of reasonable efforts to provide for the future.

7. By sending (gratuitously) to legitimate inquirers, whether

charitable agencies or private persons, reports on cases of distress.

8. By bringing into co-operation with each other, and with the Poor Law authorities, the various charitable agencies and individuals in the District, and thus preventing the mis-application of relief and the evils of 'overlapping'.

9. By making the District Committee representative of local charities and a centre of reference for all interested in charitable work, and promoting local schemes for the aid of the poor and the spread of provident habits.

10. By repressing local mendicity by means of investigation tickets and otherwise.

By 1914 there were some significant changes:

ON THE PART OF DISTRICT COMMITTEES. (1913–14)

1. By learning how to befriend persons in distress in the best way, and spreading this knowledge among all those who have dealings with the poor by way of charity or under the Poor Law.

2. By bringing official and voluntary agencies and charitable persons into co-operation with each other, by means of mutual registration and in other ways, so that all relief given in the District may be well bestowed.

3. By making the District Committee representative of local charities and social agencies, and a centre of reference for all interested in charitable and social work, and by promoting local schemes for the aid of the poor and the spread of pro-vident habits.

4. By training workers among the poor in the best principles and methods.

5. By arranging meetings, lectures, and circles for the study of social questions bearing on the work and methods of charity organisation.

6. By receiving and dealing with applications for charitable help as a means of attaining the above-mentioned objects.

7. By careful inquiry in all cases in order to test the truth of the applicants' statements; to ascertain the cause of distress; to establish the fitness of the case for assistance by charity rather than under the Poor Law; and to discover the reme-dies which are likely to make the applicant independent.

8. By recommending for pensions from charities and private persons aged and infirm people in regard to whom there is evidence of good character, industry, and reasonable effort to provide for the future, and whose friends and relations are willing to give reasonable assistance.

9. By obtaining the various kinds of help required from those who are interested in the applicants by reason of relationship, services rendered, or official position, e.g. the clergy and local endowed charities, and by seeking the aid of the charities which have undertaken the special care of such cases.

10. By endeavouring to procure from other sources the help which these agencies and persons are unable to supply, provided that the attainment of the above-mentioned objects be not thereby hindered.

11. By sending gratuitously to legitimate inquirers, whether charitable agencies or private persons, reports on cases of distress.

12. By repressing local mendicity.

The Committee Members and other Workers

Who were the people who did the work of the District Committees in this first phase of the Society's development? It was agreed that 'the District Committees, consist, as far as possible, of Ministers of religion, guardians of the poor, and representatives of all the principal local charities'.[16] The pattern worked out then was to persist, with slight modification, well into the twentieth century. The organisation was federal in structure: each District developed its own special interests and, for the most part, recruited its own members. When the first District Offices were established many areas had both rich and poor living within their boundaries. A generation later the better off were moving out to more spacious suburbs or into the surrounding countryside. But even in the late 1860s and early 70s certain districts were already predominantly working class, where poor housing and much overcrowding were common. These conditions were reflected in the staffing of the District Offices, for the C.O.S. depended upon voluntary help. Areas like Poplar and Shoreditch, where there were few members of the leisured class, relied on volunteers from such districts as

Chelsea or Hampstead. Islington could draw to some extent on its own residents until industrial and population changes compelled them, too, to look further afield.

In the 1860s it was still not customary for women to take an active part in public affairs. If they had interests outside their homes, such as membership of a charitable society, the more responsible work would naturally be done by men: men formed the executive committee: a man always acted as treasurer. This practice was reflected in many of the early C.O.S. District Committees. Islington, for example, for the first five years had men only on its committees. Lewisham reported as late as 1881–82 that there was now 'the addition of ladies to the committee'. Others had some women on the general committee but none on the executive. Marylebone District was an exception. It inherited the traditions built up by Octavia Hill and her band of House Property Managers. Octavia herself and a substantial proportion of women, even though still a minority,* took an active part in each committee and Octavia also represented them at 'Central'. Gradually, in all the Districts, more women were accepted to help in a variety of ways, many of them as Honorary Secretaries. Islington, in the year 1876–77, formed a special 'morning committee of ladies to consider cases of relief'.

In many Districts the clergy were the nucleus of the committees. They were mostly Anglican, though here and there a Minister of the Free Churches was induced to join.† The Chairman was often a local clergyman. They had the advantage of knowing the needs of their parishes and were familiar with the social conditions. Retired admirals or generals or past members of the Indian Civil Service were much favoured as recruits to C.O.S. voluntary work. They often brought a different point of view to the deliberations but were not always familiar with local conditions. Often, too, they resided outside the District in which they served. Many committees enlisted the help of local businessmen, doctors, and others who were also engaged in a variety of public activities, and would bring a wide experience to the general discussions. A doctor member usually acted as Honorary Medical Consultant. The Committee often had at least one representative of a kindred

* In 1872 there were fifteen women and twenty-five men on the committee.
† Some Districts headed their list of committee members 'all members of the Clergy in the District'.

social work organisation such as the Society for the Relief of
Distress. Occasionally it included a member of the local Board of
Guardians. Those members who could spare most time served on
the smaller relief or 'investigating committee'.* If they acted as
Honorary Secretaries they had usually to be in command of
considerable leisure.†

The C.O.S., in pursuit of its ideal of Charity, had prided itself
on seeking to break down all class barriers. Consequently the
Districts discussed from time to time how they could attract the
working class to support their efforts. Could they get a representative of the artisans on their committee? Would an address by
a local trade unionist at a special C.O.S. meeting lead to closer
association between them? Later still they were asking 'would not
the establishment of a Workers' Educational Association group in
the District bring an opportunity to have a more representative
committee?' Although some Districts reported hopefully that these
and similar efforts brought better understanding, they had little
or no success in winning active help. Committees which met
during the day could not expect it. Those who held evening
committees found that artisans had other interests after their long
day's work. St Olave's Committee was one of the few Districts
able, in 1896–97, to report some success. They convened a
Conference, and representatives of several Friendly Societies
present were invited to attend the resulting Committee. As a
result members of the Foresters, Manchester Unity of Odd-
fellows, Hearts of Oak and Rechabite Societies were subsequently
elected to the C.O.S. District Committee.

The C.O.S. was very conscious of class distinctions. Although
it tried, mostly unsuccessfully, to interest members of the working
class, it also guaranteed the standing of its committees with
distinguished Presidents and Vice-Presidents who were usually
titled. Some, like Lord Lichfield, were hard-working members,‡
but the majority lent their names and gave a donation, and otherwise took little part in the proceedings. They had prestige value.
The only representative of working people closely involved in

---

* St Marylebone Committee was so named.

† Though C. S. Loch, who was for a time Honorary Secretary at Islington,
did most of his work for the Society in the evenings.

‡ Lord Lichfield was Chairman of Marylebone District Committee as well
as being active at 'Central'.

C.O.S. activities was the paid agent.* He received a weekly wage, although occasionally a man of 'superior quality' was employed on a salary basis.† Most of the agents were either ex-servicemen, or retired police sergeants, or others of similar standing who could provide references of excellent character. Though some were said to be unable to spell, this did not necessarily betoken lack of intelligence.‡[17] One agent, who later became famous as Lord Snell, was the son of an agricultural labourer. As we have seen from an account of a District Committee's conduct of its work in the early days, § it was the agent who interviewed the applicants. He was often the only C.O.S. officer to do so from the beginning to the end of 'the case'. But he did not attend committee meetings. He submitted all the routine information in writing. The C.O.S. Central Council was much concerned in the mid-70s that some Districts left most of the work to the agents. They suggested that 'a member of committee might act as a visitor to the persons whose cases were investigated at the office'. Lewisham, reporting this in 1876–77, made it clear that the visit was to be of a friendly character only . . . it was to be 'natural but not intrusive'. By 1890 it had become a general rule that only voluntary workers should undertake 'the responsible duty of interviewing'. Factual information was still verified by the agent.

Not all committees conformed, however. Their membership illustrated how wide was the appeal of the C.O.S. to people of many different points of view. Woolwich, where Grinling was paid Secretary‖[18] and Snell the agent, offers an outstanding example of contrasts. As Lord Snell recorded much later,[19] he was actively engaged in his leisure time in the conduct of Labour propaganda in the area: he did this openly and felt that it did nothing to affect his loyalty to the C.O.S. But some members of the committee were alarmed and, as Snell wrote, 'an effort was made by one of the local clergymen to secure my dis-

* Many District Committees also had collectors but these worked on a 'poundage basis'.

† Following the custom of the time a member of committee is designated 'A. Brown *Esquire*'—the agent appears either as 'A. Brown' or as 'Mr Brown'.

‡ C. L. Mowat refers slightingly to this lack of ability to spell. Alas, it applies to some University students today and affords no criterion of ability in other directions.

§ Page 57.

‖ Grinling was described by George Lansbury as one of 'the socialists who welcomes the conscious co-operation of the working classes'.

C

missal, an effort immediately and effectively resisted by other clergymen who had more tolerant views'. Snell's account of three of these who prevented the Committee from being stampeded into dismissing him indicates what varied experience some of the C.O.S. members brought to the work. One was Canon Horsley who had served as a prison Chaplain and was an ardent reformer 'on the lines of the Christian Social Union'. He had been very active 'in forcing property owners to cleanse the area of vile slums, etc.'. The Chairman of the C.O.S. Committee, Canon Escreet, Rector of Woolwich, was another who gave vigorous support to Snell. He was a member of the Guild of St Matthew, a Socialist organisation, and was 'courageous and gentle'. Another member, The Reverend Walter Wragge, had been connected with Toynbee Hall and 'had very wide sympathies'.

That Grinling himself should have chosen to work for the C.O.S. as a paid secretary is in itself remarkable, considering the anti-socialist views of C. S. Loch and the majority of his colleagues.* It is not surprising to find that Grinling, true to his socialist principles, 'treated his fellow workers of all grades as equals'. Snell not only reported facts, but was consulted about treatment. He was even invited, sometimes, to attend committee meetings, 'a quite unorthodox procedure'.

The C.O.S., since it paid the salaries of most of the District Secretaries, could always remove them if they were too unorthodox. It hesitated to resist a strong local committee, however. From time to time secretaries were sent to other areas, often to the regret of their old committees, but the reason given was usually an acceptable one: e.g. the need of another area for an experienced worker.† In 1890 the post of Organising Secretary was created for a few experienced C.O.S. secretaries who should help to promote training and organisation in a group of Districts.

The number of salaried staff employed in the Districts gradually increased but until the First World War the C.O.S. still depended for the greater part of its work on volunteers.‡

* A few years later Grinling was constrained to resign. He found himself increasingly at odds with the C.O.S. Snell followed soon after.

† A less satisfactory reason, which was heard most often in post-war periods, was the need to retrench. The amalgamation of Districts in the Society's later history led to considerable redistribution.

‡ Chelsea had no paid secretary until 1918. The contribution of voluntary workers to the Society is so great that it is given separate treatment in Chapter 14.

In the twentieth century fewer clergy were to be found on the District Committees. Gradually more representatives of other local charitable agencies agreed to serve and, in some Districts, by the end of the first decade, men and women of the leisured class were in the minority. Some secretaries were reporting their regret at the loss of the 'experience and sympathy' of the clergy. In the past they knew that they could call on certain members to visit in particularly difficult cases. They now found that the majority of the members were fully engaged with the work of their own societies. They could not be counted on, in fact, to attend committee meetings regularly, whereas the clergy had usually managed to do so. The new pattern of representation had certain advantages, however, not least the greater co-operation now possible between social workers in the field.

By this time training schemes,* started by the C.O.S. in the mid-1890s, had raised the standard of work of secretaries and of many of the voluntary workers. The workers had a better knowledge of social conditions and had gained from the shared experience of other workers in the Society. They were expected to know what voluntary and statutory aid was available in their own Districts and they had the invaluable *Charities Register and Digest* of the Society to guide them in the choice of other sources of help. A renewed spirit of confidence and optimism was abroad. As Poplar reported in 1913: 'it had been at work for 40 years and whereas at first it was a voice crying in the wilderness it now had many allies'.[20]

Loch was certainly right in describing much of the early 'case-work' as 'pure relief'. He was right, too, in his criticism that 'the indifferent work of many committees had led to some justifiable unpopularity'. He had written in his diary, 'there is constant pressure towards relief work without corresponding increase in personal charity'. As late as 1904 Loch was calling attention to the fact that 'in one-third to one-half of "case-work" nothing is done'.[21] The C.O.S., in his view, had had to pay dearly for the haste with which District Offices had been founded. Many workers were inexperienced. The numbers dealt with rather than the quality of the assistance seemed to be the chief concern.

* See Chapter 12.

The Kind of Help Given

We have a long record of the kind of help given at different stages of the Society's development, since Districts were required to send in annual reports to the C.O.S. Council. Statistics were classified according to Central Administrative requirements.* Districts, with an eye on their subscribers, also gave a more general account of their activities, usually illustrated by 'case histories'. Many showed a genuine concern for the family in distress and a constructive plan of assistance. But later generations, looking back on these early records, tend to note chiefly the censorious attitude of many of the early investigators. There was, for example, the family which had been recommended as 'highly respectable' by a church worker and was apparently thought well of by neighbours, but thorough enquiry by the C.O.S. revealed that the man and woman were in fact co-habiting. They were therefore deemed unworthy of assistance, though there was no doubt of their need.[22] In another instance good character and gratitude were triumphant. The report shows an enquiry officer who must have been both compassionate and observant:

> The case was sent by a clergyman. The Enquiry Officer visited and found the following situation: 'it was a back room on the first floor of a house in a small street in a poor district; in this 'home' there was no furniture whatever except one old mattress without any covering; the poor people had very little clothing on, and no fire (it was the month of January), and there was no food in the house. They bore an excellent character; the husband had been unfortunate in business, he had saved money and opened a shop and failed, and subsequently had been attacked by consumption and was unable to work. The wife was also unable to work through not having clothes fit to go out in. The Society gave her a grant for this purpose; she got work as a milliner, and the Officer met her some time after in high spirits, when she said she had plenty of work, and was full of gratitude to the Society.

It is only in the context of the current Victorian emphasis on morality that we can understand the inclusion of the first example of C.O.S. thoroughness. For the same reason, no doubt, accounts

---

* See Tables 2 and 3.

of 'cases dismissed' appeared first, both in the statistical tables and in the general body of the reports. An example from the First Annual Report of the Islington Committee[23] is of interest in view of Loch's later report on this District. Class I showed that, of the 1,177 cases 'decided on' by the Committee, 421 were dismissed for the following reasons: undeserving 174, not in distress 72, ineligible 67, gave false address 46, not requiring relief (e.g. because work meanwhile found) 14. Included in this category were also 35 who withdrew their applications and 13 who left their address and could not be found. Class II—Applicants referred to other Agencies—is of interest since it shows the C.O.S. trying to make good its claim that it was not competing with existing charitable societies. As Islington reported in the following year: 'it is not designed to be an institution for the distribution of alms; it does not intermeddle with the ministration of the local charities that are endeavouring to relieve distress . . . private benefactors and other charities should be helped by the work of the C.O.S. Class II of Islington's first report showed that of 446 applicants referred, 104 were to the Poor Law, 158 to other charitable agencies, 62 to private persons, 37 to charitable institutions, e.g. children's homes, and 85 to other District Committees. It was pointed out in many Districts that the reference to private persons usually entailed a great deal of work for the Secretary.

Class III—Those Assisted—is the smallest in number, namely 310. If we exclude 'in kind', mostly vagrants and others relieved with bread (total 193), the proportion is small indeed. In fact, the Districts used the method of 'relief in kind' less as the years went by and the sub-division was soon omitted from the tables. These statistics are followed by six comparatively long accounts of the undeserving, mostly impostors. The kind of relief work done at this time is summed up in brief paragraphs.

When Districts were well established, such as St Marylebone, St George's (Hanover Square), Kensington and Paddington, who were issuing their third annual reports in 1872, they tended to play down the 'detective' side of the work and to emphasise the more positive aspects. The first three of these gave no 'case histories' to their subscribers. Cases quoted as 'specimens' by Islington in the year when C. S. Loch was a member, give a good idea of what the Committee felt was typical of their work. They are all, of course, 'success stories' since the main purpose was to satisfy their subscribers and to appeal for more public support.

The first group included: an enquiry on behalf of a gentleman who gave a persistent caller a C.O.S. ticket—it was shown that all the applicant's statements were false; an enquiry about an applicant said to have an excellent character—he was found to be living entirely on charity, supported mostly by benevolent ladies; another enquiry showed false information given and 'the surprised applicant withdrew'. These were followed by several examples of constructive help which enabled the applicants to return to work. They are briefly told but nevertheless reveal something of the District's work in situations by no means rare in the 1870s. One will suffice to illustrate the misery endured by one family in 'hard times':

> A widow whose husband died a few months back. She and her four daughters gained a scanty livelihood by needlework, earning between them about 9s. a week. Work became slack, their small earnings decreased, and they were reduced to the utmost straits. Their case was brought to the notice of the Society through a Bible woman who lived in the same house. On hearing of it the Enquiry Officer called at once on a Monday afternoon and found that with the exception of a little food the Bible woman had given them in the middle of that day, they had literally had nothing to eat since Saturday. Being people of great respectability the Officer was of opinion that they would rather have sat still and starved than beg in any shape. Of course, immediately, relief was given and subsequently the Society procured them a sewing machine and they got good work.

It must be remembered that the only available statutory assistance at that time was provided under the Poor Law. Outdoor relief was administered grudgingly, often harshly, and few who valued their self-respect would apply. The pittance given was often so small that, although by law destitution had to be relieved, it was by no means unknown for a pauper to be found dead 'from exhaustion through want'.* As late as 1904 it was reported by the C.O.S.†[24]

---

* This is borne out by the Returns of the Number of Deaths in the Metropolitan Districts. Deaths where there had been a Coroner's Inquest were noted and verdicts of 'Starvation accelerated by Privation' recorded.

† An editorial note was concerned with 'the unwisdom of inadequate relief to old people'.

that a widow aged seventy-three had been found lying dead on the floor of her room. It was stated in evidence before the Coroner that she was in receipt of 4s. a week from the Parish and did a little charing. . . . Death was found to be due to syncope and neglect. The Coroner remarked 'this is something for the Guardians to think over. What is the use to give 4s. a week to a person in this condition?'

Sometimes exceptional conditions led some of the District Committees to relax their rules. In the year 1878–79 there had been a long and very severe winter. The building trade was slack and labourers were out of work; ships were delayed and dockers were unemployed. One District Committee, in reporting aid given to 'out of work cases' which would not ordinarily be considered eligible, recognised 'the strain on the resources of even the thrifty among the working classes'. Yet they could not resist a moral lesson: 'Advantage was taken by the members of Committee who visited and dispensed relief to these destitute ones to inculcate maxims of providence in the future. . . .' They add 'this advice was well received, and in some cases they hope will prove of far more benefit than the temporary assistance given'. One wonders if the visitors ever considered what might be going on in the minds of 'these destitute ones' as they accepted assistance and advice in their dire necessity. Visitors still had much to learn. They often found it difficult to understand why the C.O.S. was 'so misunderstood'.

From time to time the work varied as conditions changed and new needs were revealed. In 1872–73 St George's and Westminster District Committees had reported a plan for the migration of industrious families, especially widows with children between the ages of eight and eighteen. Such families were helped to move 'from the overcrowded labour market of London to the manufacturing areas of the north where it was ascertained by careful enquiry they could obtain employment'.* Emigration to Australia or Canada gave other families the new opportunity they sought.† The C.O.S. Committee usually helped to supply the whole family with clothes and often made a loan or part payment towards the fare. Lewisham, for example, helped some 161 families

---

* This scheme was paid for by one of the voluntary members, p. 85–6.

† The selection and casework were done by the Districts—the scheme was organised by 'Central'.

(458 men, women and children) to go to Adelaide, Melbourne and Sydney where the C.O.S. had contacts with employers. In one instance arrangements were made with an employer in Queensland on behalf of three young men. In this case the employer guaranteed free passage, board and lodging with £16 a year for one or more years with the prospect of a bonus of £5 for good behaviour and satisfaction. In times of severe distress emigration accounted for the largest single category of help given by many Districts. But the numbers were a small proportion of the total in need.

In the early twentieth century the Districts were much concerned with their inability to do anything effective for the increasing number of unemployed. In some areas they worked closely with the 'Distress Committees'. In South West Ham, for example, the Distress Committee was dealing with over 4,000 cases. It was this Committee which asked the C.O.S. to help. 'Central' agreed to pay the cost of setting up a C.O.S. District Committee to which the Distress Committee nominated nine members and the C.O.S. six. The first committee included two Borough Councillors amongst its honorary officers.* Lewisham had reported in 1902 that the return of the Reservists from South Africa and the discharge of men from Woolwich Arsenal had added to the distress in their area.

---

* The first meeting was held in July 1906. For a further account of this Committee, see pp. 84–85.

CHAPTER FOUR

Trends since the 1880s

1. Health and Social Conditions: Examples of Casework

The Charity Organisation Society, like many others at the time, had been alarmed when the Poor Law Board asked, in the report 1869–70, 'how far it may be advisable, in a sanitary or social point of view, to extend gratuitous Medical Relief beyond the actual pauper class'.[1] But, in the 1880s, C.O.S. District Secretaries were increasingly asked to help families where sickness, disablement or infirmity had caused or increased the distress. A new type of 'long term case' was being reported. There was much concern about the ravages caused in a family when the breadwinner was discovered to have 'pthisis' or 'consumption'. The C.O.S. described the new convalescent homes where 'beds' were secured by the C.O.S. for patients sent by the Districts.*[2] The value of convalescent treatment in the 'step-by-step' method, 'undertaken with the utmost care and circumspection', was recognised where 'permanent improvement' was likely. We then find members of the District C.O.S. Committee visiting the families after the patient's return, making an allowance for extra milk, getting in touch with the employers to see whether lighter work could be found, and sometimes giving 'moral support' to the family for a long time until conditions were stable. During the first decade of the twentieth century some of the Districts were asking whether they could go on with such cases, which took up so much time and were so costly. 'Would it not be better to concentrate on Preventative Work?'

In the early 1890s many Districts had reported their general concern with families where a patient was suffering from 'the after-effects of sickness or disablement where there is a striking

---

* 'The Convalescent Home is a charitable institution of comparatively recent date; its usefulness is well known to those who try to help the poor.'

C*

lack of follow-up after treatment'. When the newly appointed almoners*[3] began referring such patients there was much closer co-operation. Islington, at the same time, was using its voluntary workers 'to find out by visiting whether those not helped with money could be helped by friendliness and watchfulness'. The Committee suggested that the volunteers might visit 'all those who came to the office in distress'.

The assistance given to the sick, the infirm and the disabled challenged many District Workers to reconsider their attitudes. The old category of 'undeserving' was becoming an embarrassment. By 1886 C.O.S. Central was omitting the sub-heading from its classification and substituting 'not likely to benefit'. Shortly afterwards all taint was removed when the revised heading appeared 'not assisted'.

A reading of old case papers at this period shows the C.O.S. workers making their plans and following through their decisions until they were satisfied that all that could be done to set individual families on the way to independence had been done. Most of the applicants were poor but not destitute. The majority, though not all, were manual workers. Widows from many walks of life were frequent applicants. The C.O.S. was in close touch with orphanages and, occasionally, with country families willing to take charge of a fatherless child. From time to time Districts included examples of help they were able to give to musicians, school-teachers and others of similar standing. For example:

In 1897 Lewisham was able to raise a large part of the fees to enable a school-teacher to go to a training college. A later example, in Kensington,[4] is of a headmaster of a country grammar-school who, when his health broke down, gave English lessons to foreign students. After twenty-five years his wife had an expensive illness and his own health broke down again; when 'the case became known to the Relieving Officer they were on the verge of starvation. The C.O.S. took up the case and the whole family, which included two children, was kept afloat for more than three years.'

The Districts were anxious to let it be known that applicants of

* Miss Stewart, the first 'lady almoner', was appointed to the Royal Free Hospital in 1895. She had been an experienced C.O.S. worker in North St Pancras District. See p. 104.

any class would be welcomed if they had fallen upon hard times. The term 'problem family' had not yet been invented but several Districts were becoming involved with families in similar complex situations. As the District Committees became more representative of other social agencies in the area, it was found that some families were known to several members. 'Difficult families' were being visited by a number of social workers. The evil of overlapping and the necessity for developing a method of case discussion led to what was later to be called a 'case conference'. Chelsea affords an early example of this method when in 1907–08 it invited members of its scheme for the Mutual Registration of Assistance[5] to attend a monthly conference: 'Difficult cases have been discussed where there has been overlapping, with a view to systematising the work', they reported in 1907–08. The following year they called a meeting to discuss the whole question of 'overlapping in Visiting and Enquiry work'.[6]

With the higher expectation of better quality casework, it was necessary to consider further the training of voluntary workers. The Districts had to provide the experience and much of the training, but some of them soon realised what a responsibility this placed on them. 'It is difficult', they were reporting in the early twentieth century, 'to find anyone who has time and is qualified to give individual attention to the training of visitors'.*

In the late nineteenth and early twentieth centuries, the C.O.S. Council was increasing its pressure on the weaker Districts to bring them up to the required standards. *Occasional Papers* by secretaries of the experienced committees were published to show what were the approved methods of working.[7] Addresses at conferences were reproduced in the *C.O. Quarterly*, amongst the most effective of which was that by C. S. Loch in 1904: though he acknowledged the good work done in the Districts as a whole, he left no doubt as to the harmful effects of indifferent work in some areas. Some extracts from two C.O.S. *Occasional Papers* will give an idea of the conditions and mode of work in many offices. It is as well to remember that telephones were not then installed: the first, paid for from Central Funds, was reported in 1906. Typewriters were rare. Reporting and letter-writing were done in long-hand. The first paper issued in 1896 is headed *The Work of*

---

* See Chapter 12.

District Committees; the second in 1903 *The Report of a C.O. Committee*.

. . . Most offices now have a staff of workers varying in number according to the accessibility of the office and the capacity of the Secretary or Hon. Secretary in setting them to work. Each office still has some paid officers; they bear only a very small proportion to the whole body of workers; but whether paid or unpaid it is essential that the work should be carried on *con amore* and with a certain amount of the 'enthusiasm of humanity'. . . .

Assuming the staff of workers, what have they to do?

Most offices have some place where applicants can wait, a room where they can be interviewed and tell their story to some one person without being overheard by others, and another room for ordinary business.

By the time the morning's letters have been opened and attended to there comes a succession of callers. . . .

(Examples of these, including subscribers, the relieving officer, a district visitor, a curate are given, together with the nature of their enquiry, etc.)

Meanwhile, in another room, applicants for relief are being seen one by one. . . .

(Some descriptions of applicants and their requests follow.)

. . . When the tide of applicants has ceased to flow the necessary letters on each case are written. Other C.O. Committees are asked to inquire at past addresses and of employers in their districts. The clergy are asked for information, and references are verified. Some worker is told off to go to the home of the applicant, see the rent-book and notice how regularly the rent is paid, whether the pawn-tickets are of recent date, and what is the condition of the room as to cleanliness. Relations are seen and asked if they can help in the emergency, employers called upon and wages verified, and the relieving officer is asked if he knows the case.

When all particulars have been obtained the case is ready to be put before the Committee. Each case is read out to the Committee—first the statement of the applicant, and then all the information which has been accumulated. It used to be the custom at some Committees to allow the applicant to appear before them, but this is now generally given up. It was found to act unfairly, as a nervous person was at a disadvantage, and a glib tongue might influence unduly. It is also quite unnecessary, for, if the case is read out by one who is conversant with every detail, the Committee can see with their mind's eye the person whose case they are discussing.

As every Committee has both men and women on it of various temperaments—some inclined to be very hard upon a fault, others to take a more lenient or sentimental view— each case is pretty sure to be discussed in all its bearings. A decision is always come to under a strong sense of responsibility, and there are certain definite lines on which it is based; . . . nothing must be done which could injure the self-respect or diminish the power of self-help on the part of the applicant. . . .

(There follows some account of the decisions made in a number of instances and the action taken.)

At this point a comment is added which might surprise workers of a later generation: 'All this', says the writer 'represents only one side of the work of a district office—*mere** casework.'†8

However the Districts might vary in their ability 'to make charity wise and thorough', they all followed certain prescribed methods which, it was claimed, kept the personal link between the giver and the receiver.

This is emphasised in the 1903 paper in the account of the *Special Case System of Help*:

> . . . help is first obtained from relations, friends, neighbours, employers, and other friends already connected with the applicant; next from the clergy and charitable institutions; finally by selection from a list of benevolent persons willing to contribute to a good case up to a certain amount in the course of a year. It is more in accordance with personal charity to interest a donor in the fortunes of some one family than to receive money for relief to be given at our discretion. The

* Italics mine.
† Marjorie J. Smith concludes that the Society made no pretence of being primarily concerned with casework until World War I.

Committee possess no funds for general relief, all money spent in that way being obtained for the individual cases by the labour of their officers or members. . . . 'Our work cannot be estimated by forms of relief or cash expenditure; its value consists in the field which it offers for well-directed personal endeavour.'

Many of the Districts experienced hostile criticism from those who persisted in looking upon the C.O.S. mainly as a 'relief organisation'. The critics made much of the fact that administration accounted for the greater part of the expenditure. It was difficult for some of the Districts to convince their opponents that their casework was advisory and consultative and only in small part grant-making, and that their function was also to organise and administer. The majority of cases quoted after the mid-eighties have some reference to medical assistance. They show the Districts making sound practical arrangements, looking both to the immediate need and to the future well-being of the family. Many of them demonstrate the business-like way in which plans were made and individuals encouraged or 'induced' to carry them out. Some also show a great understanding of the difficulties and sympathy with the feelings of families in need. The example given by Islington in the year 1906–07 under the heading 'A Widow's Story' shows the workers counselling the mother, and the mother discussing possibilities with her young son, with much understanding of the need to involve all concerned. The language belongs to its own day; psychological terms had not yet been brought into the discussion of casework, but the mother and the workers, with the help of other interested friends seem to have worked together to good effect to enable this large family to enjoy a happier future:

A Widow's Story

Nearly eight years ago a widow came to us for help and advice. Her husband had died eight months before, leaving her with nine children—the youngest only four months old. She had struggled on bravely without asking help from the parish, or indeed from anyone, until she felt that she could struggle alone no longer. A sympathetic talk with her encouraged us, for she appeared intelligent and steadfast, and we felt that she was capable of co-operating with us in overcoming her difficulties. Her husband had been steady, had belonged to two clubs, and had worked under the same employers for many years; her two eldest sons, aged eighteen and seventeen, were working for the same firm, and were therefore able to help a little besides paying for themselves. But how could the poor burdened mother work at her trade as machinist, and look after her children as well? What wonder that none of them were quite strong, and that the baby now a year old was puny and delicate? As we talked it out together, she agreed that if three were placed in good schools, she could manage. First then, we approached the late husband's employers, for she had no relations in a position to help, and they generously responded, offering to pay for Tommy, age six, for a year, in the first instance. An application was at once made to the Church of England's Homes, and the little lad was placed in a small farmer's home in the country under the supervision of the Vicar.

Having settled Tommy, we had to find a home for May, age four, and Freddie, nearly three. This was more difficult, because the mother naturally wanted them to be together and not too far away. At last after much correspondence we found an excellent small Home in a healthy suburb of London, and there they remained well cared for and taught until Fred reached the age limit for boys, seven, and came home. By this time his mother was able to keep him, the other children being old enough to be off her hands. May remained two years longer, and then her mother came to ask that she should be sent home too, for her children were all doing well, and they could quite afford it. And then came news about Tommy, now in his fourteenth year; his foster parents were so grieved at the thought of parting with him that they begged to be allowed to keep him without payment, and they would bring him up as their own son, on the farm. Of course this required grave consideration, but the Vicar, who had supervised him all these years, urged it strongly, and the farmer came up to London to see the mother and talk it over. He brought Tommy with him, and the mother wisely decided that it was too good an opening to lose. The boy had set his heart on being a farmer, and when his mother asked his opinion on the matter, he said, as he looked at the small back yard, 'Well, mother, I should have no scope here, I should like to remain in the country.' So the matter was settled. The mother now feels that the path lies clear before her—life will still be a struggle of course, but her delicate children are now all strong and on the right way to become good workers and useful citizens.

Now at the end of this story all seems to have gone very easily—but, in truth, it has meant continuous work for us all. It has been no light matter to raise the necessary money. Roughly speaking, we have had to raise more than £160 for this case. The employers have helped, we have appealed to friends and enlisted their help. The Society for Relief of Distress have also helped, and one of the owners of property in this 'dreary' neighbourhood, as it has been called, came forward generously when appealed to. And all this happened in the very streets where the journalist has said the parents are hopeless, and the sooner the children are taken right away from them the better!

The greatest difference between the work of the Districts in the 1870s and in the early twentieth century lies in the changed attitude. A patronising, often censorious, approach as in early days was not now officially acceptable, although it was still to be found, here and there, in individual workers. By 1914, it was claimed, 'those who deserve least sympathy sometimes need it most . . . the immediate issue should be dealt with on its merits, and we should not assume that it has no merits because there is a record of previous convictions. . . . given sufficient forces of help there is no such thing as an unhelpable class'.[9]

The study of the 'casework' of District Committees in this first period may be concluded by quotations from the last set of annual reports issued before the outbreak of the First World War.

In introducing the bound volume of forty-one District reports in 1914, the Central Council refers optimistically to the future. The Society, it believes, 'is gaining more and more the confidence of the public. . . . In spite of the increase in State aid and in the number of relief agencies, mostly haphazard and unco-ordinated, the C.O.S. District Committees have been able to provide "a network of intercommunication", a machinery of potential social usefulness which is unique'.

The Deptford Committee is quoted as saying, 'it is necessary to realise to what an extent the Society is the handmaid of other societies, and its offices centres for consultation, inquiry and advice'. In this respect they seem to have been forerunners of the Citizens Advice Bureaux set up some thirty years later. Other Districts record their satisfaction that so many agencies referred applicants. The list given by Battersea of 'agencies and individuals who have referred to the Committee persons for assistance or who have co-operated with them' illustrates a common practice of this period: Hospitals 218; Clergy and Missions 86; Various General Charities 80; Tuberculosis Dispensary 54; Regimental Charities 35; School Care Committees 27; Relieving Officers 17; The Settlement 16; Local Doctors 13; Juvenile Labour Exchange 11; Bermondsey United Charities 8; Invalid Kitchen 7; District Nurses 6. Private Persons sent 85. It will be noted that a high proportion, some forty-five per cent of the total, are referred on medical grounds.

The Council now comments on the fact that 'all committees find a common ground in their casework; although many do much besides, it is the casework which forms the bulk of the work of the Society throughout London'. The Council notes steady improvement in the quality of the work, 'and that the standard is much higher and more uniform than it was only a few years ago'. The cases quoted are interesting since they indicate what the Society considers satisfactory.

The first example is taken from Lewisham to illustrate the reward of perseverance. Lewisham itself adds 'patience and firmness' to the qualities needed by the workers if they are to give 'any real help'. The account is best given in their own words:

C., a girl suffering from anaemia, was sent to us by a hospital for convalescent treatment for three weeks, but she returned not much improved. The physician wished her to remain under his observation for a time, and did not recommend us to send her away again. C. was the eldest of a very large family living in a house of four small rooms under very bad conditions; so after a few weeks, with the physician's approval, we found her a light place where she would have good food, plenty of fresh air, and be allowed to attend the hospital. However, the parents would not let her go, as her mother wished to have her help at home. A few weeks later, during her mother's confinement, C. had to nurse her and look after twelve other people. It was small wonder that she became seriously ill, and we were asked by the hospital to send her away again. This time we made it a condition that C. must go to service as soon as she was fit, and must not return to the bad conditions at home. We sent her away for six weeks and at the end of that time she was helped to find a place in the country. As she had outgrown her clothes, we helped her to get a new outfit, on the understanding that she should repay part of the cost out of her wages. This she has done. She has now been nine months in her place, and is very happy and doing well. The family has been induced to move to a larger house.

A later example, from Fulham, is of interest in showing a significant change of attitude when immorality was discovered in a family needing help:*

M.E., a young widow with three children, lately come from a country town. Sent by a clergyman for financial help and employment. She appeared to belong to the superior 'servant' class, and it was hoped it might be possible to place her, with a little daughter, in good service, to apprentice her boy of fourteen, and to get the third child into an orphanage. It was not easy to arrive at truth here, but at last the real difficulty became plain. The woman had for some time led an immoral life. The children suffered in various ways as a result. Every possible effort was made to induce Mrs E. to turn over a new leaf. She was offered treatment in hospital and convalescent home, with work, under kind supervision afterwards, and help for the children. But she would have none of it! The boy of fourteen was then taken in hand, and finally sent off to Canada with delightful fosterparents, and to good work. He is doing well. The youngest child was sent to the infirmary and, on learning the real character of the mother, the Guardians have decided to keep her and educate her. The

* Cf. example, p. 68.

elder girl is being watched by the workers of a Preventive
Society, and it is hoped that she, too, may soon be placed in
better surroundings. Our efforts have failed so far as regards
poor Mrs E., but, as a result of knowledge of facts, we have
been able to help the children.

2. *Other Work of Districts: Local Co-operation in Various Projects. Mutual Registration of Assistance. 'Bad Areas'*

Although most of the Districts were chiefly interested in
casework, some had also attempted to organise charity in their
Districts. A few had found the task too heavy. Islington had
written in 1883: 'The idea of organising the charity of nearly
300,000 persons (givers or receivers) was itself so utterly pre-
posterous that the marvel is how any committee could have
undertaken such a task.'*

Other Districts, however, felt that they had a special responsibility for organising charity. Chelsea was able to report in 1889–90
that they had suggested a scheme for the interchange of information 'for the prevention of overlapping' and 'as a means for getting
to know each other better'. The problem of overlapping continued
to be discussed at intervals throughout the history of the C.O.S.
It was still being considered in the mid-twentieth century, by
which time the number of voluntary and statutory social services
had multiplied.†

But Chelsea was optimistic when in 1903–04 it took its 'first
tentative step forward' in setting up a Charities Register. By
1909–10 some twenty-three C.O.S. Districts had adopted the
scheme for *the Mutual Registration of Assistance*. Chelsea, as the
pioneer, found itself a centre of consultation for visitors from the
provinces and overseas. Yet M.R.A. was looked upon with
suspicion by some of the clergy and by quite a few of the charitable
agencies throughout London. Some of the Boards of Guardians
refused to co-operate. Enthusiasm for 'the prevention of over-

* This was a reflection by the Islington Committee after it had been forced
by lack of sufficient workers and funds to give up the northern half of its District,
Holloway, in 1883.

† The P.E.P. Reports of the late 1930s and the Younghusband Reports of
the mid-century emphasised the need to deal rationally with the situation. The
problem was still with us in the late 1960s.

lapping', was thwarted by hostility to 'the Rogues Gallery'. This limited some District efforts to extend the scheme.*

In view of renewed interest, some sixty years later, in the possibility of setting up a statutory scheme of mutual registration, in which voluntary societies would be asked to participate, it is worth noting the methods used by the C.O.S. in the pioneer efforts. It was described by Chelsea as follows:[10]

> The scheme is a simple one. Every agency anxious to prevent overlapping is asked to send in weekly or monthly a list of their cases, and when it is found that two or more societies know the same family, each is notified in the hope that they will agree to work together in the assistance of the particular family in whom they are mutually interested, and so make their work more effectual.

Chelsea had earlier explained that the lists were *confidential*.

In considering the work of the District Committees, it is their individuality which is of special interest. In spite of constant guidance and surveillance by the Central Council, each District office was shaped by the vigour and personalities of its committee and its secretary. We have seen how Woolwich, under Grinling and his forceful Committee, managed for some years to take its own path. Under Grinling's successor, the District became entirely orthodox. West Ham in the early twentieth century offers another illustration in contrasts. The North West Ham Committee was set up in 1900 in the more spacious residential and shopping area of the Borough. It worked on conventional lines drawing most of its members from the better-off sections of the area. When a separate committee was formed for the dockland and industrial area of the south it struck out immediately on its own. Its first report made clear that 'those who apply or are referred . . . will never be considered as cases but always as men and women and fellow-citizens'.[11] Two years later it was announcing that: 'It decided to study the ideas of the people rather than to impose ready-made ideas upon them.'[12] When it went further, to challenge the underlying theory of the Society, there must have been distinct misgivings at Central: 'in poor industrial areas such as this

* In Chelsea even though the Guardians did not join the scheme of M.R.A. there was often much unofficial exchange of information between the R.O. and C.O.S. workers.

voluntary effort alone cannot do all or even a large part of what is necessary. It would seem that in some shape or another the State must itself organise the different kinds of social work'.

Yet, in spite of the anti-collectivist official C.O.S. policy, C. S. Loch and his colleagues had always stressed the importance of Municipal responsibility and of Governmental action in appropriate spheres. Loch went so far as to urge the District Committees 'to hustle Local Authorities', especially in the field of housing and sanitation. The great interest in 'Artisans' Dwellings' led many Districts to set up special committees to prod the Local Authority into dealing with insanitary and overcrowded houses. The Districts sometimes participated directly in schemes; for example, Islington made itself responsible for a block of working-class houses in 1893–94*; managers and rent collectors were put in charge. The C.O.S., as such, did not manage the buildings but they were behind the scheme. They were soon adding a Provident (Thrift) Group and other similar activities.

A number of Districts formed 'Sanitary Aid Committees', either by starting the Committee themselves or by co-operating with an existing group like the London Reform Union. The Committees dealt with a large number of complaints by local residents. The formation of Provident Friendly Visiting Societies was a common activity in the 80s and 90s. In addition to securing working class depositors, the Committees usually formed a band of visitors who collected the small sums regularly. They often added other services such as issuing leaflets giving the depositors details of 'desirable men's clubs' to join, or of a movement for a free library in the area. Islington was reporting in the year 1889–90: 'We are hoping by this addition to our work to come into friendly co-operation with the artisan class, and by so joining hands, complete the circle of our fellow-workers.' They hoped 'to bring a new element into a district where there is little that is enlivening or entertaining'. One of the suggestions was for a University Extension Course.

We find other areas particularly concerned with employment difficulties; an experiment to set up a Labour Enquiry Office had been made in 1870 in Soho, by Mr Alsager Hay Hill. In connection with this pioneer effort Mr Hill issued *Labour News*, and, in order to get first-hand information, went with a colleague on two tours

* The Popham Street Scheme.

of the cotton districts of the north. He was anxious to assess the prospects for Londoners and other southern workers. This was followed up in 1872 and 1873 by St George's (Hanover Square) Committee who employed a paid agent to keep information up-to-date. All the earlier work was done by voluntary effort. A number of District Committees took advantage of the scheme.

In several other areas Skilled Employment and Apprenticeship Committees were being considered: centres were often set up on C.O.S. premises and, in many instances, were run by C.O.S. District officers. A lively interest was taken by some Committees in apprenticeship schemes. The work of many of the Committees was, in fact, 'casework', since much care was taken not only to find the right job, but to look after the welfare of the boy or girl. The Report of the St Marylebone Skilled Employment and Apprenticeship Committee[13] notes that visitors often arrange for medical examinations, and treatment follows. 'We like, if we can, to get a "guardian" for each of the children we place. . . . The intimate relationship thus established is of great value. . . .' The Committee give an example of persistence by their own workers and by the boy concerned:

> The boy was sent to a printer on trial but 'at the end of three months the firm said his reading and spelling were too poor for apprenticeship. We pleaded for another chance, which was granted, and arranged evening classes, at which L.E. worked so hard, that in another couple of months he was triumphantly indentured'. This Committee attributes what success it had 'to the parents, some of the poorest showing great intelligence and unselfishness, to the teachers who are invaluable in advising the committee about the children and to the co-operative employers'.

This enlightened Committee looks forward to the Trade Schools—feeling that their own work covers a transition period.

A second example illustrates the hard work of another C.O.S. committee[14] in the effort to apprentice a disabled boy:

> . . . A case . . . which caused us a good deal of anxiety but was satisfactorily carried through. A lad was sent to us from a cripples' home, where he had learned something of boot-making and they asked us to start him in life. . . . Our secretary . . . found out someone in the Midlands who was

wanting a boy, then had every sort of enquiry made about the character of the proposed employer, on whose kindness the future happiness and welfare of the lad greatly depended. Everything being found satisfactory, a friend interested in the lad had the indentures drawn up and paid the premium required. All this entailed much labour, and could not have been done in the same manner by any private individual, however well disposed and kind-hearted.

Sometimes members of District Committees were seconded to help start an Infant Welfare Centre, or an I.C.A.A. Office.* It was an experienced C.O.S. officer who was invited by the L.C.C. to organise the new Children's Care Committees.† It was another such officer who became the first hospital almoner.‡ Sometimes the Districts lost their most vigorous workers who started new ventures and stayed on to see them through, e.g. one of the Honorary Secretaries at Fulham set up a Social Education Council and was obliged to give up her work for the C.O.S. Many workers were manning the new 'anti-tuberculosis' dispensaries. The Districts usually reported these secondments with some pride even though they missed the help of such experienced workers. In the twentieth century many of the Districts felt that they had a contribution to make to 'the betterment' of their areas.

In 1911–12 the Districts were encouraged to move out into yet more ventures. The Council of the C.O.S. in 1912 passed unanimously a resolution: 'That it is desirable that the Society should undertake the work of improving bad local conditions and bad areas, and that District Committees, wherever it is possible, should initiate this work in their districts.'

Loch, in an *Occasional Paper*,[15] refers to this as 'a new step— new, yet not altogether new'. He had for years tried to take the Society along with him in his plan 'to form a community of neighbours'. It was part of his ideal of charity in its fullest sense. Now, at last, a drive was to be made to attack some of the worst abuses of a neighbourhood 'by making friends of the local people' and at the same time organising a corporate scheme to secure better conditions.

In 1913 the C.O.S. was able to report considerable success in

---

* The I.C.A.A. had been started by the C.O.S. See p. 101.
† Miss T. M. Morton.   ‡ See pp. 74 and 104 ff.

two of the 'Bad Areas' of Paddington and North Kensington.[16] The areas had become notorious for their insanitary overcrowded houses—once prosperous large houses now let out in squalid, furnished rooms. This problem, too, is still with us as the spacious houses of Loch's day, built for one family, are now occupied to overflowing by numerous families. (The 1960s have had the Notting Hill outcry and the television play *Cathy Come Home* to make a wider public aware of the misery which may result from such conditions.)

True to C.O.S. methods of tackling problems, one by one, through individual families and neighbourhoods, the C.O.S., before the First World War, set about organising a 'betterment scheme' as a combined operation. The Society co-operated with members of the local Borough Council, the Board of Guardians, representatives of the Churches 'of all denominations', and many of the charitable organisations, all of whom were already interested in improving conditions. This time the C.O.S. was successful in securing the support of a certain number of local working men. In consequence there was a strong committee to discuss and plan the methods of advance. The C.O.S. was then able to interest the L.C.C., especially the Medical Officer of Health and the Public Health Department. The objects agreed upon were: first, temperance; second, the provision of means of recreation and education for the boys and girls; third, rational amusement for adults, especially devices for 'healthy rivalry'. One example of the latter was the suggestion for a competition in window-boxes. The C.O.S. was able to report considerable success which began with the purchase of five houses, 'the nucleus for an open space'. The constructive aspects of this scheme were emphasised with the urgent plea that people would no longer refer to them as the 'Bad Areas' but rather stress all the improvements made. Later generations were to appreciate the psychology behind such thinking when they renamed the 'Depressed Areas' the 'Development Areas' in the 1930s.

Since 'casework' had, in fact, formed the bulk of the work carried out by the Districts in the period before the First World War, a review of this period may be fittingly concluded by a comparison of the Statistical Reports of the year's 'casework' in 1883–84, when forty offices were included, and those of thirty years later, the last full year before the outbreak of war and the last year of C. S. Loch's effective working life. By then forty-two District Offices were included in the returns. (See Tables 2 and 3.)

RETURNS FOR 1883–4.

The following is the Tabular Statement of Cases for the year 1883–4 returned by the District Committees :—

DISTRICT COMMITTEES.	Not requiring Relief, or Withdrawn	Undeserving	Ineligible	Poor Law	TOTAL	Total Number of Cases Assisted	GRAND TOTAL	Recommendation to Guardians	Recommendation to Private Persons	Recommendation to Institutions or Local Agencies	Committee	TOTAL	Medical Assistance	General Institutions	Grants	Loans	Pensions	Employment	TOTAL	Referred to other Districts or to the Central Office	Vagrants dealt with	Inquiries for other Committees or for the Central Office	Reports sent out
WEST :—																							
Kensington	210	139	427	25	801	278	1079	16	64	85	160	325	40	20	213	13	10	22	31	163	182	374	1240
Fulham Union	122	78	117	85	402	364	766	3	52	29	332	416	257	11	134	14	2	5	427	17	1	146	200
Paddington	106	64	165	57	392	367	759	7	83	68	274	432	97	26	210	30	31	60	464	12	..	308	226
Chelsea	29	32	86	55	202	155	357	20	39	67	69	195	44	9	83	8	3	44	231	20	2	205	412
St. George's Union :																							
St. George's Division	104	16	32	76	228	147	375	74	45	59	..	178	57	4	65	1	7	16	170	131	25	659	1117
Westminster Division	130	57	48	177	412	168	580	2	76	56	58	192	79	4	89	8	2	20	197				
Westminster Union :																							
St. James's & St. Anne's, Soho	84	18	69	34	205	176	381	3	76	80	70	229	46	12	134	13	5	19	234	75	..	347	155
NORTH :—																							
St. Marylebone	158	..	234	62	454	599	1053	5	115	222	319	661	178	..	354	43	37	11	623	122	..	543	404
Hampstead	45	5	39	30	119	213	332	7	69	80	99	255	90	5	115	32	3	8	253	10	56	123	130
North St. Pancras	59	34	26	36	155	287	442	8	108	119	86	321	90	9	131	16	1	4	258	14	5	193	157
South St. Pancras	123	30	166	149	468	383	851	37	278	154	33	502	130	44	286	32	7	11	510	..	..	405	208
Islington	174	91	63	96	424	156	580	..	126	42	43	211	64	52	105	22	9	15	271	200	3	355	353
Hackney Union	137	..	127	74	338	254	592	8	113	156	89	360	97	18	168	34	4	14	331	44	5	223	183
CENTRAL :—																							
St. Giles's and Bloomsbury	84	51	50	42	227	156	383	1	85	74	44	204	35	10	133	9	4	28	219	74	..	373	366
Strand Union	107	37	129	70	343	187	530	1	66	109	97	273	43	65	122	36	1	11	277	160	50	276	165
Holborn Union	34	14	37	34	119	165	284	..	22	20	144	186	19	21	107	31	3	3	184	50	3	366	268
Clerkenwell	51	23	80	31	185	150	335	4	43	59	136	241	41	11	94	24	1	7	182	15	2	456	99
City Union	9	6	51	33	99	161	260	4	27	16	139	186	16	18	99	53	..	12	189	102	2	1639	234
EAST :—																							
Shoreditch	31	24	105	105	265	190	455	1	21	52	128	202	56	..	159	8	..	..	223	9	..	429	795
Bethnal Green	66	14	117	40	237	296	533	4	84	183	154	424	79	8	237	29	8	3	364	41	..	315	372
Whitechapel Union	83	16	147	18	264	270	534	3	41	123	151	318	106	13	218	8	1	12	358	63	3	330	266
St. George's-in-the-East	113	31	117	77	338	355	693	11	30	168	146	355	86	11	347	6	2	22	474	62	..	230	152
Stepney Union	43	26	79	81	229	309	538	7	57	185	145	394	32	55	247	6	8	7	337	2	..	160	342
Mile End Old Town	114	14	28	110	266	312	578	1	56	175	151	383	40	94	245	13	6	10	409	28	1	248	424
Poplar Union	156	19	191	163	529	440	969	3	102	149	316	570	213	17	282	32	8	22	574	10	10	358	
SOUTH :—																							
St. Saviour's Union, Southwark	62	43	138	78	321	221	542	5	76	69	143	293	79	11	155	31	2	8	256	50	..	249	116
Newington	171	36	233	143	583	458	1041	2	151	239	239	651	230	14	336	35	2	25	642	47	2	390	203
St. Olave's Union, Southwark	78	12	165	38	293	392	645	..	84	190	146	420	125	3	213	46	6	17	407	9	..	237	29
Lambeth	126	52	348	63	589	465	1054	5	104	237	204	550	158	68	341	29	2	7	600	34	20	257	156
Brixton	10	13	..	45	68	180	248	5	9	48	137	199	40	8	112	37	..	3	184	18	62	57	32
Wandsworth and Putney	17	10	14	36	77	89	166	2	17	24	63	106	45	13	32	13	3	..	148	13	4	174	138
Batterses	55	58	66	17	196	144	346	1	13	43	57	144	42	..	98	5	1	..	42	74	68	95	166
Clapham	6	..	18	15	39	35	74	..	13	7	27	47	5	..	26	8	2	1	42	74	..	244	
Camberwell & Peckham	71	37	211	191	510	297	807	1	118	84	170	373	80	2	253	20	1	16	322	340	..		244
Greenwich	37	16	43	11	107	157	264	4	149	9	26	188	91	5	29	27	6		127	21	4	171	191
Deptford	28	7	72	51	158	219	377	5	55	41	118	219	27	27	139	31	4	10	97	3	1	126	27
Woolwich Union	30	8	9	11	58	101	159	2	15	11	80	148	9	20	51	7		10	136	10	349	33	96
Lewisham	30	5	20	1	56	96	152	3	34	14	97	148	37	..	77	21	..		243	..	1361		
Eltham	..	..	..	..	..	245	261	2	..	..	..	243	243 126	..	74	28	..		243	..	..	37	55
Sydenham	3	11	2	..	16																		
TOTALS	3096	1147	4699	2460	10772	9037	20409	367	2715	3545	5183	11710	3103	695	6314	832	247	1291	11961	1747	2936	10726	19062

TABLE 2

RETURNS

The following is the Tabular Statement of Cases for the year ending

COMMITTEE	Referred to other District Committees	Enquiries for other District Committees	Number of Applications made	Number of Applications decided	Number of Applications withdrawn	Number of Applications not assisted	Number of Applications assisted	Sources of Assistance				
								By Institutions	By Guardians	By Individuals	Applicant's Relatives	Other Sources
Kensington	100	785	1147	1011	148	351	521	377	43	68	110	120
Hammersmith	21	471	580	528	..	..	..	148	1	67	22	22
Fulham	—	579	728	..	..	..	..	271	4	168	47	21
Paddington	17	802	711	667	241	266	401	265	17	163	87	83
Chelsea	89	309	275	289	264	148	122	70	3	94	23	10
St. George's H. Sq.	163	861	546	455	151	196	108	73	7	37	37	11
St. James's	133	1634	340	317	126	96	95	88	12	14	32	20
St. Marylebone	17	860	647	632	100	227	305	183	22	161	55	11
Hampstead	109	313	605	324	89	72	302	188	46	173	35	163
North St. Pancras	78	427	422	429	138	164	127	71	7	42	26	54
South St. Pancras	13	723	564	571	140	159	272	155	..	201	3	..
Islington	99	771	920	890	150	339	401	304	2	61	63	145
Holloway	89	406	339	408	81	124	204	134	16	85	64	53
Hackney	20	423	423	436	72	166	198	131	1	7	..	24
Dalston	121	547	452	386	142	112	132	174	11	11	13	9
Finsbury	134	729	562	391	66	262	158	136	4	13	6	9
Shoreditch	37	527	615	615	169	257	189	184	..	38	46	..
Bethnal Green	12	260	383	360	104	139	117	77	3	3	28	23
Whitechapel	50	518	229	201	28	87	114	85	1	37	18	29
St. George's East	53	183	323	309	20	152	137	98	6	6	..	27
Stepney	103	466	382	364	61	184	119	107	13	40	23	8
Poplar	48	561	324	292	32	177	115	47	..	28	2	57
North West Ham	32	457	262	263	18	103	142	75	4	18	21	79
South West Ham	20	267	293	..	56	121	116	49	2	10	2	70
St. Saviour's	48	675	442	360	81	136	146	116	7	10	5	57
Newington	11	820	616	623	90	287	310	378	14	146	151	81
Bermondsey	14	380	706	616	146	243	326	260	2	38	135	..
Vauxhall	56	778	669	628	124	179	325	567	6	136	127	15
Lambeth	60	528	312	266	51	88	182	156	3	19	..	2
Brixton	125	477	340	309	122	105	95	68	1	40	35	27
Wandsworth	66	324	406	363	68	201	152	103	1	79	52	3
Battersea	61	548	571	567	44	261	262	221	9	139	65	4
Clapham	103	553	423	416	101	91	227	289	14	94	15	44
Camberwell	182	630	587	432	107	173	208	208	25	17	70	30
Dulwich	36	180	250	218	82	114	104	141	2	20	53	19
Greenwich	51	158	361	365	64	99	183	191	1	62	62	..
Deptford	16	394	252	257	33	124	100	86	2	46	56	10
Woolwich	1	267	252	238	34	117	102	103	..	37	32	14
Lewisham	55	229	257	240	71	79	90	74	1	32	22	17
Norwood	57	114	213	200	36	79	120	96	..	106	36	40
S. Kilburn Ward	11	80	131	119	34	46	73	45	1	21	26	22
Westbourne Wd.	8	137	214	209	29	77	108	48	6	39	7	19
Totals	2,522	21,150	19,074	16,564	3,714	6,399	7,508	6,648	329	2,624	1,712	1,462

Friendly visits, e.g. to pensioners, not included in the above.

FOR 1913-14.

September 30, 1914, returned by the District Committees:—

Reports sent out	Some forms of Assistance						COMMITTEE
	Employment and Apprenticeship	Emigration	Sanatorium Treatment	Medical, Surgical, and Convalescent Aid	Pensions	Other forms of Assistance	
1493	39	2	2	203	12	169	Kensington.
482	1	1	3	55	..	157	Hammersmith.
712	42	2	8	209	9	155	Fulham.
1040	62	1	3	144	17	229	Paddington.
963	17	..	4	61	4	57	Chelsea.
431	12	..	..	73	1	35	St. George's H. Sq.
1101	18	..	2	52	4	50	St. James's.
569	45	1	3	121	10	154	St. Marylebone.
407	86	15	5	144	17	231	Hampstead.
836	8	..	2	69	2	43	North St. Pancras.
597	4	3	..	98	3	180	South St. Pancras.
799	14	3	4	231	4	192	Islington.
636	20	1	3	98	4	62	Holloway.
389	4	2	..	127	6	59	Hackney.
543	3	1	..	102	..	39	Dalston.
780	14	2	3	67	4	28	Finsbury.
448	2	..	7	76	2	109	Shoreditch.
707	5	2	..	65	4	34	Bethnal Green.
191	3	2	..	32	7	70	Whitechapel.
313	1	..	..	13	6	78	St. George's East
461	18	3	4	58	8	51	Stepney.
201	..	..	..	37	..	78	Poplar.
247	7	1	1	77	2	64	North West Ham.
330	4	2	..	48	2	77	South West Ham.
528	9	..	2	94	6	54	St. Saviour's.
985	11	3	18	220	7	88	Newington.
531	13	3	25	182	6	111	Bermondsey.
839	17	..	6	252	4	115	Vauxhall.
315	10	1	..	91	7	78	Lambeth.
379	9	..	2	49	2	26	Brixton.
746	17	..	1	95	1	49	Wandsworth
487	14	2	4	164	9	92	Battersea.
1336	32	3	1	135	6	157	Clapham.
593	1	..	..	161	2	32	Camberwell.
262	5	..	1	73	2	31	Dulwich.
301	3	..	..	121	4	93	Greenwich.
141	3	..	3	53	..	39	Deptford.
253	2	2	2	36	1	64	Woolwich.
420	7	1	1	47	5	39	Lewisham.
191	8	4	1	51	6	62	Norwood.
138	5	..	..	45	1	25	South Kilburn Ward.
..	4	2	2	31	5	64	Westbourne Ward.
23,121	599	65	123	4,160	202	3,620	

G

TABLE 3

CHAPTER FIVE

Achievements of 'Central'

1. Scheme For the Homeless, the Handicapped, the Sick, etc.

When in 1874 Bosanquet published *The History and Mode of Operation of the Charity Organisation Society*, it is significant that he left the account of the Central Council till near the end. The emphasis in the early years had been on the formation of District Committees and the establishment of a federation of committees; yet the achievements of 'Central' were still considerable. Under Bosanquet's successor, C. S. Loch, 'Central' was to play a dominant role in the development of the Society.

In considering the purpose of the Council Bosanquet had noted:

> It is essential that such a federation of Committees . . . should have a strong central body to assist any Committee that requires assistance, to preserve unity of action, and to represent the Society in Metropolitan, as distinguished from local matters, and indeed in all cases in which it is necessary that the Society should act as one body.

During the first years of rapid organisation the Central Council had not only established District Committees in many parts of London, but had started a District Aid Fund,* whereby wealthier Districts assisted committees in poor areas; it had set up an Inquiry Department 'which enquires into suspicious charities, and into cases of begging letters and other impostors whose operations are not confined to the district of any one committee, and keeps up communication on these subjects with kindred societies at home and abroad, and, when necessary, with the police'; it had begun

* See Chapter 15, p. 308.

the collection of reports and documents which was to form a valuable library under the direction of C. S. Loch: already, metropolitan charities had agreed to send in annual reports; Acts of Parliament, Reports of Parliamentary Committees, and other publications bearing on Charity and the Poor Law, were available for reference; the Society expressed its willingness to supply information to 'all who liked to apply for it'.

In these first five years the C.O.S. had also carried out an extensive review of metropolitan charities and had reported on Night Refuges, Soup Kitchens, Public Day Nurseries and Voting Charities. It had set up a Standing Medical Committee which had prepared rules for Provident Dispensaries, 'to relieve Medical Charities'. The Council had been discussing employment migration, emigration and the promotion of provident habits 'with regard to the bearing of each on the elevation of the poorer classes and to the most appropriate agencies for dealing with them'.[1] Bosanquet also reported that 'in pursuance of that part of the place of the Society which contemplated dealing with causes rather than symptoms of pauperism, a large Special Committee was formed in 1873 to consider how the dwellings of the London poor could be improved'.* This method of the 'Special Committee', to consider social questions of public importance, was one which the Society was to employ with good effect in subsequent years.

Though mainly a London Society, the C.O.S. looked further afield than the Metropolis. It compiled a list of all relief agencies at home and abroad which seemed likely to be able to assist one another with information: 'They have always recognised the duty of giving all the assistance they can to those who are interested in similar work elsewhere, and the importance of obtaining help from them.' As an instance of its wider contacts, Bosanquet gave an account of the Special Committee, formed in 1871, comprising representatives from all parts of the country to consider the best mode of repressing vagrancy. (The C.O.S. felt that vagrancy had become an alarming problem and the Committee considered various plans adopted in different parts of the country to deal with it.)

The work done in this early phase of the Society's history is an

---

* It is instructive to note the steps taken to make the Enquiry effective (see Chapter 5, 2.).

impressive record, considering the few resources available, but hardly equal to the inflated claims made for it in 1875:

> We have now risen to the dignity of a volunteer society, equal in work and usefulness to a Government Department, and it well behoves the Council to consider this high position we have attained, and to make it efficient and homogeneous, and not inferior to the high class of officers whom we have been fortunate enough to engage in our service to carry on the great work which is before us.*[2]

There is no doubt that in its early years the C.O.S. had its greatest publicity and earned the widest hostility from the work of its Enquiry Department. Ignoring unpopularity the Society was determined to stamp out malpractices, whether of blatant fraud or of unsound method. Begging letter writers were thriving on the sentimentality of the age: fraudulent organisations were profitable, since the law had many loop-holes: mendicity was practised on a wide scale. The C.O.S. prosecuted whenever possible; it publicised malpractices extensively and drew up a cautionary list of organisations, which proved very effective, particularly when a court case upheld C.O.S. action as 'not libellous'. But when the C.O.S. went further and attacked some wellknown institutions for lax methods and unsound organisation, it was not so successful. Dr Barnardo's was the first to be the object of investigation, in 1877, by a C.O.S. ad hoc committee. Some inefficiency was uncovered but no fraudulent practice. Dr Barnardo's continued to flourish under its dedicated leader, with some tightening up of administration. The Salvation Army was the next considerable organisation to come under scrutiny, this time by a critical letter to *The Times*. But, however much the C.O.S. might consider the direction irresponsible and sentimental, 'the Army' had captured the imagination of a wide public and was doing work in districts where no others had penetrated. The C.O.S. did not come out too well from the encounter. However, the Department continued to flourish and developed later into a widely used 'Information Department'.

One of the Society's most constructive contributions was its

---

* Loch, a newly appointed 'high class of officer', was to be severely critical of the quality of some of this early work, undertaken, he thought, in too great haste.

activity as a centre of information on social problems. It directed public attention to a variety of questions with some skill, carrying on propaganda and exerting pressure in influential quarters. This was particularly apparent during the secretaryship of C. S. Loch.* Its methods were various: one, as we have seen, was the use of the experience of District Committees. The Central Council would, from time to time, discuss a matter of public concern, outline the question on which further evidence was needed and ask its District Committees to send in any examples met with in the course of their day-to-day family social work. Armed with this material they would prepare a memorandum, send a deputation to those concerned, either Government Department or Local Authority, and give the question all the publicity within their power to get the matter discussed and dealt with. Their valuable fact-finding work on money-lenders and hire purchase evils was done, later, in this way.

Two points must be specially noted in considering these early efforts of the C.O.S. First, that in spite of its 'Individualism' the Society was prepared to advocate statutory intervention, both at local and national level, on questions such as public health and housing, when the 'betterment of the community' was at issue. Secondly, that their committees of enquiry were conducted with administrative efficiency and with a thoroughness in investigation which was an innovation in the proceedings of a voluntary society. Did the Society rate its contribution as a pioneer too high? Council reports and 'short histories', referring later, with some pride, to the successful outcome of C.O.S. efforts, tended to claim full credit for resulting legislation. There is no doubt that Kay-Shuttleworth used his experience on the C.O.S. 'Dwellings' Committee to good effect. Octavia Hill's work was quoted in the debate in the House on the Cross Bill. The C.O.S. organised deputations and sent letters to *The Times* keeping up a constant interest in the Bill as it went through Parliament. The Society certainly played a valuable part in collecting evidence, in making recommendations and in keeping the matter before the public. It did useful work later in trying to prod the authorities into action when there was delay in carrying out legislation. It claimed to

---

* Loch perfected procedure by organising the hearing of evidence before 'select committees'—question and answer on the model of an official Public Enquiry—followed by reports, very like 'Blue Books'.

have been instrumental in getting the appointment of a Select Committee of the House of Commons to examine the unsatisfactory results. But the Artisans Dwellings Act of 1875 was the culmination of many ideas and improvement schemes, not least those of Joseph Chamberlain in Birmingham; and, as Mowat has pointed out: 'Its (working-class housing) promotion fitted in with the social programme of Disraeli's new government.'[3]

The C.O.S. also took up the question of the 'Homeless Poor', which was closely linked with its interest in Vagrants. It was noted that whenever there was an increase in unemployment the ranks of the homeless were swelled. In 1881 Mr Alsager Hay Hill raised the question at the Central Council, pleading for the more humane treatment of the Homeless under the Poor Law, and considering what might be done by the Districts for those in Common Lodging Houses. In keeping with the attitude of his time, Mr Hill asked for 'a careful sifting of applicants'—the better class to be treated with a view to recuperation, while genuine vagrants were dealt with by the criminal law. The question of vagrancy, raised by Sir Baldwyn Leighton in the House of Commons, led to the Casual Poor Act of 1882, but it did little to solve the problem of the Homeless.*[4] Some of the C.O.S. Districts were trying to assess the need and to see what constructive work could be done in co-operation with a Hospice and a Casual Ward.[5] The results were not encouraging but, as Helen Bosanquet pointed out, 'experience was gained which indicated some of the defects in the existing administration'. So far little was known about the extent of the need or the numbers of Homeless Poor. Consequently the C.O.S. decided in 1891 to investigate. A representative Committee was set up including members of London refuges and of the Local Government Board. It took evidence from police inspectors and from two habitual frequenters of casual wards, as well as from managers of shelters and from Poor Law Officers. The Commissioner of Police and the Local Government Board also placed information at the service of the Committee. As a result a report was published[6] which filled in many of the gaps in knowledge and recommended some very practical measures. One of these was the setting apart of small

---

* As H. Bosanquet comments, it enabled the Poor Law authorities to detain the casual paupers long enough to execute a fair task of work.

houses for careful treatment of the homeless. As might be expected, the recommendations also included:

(1) Investigations into the condition and antecedent of each person applying for admission to a Refuge, with a view to ascertaining the best form of assistance, and (2) co-operation between the Poor Law and Charity and between the various charitable institutions concerned with the Homeless.

Both 'Central' and individual District Committees continued to report on their efforts to help the homeless,* but the results were meagre until, in the 1920s, the L.C.C. took up the question. Only then was the co-ordination of statutory and voluntary enterprise effective and the valuable Welfare Centre by Charing Cross Bridge set up. The C.O.S. was consulted as negotiations proceeded[7] and it was claimed that 'our Council has borne an important part in securing the present Metropolitan arrangements for his [the homeless man's] true welfare'.[8]

If there had been considerable public interest in dwellings for the workers, and rather less for provision for the homeless, there was very little for the vulnerable groups which included the mentally defective, the deaf, the epileptic, and other physically handicapped persons. The blind had attracted rather more support, but, even here, certain important fields had been neglected and there was great need for co-ordination of the many scattered and overlapping efforts.[9] In 1874 the C.O.S. had set up a special committee to consider 'what more can be done to promote the welfare, especially the industrial training, of the blind'. It was successful in bringing together on the committee representatives of nearly all associations and institutions for the blind in London, and of others who were in touch with work in the provinces. It considered evidence from abroad, especially from Vienna and Saxony, on training. The Committee reported the following year and its recommendations were in line with principles generally accepted today. They included:

The treatment of the blind, so far as possible, on the same principles as those who have their sight; the management of workshops on a businesslike footing; application to the

* The C.O.S. Annual Report 1895 gave a description of the Society's work for 'Homeless Cases'. See also the reports of Paddington where an Association was formed in 1911.

D

Guardians to make full use of their legal powers; co-operation between charitable institutions for the welfare of the blind;
the formation of a Central Representative Council, and the setting up of a Royal Commission to enquire into the subject
of state aid towards the education and training of the blind.

The Council noted with satisfaction the passing of the Education (Blind and Deaf Children) Act, 1875, and commented: 'The
C.O.S. feels that only the State can cope on a wide enough scale
to aid fully the education of these classes.'* The Society thought
that statutory powers and duties were insufficiently known and,
in order to publicise them, published a summary 'of all existing
legislative enactments on behalf of the various classes of the
afflicted poor'.† C.O.S. principles were clearly stated by the
Council when the decision to circularise a summary of the Act
was discussed. 'It is well known that in all parts of the country
there are large numbers of afflicted children of poor respectable
people who, through want of sufficient funds are now growing up
a drag upon their families and are an injury to the children around
them, without receiving the advantages of the special instruction
which would alleviate their condition and render them to some
extent self-supporting and useful.'[10]
It was the educational aspects of legislation which particularly
interested the C.O.S. In 1877 the society was also noting with
satisfaction, the action of the London School Board in giving
opportunities to blind, deaf and dumb children.[11] For several
years the Society kept in close touch with developments, particularly on the vexed question of the use of types, sending deputations to the School Board, and notices to the Provincial Towns.‡[12]
Elementary education for blind children could make no progress
until the question of the most satisfactory type had been finally
settled. The knowledge acquired by the C.O.S. was put to good
use, in the early 1880s, in giving publicity to urgent and outstanding needs. Mr Gardner had left a large bequest for the
Welfare of the Blind with instructions for its use under four main
headings: the first two were concerned with education, training

*This was to take the form of Government grants and inspection.
† The summary was prepared in 1875 by W. M. Wilkinson, a barrister and a
staunch supporter of the C.O.S.
‡ Council drew attention to the agreement of Mr Fawcett, M.P. with the
C.O.S. findings.

and instruction in suitable trades, handicrafts and professions. To carry out this purpose the Trustees to the Fund were considering setting up a large institution and were already discussing suitable sites when the C.O.S. made its protest. It addressed a letter to *The Times* and followed it up with another to the Trustees of the Fund, with the result that the idea of an Institution was dropped and the income was used instead for grants to existing institutions, for scholarships, assistance to individual cases, and pensions. The C.O.S. noted regretfully that its suggestion for a representative Council was not followed. It was to be many years before the co-ordination of the various activities for the blind was achieved. The C.O.S. continued, however, to have a very close connection with the Trustees which was particularly useful when it applied for assistance for blind persons.

Another of the 'afflicted groups' of concern to the C.O.S. was the feeble-minded, then known as 'improvable idiots'.* It had been difficult for some of the enlightened pioneers, such as Dr Duncan, to get public sympathy on their behalf. The C.O.S. did much to publicise the need and to stimulate action, both voluntary and statutory. The question was taken up by Sir Charles Trevelyan when, in 1875, he gave notice of six resolutions which he proposed to move in Council. He stressed the confusion of existing legislation and his intention to frame a single consistent plan. He had the general approval of the Commissioners in Lunacy. (It is of interest to note the introductory statement of his change of attitude on the ability of a private charity to make adequate provision for Idiots and Imbeciles.) According to its usual practice, the C.O.S. set up a Special Committee, which attempted to cover the whole range of the mentally handicapped, and its report was submitted to the Local Government Board in 1877.[13] A sidelight on this venture is given by Helen Bosanquet who records the fact that one of the members of the C.O.S. deputation to the Local Government Board was Lord Shaftesbury, then Chairman of the Commissioners in Lunacy: 'Four years earlier, when the Organising Secretary raised the question of criminal lunatics, he (Lord Shaftesbury) wrote reproaching the Society for "erecting yourselves into a grand association for the control of everybody and everything. I certainly shall refuse to

* For a more detailed discussion of the development of voluntary and statutory aid for this group see Rooff *opus cit.* Part III.

become, or perhaps remain, a member of a body so fearfully
ambitious".' Helen Bosanquet comments 'the Society proving
irrepressible, he fortunately thought better of it, and supported
it on many occasions'.[14] After a promising start, the Bill which,
according to the C.O.S. embodied a large part of its programme,
was withdrawn. The Council went on to consider how it could
stimulate Boards of Guardians to use their permissive powers
more consistently (practice varied from Union to Union) for the
care and maintenance of these groups, and again set up a committee to investigate.[15]

In 1890 a measure for the elementary education of defective
children was passed, but it was not until 1903 that a Royal Commission on the Feeble-Minded was set up after much pressure,
not only from the C.O.S. but from other Associations, particularly
one established in the 1880s to promote the welfare of this group.*
Loch was invited to serve on the Royal Commission. In 1910 the
C.O.S. called a Conference to promote public interest, and by
1913 the first effective Mental Deficiency Act was on the Statute
Book. During the 1920s the Society continued to give publicity
to the question, 'since interest in this group so quickly dies down'.
They co-operated with other organisations as needs were identi-
fied. For example, in 1923, in conjunction with the Central
Association for Mental Welfare and the Invalid Children's Aid
Association, they tried to get support for special Convalescent
Homes (ordinary convalescent homes could not cope with the
difficulties). In 1927 they were able to welcome the second
Mental Deficiency Act.

The Society took up other causes as they saw the need: for
example, that of Italian Children in the late 1870s. With their
usual thoroughness the C.O.S. committee collected evidence of
the evils of the *padroni* system of importing Italian children to
sing and dance in the streets during the day and in public houses at
night. Boys and girls were housed in depots under miserable
conditions by the *padroni* who made a profitable business out of
the exhausted children. The C.O.S. secured the co-operation of
the Italian Ambassador and others in presenting the evidence to
the Home Secretary. As a result public sympathy was aroused,
the police were vigilant and the iniquitous trade was gradually
suppressed.

* The National Association for the Care of the Feeble-Minded.

Another illustration of the effectiveness of the Society's pioneer work is the foundation of the Invalid Children's Aid Association in 1886. This is of special interest since it illustrates the readiness of the Society to 'hive-off' a project once it had proved its worth and gained sufficient support. The close co-operation of doctors was assured from the beginning since the surgeon to St George's Hospital had helped the C.O.S. to draw up the scheme. It was shown that the advisory service offered to mothers was a way of using the hospital service more effectively. True to the usual pattern, the bulk of the work was done in the initial stages by volunteers. In the first year 'some 300 ladies' offered to visit the families in different parts of London. Progress was made when the Nursing Association agreed to take part, by visiting the children who required more skilled attention. After two years, in June 1888, the C.O.S. pioneer* who had been the inspiration behind the scheme, and who guaranteed its expenses for the first year, decided to carry it on as an independent venture. In a letter to Loch he writes: 'I trust that the fact will always be remembered—remembered to the advantage of both parent and child—that it was the offspring of the Charity Organisation Society.'[16] C.O.S. District Committees were in future to work closely with I.C.A.A. committees in every part of London.

The Central Council was less happy in its attitude towards the feeding of necessitous schoolchildren. In this field it was guided by strict adherence to its social philosophy of family responsibility. It was also convinced that partial assistance through an Education Authority was the wrong approach. The service violated the principle that the *total* need of a necessitous family should be adequately met. The C.O.S., at first, argued that this could only be done through the Poor Law which had a duty to give sufficient relief to enable the children to be properly fed. If the family were in temporary difficulty then Charity could step in to re-establish them. Whenever the Education Authorities proposed partial schemes, the C.O.S. felt bound to resist and to support the alternative: that there should be 'constant endeavour to supply the needs of the children by improving the position of their families'. The Society continued into the twentieth century its already out-dated policy as it opposed the new provisions in the Education (Provision of Meals) Act, 1906. It earned considerable un-

* Mr Allen D. Graham, a staunch C.O.S. worker.

popularity in its own day and projected an unfavourable image for future generations since this action, together with the Society's opposition to the Old Age Pension Scheme of 1908 for similar reasons, was frequently quoted to brand the Society as a reactionary body.

Yet, in fairness to the Society, its constructive proposals and its own early pioneer efforts on behalf of schoolchildren should also be remembered. As it pointed out in a letter to *The Times* in November, 1906, C.O.S. opposition was to the *mere* feeding of necessitous children. It wanted more thorough and adequate care, which should include medical inspection, assistance to the families of such children, the setting up of school care committees on the lines of experiments which had already proved successful, and an increase in the number of day industrial schools. The C.O.S. claimed that its pioneer work for the general welfare of poor schoolchildren, in relation to family needs, led directly to the Children's Care Committee system established by the L.C.C. That there was some truth in this claim is evident as we look back at some of the Society's earlier propaganda and experimental work.

In November 1889, a letter to *The Times* had recommended: 'That arrangements be made between a few bodies of school managers and a few of its District Committees to allow for an enquiry into the causes of distress . . . of children thought to be in want of food, that in close communication with these school managers, a body of almoners should deal with each case personally, and as thoroughly as possible . . .' The letter pointed out that already there was co-operation between the School Board and the agencies and they would carry on 'until a better system takes the field'. The Society followed this up by appointing another Special Committee, which undertook 'a careful study of 101 families of which the families were attending schools in poor districts'. A report followed which described and analysed the findings 'showing how even those apparently hopeless had been successfully helped by dealing with the family as a whole'.[17] During 1890 further experiments in 'individual treatment' were made in five schools: representative committees of school-teachers and local agencies were formed and 'Provident Visitors' helped in difficult cases. 'Thus all the cases of delicacy and illness were at once attended to, and the school managers arranged that a

district nurse should be at hand on certain days of the week.'
Another useful Report was published, but progress was slow. It
needed the drive of Miss Frere and the L.C.C. Education Committee to use the new statutory powers of 1907 (for medical
inspection and school meals) to set up Care Committees throughout London.

The C.O.S. pattern of a salaried organiser with volunteer
workers was adopted and the C.O.S. immediately sent in lists of
suitable volunteers who were willing to serve as members of the
Children's Care Committees and of the new Local Associations.
To help with the preliminary planning for this unique and comprehensive scheme, the C.O.S. seconded one of its most
experienced secretaries, Miss Morton, who was employed by the
L.C.C. to superintend the investigation of cases in selected
schools. As with other earlier 'loans', for example the first hospital
almoner, the C.O.S. lost the services of Miss Morton* when she
was appointed in 1907 as Organising Inspector of London's
Children's Care Committees. The total welfare of families was
recognised as a vital factor in the welfare of schoolchildren, and
C.O.S. Districts continued to work in close co-operation with
Children's Care Committees throughout London.

One of the most valuable and persistent activities of the Society
was its advisory and practical work in the field of health. The
Central Council had, in 1871, established a standing Medical
Sub-Committee which was 'to deliberate and advise on medical
charities'.[18] Throughout its long history, this Committee was
successful in securing the services of eminent medical men and
others distinguished in public life. At first, in line with general
C.O.S. policy, the Committee was much concerned with the
scrutiny of dispensaries, sick clubs, etc. getting as much information as possible on doubtful practices. It soon opened a fullscale
campaign for the better administration of medical charities.

It was through the initiative of the doctors that the C.O.S.
turned its attention to the overcrowded out-patients' departments
of voluntary hospitals. A committee of doctors, formed in 1870,
invited the C.O.S. to help them to solve the problem. Two
approaches were made; one through the establishment of an
alternative, namely, Provident Dispensaries, which, it was hoped,

* Miss Morton came back years later, after her retirement from the L.C.C.,
to act as tutor in the C.O.S. training schemes.

would replace the Free Dispensaries already operating in some
areas; the second through the improvement of the out-patients'
departments by enquiry into the circumstances of the patients
attending. The C.O.S. had only a modest success in the first
approach, although it had the co-operation of the Friendly
Societies, the Hospital Saturday Fund (both representing working
people), and of some of the hospitals; a Metropolitan Provident
Medical Association was formed and registered under the Friendly
Societies Act in 1880. The C.O.S. was represented on the
committee and one of its members acted as chairman for many
years. Once launched, the scheme became independent of the
C.O.S. Sir Charles Trevelyan was, meanwhile, active in promoting
the Provident Dispensary Movement in the Provinces. But, overall, the schemes did not do much to relieve the pressure on the
voluntary hospital outpatient departments. The Provident Dispensary in London did not get the support of poor families
accustomed to free treatment in hospitals.

In 1888 a special committee of the C.O.S. prepared a petition
to the House of Lords asking for a Select Committee or Royal
Commission to investigate the work and management of Medical
Charities and their relation to infirmaries and other Poor Law
Institutions. The petition included a full statement of the main
issues drawn up by the C.O.S. in its preliminary discussions. The
C.O.S. was strongly supported by the medical profession, and, in
1890, a Select Committee of the House of Lords was set up to
enquire into the conditions of the Metropolitan Hospitals. The
C.O.S. gave evidence, but the special features of the C.O.S.
recommendations, the establishment of a Central Board and of a
uniform ˙system of accounts, although approved by the Select
Committee, were not implemented.*

The Hospital Almoners

The C.O.S. was more successful in its persistent endeavours to
get what later developed into a casework service in out-patient
departments. It deserves full credit for the appointment, in 1895,
in association with the Royal Free Hospital, of the first hospital
almoner, Miss M. Stewart, one of the most experienced of the

* Central co-ordination was not effected until 1948 under the National
Health Service Act, 1946.

C.O.S. workers.* She was at first seconded for three months, with salary paid by the C.O.S. There was an interval of six months, when she returned to St Pancras, while the hospital debated the financial aspects. To break the deadlock two C.O.S. members of the Medical Committee gave donations to both the C.O.S. and the Hospital for joint payment of her salary—and Mary Stewart returned to consolidate her work as 'Lady Almoner'. The C.O.S. remained closely associated with this venture, since it recruited and trained the almoners who were gradually being appointed, both in London and in Provincial Hospitals. In 1907 the practice was sufficiently strong for the formation of an Independent Council, on which the C.O.S. was represented. The Society continued to offer practical training in its District Offices for intending hospital almoners, and close co-operation was a feature of subsequent development.†

Another valuable contribution of the Medical Sub-Committee which persisted into the modern era was its work in relation to Convalescent Homes. Arising out of the Society's interest in efficient administration, the Committee concentrated on two reforms: one, the abolition of the need for 'letters'‡ before admission to a Home could be gained; two, the need for centralised information on vacancies in the scattered Convalescent Homes. The organisation of the whole system was begun by the C.O.S. in 1879, by a special Convalescent Committee soon to be grafted on to the Medical Sub-Committee. It immediately collected information for the publication of a catalogue of Convalescent Homes, which it thereafter kept up-to-date (first issue 1879). The Council offered to receive lists of vacancies from the Homes; the whole scheme was well publicised and, by 1881, some thirty-six Homes had responded. The C.O.S. began sending patients and very soon an efficient system of supply and demand was organised; the Society arranged a scale of charges based, when necessary, on the full costs, since the C.O.S. was prepared to raise funds for the

* She had been a District Secretary in North St Pancras; see the account of Miss Stewart's contribution and that of her successors in E. Moberly Bell's *The Story of Hospital Almoners*, Faber, 1961.

† In later years experienced hospital almoners were invited to join the Medical Advisory Committee.

‡ The Society had a long fight against this practice not only in connection with in-patient treatment in hospitals, but also with the acceptance of candidates for pensions, or of children in orphanages, etc.

D*

assistance of individual patients. The Society had the support of benefactors for its own administrative expenses as well as for its Relief Fund, and it was able to appoint a special secretary for the work.*

The District Committees found the central organisation of convalescent treatment of great value.† As part of the C.O.S. aim to secure the full medical and social benefits of co-operation, the Medical Secretary consulted the hospital staff on the needs of the families of all the 'breadwinners' who were already patients, and who were 'capable of being assisted'. 'Central' then asked the District Committee in the man's area to enquire and to assist the family. It is indicative of C.O.S. thoroughness that rather than keep applicants waiting for a place in a Convalescent Home, they arranged for those 'who needed only good food and air' to be boarded out, either in private homes or in lodgings. Children were, whenever possible, boarded with the families of villagers 'under the supervision of ladies and others'. Closely linked with the other medical work of the sub-committee was the surgical aid system[19] which was also extensively used by District Secretaries in an era when statutory services made no provision for this need.

The social evils of tuberculosis were another special interest of the Medical Sub-Committee in which fact-finding and propaganda did much to make the need better known. At the end of the nineteenth century the public knew little about the infectious nature of 'consumption', but convalescent homes were seldom willing to accept patients with diseases of the chest. Some convalescent homes were, however, already offering open-air treatment and the C.O.S. arranged for everyone of these to be visited with a view to the Council 'renting some beds'. As a result, District Secretaries were able to send applicants in the early stages of the disease, without the long and almost hopeless wait of earlier days. In 1899 the C.O.S. issued a memorandum stressing the need for preventive measures. Other papers followed in which both the training of the patient 'in hygienic living' and the 'follow-up' or

---

* Colonel Montefiore, who gave twenty-five years' service before his retirement in 1909. He was assisted by voluntary workers who undertook the regular visiting of the Homes. See below, The Volunteers, Chapter 14.

† In a paper read to the Council in November 1901, the Medical Secretary included a table showing that in four years the C.O.S. had assisted some 5,890 patients to have convalescence. In later years (e.g. the 1930s) the average was about 400 patients per year.

'after-care' when he had returned to his family were important elements. The C.O.S. compaigned also for open-air treatment and for more Sanatoria.*[20]

Their fact-finding enquiries led them to examine the work of the Anti-Tuberculosis Dispensary in Edinburgh and one of the Sub-Committee's Reports (it was now called The Medical Advisory Committee) outlined, in 1907, a scheme for bringing into co-operation the hospitals and health authorities with a dispensary for tuberculous patients in every District. The C.O.S. claimed in its Annual Report 1913, that 'without the evidence which they were able to produce, it is doubtful whether the Departmental Committee, appointed by Government to consider how Tuberculosis throughout the country is to be dealt with, would have recommended their provision as the chief unit in a national scheme'. However, there were other influential forces, particularly in the medical field, and it is difficult to apportion merit; but there is no doubt that C.O.S. 'Central' had assembled valuable factual material and had given useful publicity to the campaign. Moreover, the Districts were co-operating closely with the Dispensaries: in a few cases District Committees had initiated the organisation of the unit, which was, of course, independent of the C.O.S. The work had been very costly for the Society and C. S. Loch had the backing of *The Times* in his appeals for special funds. Districts had also to raise their individual funds for helping each family of an assisted patient.

C.O.S. interest in preventive work was shown, too, in their relation to the new Health Societies, and in Health Visiting,† and in this sphere they worked closely with the Medical Officers of Health and the Poor Law, as well as with voluntary organisations such as the Nursing Association. They gathered information on behalf of various statutory bodies, for example in 1918–19 on the supply of dentures to nursing and expectant mothers and the services to children up to five years of age in Maternity and Child Welfare Centres, at the request of the Local Government Board, and on the cost of medical treatment to schoolchildren, for the L.C.C.

---

* H. Bosanquet points out that 1899 also saw the foundation of the National Association for the Prevention of Consumption.

† The C.O.S. Annual Report 1907–08 gives an interesting account of co-operation in the Battersea District where a Health Visiting Society was started. Loch had already called attention to the opportunities in 1905.

From time to time the Medical Advisory Committee had suggested the need for further research into specific problems; the Society itself had not the means for such an undertaking until, in later years, the Charitable Trusts provided funds. It was ready to point the way to others: for example, in 1886, when it considered whether and how far Poor Law Infirmaries should be thrown open for medical research.

The gradual introduction of statutory services reduced the necessity for some of the specific pioneer work of the Society, but the C.O.S. continued to act as watchdog; it considered the effects of successive measures on the needs of the family as a whole, for example the Social Insurance Schemes from 1911 onwards, and the Local Government Act, 1929. It pointed out unmet needs, for example, of children suffering from rheumatic heart disease; it offered advice, for example, on the desirability of a course on social problems in the training of health visitors. It also continued to keep its own District Secretaries informed of useful work being carried out in the field of health, for example, on nutrition.

The most valuable work of the Medical Advisory Committee had been done in these pioneer days, before the community accepted collective responsibility for social security and welfare. After 1948, there was no longer the need for the wide-ranging assistance common in the earlier periods of the Society's history. But between the two World Wars the Committee's work was a valuable part of the contribution of 'Central' to the health and well-being of the community. (See Chapter 8.) The Sub-Committee remained in existence for some years longer as an advisory body,* but it no longer claimed a separate and substantial place in the Family Welfare Association's Annual Reports.

Two contributions by the C.O.S. which affected the social policy of the future deserve special mention. One was the strenuous service given by C. S. Loch and other prominent members of the Society on the Royal Commission on the Poor Laws, 1905–09. The Majority Report was strongly influenced by their efforts. The propaganda of the signatories of the Minority Report,

---

* One of its latest deliberations took up the current interest in birth control with the cautious statement: 'This Sub-Committee realising that a knowledge of wrongful methods of contraception control is widely spread, is of opinion that information as to safe methods should be available for suitable cases.' (2.2.1956).

organised conspicuously by Beatrice Webb, tended to dominate subsequent discussions. The positive recommendations common to both reports, together with the specific suggestions in line with C.O.S. thought, were later reconsidered in relation to the Welfare State in one of the Loch Memorial Lectures.*[21]

One of the most valuable and lasting contributions was that of education for social work, following logically from the Society's principles and methods. If respect for the individual was of first importance, if the family was to be helped in relation to the total environment, if all help given was to be thorough and appropriate to need, then the helper must be adequately equipped for the purpose. During the 1880s the C.O.S. worked out, empirically, methods by which voluntary workers in District Offices were prepared for the various tasks they had undertaken. The great step forward came when experienced workers reflected upon methods of training and shared their experiences in discussions and written papers. The 1890s were fruitful years for the discovery of the essential elements of training. In the early twentieth century these new concepts of education and training resulted in the establishment of a School of Sociology and (at the suggestion of C. S. Loch)[22] the association of social work training with the universities. These and later developments which led to wide recognition of professional education for social work will be considered in more detail in Chapter 12.

2. Example of a C.O.S. Special Committee

The Improvement of the Dwellings of the Metropolitan Poor

The Special Committee set up by the C.O.S. in 1873 included Members of Parliament, representatives of the principal Dwellings Improvement Councils, Medical Officers of Health and other specially qualified members, such as Octavia Hill and Kay-Shuttleworth; Lord Napier and Ettrick† became Chairman. In 1873 the Committee recommended that it should be made the duty of some duly constituted public body to initiate improvements, under compulsory powers, in the worst parts of London.

---

* In addition to this paper by Una Cormack, there is an interesting discussion in Calvin Woodard's thesis, *The Charity Organisation Society and the Rise of the Welfare State:* Cambridge University Library

† Lord Napier and Ettrick had been specially interested in such questions when he was Governor of Madras.

They pointed to the success of such compulsory schemes in Glasgow and Edinburgh, and proposed to submit a memorial on the whole subject to the Government.[23] The following year the C.O.S. joined forces with the College of Physicians for the preparation of a memorial and then produced another of its own for presentation to the Prime Minister and the Home Secretary. 'As a result', the Society reported, 'Mr Kay-Shuttleworth in consequence, as he stated, of information which he had acquired as a member of the special committee, moved a resolution urging the Government to take action. . . .' The Home Secretary promised that the measure would be put forward. 'The Cross Bill now before the House is a result. In its general scope, and in the authorities designated for carrying it out in London, the Bill is in exact accordance with the Report and Memorial.'[24]

The following year we find the Council welcoming the Cross Act, with the proviso:

It is hoped that some other points of great importance in connection with the dwellings of the poor, to which the special committee referred in their report, may not be over-looked, especially the necessity for improving the Metro-politan Building Act of 1855, so that builders may be effectually prevented from erecting new houses which can only be described as unfit, from the first, for habitation, and the expediency of enabling the Metropolitan Board as well as the Local Boards to avail themselves of the summary powers conferred on the latter bodies.[25]

The Society continued to watch the whole question closely. They next took up the subject of the bad landlord and of depreciation, and reported in 1880:

Owing to many complaints, a special sub-committee of the C.O.S. investigated the operation of the Artisans Dwellings Act. They made the following recommendations, which were forwarded (with a statement and minutes of evidence) to the Home Secretary:

(a) Local authorities should have power to demolish, on owner's neglect to rebuild, property which had been allowed to fall into a disgraceful condition, and should compensate only for the value of land and materials.

(*b*) Persons holding the local enquiry under the Act (in regard to loss in selling areas), should obtain evidence as to the number of persons for whom it was necessary to make provision on the spot. Space should be allotted for the dwellings of those only whose work required that they be so accommodated (probably about one-third of the present number of inhabitants).

More investigations are being made.[26]

Further investigation of the Special Committee resulted in another report with recommendations, in 1881.

(1) The scale of compensation under the Artisans and Labourers Dwellings Acts of 1875 and 1879 should be reduced and the mode of procedure simplified.

(2) These Acts should be converted into a Towns Improvement Act. Needs of labouring classes should have due consideration; no rigid rule concerning replacing dwellings on cleared sites should be made.

(3) Effectual means should be taken to enforce Towns Acts in London and Sanitary Public Health and Building Acts in London and suburbs.

(4) All Railway Companies should be required by law to run cheap workmen's trains similar to those on the Great Eastern Railway to Enfield.[27]

CHAPTER SIX

The First World War

At the outbreak of the First World War the Government was totally unprepared to meet the immediate needs of families whose breadwinner had enlisted or was called up as a reservist. The C.O.S., like other voluntary organisations, was at once under pressure to help bridge the gap while the Soldiers' and Sailors' Families Association was getting into working order, while the Mayors were setting up their Relief Committees and while the Prince of Wales' Fund was being organised on a national scale. C.O.S. workers at 'Central' and in the Districts were called upon to help man the emergency committees formed to meet the widespread distress, while the Government was belatedly organising servicemen's dependants' allowances. At the same time the Society was trying to deal with the day-to-day applications at their own District Offices. When funds became available for those in distress directly due to the war, the Society found that many sick, infirm or disabled applicants did not fit into this category: the needs of pensioners, chronic invalids and sick children must be met when the ability of relatives to contribute was reduced. An increasing number of enquiries of all kinds had to be dealt with. The C.O.S. Secretary reported that in some Districts, as the war went on, 'they were left almost alone to wrestle with the intricacies of food economy, war savings, war pensions, school care committees, infant welfare, day nurseries, tuberculosis after-care, Belgian relief, and kindred forms of social effort'. It is no wonder that he added, 'at ruinous sacrifice of the health and strength of our workers, and of our slender reserves of money'.[1]

Many of the most experienced workers devoted their whole time to other services, and the local C.O.S. offices had to recruit and train volunteers to carry on normal C.O.S. work. Yet it was in the year 1915–16 that the C.O.S. offered a one-year training course for volunteers.*

It was soon decided that the Society could make a useful contribution to the reduction of chaos by building up its schemes for the Mutual Registration of Assistance. Islington reported in 1915 that some of its volunteers were working full-time from 10 a.m. to 6 or 7 p.m. to organise M.R.A. on as wide a basis as possible.

Long before the Curtis Committee reported, when there was no statutory provision outside the Poor Law for children deprived and neglected in their own homes, the C.O.S. was pointing the way. Many Districts increased their work for the care of children during the war. Fulham, for example, reported a variety of help: great care was taken to find the right home in the country for delicate or orphan children. Sometimes a foster parent had to be found; in 1916–17 a day hostel was set up for forty children of school age whose mothers were out at work; the children had breakfast, dinner and tea, followed by games until their mothers could fetch them; this venture was started by a C.O.S. worker, but it was run independently and developed later into a Play Centre where the Honorary Secretary and several of the helpers were C.O.S. members. In 1917–18 the same committee was much concerned with young widows with large families. Fulham was reporting in 1918–19 that it had placed fifty to sixty children temporarily or permanently in country homes to help mothers who complained that their children were unruly. Fulham, like many other C.O.S. Districts during the war, was doing what it could to keep families together: a common form of assistance was the arrangement made for the care of children while the mother went 'with an easy mind' to hospital. As Fulham reported, they took great time and trouble to place the children 'often with a cheerful family in the country'. Under an arrangement with the Home Office (Reformatory and Industrial Schools Department) the Society had undertaken to enquire into and report upon the home conditions when Managers of a school proposed to return a child to its parents. Where necessary the Society kept in touch with the child after its return home.†

* A certificate was given on the successful completion of the course.

† During the year 1918–19 the Society was concerned with 353 such children and their families.

By now the C.O.S. was being asked to administer funds from
various sources. Some, such as a fund to help widows and mothers
of soldiers killed in the war, were administered in close co-operation
with other charities. The Society was also reporting that its
offices were more widely accepted as 'advisory and consultative
centres'. At the same time they were being used to a much greater
extent to supplement statutory aid; for example: although Infant
Welfare Centres were subsidised by the Borough Councils and the
Local Government Board, many centres referred people to the
C.O.S. District Committees if investigation of circumstances was
required, or if extra help was needed. Insurance Committees were
attempting to fulfil their obligations to patients, but no one could
expect to pass directly from a sanatorium into the labour market:
the supplementation of part-time earnings, as well as the provision of adequate diet and clothing, or of suitable accommodation,
were left to voluntary societies. Regulations pressed hardly on
some families; for example, applicants who found that they did
not qualify for aid under the War Pensions Act often sought help
from the District C.O.S. Discharged servicemen, waiting for their
pensions to come through, or for a place in a Government Training
Centre, were often 'tided over'. Many statutory allowances were
quite inadequate if any urgent need arose: for example, Old Age
Pensioners, with the statutory 10/– a week, or men out of work
through illness with sickness benefit of 15/– a week and no
allowances for their families. A case quoted by North Lambeth
illustrates the thoroughness typical of C.O.S. work:[2]

C.L. is a young ex-regular soldier discharged after nine years'
service with a slight disability and a small pension. He had no
civilian trade, made vain efforts to get work, and put down his
name for training under the Government scheme. Time went
on; his unemployment donation was nearly ended and his
wife was suddenly taken seriously ill. At this moment he was
referred to us by the hospital, and for nine months or more
we helped the family, first supplementing the donation and
pension and later maintaining the family entirely except for
the pension, which just covered the rent. Every effort was
made both by C.L. and by us to secure work or training.
There were delays at every turn, but at last he was sent for, to
start training, only to be told that he was medically unfit. He

was referred to hospital, but another three months elapsed before allowances were granted, owing to the fact that no report had come through from hospital. At last, after harassing delays and urgent appeals, the allowance came through and he is now waiting to be declared fit for work and start training. The amount of money spent in helping him was large, but even so it gives little indication of the time and trouble which we expended in negotiating with the Ministries of Labour and Pensions before they could be induced to take action.

Most Districts were reporting similar cases and were noting the greater readiness of 'Town Hall Officials' and other statutory officers to refer people in trouble. The role of the C.O.S. in supplementing statutory aid is summed up in the Lambeth comment:

It would be easy to prolong the list of instances in which the public help rendered would have been of comparatively little value had it not been for the timely and more directly personal assistance of the Committee. These, however, have been mentioned in order to exemplify and render clear the importance of such agencies as the C.O.S. alongside the machinery provided by the State and the local authorities.

A slight change might now be discerned in the C.O.S. attitude towards public social services. The Council reported in 1920: 'No one, of course, will deny that a great deal of the action of the State in this direction' (they had been considering Public Assistance) 'is inevitable, or that much of the money had been well spent'; but they added 'whether or not there are financial limits to what the State can do, there are limits to what it can do effectively, and therefore to what it ought to undertake'.[3]

However, there is no doubt that the C.O.S. found considerable satisfaction in the opportunity to co-operate with Local Authorities and with Government Departments. The Society had been asked early in the war to serve on the Departmental Committee on War Charities. They were glad to show that their activities were not confined to London but that they could call on help in many parts of the country.* In the year 1918–19, for example, the

* From time to time in their subsequent history the Society claimed to be national in scope.

C.O.S., at the request of the War Relief Trustees, 'co-operated in the appointment of Almoners and the obtaining of the necessary information in respect of some hundreds of civilians resident in various parts of the United Kingdom'. They also undertook the administration of the *ex gratia* awards made by the Treasury in certain cases of distress caused by air raids.*

The C.O.S. kept in touch with other Government Departments and continued, whenever it saw a need, to offer information and advice. Such an instance occurred in 1920, when, looking ahead to the probable increase of unemployment, it formed a working party to devise a scheme; although it had no influence on this intractable problem, 'Suggestions for Relief of Distress caused by Unemployment' showed the C.O.S. with a more understanding attitude than in the past.

One of the methods used by the Society in the promotion of a cause in which they were specially interested was that of offering the hospitality of Denison House for the meetings of an *ad hoc* committee or conference: 'The Denison House Public Assistance Committee'† was among the most famous. Formed in 1917 with Mr Geoffrey Drage, a member of the L.C.C., as Chairman, and Mr Woollcombe of the C.O.S. as its Honorary Secretary, its purpose was the formulation of a scheme for the reconstruction of the Poor Law and other public relief authorities. As a first step the Committee submitted a memorial to the Government in which they petitioned for the publication of a complete Return showing the growth of public expenditure on public assistance. A deputation met the President of the Local Government Board, and, eventually, a motion in the House of Commons was passed in July, 1919. The issue of the 'Drage Return' proved to be a useful addition to the information on public social services, in a field where adequate statistics were often lacking.

Among the roles the C.O.S. was anxious to maintain was that of adviser to other charitable bodies. This was exemplified during the war in its relations with 'The Professional Classes War Relief

---

* The C.O.S. representative of the War Relief Trustees was Mr Woollcombe. The Society was able to call upon the services not only of its District Committees in London, but of fifty-nine charity organisations and kindred societies and 199 private individuals in various parts of the country.

† Other groups were 'The Care Committee Group of Voluntary Workers', and the 'Conference on the Employment and Maintenance of Elderly Educated Women'.

Council' formed in 1914 to relieve temporary distress among members of the professional classes. Mr Woollcombe was again one of the active members of its executive committee, and the C.O.S. kept on very friendly terms throughout. The work was efficiently organised and valuable help was given in education and training, as well as in employment, to musicians, artists and others. The C.O.S. annual report for 1919 noted that 'an experience was gained and the need for thorough investigation was recognised; the case-work of the Council became more and more constructive. Over 11,000 cases were dealt with on those lines'.[4]

Towards the end of the war the C.O.S. took part in discussions on the desirability of promoting Councils of Social Service in all London Boroughs. When a Joint Committee was appointed to consider matters of common interest it was significant of the new attitude that when an amendment was moved that the same end was more likely to be obtained by adapting 'our own Society' to changing conditions, it was lost.[5] However, as the Councils were still in an experimental stage the C.O.S. decided to set up a 'Standing Conference on Social Work' to bring together representatives of charitable societies for consultation and discussion. It was to be 'a sort of Parliament of Charities'.* The C.O.S. envisaged for the future a 'unified Public Assistance Authority, the Council of Social Service, and the C.O.S. working together in harmonious co-operation, each dealing with a part of the field, but each equally interested in the whole'.[6] The C.O.S. was, in fact, represented on each of the Councils of Social Service in London as they came into existence, but the pattern eventually worked out was rather different from that expected by the C.O.S. When the National Council of Social Service was formed in 1919, with the approval of the Local Government Board and of other Government Departments, the C.O.S. was only one of the many charitable organisations represented. But although the first Secretary of the N.C.S.S. had gained much of his experience of social work as a C.O.S. District Secretary,† the National Council took an independent line. It was successful in promoting representative groups in many parts of the country and, in some instances, was

* The Conference discussed various questions in relation to proposed legislation, e.g. the unmarried mother and her child; suggestions for the compulsory registration of Charities were submitted to the Charity Commissioners.
† Mr Lionel Ellis.

able to achieve the co-ordination of voluntary and public effort
which had eluded the C.O.S. Starting afresh in a period of goodwill, and unhampered by an outdated social theory, the N.C.S.S.
established its own public image as a co-ordinating body. The
Charity Organisation Society and the National Council of Social
Service were to work together on several worthwhile ventures,
notably the establishment of Citizens Advice Bureaux some
twenty years later, but they continued, for the most part, 'friendly
but aloof'.*

It is difficult to give in statistical terms an idea of the volume of
work done by the Society during the war. Some forty District
Offices had been maintained.† There had been an overall drop in
the number of applications for assistance, though less than might
have been expected.

Full employment and the consequent rise in the general
standard of living of the industrial workers, together with the
greater employment of women, had raised many families to a
condition of prosperity never before enjoyed. The rise in prices
was offset by an increase in wages for those in employment. This
served to make the relative position of widows with children, of the
elderly, the sick and the disabled even harder to bear. The bulk
of those who sought the assistance of the C.O.S. came within these
categories. A comparison of the average numbers of applications
for the years 1910–14 with the average for 1914–18 shows that a
greater proportion were assisted.

Year	Number of Applications Decided‡	Number Assisted	% of Cases Assisted
1910–14 Average	17,587	7,439	42
1914–18 Average	11,263	6,329	56

The above figures do not show the substantial volume of enquiries and
advisory work of the Districts.

* All the same, the C.O.S. continued to be represented on the Council and
the N.C.S.S. took an active interest in the C.O.S. In the *Review* of the Family
Welfare Association its Director, Sir George Haynes, gave valuable service as
Chairman of the Steering Committee.

† Starting with forty-two, two had had to be amalgamated with others by
reason of staff shortage and diminution of funds.

‡ 'Decided' was the term used when an application had been considered by
the Committee and dealt with.

In 1917–18 the main form of practical assistance was 'medical, surgical and convalescent aid', for 4,151 persons; sanatorium treatment was separately listed, 69 persons; employment and apprenticeship accounted for 214; pensions for 115; emigration was again starting with 9 persons assisted; other forms of assistance totalled 2,004.

Throughout the war the Society had regularly published its substantial annual reports. A number of *Occasional Papers* were also printed. A selection of these indicates the topics of interest to the Society at this period of development; a short history: *Fifty Years of Charity Organisation*;[7] a contribution from Bernard Bosanquet on *The Philosophy of Case Work*;[8] one from Sir Arthur Clay on *Social Organisation*;[9] and from Miss Sewell on *Changing Social Ideals*.[10] The last of the war-time series, in 1918, was, appropriately, *Thought and Practice*.[11] 'No time to think' was to be a recurrent cry in the years ahead.

As we survey the years during and immediately following the First World War we can appreciate the efforts made, under considerable strain on personal and financial resources, to preserve the former standing of the Society; to maintain continuity with the past while trying to meet the emergencies of the war, and to prepare for reconstruction in the future.

Some of the Districts, more aware than others of the changing social order, were urging a review of the Society's Machinery and Methods. Discussion at 'Central', in 1917, led to the appointment of a committee 'to consider the best way of making the Council more effective'. It discussed a number of criticisms 'to account for widespread dissatisfaction'.* Besides making recommendations for administrative reform it advocated a change of name on the grounds not only that the title 'Charity Organisation Society' was out of date but that 'The Society's name is undeservedly, but none the less finally, objectionable to many people, including in a notable degree the industrial classes, and that its sub-name has a tone of patronage unsuited to modern conditions'. After considerable discussion it was agreed, on 18th February, 1919, just fifty years after the Society's foundation, that the name should be changed, but a decision on the date, and further consideration of an alternative title, were postponed. At the end of the year the

* Amongst other criticisms we find; 'too little discussion'; 'older members too talkative'; 'Council had ceased to exercise proper control over policy'.

resolution was reversed; the name 'Charity Organisation Society' remained till after the end of the Second World War.

However, changes had taken place in the constitution, 'to secure better division between its domestic administration and its larger purposes'.[12] The Society was still anxious to emphasise 'the larger purposes' which Loch had kept in the forefront of policy. They were to find it increasingly difficult as the high hopes of the nation for reconstruction gave way to 'the troubled decades which bridge the two world wars'.[13]

What were the qualities of the Secretary, J. C. Pringle, who was to guide the Society during these years?

Part II

BETWEEN THE TWO WORLD WARS

CHAPTER SEVEN

John Christian Pringle 1872–1938

Secretary of the Charity Organisation Society 1914–18 and
1925–36: Director and Consulting Secretary, 1936–38

In Loch's last years with the C.O.S. he had as his chief colleague
at 'Central' J. C. Pringle, whose rôle was to be important, though
by no means as dominant as Loch's, in the history of the Society.
A general review of the main incidents in Pringle's life and of his
contribution to the Society will give something of the atmosphere
and background of the period.

John Christian Pringle was born in Edinburgh, 27th August,
1872. He was educated at Cargil Field, Edinburgh, at Winchester
(as a Scholar) and at Exeter College, Oxford (as a Scholar). He
took a 1st Class in Classical Moderations in 1893 and a 2nd Class
in Literae Humaniores in 1895. All his written work abounds in
quotations from the Classics, from the Bible and from contemporary plays. His annual reports often read like studies in Greek
literature; Pirandello later became a source of inspiration. His
reading also included history, sociology and psychology. He
seemed to one colleague to 'relate everything that he had ever read
or thought to the work and principles of Charity Organisation'.[1]

Pringle married Constance Mary Warburton, a fellow C.O.S.
worker in Poplar where he was a curate (1902–05). They moved on
to join the Hackney District Committee when Pringle became
curate of St John's (1905–09). The only other member of Pringle's
family of whom we have record is his sister, Dr Julia Pringle, whom
he thanks for her encouragement in the preface of his first book.
He lived with her after the death of his wife.

Pringle was a great traveller. On leaving Oxford he had joined
the Indian Civil Service and served in Sind, 1896–1901. He
returned to England to train for the Ministry at Cuddington,
1901–02, and was ordained in 1903. In 1909 he went to Japan to

become Professor of English at the Hiroshima Higher Normal College. In 1912 he accepted C. S. Loch's invitation to come and help him at the Charity Organisation Society's headquarters. When Loch retired, Pringle was his natural successor. Towards the end of the First World War Pringle had leave of absence to serve as Chaplain to the Royal Garrison Artillery and was abroad from May 1918 to January 1919. He did not, however, return immediately to the C.O.S. as Secretary; but he was closely connected as a member of the C.O.S. Council. He became Rector of St George's-in-the-East from 1919–25, where he took an active part in social work and was well known at Toynbee Hall. During the year 1922–23 he was a member of the Mission of Help to India.

Meanwhile, H. L. Woollcombe, who had been Organising Secretary, carried on the traditional work of the society, and when he died in 1923, Fox-Strangways succeeded him, temporarily. When Pringle decided once more to take up the Secretaryship at 'Central', in 1925, his interest in overseas developments kept him in close touch with the United States, Australia, and with other areas where C.O.S. principles were accepted. He paid frequent visits abroad, especially to America.

Pringle's experience had brought him into close touch with the conditions under which the manual workers were living. He had seen the Poor Law at work in the East End of London. In 1906–07 he had served as Expert Investigator for the Royal Commission on the Poor Law. He became a member of the Board of Guardians for St George's-in-the-East from 1922–25. From 1930–33 he was co-opted member of the London County Council Public Assistance Committee. He was also Vice-Chairman of the local committee of Poplar, Stepney and the City (Area I).

In 1933 his first book was published: *British Social Services, the Nation's Appeal to the Housewife and Her Response*. His second and last book was a study of the Metropolitan Visiting and Relief Association, published in 1937, under the title *Social Work of the London Churches*. Pringle prepared this under the direction of the Executive Committee of the M.V.R.A. in co-operation with the London Association of Voluntary School Care Committee Workers. He was Honorary Secretary of both Associations.

What kind of man was Pringle and what was his influence on the development of the Charity Organisation Society? Those who knew him at home and abroad were captivated by his natural friendliness. They found his company delightful. Yet, 'in public controversy he was fiercely partisan, while always regretting the party spirit evinced by his opponents; but the Gallic ferocity with which he fought for what he believed to be right never affected his personal relationships'.[2] It might be added that Pringle was the master of invective. His return to the C.O.S. in the mid-1920s is immediately apparent in successive annual reports as he attacks institutions and groups whose ideas were opposed to his own, whether economists, Bolshevists, the Webbs, Trade Unionists or 'the guileless students of the London School of Economics'.[3]

Pringle had greatly admired the work of C. S. Loch and, in many respects, modelled himself upon him. This strongly affected his attitude in resisting change within the Society. He was proudly proclaiming in 1927[4] that the C.O.S. had not changed one 'jot or tittle' since Loch's time. We have seen that Loch's chapter in successive C.O.S. Handbooks was kept inviolate till the mid-1930s. It was Pringle who convinced the Council of the demand at home and overseas for a reprint of Loch's books for the use of students.

Pringle paid tribute to Loch at some length in 1937[5] where he refers to Loch as 'our Greatest Ally' with his 'fire, initiative, and originality'. The one criticism Pringle allowed himself was connected with Loch's 'most heroic blunder' in the eighties and nineties in the restatement of religion: 'that here, and nowhere else, was to be found the real step in the onward march for social betterment'. Pringle goes on to summarise 'Loch's proposition':[6] 'Man's neighbourly (or parochial) service of his fellow is the sphere and expression of his true greatness, goodness and beauty: in that service the ordinary man has by far his best chance of finding, understanding, serving, and worshipping God.' These words, slightly misquoted, were inserted by the C.O.S. in successive introductions to the Loch Memorial Lectures until the late 1960s.*

Although Pringle carried on the main principles and practice of the C.O.S. of Loch's day, he lacked Loch's realism and administrative flair. Loch had had a firm grasp of economic and social

---

* See the Loch Memorial Lecture, 1966, by Mary Stocks: p. 3 of the Introduction repeats the customary reference to 'Loch's own words'. The quotation was, in fact, a précis made by Pringle of entries in Loch's Diary. E.g. entry for the 30th May, 1882. (When the mistake was pointed out a correction was made in the introduction to the 1967 Loch Memorial Lecture.)

issues, and had kept a balanced view of the normal family. Pringle 'often had his head in the clouds'.* One social worker, writing in 1931,[7] tries to follow Pringle's flights into the literary world:

For some years we have vaguely known that Mr Pringle . . . has a particular point that he tries to hammer home. . . . In the stress of the day's work, it seems excusable enough that it should remain a mystery as to why he invites us to the study of the writings of men so far removed, seemingly, from the problems of case-work as Jung, Adler and Pirandello. Why, at an annual meeting of the Society in Coventry, he addresses us upon the subject of the Berber people, and at the Cheltenham Conference delivers a discourse upon King Lear, the applicant, and Kent, the Case-Worker. Why, failing to awake our interest in any connection with either Jung or Adler, or Pirandello or Shakespeare, and the decay of a Mediterranean civilisation, he begs us to study the history and personalities of Old Testament history and fulminates with such 'amazing wrath' at the Cambridge Conference against the system responsible for the over-taxed powers of a certain Public Assistance Committee, who, exhausted, tired and hungry, was expected to deal rightly with the innumerable applications brought before it at a sitting.

We pretend not to understand, but in reality we know that he attempts to direct our attention to persons and subjects in which character, its effect upon circumstances, and again, the effect of action upon character, is the theme. He knows the study to be of supreme importance. For some reason he fears that it has ceased to take its right place in case work.

Yet Pringle could also write simply, with first-hand knowledge, of the difficulties facing some of the manual workers in overcrowded neighbourhoods. He had special sympathy with the hardworked mother of the family.[8] His writing as a whole certainly reveals some eccentricity: the annual reports and some of his articles in the *Charity Organisation Review* seem further removed from the modern outlook than do those of C. S. Loch. What are we to make of the appeal to 'the Cock Robin Spirit' which

* This was said of him by one of his younger colleagues as she 'reminisced' after her retirement.

dominates the Annual Report of 1933? Pringle's last reports as Secretary show some of the main interests of the C.O.S. at that period. They illustrate also the literary style of the writer. One section is headed 'National Services of the C.O.S. in 1936':

The C.O.S. offers today, as its founders—Gladstone, Ruskin, Maxse, Bosanquet, Octavia Hill and their friends—offered in 1869, what they called, and we still call, a 'general family case-work service'. The Society was, and is, prepared to tackle the whole problem presented by a citizen or family in need, perplexity or trouble. This was a sufficiently arduous task in 1869, when a quite enormous array of charities designed to satisfy some detailed passing need were constantly springing up. But in those days it was still possible for responsible people to think and act in terms of persons and families. Today the C.O.S. is alone in making any such attempt consciously and systematically. The public services designed to aid and remove distress are broken up, both nationally and locally, into many departments, the effective co-ordination of whose work presents acute practical diffi- culties. The numerous applications of science to the problems arising from human affliction are all of them specialised, and, as time goes on, constantly more and more narrowly special- ised. Both of these are processes endowed with irresistible force. In tune with them statesmen, the public, the press, and the advertiser, think along departmental and specialised lines. But human beings remain obstinately unified; nor can they evade the necessity of being born in families. It follows that these departmental services and specialised sciences peremp- to- rily require the aid of some long-suffering agency which will persevere, both in study and treatment, upon the old personal and family basis. It is this indispensable ancillary service which the C.O.S. continues to offer, alike to the public departments and to the specialists, in this its seventy-eighth year. It offers it to all alike. The six examples which follow are merely those which stood out most prominently in 1936. In every instance the Society's help has been cordially recognised by the bodies concerned.

There follow six examples, which may be briefly summarised:

1. Forlorn Migrants in the New Housing Estates

The C.O.S., co-operating with leading social workers, opened a centre in Hendon, extended its work into Willesden, Chiswick, Tooting and Balham. It had already developed facilities in the great housing estate of Downham.

Hire Purchase and the Tallyman who aggravate family troubles. This example rouses Pringle to one of his typical literary flights as he recalls the troubles which beset the housewife:

> Forthwith her footsteps are dogged by Fates and Furies not less dread than those of Greek tragedy. If Clotho* be her doubled rent, and Lachesis the inexorable instalments on her 'suite' and curtains, Atropos is the moneylender called in to help her meet either or both of them. She can survive by means of subtle adjustments built up through unnumbered generations by countless wise old forebears dead and forgotten, but unrooted and pitch-forked into a dormitory suburb she pines away and dies.

* Clotho colum retinet, Lachesis net, Atropos occat.*

An extract from Macbeth follows, after which we hear that:

> The C.O.S. is much comforted that a Hire Purchase Bill—albeit only a private member's one—is being promoted, designed to stand—as Aaron stood between the dead and the living—between the shortsighted fancies of the people and the wrath of Hades or Set enthroned in the County Court.

The whole section ends with an extract from Sophocles' *Antigone*.

2. Almoners in the L.C.C. Hospitals

Pringle reports a great increase in co-operation between the hospitals and C.O.S. workers as a result of the appointment for the first time of Lady Almoners in the L.C.C. general hospitals: 'an offensive and defensive alliance between the lady almoner within the gates and the social services without'.

3. Nutrition and Child Care

Pringle characteristically recalls the work of Sir Charles Loch who 'was one of those most instrumental in making known to

* Pringle's footnote.

social workers in this country the researches of Atwater and Chittenden (1905 and 1909)'. Pringle then notes the L.C.C. nutrition centres where *Individual* care and the awareness of personality problems endorse the C.O.S. idea. He adds that a majority of C.O.S. members have been members of the School Care Committees during the thirty years of their existence.

4. The C.O.S. welcomes the opportunity to co-operate with the newly-formed P.O.I.P.H. (Council for the Promotion of Occupational Industries among the Physically Handicapped). Pringle asks 'Did not the mother of Achilles arrange another occupation than war for him because his heel was vulnerable?' Pringle then discusses the special investigation made by the C.O.S. Medical Advisory Sub-Committee since 1930 to see whether the belief hitherto held that the finding of suitable tasks whereby the physically handicapped could earn their own living was in fact sound policy. He discusses lack of incentives where there is 'endowed idleness' and welcomes the efforts of P.O.I.P.H. to encourage the handicapped to escape from such a life. The partially blind and the epileptics in whom the C.O.S. had taken an active interest for a quarter of a century or more will also be helped by the new P.O.I.P.H. The C.O.S. is represented on the Joint Committee of the new body.

5. *Maudsley Hospital (L.C.C.)*

Pringle welcomes the 'understanding' report of the Medical Superintendent of the Hospital and notes C.O.S. co-operation in the work. Pringle's comments on the effect on the family are worth noting in view of the recent emphasis on 'community care' of the mentally ill.

To a society like the C.O.S. which takes cover behind no speciality, but as a general case-work agency, and for the most part the only one in the locality, has its doors wide open to every kind of human affliction, cases in which mental trouble is an element are fraught with the utmost anxiety. Not only may the peace and comfort of the home, and the means for its support, be threatened momentarily with destruction, but the lives and safety of its most helpless members imperilled.
E

There are signs that, with the passing of the Mental Treatment Act, 1930, and the development of hopes of effective
cures on 'voluntary' and 'temporary' lines, official sympathy
has, to some extent, moved away from the protection of the
patient's family. They must take their chance while a psychiatrist is humouring the patient by week-end leave home, etc.
The former prompt and resolute action of the lunacy officer
seems to be a little out of date. We have great confidence in
Dr Mapother as an officer not likely to let such tendencies
go too far.

6. *British Repatriated from Spain*

Pringle describes the plight of many hundreds of persons whose
legal status was British, but who were none the less integrated
members of Spanish society in August, 1936. The Civil War led
the Foreign Office to exercise its responsibility by putting the
refugees on British warships, landing them at Marseilles with a
railway ticket to *Londra*, plus ten days' maintenance. Pringle's
comments on this situation show his delight that voluntary help
was generously forthcoming. He pours scorn on the 'so-called
statutory rights' which failed to include 'these worthy unoffending
folk whom the exigencies of the crisis had wrenched away from
their homes and "dumped" in a strange and remote land'. Pringle
uses the opportunity to confound the critics:

> Not many weeks before, a writer in a medical journal had said
> of all voluntary charity, and of the C.O.S. in particular, that
> it was 'pathetic' and 'paradoxical' that any such work should
> go on in an era which no longer required or wanted it. Aware of
> the continuance of this pathetic paradox, the Foreign Office,
> in consultation with the Ministry of Health and the London
> County Council, decided that it was, without the slightest
> doubt, the appropriate resource for the succour of these
> refugees. It invited the C.O.S. and any other persons
> interested to raise the necessary funds by direct appeal to the
> charitable public; . . .

and so,

> . . . wisely as we think, they fell back together on something
> bigger and deeper even than 'social security by statutory

enactment', the urge in the heart of the common man to open his purse to a fellow creature in undeserved distress. . . . The story of the British repatriated from Spain makes a bright page in the chronicle of 1936.

The above passages reveal Pringle's attitude as he led the C.O.S. in the last years of his life.

Pringle had been singularly unfortunate in his prophecies. He was convinced that the early 1930s saw the beginning of a new era, with C.O.S. principles vindicated. For this reason he welcomed the Final Report of the Royal Commission on Unemployment Insurance. He rejoiced over the Ray and Lovat reports, both issued in November 1932, on Local Expenditure, with their emphasis on the responsibility of the 'household'. He affirmed that collectivism was a 'phantasm'. He made slighting references to what he called 'Beveridgism'. He quoted the 1869 *Goschen Minute* with approval as he recalled the C.O.S. to the principles of its founders.[9] It was unfortunate that Pringle had so little understanding of the political, social and economic changes which had transformed conditions since the First World War. He kept many of the forms and practices of a past age long after they were out of date.

Yet within a limited range Pringle was a man of ideas. He kept abreast of new thinking at home and overseas in the field of social work. It was he who arranged for the first family case worker from this country to study in the United States.* He saw the value of psychology for the better understanding of relationships within the family and between workers and clients.

Pringle's last book *Social Work of the London Churches* revealed more of himself than of the Metropolitan Visiting and Relief Association;† it showed how closely he related the district work of the C.O.S. to parochial visiting. He was essentially the pastor and crusader.

By the 1930s criticism of the Society's 'stagnation' was already being heard inside the C.O.S. A clear example is given in the speech at the Conference of Charity Organisation and Kindred

* This was Miss Crosse who was later the close colleague of Astbury, Pringle's successor. A group of psychiatric social workers had already found this experience valuable.

† Its subtitle was 'Some account of the Metropolitan Visiting and Relief Association'.

Societies in 1931 by Mrs Milnes: she was probably reflecting the views of many of the Social Science Departments of the universities. Opening with some consideration of 'the gloomy prognostications which had been forecast by the C.O.S. as a result of State Action', she continued:

> They have not been fulfilled, and probably those working for the C.O.S. fail to appreciate this point because their work is chiefly among the failures in this life. . . .
>
> While your much beloved Secretary may be able to quote (and probably will) St Paul, the Ephesians, the Corinthians, Mahommed, Buddha, Plato and the other Greek philosophers, to say nothing of the writers of the Middle Ages, in order to crush me with his weight of evidence that human nature doesn't much change; in spite of it all I shall continue to insist that a Society that adopts a case front for its family casework, which . . . has not been altered since about the year 1911, is a Society which proves that in many ways it is stagnating. It is just out of touch with the times and this is seen in the little support it gets from the young generation. . . . It is just because I for one believe so greatly in the value of family casework, though not as Mr Pringle would, with his belief even in the family casework of the United States (which struck horror in my soul, so little seems sacred to them) but because I believe in a reasonable family casework, that I deplore the rigidity so often found within the sphere of the C.O.S. . . .

It was characteristic of the C.O.S. that it included this speech in the next issue of its journal.[10] The Society was accustomed to criticism and took some pride in reporting it.

In considering the last years of Pringle's work for the C.O.S. we should note that for some time he had been a very sick man who faced personal tragedy with courage. Like C. S. Loch, he never spared himself, and he roused great devotion in his followers. Some indication of his personal quality and of the Society's concern for his health is indicated in the reports of the Administrative Committee between 1930 and 1932. He was urged to take a holiday, to take days off for rest, to accept a donation towards medical expenses, to come for two days a week only, etc. Throughout the period, Pringle was sending in suggestions for a book on the C.O.S., notes for District Committees and a paper on Family Income.

When Pringle died in 1938, the influence of Loch was still strong. It was clear from the *Memoirs* that Pringle was adjudged a faithful follower. This was summed up by Islington with the words:

> As the spirit of Elijah rested on Elisha so Mr Pringle carried on the work of Sir Charles Loch, who inspired him with his own belief that 'Charity has a social purpose, requires a social discipline, works through sympathy, depends on science and in fervency is religious.'[11]

A Memorial Fund was opened to be devoted to 'the encouragement of the Study of Family Casework by meeting the costs of publication of material and dealing with casework and the training of social workers'.*

There is no doubt that Pringle's personal qualities, and not his writings or his social theory, had most influence on the C.O.S. It was the day-to-day work in the Districts in those troubled years between the wars which taxed the secretaries nearly to breaking point. It was Pringle who understood the strain which many of the workers had to endure; he had the gift of putting new heart into people when things looked almost hopeless. His successor, Astbury, remembered him as a source of inspiration. The only sense in which Astbury would allow that Pringle 'had his head in the clouds' was that 'since he was a great scholar he often spoke above the heads of his audience at Conferences: that was a compliment he paid them. In actual fact he was one of the most humble-minded persons I have ever known'.† On Pringle's death in 1938 tributes to his ability to inspire others came, not only from workers at home, 'but from every country in Europe, from the U.S.A., India and every other country in the British Commonwealth'. They came, too, from people of other religions. As Basil Henriques said: 'he helped me to understand his Christianity, he was always ready to try to understand my Judaism'.[12]

Was Pringle's term of office a period of stagnation as some had

---

* Professor Marjorie Smith made a study of *Professional Education for Social Work in Britain* which was published, in 1952, for the Pringle Memorial Fund.

† In a private letter in my possession.

affirmed? Or was it 'a holding operation' at a time of considerable strain for the country in general and at a critical period for voluntary organisations in particular? There was little that was creative as Loch's term had been creative, unless we accept the new psychological approach as such. We should note, too, that at a time when fragmentation of the public social services was increasingly apparent, Pringle seized every opportunity to proclaim the necessity for family-centred social service. His diatribes against many of the statutory services were directed chiefly against their departmentalism. *Family* social work was the main contribution of the C.O.S. in the years between the First and Second World Wars. C.O.S. thinking and practice were centred on the well-being of the *family as a whole*. A closer study of the development of the work of the Districts in the 1920s and 30s will help us to judge the results more truly.

With the death of Pringle the era of the scholar-gentleman who gathered round him a group of like-minded men from public school and university had ended. The new Secretary was 'a man of the people'.

'Central' and the Districts: Stagnation or Consolidation? Local Co-operation in Health and Welfare of Families

The years between the two World Wars held an unstable balance between continuity and change. It was an age of contrasts: improvements in the standard of living for many of the wage earners, severe unemployment and poverty for others: fundamental changes in the social and economic structure of society, side by side with the persistence of traditional ways of life. The air of expectancy and the hopes for reconstruction following four years of exhaustive war gave way to a mood of depression and gloom.* Developments in world economy which had reduced the overseas markets for many of the staple industries were already affecting production: the changeover from a war economy to peace was a further cause of severe dislocation. The concentration of unemployment in the areas of heavy industry was a new factor. 'The Great Depression' caused distress not only in shipbuilding, iron and steel, and mining districts, but in the country in general. The nation became more sensitive to the economic and social wastage of unemployment and poverty.† The fact that the severe economic depression of the early 1930s was shared by other leading industrial countries did nothing to lessen the despondency. Yet the first decade, in contrast with the second, might be described as 'the hopeful twenties'.[1] The increase in the real income of the wage earners made possible the enjoyment

* In the eighteen months following upon the armistice, employment in London was available for the majority who sought it. By 1921 unemployment figures were rising; post-war economic depression had begun but had not yet reached the proportions of the early 30s.

† More facts were available since the extension of unemployment insurance: greater publicity was possible with the concentration of unemployment in 'depressed areas'.

of new opportunities. The new technological changes had brought the cinema, broadcasting and the motor bus. The popular papers had a wide circulation. New fabrics and new fashions made for greater equality in dress. It was the age of electricity, and of greyhound racing.* Great estates were breaking up but new suburbs were being developed. The building of houses and blocks of flats brought more homes within reach of the working classes.

One of the most publicised issues of the post-war years was the change in manners and morals. Old rules and customs were being challenged. Religious faith was suspect; psychology† and the new physics were coming into the range of popular discussion. There were two main reactions: there was the cynicism of those who asked: What's the use of anything?[2] By contrast local labour parties were active; there was some good liberal research (e.g. the 'Yellow Book'); there was enthusiasm for C.O.P.E.C. (Conference on Politics, Economics and Citizenship).‡ A new equalitarian spirit was abroad. By 1924 a Labour Government was in office, though not in power.§

Yet the older generation still dominated politics and industry. They held the highest posts in the civil service and the professions. Traditional elements were strong in these spheres, as they were in the administration of charitable organisations. But taxation and death duties were reducing the incomes of the well-to-do. Domestic servants were scarcer and young women from the 'leisured classes' were seeking paid employment.

Many charitable organisations were viewing their future prospects with alarm. The Charity Organisation Society had little doubt that its work was more than ever necessary,‖ but it had to make drastic reductions in its expenditure. It withdrew grants from several Districts and reduced them in others. As a

* Greyhound racing began in Manchester in 1926. In London attendances increased from three million to eight million between 1927 and 1929.

† Freud's works were translated into English and published in the 1920s.

‡ William Temple was the inspiration behind C.O.P.E.C. in 1924 and he was in close touch with other social and educational organisations of the 1920s and 30s.

§ Both in 1924 and 1929 the Labour Party was dependent upon the support of the Liberals. The mood of the country was anti-conservative rather than pro-socialist.

‖ Some C.O.S. Districts were reporting that steady subscriptions were tending to become donations and then to disappear altogether. The percentage of cases in which relatives were able to help fell from sixty to forty in the early 1920s.

consequence, offices in North and South West Ham and Lewisham, which could not get enough local support to make good the deficiency, were forced to close. Sydenham, Woolwich and Norwood were also casualties of the financial crisis. Other offices were amalgamated. By 1922 the number of District Offices had fallen from forty to thirty-two. The following year four more were closed. It is interesting to note that the decision to close the Poplar office was influenced not only by financial difficulty but by incompatible social theory: 'We feel that they (the Borough Authorities) proceed upon a too mechanical conception of human nature and human frailty. . . . Our Society, while believing that the spread of social truth is perhaps more necessary in Poplar than in most places, believes that for the present there are more promising fields for the particular application of those truths.'[3] As soon as economic circumstances allowed, the C.O.S. determined to restart some of its offices, for example, in Lewisham in 1927. When the Great Depression lifted, the Society discussed the possibility of further extensions;* a second office was opened in Lewisham in 1935, since local support was assured. By 1937 the Society had sufficiently recovered to consider further extension, outside Metropolitan London. They did not return to the old industrial district of West Ham but concentrated on the areas of growing population in Greater London. One of these was Hendon whose committee, established in 1937, was to do some excellent work until the early 1950s, when re-organisation of areas once more compelled restriction to Metropolitan London.

If financial anxiety brought recurrent crises to the C.O.S., the fluctuation in the numbers of voluntary workers was equally serious, since the work of the Districts was largely dependent upon their services. Many secretaries were reporting losses. Sometimes special activities had to be given up; for example, Islington found it impossible to carry on the Provident and Friendly Visiting Society which had been working in the District with voluntary help for some thirty years. The scale of the operation in six or more localities was such that no other agency

* In spite of shortage of funds the Society decided that a travelling secretary must be appointed once again. It had proved very successful in the past, especially in starting new agencies in the Provinces. (Started originally in 1905 with Mrs Marsland, the work went on until 1923, when the Secretary had to retire through ill-health.)

E*

in Islington could take it over.* The loss of the friendly visiting part of the work was deeply regretted. A number of Districts were obliged to give up their Mutual Registration scheme through shortage of voluntary workers, as well as loss of financial support.[4] 1921 had seen the end of the *Charity Organisation Review*, after thirty-six years.†

An important step towards meeting staffing difficulties was the decision made by the C.O.S. to raise salaries 'to compare more favourably with those obtainable by educated women elsewhere'. The C.O.S. had been forced to realise that many young women were no longer content, even if they could afford it, to work for a 'token salary'. There was greater readiness to take a training course if it promised a professional career. The course offered by the London School of Economics and the scheme arranged by Bedford College in co-operation with the C.O.S. were now well established. By 1920 the Society was taking students for practical training not only from these two colleges but also from King's College, London, the Battersea Polytechnic, and the Council of Hospital Almoners. As a result the C.O.S. received more recruits, but they reported regretfully that although there were applications from young women, 'the young man is more difficult to attract. Yet a short term of years as a C.O.S. Secretary would be no bad training for public life'.[5] It was not suggested that a young man's salary would be comparable to that obtainable by educated young men elsewhere. He would not be expected to make social work his career unless he had private means.‡ In practice, 'educated young women' found it difficult to keep up their accustomed standards unless they, too, had a private income, or were subsidised by their families by living at home. The majority of C.O.S. Secretaries were, for many years, drawn from the well-to-do middle classes.

Policy and Practice of the C.O.S. in the Years Between the Wars

What was the influence of the new conditions on C.O.S. policy and practice? First, they had to look again at their attitude

* All that the C.O.S. could do when the main visitor died suddenly was to arrange with the depositors for transfer to War Savings Banks and to the Post Office Savings Bank.

† It was replaced after a short lapse by the *C.O. Quarterly*.

‡ The C.O.S. in the years between the wars had, in fact, several such men on their staff.

towards the Poor Law. The Society now accepted the fact that 'a great extension of out-relief is inevitable, and it may fairly be said that, apart from certain notorious cases, it is well and wisely administered'.[6] In London the numbers in receipt of Poor Relief rose from 164 per 10,000 of the population in 1920, to 463 per 10,000 in 1921, and 501 per 10,000 in 1922. What could a voluntary society do? 'The thorny question of how and when we can co-operate usefully with out-relief has met us at every turn', said the Islington Committee: 'This question of co-operation with the Guardians is no longer so simply solved as in the old days when we either "took a case off the Poor Law" or "left it to the Poor Law". The line of demarcation is less clear and the interpretation by Guardians of their duties and powers has become more elastic'. The C.O.S. Council reminded the Districts that 'It is not possible or desirable for a voluntary society to compete with the State in paying allowances to men out of work. Sometimes a little temporary assistance, or medical or convalescent treatment, will help a man to get back into work, sometimes an insurance difficulty may be put right, or an adverse decision of an official body may be modified on a full report of the facts; but there remain a distressingly large number of cases where employment is the only need, and the one need which cannot be met'.

Some of the Districts went further. Islington decided in 1922 that, in the abnormal conditions, they were justified in recommending money grants from regimental and other funds 'in cases where the Guardians' Allowance leaves no margin for things sorely needed to keep up the ordinary standard of living in the family'. The C.O.S. had moved a long way from the attitude at the beginning of the century when Mrs Bosanquet wrote: 'The fact that a man is out of work may be explained mainly by his own character or mainly by the conditions of trade; but in the majority of cases both causes will be involved.'[7] The economic conditions between the wars made such sentiments intolerable. In fact economic events had been shaping the policy of the C.O.S. without the chief officers of the Society being fully aware of what was happening. Many of the Districts were in closer touch with reality.

In the 1920s, the question of co-operation with statutory bodies, particularly with the L.C.C., was one of the principal issues discussed at Central. With the changes consequent upon the passing of the Local Government Act and the setting up of the statutory Public Assistance Committees, in 1929, to replace the old Boards of Guardians, the C.O.S. was anxious to secure an influential voice. Pringle had been in close consultation about submitting a list of persons suitable to serve on the P.A.C.s. The Conservatives were in a majority on the L.C.C. and were likely to be generally sympathetic to voluntary effort.*

The Public Assistance Committee resolved to continue the grants made hitherto by the Boards of Guardians to some twenty-seven organisations. The C.O.S. was one of these and the grant was to be paid in respect of the Mutual Registration of Assistance in selected areas. The L.C.C. recommended schemes of co-operation which set out in some detail upon what basis assistance should be given to 'suitable persons who would be likely to secure complete rehabilitation or derive lasting benefit from assistance afforded by a voluntary agency'.[8] This was an excellent summary of C.O.S. aims. The Report of the P.A.C. in December, 1932, is of special interest as it includes a statement of the ideal to be achieved by the Council in its policy of co-operation with voluntary agencies. It also shows that there was a vociferous minority which moved, and lost, an amendment seeking to remove all reference to co-operation with voluntary agencies. The approved statement read:

> Co-operation between the statutory and voluntary agencies concerned in Public Assistance has long been one of the ideals of persons interested in the welfare of those who are compelled to seek relief. While the adequate maintenance of individuals or families who fall into a state of dependence must be the immediate care of those responsible, the ultimate aim must always be their restoration to independence. It is in this constructive work, lying largely outside the sphere of the statutory authority, that the services of voluntary agencies must be especially valuable.

C.O.S. members must have rejoiced in this statutory support for

* In fact, the Chairman of the C.O.S. Administrative Committee, Sir Francis Morris, was Vice-Chairman of the L.C.C. Public Assistance Committee. He was also a member of the L.C.C. Public Health Committee. Pringle was a co-opted member of the P.A.C. and a member of the General Purposes sub-committee.

their main object. The L.C.C. P.A.C. showed, moreover, that it had a thorough grasp of the traditional basis of its policy as it went on to refer to the *Goschen Minute* of 1869 'which still remains the standard official statement of the principles involved in co-operation between public assistance and voluntary agencies, and was accepted in the Majority Report of the Royal Commission on the Poor Laws and Relief of Distress in 1909'.

As soon as there was a Labour majority on the Council the policy was reversed. The general scheme of co-operation 'was not acted upon' after November 1934. Co-operation in the Mutual Registration of Assistance was terminated on 31st March, 1935.* An amendment by the Conservative minority asking for con- sideration of the best means of effecting co-operation with voluntary organisations was lost. There was by this time very strong feeling in Labour circles against C.O.S. social theory. For many years Pringle, the C.O.S. Secretary, had been using all his powers of invective against 'socialist philosophers'. He believed that their day was done; it must have been a sad blow to him when the L.C.C. was captured by his enemy. Not only was there a wide difference between the two social theories, but there was also the question of the effectiveness of the existing schemes of co-operation; the original project had been experimental, for three areas only in the first instance. Careful assessment of the results by the L.C.C. led them to conclude that they had not received benefits worth the labour entailed by registration.[9]

District reports, in the 1920s and 30s had frequent references to increasing co-operation with private and public bodies. In addition, Fulham believed that there was a call 'to give serious thought to, and effort towards, helping to carry out one or other of the many legislative schemes passed by Parliament'. Although the Society had opposed many of the Bills in the past there was general agreement that, now that the Acts were in operation, the District workers must do their best to see that the services were effectively administered. It was, in fact, accepted that 'a voluntary society can do little by itself: it can do much by co-operating with public institutions. . . . as an executive power the voluntary system may be considerably restricted, but in its advisory capacity it has a future of boundless usefulness.'[10]

* The C.O.S. reported 'Grants have ceased with their withdrawal of the scheme. This means a serious loss.'

Fulham was an example of the good relationship with other agencies. It listed, in 1921–22, all those who referred applicants for help: they included: 'Hospitals, both general and special, from all over London; Regimental agencies, as well as Navy and Military Charities of every kind; School Care Committees, After-Care Committees, Town Hall Committees (unspecified); the T.B. Dispensary (taken over by the Borough from the C.O.S. the previous year); the Poor Law Guardians*; the Day Nursery, District Nurses, Infant Welfare Centres; the Clergy, Doctors, Church Workers and others; the Home Office, Colonial Office, War Office, India Office, etc.' Fulham also drew attention to the outside activities of its own members. C.O.S. workers were engaged in a variety of statutory and voluntary work; every member of the C.O.S. served on one or other of the local committees, and the C.O.S. Secretary was a member of one of the Statutory Committees. The C.O.S. was 'in closer touch than ever with municipal work'. Fulham was also especially interested in the Housing Association, and reported, in 1928–29, that it had been able to invest £1,000 in the Fulham Housing Improvement Society, 'through a generous donor'.

Other areas, too, were seeking to extend co-operation in various ways: Islington was typical of many. They reported as examples of co-operation in 1923: the loan of their committee rooms, regularly, to four committees; two organisations were housed beneath their roof; the C.O.S. did all the casework for the United Services Fund (this was continued for three years) and this, in turn, strengthened the association with other organisations. There was co-operation in the Government schemes for emigration†[11] (the Government schemes made no provision for clothing or for landing money); they worked very closely with the hospitals (through the almoners) and much casework resulted from this source of referral. M.R.A. (Mutual Registration of Assistance) was given greater publicity by the Society and many Districts were noting increased activity. Some went so far as to report 'we

---

* In 1923–24 a grant of ten guineas was received from the Board 'in recognition of their work on cases'. By 1927–28 there were five members of Boards of Guardians, headed by their Chairman, on the C.O.S. Committee.

† The C.O.S. Emigration Committee had done some very thorough work in the past. It was in line with this policy that the Society sent the secretary of this Committee, in 1921 (a difficult year financially for the C.O.S.) 'to make an exhaustive visit to Overseas Dominions'.

wonder how we ever got on without it'. All the District Committees did a considerable volume of enquiry and advisory work
on behalf of other agencies; this, in turn, sometimes led to casework. An example to illustrate this was given in connection with
an enquiry on behalf of the Royal Engineers' Benevolent Fund:

> it concerned the widow of an ex-sergeant major who lived
> with a delicate widowed sister. The C.O.S. visitor found
> them 'plunged into destitution'. The C.O.S. were able to
> report to the Fund on the urgent need of the first widow,
> but the sister was not eligible. Help was therefore given to
> the sister by the C.O.S. It proved to be one of their most
> difficult cases and the Society undertook 'a formidable task' in
> seeing the case through to a satisfactory conclusion. [12]

What Needs were Identified in the Period between the Wars and How Did the C.O.S. Meet Them ?

As we have seen, while, in the early 1920s, certain sections of
the community were in a hopeful mood, others had no share in
the recovery. These included the traditional poor: the old and
infirm, the sick and disabled, the widows with children, and the
unemployed, and the so-called 'new poor', particularly those
whose fixed incomes were insufficient to meet the rising prices.*[13]
The Society was noting that an increasing number of their
applicants were coming from 'a higher social class'. The term
'decayed gentlewoman' had dropped out of the C.O.S. vocabulary,
though not yet from that of some of the older charities. The
great majority of those who applied to the C.O.S. for help and
of those who went to the Relieving Officer still belonged to the
'traditional poor'. The C.O.S. could, in any case, assist only a
small proportion of those in need.†

In 1921 the Districts found that unemployment was the
greatest single cause of distress amongst the families who applied
for help. It was a problem too great for them. In these difficult

---

* Savings were estimated to have been reduced by about one-half or one-
third.

† Applications to the C.O.S. in 1919 were approximately 10,600 rising
to approximately 12,800 in 1920. The increase in the Poor Law figures in
Metropolitan London in the same year was from approximately 65,000 to
approximately 74,000.

years the service most frequently offered was that of medical, surgical and convalescent aid. National Health Insurance, in spite of some modifications, did not cover a working man's dependants, while his own benefits, if he fell sick, were still very limited.

But the nation had become more health conscious. War-time regulations on venereal disease, propaganda on the prevention of tuberculosis, the School Medical Service and the Infant Welfare Service were all stressing the need for personal hygiene and concern for positive health measures. One relatively minor health factor was to affect the C.O.S. out of all proportion to the numbers assisted. In the propaganda against the dangers to health of pyorrhoea, doctors and dentists had been advising the extraction of teeth. During the 1920s and 1930s the C.O.S. were having an increasing number of applications to help supply dentures: to mothers of families who felt depressed because their teeth had been extracted, often months earlier, or to fathers who, without teeth, were unable to look and feel their best when applying for a job. The psychological effect on the individual, and consequently on his family, was often the determining factor in the decision of the C.O.S. to help. Their claim that the supply of teeth was constructive case work was often well-grounded. The Central Council, in its annual report for 1928, quoted an illustration from Stepney: help was given to a family where the initial application for teeth led also to the provision of glasses, the restoration to health of the overwrought mother (she had three children and a delicate husband) and the finding of a job so that she could help support her family. The family had been living in very over-crowded conditions but, as a result of renewed self-confidence, the mother took the initiative in applying for a Council house, and the C.O.S. had the satisfaction of seeing the family happily settled. This was 'a success story' indeed.

Ten years later the C.O.S. was still quoting similar cases:[14]

Take, for instance, Mrs W. who was sent to the Camberwell Committee for a set of artificial teeth. Mr W., a boot repairer, found it difficult to make a living in a poor locality; and one daughter suffered from tubercular spine and legs, and usually went about in an invalid chair. The Camberwell Committee provided Mrs W. with her teeth, and did what they could for the invalid daughter, and then sent the whole family away to a country cottage for a holiday. (As a result the family determined to settle in the country) . . . so with Camberwell's help, Mr W. exchanged boot repairing for work as a car-park attendant, Mrs W. and one daughter found daily work quite easily, and the invalid daughter, as a result of fresh air and treatment, soon learned to walk.

But, in general, the secretaries had difficulty in keeping up the interest of students who were often asked to pay the first 'home visit'. As one District explained: 'The aim of all our work is to make those whom we help self-supporting and there can be no doubt that a good set of teeth often plays a large part in this endeavour.'[15] But another reported to Central: 'We cannot always remodel the outlook of the entire family because one member of it requires teeth.' Fulham was determined not to give the impression that they were 'absorbed by convalescence and teeth'. They assured their supporters that they were 'concerned with the larger question of raising the character of work in the District'.[16] However, since the applications continued and the Society accepted the need to carry out this particular service, the Districts had to come to terms with necessity.

As the C.O.S. had difficulty in interesting students so they had difficulty in influencing individual donors to subscribe towards the cost of teeth.* In spite of some help from various sources, anxiety in trying to finance so many cases almost overwhelmed Districts until, in 1934, Ivory Cross came to the rescue with a fund for this purpose. From 1935 until the Second World War 'dentures' were separately classified in the C.O.S. reports on the kinds of help given. (See Tables 4 and 5.) The number was greater than for 'surgical appliances' and nearly equal to 'convalescent treatment', two forms of medical assistance in which the C.O.S. had had many years' experience. (The Districts had made great use of the 'rented beds', in the variety of convalescent homes for patients in immediate need.)

If the C.O.S., in those years of pressure, had had to concentrate largely on 'practical assistance', they had, at the same time, identified some outstanding medical needs. They were concerned to keep a watchful eye on the possibility of improvements, particularly in the provisions for the handicapped. In 1925 they

* A full set cost £4 to £6 according to the source of supply.

RETURNS

The following is the Tabular Statement for the Year ending

COMMITTEE	Referred to other Districts	Friendly Visits	Enquiries for other District Committees	Number of Applications made	Number of Applications decided	Number of Applications withdrawn	Number of Applications financially assisted	Number of Applications otherwise assisted	Number of Applications not assisted	Sources of Help					
										Recommended to and assisted by Voluntary Institutions	Recommended to and assisted by Statutory Bodies	Co-operation with Public Assistance Committees	Assisted by Individuals	Applicants and their Relatives	Other Sources of Assistance
Battersea	31	58	108	437	439	114	102	131	92	195	7	1	29	114	71
Bermondsey	8	26	109	790	701	75	285	187	154	478	52	39	72	84	—
Bethnal Green	—	5	45	273	294	81	95	35	83	125	—	—	8	30	2
Camberwell	67	65	195	1025	1008	243	380	201	184	502	88	18	126	155	39
Chelsea	6	17	113	267	233	63	83	42	45	79	15	3	6	20	17
Clapham	33	53	144	319	287	82	123	43	38	209	6	5	25	39	30
Deptford	4	53	127	325	331	46	95	136	54	186	23	5	37	42	52
Fulham	5	85	136	708	642	108	184	169	181	310	40	11	51	46	56
Greenwich	22	61	87	315	305	64	109	77	55	135	5	7	16	44	11
Hackney	46	48	233	420	375	105	74	60	136	141	3	2	14	27	22
Hammersmith	6	41	140	961	918	290	269	206	153	355	38	4	199	85	6
Hendon	13	·47	71	284	281	60	85	62	74	94	14	17	14	50	24
Holborn	31	110	849	432	435	92	142	72	129	149	20	2	13	39	42
Islington	36	193	238	1388	1203	261	466	209	267	902	111	33	64	200	134
Kensington	48	55	293	819	785	149	280	110	246	304	11	1	41	55	137
Lambeth, North	13	208	149	321	266	32	133	61	40	134	12	9	24	40	38
Lambeth, South	*7	91	265	671	702	114	247	184	157	618	2	11	65	40	—
Lewisham, East	6	46	76	717	621	72	294	102	153	313	30	3	15	141	35
Lewisham, West	8	54	69	322	316	87	92	54	83	126	19	8	23	48	25
Norwood	42	99	105	322	351	53	97	115	86	225	22	19	39	56	15
Paddington	9	69	223	874	811	219	233	103	256	256	18	2	166	41	17
Poplar	18	36	40	120	136	34	58	18	26	101	4	5	18	33	10
St. Marylebone	6	26	324	329	320	72	73	77	98	111	7	3	32	31	20
St. Pancras, North	5	97	113	686	648	113	131	223	181	342	58	2	37	48	100
St. Pancras, South	4	46	288	521	535	156	165	72	142	293	3	—	25	47	63
Shoreditch	8	121	163	468	431	54	100	138	139	138	30	25	17	40	61
Southwark	4	74	272	686	684	226	255	137	66	557	32	12	92	145	120
Stepney	55	128	60	385	354	134	103	44	63	197	21	16	49	66	20
Wandsworth	18	41	95	426	456	112	121	92	131	154	17	4	77	46	-61
Westminster	25	75	574	489	445	89	130	62	164	188	11	4	40	38	28
Whitechapel	7	16	135	388	398	52	215	41	90	204	5	16	64	66	
	521	2,174	5,839	16,488	15,711	3,453	5,219	3,273	3,766	8,121	724	287	1,498	1,956	1,256

Friendly visits, e.g. to pensioners, not included in the above

FOR 1938–39.

September 30, 1939, returned by District Committees.

Work found	Grants for Stock or Equipment	Grants for Removal	Psychological Treatment	Medical Help	Surgical Appliances	Dentures	Convalescent Treatment	Temporary Allowances	Pensions	Provision for Children	Other Forms of Assistance	Reports given	COMMITTEE
4	6	2	—	1	21	18	97	23	1	8	72	431	Battersea.
7	16	9	—	8	24	49	51	71	—	71	158	436	Bermondsey.
—	12	1	1	4	15	18	23	5	1	1	52	298	Bethnal Green.
4	42	21	5	20	48	74	58	112	2	41	196	999	Camberwell.
4	9	5	3	1	9	16	16	20	2	7	58	300	Chelsea.
2	6	6	1	5	11	19	20	60	—	5	34	413	Clapham.
9	6	10	—	13	23	28	18	17	1	14	129	337	Deptford.
8	15	13	—	4	21	31	37	35	7	6	185	463	Fulham.
7	9	3	3	—	17	21	18	10	—	5	93	460	Greenwich.
6	10	1	—	—	13	14	13	16	4	7	47	280	Hackney.
10	16	62	7	27	28	47	38	66	7	18	170	834	Hammersmith.
2	9	5	3	—	7	24	19	20	—	27	47	301	Hendon.
1	10	5	—	3	15	37	28	26	2	12	93	571	Holborn.
11	34	40	4	6	44	112	56	64	6	43	282	1,536	Islington.
11	14	2	—	—	34	52	35	49	1	9	172	743	Kensington.
2	9	9	—	3	8	19	30	17	3	10	76	316	Lambeth, North.
5	18	22	—	4	60	41	134	66	6	8	118	1,035	Lambeth, South.
7	32	6	—	9	36	33	73	80	1	31	94	357	Lewisham, East.
5	2	4	3	3	11	11	18	13	3	26	32	479	Lewisham, West.
14	10	7	1	7	18	12	20	25	4	19	95	562	Norwood.
3	5	22	—	—	9	28	22	34	3	16	241	868	Paddington.
—	3	—	1	2	6	24	5	1	—	1	38	159	Poplar.
6	8	6	1	—	11	15	15	13	1	11	73	341	St. Marylebone.
3	50	11	—	1	15	22	40	72	1	13	166	779	St. Pancras, North.
4	13	7	1	1	19	36	29	41	6	14	100	273	St. Pancras, South.
11	35	2	7	3	21	4	16	45	—	19	109	235	Shoreditch.
6	17	27	—	—	36	84	43	32	—	19	154	1,247	Southwark.
5	4	4	1	6	10	64	28	13	—	7	57	456	Stepney.
2	6	4	2	5	14	15	20	28	9	17	94	381	Wandsworth.
7	29	24	1	3	6	11	23	27	2	9	52	659	Westminster.
1	5	1	—	—	7	15	11	35	1	—	193	136	Whitechapel.
167	460	341	45	139	617	1001	1,054	1,136	74	494	3,480	16,685	

TABLE 4.

were giving publicity to work for the mentally ill and the provision of clinics for early nervous disorders. In addition to their continued interest in the mentally defective they made enquiries on behalf of epileptics,*[17] of those disabled as a result of injury or disease,[18] and of the tuberculous who needed rehabilitation.† The usual method was to ask the Districts to send in examples to the sub-committee, and, in certain cases to make a special investigation in their area. As in the pre-war era, the Medical Sub-Committee, in their turn, sent a memorandum to the District Committees to give them useful information, such as clinics available for the provision of special treatments.[19] The results of special enquiries continued to be sent to the appropriate body, for example, one to King Edward's Hospital Fund on overcrowded conditions in out-patients' departments. The C.O.S. was often asked to give evidence to the committee set up as a result of their initiative.

From time to time they were asked to supply information, for example, to the British Medical Association on the effects of National Health Insurance on Charitable Dispensaries: to the Great Ormond Street Hospital on the home conditions of children with asthma: to the L.C.C. Medical Officer of Health on the extent to which employers on the King's National Roll were including in their quota of reserve men those suffering from medical disabilities. In 1934 the Society submitted a memorandum on Workmen's Compensation to the Home Office Committee. They then gave evidence and, at the Home Office's request, submitted a study of some thirty cases showing how a lump sum had often been detrimental to the welfare of the recipient. This was followed up by another deputation.‡[20]

The long years of experience in the provision of surgical appliances and in the rehabilitation of persons injured by accidents, had also qualified the C.O.S. to offer useful evidence to the British Medical Association when, in 1936, this body was discussing with the Ministry of Health certain aspects of compensation for fractures. The C.O.S. examples of the long and patient work necessary with individual families were quoted and discussed by the committee concerned.

---

* The Society claimed that the permanent committee on Epilepsy set up in 1929 was due to C.O.S. initiative.

† This was a matter of continual interest to the Committee.

‡ This consisted of Sir William Hamer, J. C. Pringle and Miss Morton, all experienced in various other fields as well as in the C.O.S.

In 1937 the C.O.S. contributed to the Survey of Dental Provision in the London Area, made by the London Council of Social Service. They were also able to advise the Secretary of the national dental charity, Ivory Cross, on the attitude of local Public Health Authorities to the supply of artificial teeth to persons whose teeth had been extracted in hospital. They discussed the same problem with the Chief Officer of Public Assistance for London.

But, meanwhile, in the Districts, some of the customary medical work had been curtailed, the more willingly as other societies had been able to extend their work in particular fields. An example of this was the Invalid Children's Aid Association, which had opened more offices with trained workers in various parts of London, and was less in need of a general family case work service. The C.O.S. withdrew but some Districts agreed to continue to accept very difficult cases if the I.C.A.A. wished to send them.[21] No decision to withdraw could be made on work in co-operation with the hospitals, since almoners were largely dependent on the C.O.S. for family casework for their patients in the community. Hospital Almoners were often the greatest single 'source of referral' listed by the C.O.S. Districts.

In one instance we find co-operation taking a special form, a method which was to be given prominence in a later stage of the Society's development. The Secretary 'arranged a small conference of various Hospital Almoners, who were interested in the same case, in the hope that the difficulties of this particular family might be solved by the joint consideration of some of the Agencies concerned in their welfare. It was an interesting experiment, which seems worth development in the future'.[22]

As the C.O.S. had ready access to a number of charitable funds and as the family social workers had a thorough knowledge of other sources of assistance, both voluntary and statutory,* hard-pressed workers from other fields also sought the help of the C.O.S. A Probation Officer, for example, limited by her responsibility to the Court to the care of a particular delinquent, might recognise other family needs which would, in turn, help her own charge: co-operation with the C.O.S. might well be the answer; material

---

* They kept up-to-date by constant reference to the valuable C.O.S. yearly publication *The Charities Register and Digest*, which was also, of course, widely used by other Societies.

benefit, like the provision of an extra bed or help with removal to a new house, might make all the difference to a fresh start. Such instances were a common form of help towards the recovery of self-respect. Health visitors, too, who were sufficiently sensitive to social needs, were glad to call upon the services of the C.O.S. worker on behalf of a family struggling to keep up standards.* Other examples will serve to illustrate the variety of work done by the Society in this period.

Islington reported in the year 1929–30 the long term help they had given to an ex-railwayman and his wife:

Mr P. had made his application when he was still in the Sanatorium, being treated for tuberculosis. His sick club benefit had ceased and he asked the C.O.S. for an allowance for his wife and child. This was given, and was then increased when his National Health Insurance benefit dropped to 10/– and was again increased when Mr P. left the sanatorium. During the difficult period of adjustment when Mr P. was not yet fit to return to work, the C.O.S. saw the family weekly, 'in which man and wife were cheered and their courage sustained through many months of anxiety, for, . . . to quote Sir Charles Loch, "much is left undone if those who would render help forget that a large part of Charity is consolation" '. Meanwhile, the Chairman and Vice-Chairman of the Committee considered what they might do to help Mr P. to find suitable employment when the time came: 'through their influence suitable work on the L.N.E.R. was at last found for him'. The report adds, 'Our expenditure on this case has amounted to over £60 raised with great difficulty from many sources'.

Another example of thoroughness, illustrating the many agencies approached in the course of giving appropriate help, is given in the Report for 1931–32:

Mr T., a goods porter with a wife and six children, lived in two rooms at a rent of 12/– weekly. The original application

* Medical Officers of Health were not all in favour of 'intervention' by voluntary agencies and sometimes denied the need for it, publicly, while their own health visitors were in fact using the C.O.S. family casework service. In other instances M.O.H.s themselves co-operated cosely with the C.O.S. in their area.

was for general help and milk for the babies. The C.O.S. discovered him to be an ex-soldier of very good character and having a hard struggle to maintain his family. Before the C.O.S. 'closed the case' they had decided to help not only with milk for the babies, but with dentures for Mr T. Three years later they helped again: as the family had the offer of better quarters, the C.O.S. helped them to move. In order to finance these efforts the Society had secured the co-operation of Mr T.'s regiment, the Dental Aid Society, the Society for the Relief of Distress, and the Soldiers and Sailors Help Society, 'while the milk for the babies—the *fons et origo* of the application—came from the Town Hall'.

The C.O.S. continued to give help in 'child care'. An example from West Lewisham in 1935, soon after it was re-opened,* illustrates an unusual call:

The International Migration Service in New York had been asked to help an American doctor who sent a regular allowance to a Sydenham bank to support a boy aged ten in this country; the foster mother, once nurse to the doctor, had died. The C.O.S. had to discover the legal guardian (who proved to be the dead foster mother) get into touch with other foster mothers, with the bank manager, lawyers, clergymen and schoolmasters. Besides establishing the required facts, the C.O.S. considered what the boy himself would most like to do in the future. As 'he had a passion for the sea' they arranged for his training in the *Arethusa* and followed his very happy career with continued interest.

A more common example of child care was that of temporary boarding-out while there was a crisis in the family. An instance reported by the East Lewisham Committee[23] shows that very practical help with another problem followed the original child care arrangement. To quote from the report:

Mr N., a harassed young man, came early one morning to say his wife had been taken into hospital for an urgent operation, leaving him with twins of two. He had taken the

* West Lewisham was re-opened after special appeals from social workers in South London, partly to replace the Sydenham Office, closed in 1922 and much missed.

previous day off from work to try to find someone to look after them but without success. He dared not risk losing his job and was in despair. Half a dozen telephone calls and he was sent off to take the babies to a Home in the country. Payment came for them regularly until one evening he arrived looking as harassed as before to say his wife had been in a money lender's hands two years ago and he found the debt had not been wholly repaid. He could not meet it and pay for the children too. Consultation with the moneylender resulted in a satisfactory adjustment being made for everyone.

'Central' was always ready to encourage the Districts in community work. After the war the great new housing estates, consequent upon the slum clearance schemes, posed their own special problems and we find the C.O.S. taking part in plans to help meet the distress of 'social isolation'.* In 1928 the Administrative Committee instructed Pringle to consult with the new Chairman of the L.C.C. Housing Committee 'on the conditions of life in L.C.C. housing areas'.

Lewisham took a special interest in people who had moved to the new housing estate at Downham,[24] since many of the residents were far from their relatives and old neighbours. The Committee reported that the 3,071 houses with 30,000 inhabitants gave them more work than all the rest of Lewisham. Not only did they find numerous calls on their 'casework service' but they co-operated closely with the L.C.C. in the provision of community work. Their experienced Honorary Secretary† was said to be the inspiration behind the fellowship to be found in the Community Centre, with its education, youth, sports and welfare sections. The Welfare Section had a Poor Man's Lawyer, and a Bureau of Information. There was a Boot Club and a boot-repairing class for unemployed members. A Marriage Clinic was being planned. East Lewisham later reported an 'Unemployed Fellowship' at Downham, which was specially interested in a Social Club, allotments, woodwork and other classes.[25]

Most of the District Committees in the 1930s were reporting a good relationship with the Unemployment Assistance Board's

* It helped to open centres at Hendon and at Downing to meet the lack of social facilities.

† This was the hardworking and much loved Miss Locket. See Chapter 14 below.

officers.* During the Great Depression many of the Board's applicants were put in touch with the C.O.S. for replacement of clothes, particularly of boots for the family. The C.O.S. 'shop' and the jumble sale became regular features of District activities, while financial help or loans were frequently given to help the father look his best in his application for a job. The C.O.S. had often come to the help of applicants when they had fallen into the hands of moneylenders.† As the economic situation improved and houses and flats became available, hire-purchase firms and tallymen rushed in to take quick advantage of the need for furnishings and other articles of equipment. Advertisers and high pressure devices of various kinds tempted many of the families on new housing estates and elsewhere to buy beyond their means. Social workers were aware of the difficulties of keeping up payments when sickness or other misfortune occurred. Unfortunately, there were no adequate legal restraints on those who exploited the hire-purchase system. The C.O.S. were in a good position to give examples when a Parliamentary Committee was set up, resulting in the passing of the Hire Purchase Act, 1938. In this campaign the C.O.S. had taken an active part in discussions and negotiations between the trade and other social workers. They joined forces with Toynbee Hall in pressing for legislation against the unscrupulous use of the system. It should be noted that the more reputable hire-purchase firms, looked upon favourably by the C.O.S., welcomed the Act. The C.O.S. followed up their work in this field by publishing a very useful Occasional Paper on Hire-Purchase.[26]

Two examples from the experience of District Committees illustrate the 'snatch back' and the 'tack on' system:

In 1934 a man purchased a lorry from a firm in Greater London. The transaction was sold by the firm to a Finance Corporation to whom the man agreed to pay the sum of £275—a deposit of £75 and the balance at the rate of £11 a month. The payments were made regularly until some £245

* E.g. Fulham reports close co-operation in 1931–32 and in subsequent years.

† Secretaries relied largely on the C.O.S. agents to attempt to secure some relaxation in the demands for repayment. A report from Islington in 1927 praises the agent 'for his successful efforts with five out of the six money lenders'.

had been paid, leaving only a balance of £30. The man then became ill, and wrote asking for an extension of time before making the next payment. This was refused, and the man was informed that unless the instalment was paid they would take possession of the lorry, and that he could regain it only if he paid the sum of £30 within seven days. The man then applied to a District Committee of the C.O.S., who wrote to the firm enquiring whether they still held the lorry; they replied that it was still in their possession, whereupon the Committee sent a cheque for £30. This was returned with a letter to say that the lorry had now been sold. The man had lost his livelihood and had nothing in return for the £245 which he had paid.

A man trading on his own account had bought a motor coach for £1,600. Shortly before he had completed his payments he was persuaded to buy a motor haulage wagon for £800. For eighteen months he paid with absolute regularity, the debt in regard to the motor coach being repaid in full. A spell of bad trade compelled the man to default in one payment, and in a matter of hours the Finance Corporation, to whom the transaction had been sold, seized both the coach and the lorry.

This case was later dealt with by a C.O.S. District Committee, who were powerless to obtain any redress on the man's behalf.

A third example shows what could happen to an ordinary family at a time of misfortune:

Possibly the most blatant case was that of a family who had paid some £30 on account of furniture to the value of £100 bought under a hire-purchase agreement. The man died, and the widow asked for an easement in the terms. The reply was swift and certain. Whilst the widow was out representatives called, obtaining the key from the letter-box, entered the house and seized all the furniture.

Another example of casework in this period is of interest for its combination of moral attitudes and a more constructive approach. In spite of the father's conviction for bigamy, of the unsatisfactory condition of the home, and the decision to leave the assistance of this family to the Public Assistance Committee, the C.O.S. Committee decided that 'they must do something more'. They reported:

> Mr and Mrs P. presented moral handicaps in various forms. . . .when application was made to us for boots for the children (there were 12 children of whom 8 were still at home) . . . on all hands we received unsatisfactory reports of the family. We managed, however, to induce the authorities to increase their relief, to enable the family to improve their housing conditions, and various Care Committees promised to keep in touch with the children.
>
> In February of this year, they were again referred to us, as Mary, aged 11, had gained a scholarship, which her Headmistress could not conscientiously allow her to take, while living in such conditions, as it was obvious that the child could not work at home. We were asked to board her out, to enable her to take advantage of this educational opportunity, and after much discussion and enquiry, the Waifs and Strays Society undertook to pay for Mary to live with a foster mother during term time, only returning to her home for the holidays.
> We have succeeded in placing the child with a good type of working class family in the neighbourhood of the school she is to attend and, so far, the arrangement is working well. Mary is like a child from another world, in her neat school uniform, and is able to take her place among the other girls, as a member of our Committee has kindly undertaken to give her regular pocket money.
> It will be an interesting experiment to see whether environment or heredity will prevail in this case.[27]

Table 5 below gives a summary of some of the main forms of assistance undertaken by the C.O.S. between the two world wars. Amongst them 'pensions' was a valuable and time-consuming service, although it does not, numerically, come high on the list. The C.O.S. were much concerned with the plight of the elderly; much of the 'friendly visiting' (not included in 'some forms of assistance') was to old people living alone, on whose

behalf some organisation or private person had appealed to the
C.O.S. In August 1938, the L.C.C. Public Assistance Department
asked the Society to be responsible for a scheme 'whereby friendly
visits could be made from time to time to lonely old people in
receipt of Public Assistance'. Over a thousand old people had
asked to be included and it meant special appeals by the C.O.S.
for more voluntary workers to undertake such work in each of
the Districts. The Secretary, Astbury, reported a good response:
young people were particularly welcome.*

Between 1935 and 1939 'Psychological Treatment' was
separately classified as one of the forms of assistance. The
numbers were relatively small but the families were amongst
those who needed most sustained help. In accordance with the
special interest of its Secretary, Pringle, the Society had been
noting the influence of psychology and psychiatry on the practice
of casework in the United States. As long ago as 1918 the C.O.S.
had had a series of lectures by Dr Cyril Burt who, cautious about
'laboratory psychology', yet pointed to the importance of the
new 'psychology of individual differences' which should prove to
be 'a master science' for the social worker.[29]

In 1927, Pringle had written enthusiastically of Jung as 'an
unrepentant champion of elaborate individual case work'.[30] Soon
after, plans were made for a C.O.S. worker to go for a period,
under the sponsorship of the Commonwealth Foundation, to the
New York School of Social Work and the Child Guidance
Institute, where the practical training was strongly under the
influence of psychologists and psychiatrists.[31] Yet there was
considerable misgiving in the Society about the psychological
approach to casework. This was put unmistakably by E. J.
Urwick in The Loch Memorial Lecture of 1930.[32] Urwick
referred to the extravagant claims made by some psychologists
and by some of their followers 'including the younger social
workers'. He disliked the emphasis on 'diagnosis' and 'treatment'
which to him suggested a 'patient often a passive recipient of
treatment', even if the treatment was said to be skilled and
therapeutic. For him it was the effort of response which was the
necessary part of the principle of reciprocity.

However enthusiastic the younger generation of C.O.S. workers

---

* It was found that elderly ladies liked to be visited by young gentlemen,
and vice versa.

TABLE 5. SOME FORMS OF ASSISTANCE 1918–1939

Year	Numbers Assisted	Employment	Pensions	Emigration	Sanatorium Treatment	Medical Surgical Convalescence	Other
1918	5,786	214	115	9	69	4,151	2,004
1919	5,946	150	100	10	49	3,798	1,993
1920	7,169	236	111	28	64	4,366	2,842
1921	7,253	270	77	53	43	3,975	2,743
1922	7,113	307	87	69	96	3,953	2,962
1923	7,359	322	102	161	93	4,072	3,315
1924	7,814	239	98	88	90	4,653	2,993
1925	7,840	213	228	61	103	4,289	2,608
1926	8,019	194	115	81	129	4,723	2,707
1927	8,296	218	112	60	165	4,584	3,229
1928	8,567	236	296	62	87	5,059	3,521
1929	8,186	259	155	51	114	4,328	3,328
1930	8,010	258	169	17	89	4,270	3,367
1931	7,565	237	191	8	57	3,864	3,420
1932	8,016	255	177	6	35	3,948	3,908
1933	8,099	356	137	7	51	3,611	4,231
1934	9,169	391	142	7	47	3,676	5,268

Year	Numbers Assisted	Employment	Pensions	Emigration	Psychological Treatment	Incl. Dentures	Grants: Removal Equipment	Temp. Allowance	Provision for Children	Miscellaneous
1935	8,114	237	100	—	38	3,296	650	919	418	3,046
1936	7,841	272	126	—	39	3,079	680	995	419	2,755
1937	7,958	225	144	—	33	3,099	615	1,129	460	2,434
1938	8,286	203	103	—	31	3,172	759	1,307	502	2,950
1939	8,492	167	74	—	45	2,811	801	1,137	494	3,480

might be, they found it hard to practise the American way of casework in this country. Practical difficulties were too great: small interviewing rooms were almost non-existent (some Districts were forced to use one large room, hoping that when several interviews were taking place at once, the babel of voices would ensure the required privacy). In addition there were the long succession of callers, the overcrowded waiting room, the pressure to get reports made out and letters written so that visits could be paid, the endless walks along squalid streets (with some applicants always out, since the appointment system had not yet been introduced), the rush to get everything ready in time for the long weekly committee. All these factors made it impossible to command the quiet, and the leisure, necessary for a series of sustained and lengthy interviews demanded by the 'psychologically trained'.

The older members were looking nostalgically to the past when 'wider social issues' were discussed and projects planned. Several committees stressed the lack of time to organise charity in their Districts;* they had to concentrate entirely on casework. That many of the secretaries and their helpers were overworked, that 'they had no time for thought', were weaknesses frankly recognised by the Society. The problem was clearly stated by T. E. Lloyd† in a Paper read at the Conference of Charity Organisations and Kindred Societies.[33] '. . . we are defeated by our own zeal and efficiency. We have become the handmaiden of everyone who finds his duty to his neighbour too difficult and wants to be relieved of it. We have almost become popular.' Referring to the overworked secretaries he adds '. . . a social worker who does nothing but relief is in danger of losing perspective'. Other pertinent remarks are worth quoting: 'the natural tendency of every social service institution is to increase its activities'; 'there is a tendency for larger institutions to become stereotyped and overcentralised'; 'personal relationships are the essence of Social Service and thrive best in the work of small communities'. T. E. Lloyd was not too happy about American casework, not least because, 'with the increase in professionalism,

---

* E.g. Islington in 1933.

† T. E. Lloyd was in great demand as a speaker in various parts of the country. He had been an Organising Secretary of the Society until he resigned in 1914 for war service. In 1920 he was appointed as Secretary to the C.O.S. Associated Societies Committee.

there is a tendency to despise the humble volunteer'. Yet Lloyd looked forward to an increase in social equality. He deprecated the divisions and distinctions which follow from too much organisation where 'one class is always engaged in managing the affairs of another class'. Having pointed out the weaknesses and dangers, Lloyd affirmed his belief in the social workers who would have magnificent opportunities to create 'a closer and more personal relationship between all classes of the community'. Loch himself would have approved. But there was one considerable difference between the old and the new. An earlier generation had been proud of the fact that they were the 'handmaidens' of other charitable organisations, whereas Lloyd was now lamenting the overwork caused by that very fact.

One of the extra tasks, begun during the First World War and carried on for another generation, was the enquiry and advisory service on behalf of Service Fund Trustees. This was now becoming irksome since the Trustees required investigation on specific points, such as the scrutiny of 'marriage lines'.* By now the C.O.S. was laying far less emphasis on 'investigation'. In 1929 a decision was made to ask permission of the applicants before certain enquiries were made, for example of employers and relatives. In the following year it was suggested† that enquiries should not be made of neighbours or of local shops. Other general routine enquiries should not be made if it was unlikely that help would be granted. They should not be made, either, 'if help must be granted irrespective of the character of the applicant'. In practice, although the old case front was still in use, secretaries were using their discretion about filling in all the details. Consequently the methods used for establishing the genuineness and the extent of the need tended to vary from District to District. As late as 1943, some secretaries were finding it repugnant to fill in case fronts and a memorandum was sent to the Administrative Committee urging that 'enquiries should be relevant'.

Meanwhile, others were trying to solve the question of 'too much relief work' by greater attention to the question of selection.[34] The problem of the 'selection of cases' and the best use

* The Society was finding that not only their own secretaries but applicants, too, were showing increasing dislike of enquiry; e.g. Report from Islington, 1929.
† At the Domestic Meetings of the Administrative Committee.

of the skill and experience of workers in short supply continued
to worry the Society for another quarter of a century.*

The concentration of the Society on family casework in the
years between the two world wars gave them a good opportunity
to discover and record the varying needs of people in social or
financial difficulty. Reference has already been made to the
accumulated evidence of medical and other health needs and to
the many examples offered to the committee enquiring into
hire-purchase problems.† Their work in the field of child care,
long before the Children Act of 1948 gave the necessary statutory
powers and duties, had also given the Society valuable insight.
When a Departmental Committee was set up on the Adoption of
Children, the C.O.S. had the satisfaction of knowing that their
Secretary, Astbury, was a member of the Committee. A memorandum of evidence was prepared and four C.O.S. representatives
were examined by the Committee. When the Adoption of Children
(Regulation) Bill was introduced the Society congratulated itself
on 'its contribution to the solution of a grave social problem'.[35]

The Enquiry Department of the Society was still very active,
particularly in answering queries about the status of charities
which were making appeals to the public.‡ Checking allegations
against institutions and giving warning to the Districts if there
was justification were still part of the Medical Advisory Sub-
Committee's activities, but, although it entailed a lot of work, it
was a minor part. The C.O.S. had already secured the co-operation of bona fide charities and institutions: for many years these
bodies had regularly lodged their annual reports and had given
other information which was published by the C.O.S. in its
Annual *Charities Register and Digest*.

The Society was much concerned§ by the increasing number
of house to house collectors, a lucrative method used by bogus
charities. The high percentage paid to collectors on commission,
varying from thirty-three and a third per cent to fifty per cent, and
to the promoter of the scheme as salary, left very little for charity.
The law had many loop-holes and the C.O.S. was collecting evi-

---

* Culminating in long discussions and the complete review of the Society's
work in the Cunliffe Report, 1960.

† The Hire Purchase Act came into force in January, 1939.

‡ 15,000 such queries were dealt with in the year 1937–38.

§ The Society was represented on the Street Collectors Advisory Committee,
Scotland Yard.

dence and pressing for adequate legislation. A closely related form of unscrupulous preying on the charitable public was the occasion of another memorandum and of oral evidence to the Joint Committee of the House of Lords: the C.O.S. had many examples of 'Hospital or Charity Waste Collection Schemes' where bags were left at houses to be filled with materials to be sold for the benefit of hospitals or other specified charities. The Society investigated many of these schemes and found them to be purely business concerns, whose owners kept just within the law by giving occasional donations to the Charities concerned. Similar forms of bogus charity continued to carry on a profitable business.*

But the Society was not anxious to perpetuate its early image as a 'detection society'. During the years between the wars it was making high claims for its role as a casework agency in the community; 'We are prepared to struggle with any human problem you choose to send us', declared its Secretary 'and we can advise you from immediate first-hand daily experience upon the working of any particular social service, and upon the reaction of the people to it.'[36]

The first part of this all-embracing offer had led to the situation where many Districts had had to give up all thought of the organisation of charity in Loch's sense. It had resulted in the overwork of many of the staff and very nearly to the identification of the C.O.S. as another relief society—a title which they always strenuously denied. The Society claimed to select only those individuals and families where timely help would lead to rehabilitation; the list of those 'unassisted' was certainly formidable. It was the C.O.S. refusal to help those who were unlikely to respond which earned them so much hostility. The Society valued the right to discriminate: selection was essential to constructive personal work. The denial that they were a relief society was also supported by the method of financing cases. As we have seen, Districts raised the necessary sums to cover the cost of each case as it arose: there was no general relief fund. Yet, in the period between the wars, the Society was administering an increasing number of funds and some of the Districts also had local funds on which they could draw. Were the large sums available for ex-service men and their

* A favourite modern form, shown up for what it is on television programmes, is the statement that disabled workers are employed in the manufacture of certain articles, or in the re-use of collected waste, such as knitting wools.

F

dependants a temptation to give financial help more easily? B. Astbury, Pringle's successor, put the position frankly as he looked back, in 1930, to his own casework: 'that I had dealt with a vast number of people, I knew, but had I done a piece of work on their behalf, or had I taken the easier course and made it possible for them to obtain some temporary form of monetary assistance?'[37] The L.C.C. had similar doubts in 1935.* The examples quoted earlier, and many more of a similar nature, show that much care and thought had also been given in helping many families to overcome their difficulties and anxieties. At District level, difference in social theory rarely conflicted with practical concern for a family in need. The Society had trained many volunteers and an increasing number of students in the process.

DIAGRAM 1

Charity Organization Society. London (England)
Applications Decided All Offices Thirty Years 1905-1934

Finally, we should remember that the structure of the Society and its social knowledge made it a natural source of advice and organisation when emergencies arose. We have noted how quickly the Society came to the rescue of servicemen's dependants at the outbreak of the First World War. Less well known is the work of

* See page 141.

the Districts in South London when, in 1928, the great Thames flood caused much desolation. A description in the report of the North Lambeth Committee gives some idea of the co-operation which helped the C.O.S. family social workers and others to go immediately to the rescue:

The night of 6th January, 1928, will never be forgotten by those who lived through it and saw its tragic sights. On that dreadful night, the river rose beyond all recorded bounds and black water poured remorselessly down every river-side street. Sewers ran backwards, spreading foul desolation. Houses were damaged, furniture ruined, and homes destroyed. As the dark night passed, the waters subsided as silently as they had come, leaving chaos and misery widespread. When the day broke, the work of reconstruction and restoration began. We are happy to know that in that time of dreadful need our Society was not found wanting. The Rector of Lambeth lent a room for use as a Central Office. All applications had to be made there, Miss Cope dealing with those from South Lambeth, Miss Perry with St Mary's and Miss Locket with North Lambeth. Statements were taken as to the number in family, the position of the rooms damaged, and the amount of loss suffered. These were verified the same day by visitors, all of whom knew the district intimately. The Medical Officer of Health and the Guardians most kindly lent some of their officers to help in this way. Where the immediate need was for coal and bedding, it was at once supplied, and clothes depots were established in the Rectory and St John's Hall. Lady Margaret Hall Settlement took charge of the latter and spent many strenuous hours wrestling with huge bales of goods, some most unsuitable, and trying to meet the demands of those who thought that, however old the drowned clothes had been, completely new ones must be supplied in their place.

Representative Committees for each district met frequently to consider the amounts to be granted towards the restoration of furniture (including wringers and sewing machines), bedding, and floorcloth; here the representatives of the Duchy of Cornwall and the Ecclesiastical Commissioners gave invaluable advice, knowing intimately the former condition of

the homes. We must not omit to mention the close co-operation of the British Legion, who, under the energetic and
efficient guidance of Mr Booth, supplied clothes and bedding
to ex-Service men and their families who were passed on to
him from the Secretaries with a written recommendation,
without which he refused to act.

The response to another emergency, the influx of British
Refugees from Spain, has already been referred to.* It was part
of a valuable, if relatively small, effort in which a number of
Societies co-operated. A special fund was raised upon the appeal
of the Bishop of Gibraltar with the support of *The Times*; the
C.O.S. carried out the administration of the Fund, without
charge, and also supplied the Honorary Secretary to the small
representative Committee. For a while the *Catholic Times* Fund
was closely associated. The C.O.S. and the District Committees
did much of the casework involved in helping families,† some of
whom could speak only Spanish although they were of British
nationality. Some of the refugees were professional people who
had arrived almost destitute. One example will show the sympathy
and practical help given:

Mr B. had been Professor of English at three Government
Colleges in Madrid, where he had lived for 30 years. He was
a man of 53, with a wife and a little girl of 8, neither of whom
knew any English. They arrived in this country on September
11th with £9 as their total capital. It was soon found that the
most urgent need for the majority of the Refugees was that
they should learn English. Daily classes were therefore
arranged by the C.C.I.R. and Mr B. was engaged as teacher
at £4 a week. In October we received a generous donation
from the British Legation in Montevideo, and an enquiry for
someone to fill the post of Director at an institute in that city.
Mr B.'s name was given and in due course he was appointed
to the post, the Institute paying his fare to Uruguay. Mr B.
was most anxious for his wife and daughter to accompany
him, and, as it was felt that after all their unhappy experience
in Spain it would be wisest for them to start life together in

---

* See p. 130
† The total number of families assisted was 278, comprising more than
1,000 individuals.

the new country, a grant of £60 was made to meet Mrs B. and her daughter's travelling expenses.[39]

The greatest emergency which the C.O.S. helped to meet was that of the threat of war in 1938–39. The response was one for which their long experience of advisory work had well equipped them, namely, the setting up of Citizens Advice Bureaux in London.*

By this time B. E. Astbury had become the Secretary of the Society. Before we consider the development of the C.O.S. during and after the Second World War we should note the background and the quality of the Secretary who was to lead the Society into the modern period.

* See Chapter 10(i).

Part III

FROM C.O.S. TO F.W.A.

CHAPTER NINE

A New Approach

1. Benjamin E. Astbury and the Second World War

(B. E. Astbury: Assistant Secretary, 1930–36:
Organising Secretary 1936–38: Secretary 1938–56)

Benjamin Astbury was born in June 1889, one of a family of eleven children. At the age of nine, he was admitted as a Scholar to an old foundation, the Chester Blue Coat Hospital. He had hoped, on leaving school, to train for the Ministry but, as he had neither Latin nor Greek, this seemed to be impossible and he entered a solicitor's office. He was never happy in this work and eventually joined the staff of the Chester Poor Law Institution, then known as the Union Work-house. He soon became Assistant Master and was able to take a two-year external course at the School of Social Science at Liverpool University where Miss Elizabeth Macadam was in charge.[1] He qualified in the specialised course on the Poor Law in its relation to social work.

On the outbreak of the First World War Astbury enlisted as a private and served in Egypt. In 1917 he was sent home to take an Officer Cadet course and was commissioned in January 1918. On his return to the front he was severely wounded and taken prisoner at Cambrai. After the war he had to have prolonged hospital treatment. He had, meanwhile, decided to take up social work. In 1919, while he was in Liverpool, working with the War Pensions Committee and the Lord Mayor's Distress Fund, he studied other social work in the area. An important step in his career came in July 1919, when he was appointed secretary to the Council of Social Welfare in Chester. Soon after, there began a close association with the new Bishop of Chester, Dr Luke Paget, and Mrs Paget, both of whom took an active part in social work.

F*

Together they started the Federation of Boys Clubs, the Federation of Girls Clubs and the Juvenile Organisation Committee. Astbury always felt that his friendship with the Pagets greatly influenced his life. It was through Dr Paget that he met Pringle, since Pringle had been the Bishop's examining Chaplain.* As a result, Pringle invited Astbury, in 1930, to come and help him at C.O.S. headquarters in London.

Astbury's first interview throws some light on the Society at that time: when he was offered charge of the Enquiry Department he refused on two counts, firstly, that he found the manner of members of the Interviewing Committee too autocratic and, secondly, that he disliked the thought of being entirely concerned with bogus charities. Pringle, who was anxious to secure the services of this very promising young man, made two offers: that Astbury should become Assistant Secretary,† with duties which would include the Enquiry Department, and that the first six months of his appointment should be spent in visiting the District Offices of the Society.‡ This was acceptable and Astbury entered upon his long career with the C.O.S., becoming Organising Secretary in 1936, with Pringle as Director and Consultant, and Secretary in 1938, on Pringle's death.

From the beginning Astbury was critical of some aspects of C.O.S. policy and methods. He had a strong ally in Olive Crosse who had recently returned from the United States. Astbury was soon in demand as a speaker at meetings of 'kindred societies' in various parts of the country. In the early 1930s we already hear a new note.§ His address to the Standing Conference on Personal Service, November 1930, was 'A re-statement of Case Work'.[2] Although the paper was mainly a plea to re-learn the lessons of the past and to examine the factors which had led caseworkers astray since 1918, it also had some practical suggestions to offer for future developments. These concerned, particularly, new thinking about 'long term cases', and the better training of family case-

* When Paget was Bishop of Stepney and Pringle rector of St George's-in-the-East.

† Pringle made no secret of the fact that he hoped Astbury might follow him as Secretary of the Society.

‡ Astbury had asked for this opportunity of getting to know the Society thoroughly before being immersed in Central affairs.

§ See references to Astbury's work, together with that of an experienced voluntary worker, T. E. Lloyd, in the Journals and Reports for 1931.

workers. Both of these were to become vital issues for the Society. Astbury, whose experience gave him a special interest in the question, also wrote a useful 'pamphlet' on *The Homeless Man*[3] giving practical guidance to Districts on the facilities available. Astbury continued to follow up the question of housing the homeless, for example, in 1949, when District Committees were asked to send in any comments they might wish to make as to the present services of the L.C.C. to the homeless; but the subject was no longer a matter for enquiry by a Special Committee as in the early years. The emphasis shifted to homeless families; other societies, as well as local authorities, were also wrestling with this intractable problem.

Meanwhile, Astbury contributed a number of useful memoranda on questions of current interest to the Society. His paper on the results of a survey undertaken, in 1949, by the twenty-one District Committees and seventeen C.A.B.x of the Association was published in the following year under the title: *Some Observations on the Impact of the New Social Services on Family Life.*[4] That Astbury was at heart a caseworker, as well as an administrator, is evident in an article contributed, in 1946, on *The Effect of Long Separation of Family Life*. This illustrates Astbury's understanding of families trying to adjust to normal life after evacuation and demobilisation; it also throws light on the attitude to casework at that time and helps to explain the need felt by the young professional caseworkers to improve their skills in dealing with problems of personal relationships.

The annual reports, from Astbury's time onwards, were mainly factual, with no literary embellishments or classical allusions. Invective, which had enlivened Pringle's term of office, no longer found a place. The C.O.S. had become respectable. Astbury's background and experience were valuable assets as he served on many committees concerned with social questions (e.g. that on Law and Practice in regard to Charitable Trusts and on the Committee of Enquiry into the Law on Intestacies. He was also a member of the Advisory Committee on the Legal Aid and Advice Act.) They were useful, too, in his successful contacts with the various ministries and local authorities. As the statutory social services increased, it was important for the Society to have a Secretary who was anxious to improve voluntary-statutory relations.

Soon after his appointment as Secretary, Astbury's gifts for organisation were in demand in the preparation for war, and in the practical efforts of the C.O.S. to meet the dislocation of its outbreak. He now showed his quality. He threw himself wholeheartedly into the immense task of helping to plan and to organise the Citizens Advice Bureaux throughout Metropolitan London. He, like others, felt frustrated when the Government failed to take the social service organisations into consultation when the schemes for evacuation and the relief of war distress were first worked out:

> Early in 1939 the Voluntary Societies were told by the Government that their work would be regarded as of National Importance 'should a state of emergency arise'. In spite of this complimentary assurance it is a sad fact that in the mass of social legislation that has poured from different Government Departments in the last few months, there has been little or no consultation with social workers.*

It was pointed out that 'in the economic collapse in America in 1931, social workers were everywhere called into consultation. . . . It may be fairly claimed that English social workers have had equally valuable experience'.[5] But, if the Government did not take advantage of the experience of social workers in framing large issues of policy, such as evacuation, there was much greater readiness to co-operate at a local level. It was here that the organisation of charity over the years gave the C.O.S. opportunities to offer valuable service under wartime conditions.

Astbury, at Central, worked closely with a variety of agencies and some of those who knew him in those days remember how successfully he brought together rivals who had each been claiming his own field of influence.† The C.O.S. was also fortunate in having the strong support of overseas friends, and of influential and forceful British voluntary helpers.‡

---

* After the initial failure of some of the evacuation schemes, the various ministries concerned hurriedly revised their methods, and social workers were brought into close consultation—some were seconded to the statutory services.

† A less favourable view was held later when Astbury seemed to some organisations to be 'building an empire'.

‡ E.g. The Hon. Mrs Jack Crawshay, daughter of Lord Tyrrell, former British Ambassador to France. As a member of the British War Relief Society, and of the Personal Service League, she was in close touch with many influential Americans. She became the very vigorous Chairman of the Islington District Office until its amalgamation with Area 4 in the 1960s.

The Society was soon entrusted with funds from the U.S.A., Rhodesia, the Crown Colonies and others for emergency plans. The immediate response of the people of Canada in sending, through the Canadian Red Cross, large gifts of blankets, clothes and food was heartening when bombing made so many families homeless. The C.O.S. was asked in August 1940 to be the distributing centre. Richard Titmuss, in the official war history,[6] writes of 'the voluntary organisations—the Charity Organisation Society, the Society of Friends, the Settlement Workers, the London Council of Social Service and many others—who helped to hold the line . . . while the official machine was beginning to take effective action'. He continues: 'The Charity Organisation Society, for instance, had foreseen the need for blankets and clothing and through the generosity of the Canadian Red Cross had acquired stocks of 50,000 blankets, 100,000 miscellaneous garments and 50,000 tins of food. These stocks were quickly distributed to London rest centres.'* The rapid and effective distribution owed much to Astbury's drive and initiative. His own reflections, in relation to the Society's function, were recorded later: 'in those nightmare weeks in September, when "alerts" seemed to follow "all clears" without half an hour's pause, much of our time was spent in unloading huge lorries, repacking and despatching smaller vanloads to Rest and Feeding Centres, Settlements and Hospitals'. The writer pauses to reflect on the 'distribution of food and blankets' and to wonder what the founder pioneers would say—but decides that this is the beginning of true casework, even though 'only first aid', since it gives power of recovery from shock. C.O.S. family social workers could then help in plans for the future.

The C.O.S. was also asked to act as the almoner for the British War Refugees Fund when the invasion of the Low Countries brought British subjects from Holland, Belgium and the North of France. In January 1942 the C.O.S. undertook, under a Deed of Trust, the administration of this fund; it involved taking over some 1,600 current case-papers. 'New applications soon followed from refugees escaping from France, or from Spanish prisons and internment camps in Spain, Germany and France. Some were

* '11,000 blankets, 27,000 garments, 45,000 tins of soup and other food were distributed in September, and the homeless people of London were loud in their gratitude.'[7]

repatriated from Italy.' Many refugees were elderly or ailing and needed more help than was possible on their 'Prevention and Relief of Distress Allowances'. The C.O.S. also agreed, at the request of the Government of Malta Office in London, to administer, through the same committee, sums for the benefit of refugees from Malta. Much of the relief given from these funds involved practical help, such as temporary allowances, medical aid, furniture, clothing, or educational grants; but some of the unhappy situations meant long and sympathetic casework which experienced District secretaries were glad to offer. Students and voluntary helpers often gave valuable help when there were language difficulties. Soon after, the Channel Islands Refugees Committee asked the C.O.S., to help, and much of this was done through the C.O.S. affiliated Societies and the network of correspondents, many of whom were clergy.

The largest piece of work undertaken by the C.O.S. in co-operation with overseas friends, for 'British civilians suffering as a result of enemy action', was that on behalf of the British War Relief Society of the United States of America. Astbury became an Honorary Advisory Member of their committee, and the C.O.S. was entrusted with the administration of considerable sums of money for the benefit of those in badly raided towns. In the annual report for 1941–42 the C.O.S. Secretary reported the expenditure of over £66,000, on a variety of schemes which included the provision of equipment and recreational facilities for 120 Shelter Clubs for boys and girls, for 380 Hostels for Evacuated Children, and for 100 Hostels for Homeless Old People;* 16 Homes had been established for children 'shocked' in air raids; 50 Settlements had been enabled to expand their work; education grants were made to children who had lost one or both parents by enemy action; and some 600 'bombed' families who were not eligible for statutory grants or aid from the Lord Mayor's Fund, had been assisted.

Other much valued gifts for children were distributed by the C.O.S. This was very time-consuming work for all concerned but none the less welcome; the gifts included Christmas presents year by year from the Children of Rhodesia and funds for parties, held

* This had a sequel later when the same fund made a grant of £3,000 for Old People's Welfare and the C.O.S. made itself responsible for the Old People's Homes Committee and Register for the London area.

in all parts of the country; there were also the very large gifts of toys and sweets through the B.W.R.S. of U.S.A. The American Embassy also asked the C.O.S. to carry out the administrative work of the British Service Charities Committee in connection with a U.S. Army theatrical production which brought in some £60,000 for Service Charities in Great Britain.

In addition to their other administrative war-time services, the Society also helped to establish a Poor Man's Valuer Service. Specialist advice on war damage claims and compensation was arranged at the C.O.S. District Committee offices; as air raids increased in intensity, this service was in greater demand. Another service which for many years had proved its value was now administered by the C.O.S. After 1939 the Legal Advice Centres at Cambridge House University Settlement and the Mary Ward Settlement were carried on under the aegis of the Society. Citizens with legal problems were usually referred by the C.A.B.x (some 17,000 in the London area in the year 1942–43).

Meanwhile the demands on the medical services, for so long organised by the C.O.S., continued and new needs were identified. One of these was the plight of old age pensioners whose sight was failing, but who dreaded applying to the Public Assistance Committee for spectacles. The City Parochial Foundation, which had a long history of co-operation with the C.O.S., became aware of this special need and asked the C.O.S. to administer £500 for the supply of spectacles.* Within three months nearly 300 old people had been supplied through the District Committees. Many District Committees, much concerned for the difficulties of old people, had promoted local Old Peoples Welfare Committees, some of which undertook the administration of the Government's Home Help Scheme. C.O.S. 'Central' assumed responsibility for London's Old People's Homes Committee and Register. The Society argued that air attacks had only accentuated a problem which had been long known but little publicised.

The Society found time, during these exacting years, to maintain its tradition of collecting evidence and reporting on specific questions. A memorandum on 'Evacuation 1939' was sent to Titmuss for the war history. In September 1943 another

---

* The C.O.S. took over the administration of this fund in July, 1943 and the scheme came into operation in September.

report was sent in, on Rest Centres in Bethnal Green, East Lewisham, St Pancras, Islington, Camberwell and Southwark.*[8] One District Committee undertook an enquiry into housing conditions in a small slum area: a house-to-house visitation (some 400–500 houses) was made by volunteers from the London School of Economics, with the tenants co-operating. The purpose was set out as follows: 'The Committee thought that if the facts as to overcrowding, inadequate sanitation, vermin and uncared-for bombed sites could be collected and placed in a clear and forcible way before the responsible authorities something might be done. . . . Failing local action, steps will be taken to approach the Ministry of Health.'[9]

The C.O.S. was also glad to respond to the invitation to submit evidence to the Government Committee appointed in 1943 to review the whole question of seamen's welfare in ports. This included consideration of the large number of appeals for funds for welfare and benevolent purposes. The Society reported: 'It is satisfactory to note that the recommendations made by the Society are included among those finally put forward by the Committee, namely, the compulsory registration of all seamen's societies appealing to the public, the control of appeals under licence from the registering authority with power to refuse such licence on the grounds of redundancy or overlapping.'[10]

This accorded with much of the work of the Enquiry Department which had many demands made upon it: the war had brought into existence a large number of new charities (especially 'Comforts Funds'). Many firms sought the advice of the C.O.S. on the genuineness of appeals, while others asked the C.O.S. to administer their funds. The Society was able to supply evidence when the re-enaction of the War Charities Act, 1916, was under consideration. In spite of compulsory registration of charities, which included some of the unsatisfactory mushroom organisations, there were still many bogus charity promotors and begging letter writers about which the C.O.S. had enquiries. There were also an increasing number of societies which were genuine, and quite ready to co-operate in the compilation of valid information in the *Charities Register and Digest*—a publication which was still

---

* Titmuss pays tribute to the C.O.S. contributions on Rest Centres which were 'judged faithful records after an inspection of a mass of official and unofficial reports'.

greatly in demand. New editions of *How to Help Cases of Distress* were also issued and rapidly sold out.

Meanwhile, as far as bombing and other war-time conditions allowed, ordinary casework went on in District Offices. While the C.A.B.x took over much of the advisory work they sent on to the C.O.S. family caseworkers those enquirers with special difficulties who needed a trained social worker with more time to help solve their problems. In the first year, Districts reported an increase of about a thousand applications. They noticed a tendency for more 'black-coated workers' to seek help. Whatever demands were made on the Society, casework was basic to its activities.

When the flying bomb attacks occurred in the summer of 1944 the Society carried out its intensified activities not only in C.O.S. and C.A.B. offices but in Borough Information and Administrative Centres. In the next annual report the Association paid tribute to its workers:

> The Council would like to take this opportunity of recording its gratitude to and pride in the members of its staff who, in many instances, worked seven days a week—with little opportunity for rest at night—throughout the three months of the flying bomb attacks. They undoubtedly made a valuable contribution to the relief and to the morale of the much-tried citizens of London.

The professional skill of family social workers had been tested in the war years. An outside tribute to these qualities is to be found in the official war history[11] when Titmuss discusses work in the rest centres. The comment on the value of their service is illuminating in view of many past criticisms of their methods. '. . . many social workers voluntarily gave to the centres the benefit of their training. They had experience in handling distressed people, they knew the value of order, they were familiar with the detail of social provision. Unlike some—not all—of the Poor Law officials they were capable of taking the initiative, and of temporarily disregarding rules and regulations. This they did effectively.'*

---

* The C.O.S. workers were not alone in giving such services; as Titmuss adds, the need was met also by 'members of the W.V.S., teachers, local officials and clergymen. . . . In other instances ordinary people of the neighbourhood quite naturally became leaders in the centres'.

In the year 1944 the C.O.S. celebrated its seventy-five years Jubilee, and Sir William Beveridge (afterwards Lord Beveridge) gave the address. A quotation heading the Annual Report reads:

The main doctrine of your Society is based on humanity and reason . . . it is that partial, inadequate help of any kind is wrong; that the only help which is worth giving is that which is adequate and restorative. . . . Today, while you have not departed in any way from your fundamental principle that people should be helped adequately and constructively through careful study of each individual problem, your Society is very far from saying that there should not be any organised general provision to prevent distress . . . Yet, whatever the State does, since that must be the same for all citizens, there will always remain the scope for personal help, individual care of those who for whatever cause need something more or different. There will always remain the need for such a Society as yours to make charity constructive and healing.

The Annual Report noted that these words were 'particularly heartening to the Society at a time when it was engaged in reviewing its whole machinery and functions in order to adapt itself to meet the demands of a new social order which, during its seventy-five years of pioneering work, it had done so much to bring into being'.

Was this, once more, too large a claim for a Society which had opposed the Liberal measures of the first decades of the twentieth century? Had not the C.O.S. been slow to recognise the economic and social factors which had helped to shape the new order? If the Society over-estimated the role of a London charity organisation in these large events, yet it had done some valuable and lasting work. It had consistently upheld values which were an integral part of a free society: belief in the worth of the individual and respect for his rights as a person with the corollary that 'intervention' required great care. The rights and duties of the family flowed from this. Its constructive casework had pointed the way to 'rehabilitation'; it had revealed the gaps in the social services and the failure of particularised benefits unrelated to the total needs of the individual or his family. Not only had the

C.O.S. identified needs, especially in the field of health, but it had achieved practical results in several pioneer experiments. It had also publicised social evils and instigated legislation to deal with them, of which the Moneylenders and Hire Purchase Acts were good examples.

As the Society approached the post-war years it carried forward not only a new attitude to 'community responsibility for universal needs', but a tradition of family social work which had much to offer in a period of re-adjustment to a more normal way of life.

2. *The Transition Period*

Many of the C.O.S. members and workers were now convinced that the old attitude towards statutory responsibility for health and welfare services must be reversed.* Mr H. W. Willink, one of the staunch members of the C.O.S. Council, was welcomed as the new Minister of Health; the Society appointed a special committee to consider the Beveridge proposals for Social Security;[12] a memorandum followed, warmly welcoming the recommendations. Pringle must have turned in his grave.

The Society had at the same time been considering a change of name to mark the new attitudes. Agreement was reached on 4th December, 1944, on a memorandum sent in by the secretaries in May, though the change could not be effective for nearly two years. The C.O.S. became the F.W.A. in 1946.

But if the traditional social theory had been reversed, the principles and practice of casework had not; nor had the experience of organising help on behalf of people in distress. All the same, when in 1948, the State undertook responsibility on a much larger scale for the welfare of the community, the F.W.A., like other voluntary societies, had to re-examine its function. It would no longer need to 'fill the gaps' in the health services. A Child Care Service was established (although only for children deprived of normal home life), and Social Security would, it was hoped, remove 'financial aid' from the Association's categories of assistance. There remained important human needs, other than material, which the F.W.A. had always recognised as its primary concern. The War and its consequences had emphasised some of

* In 1942 the old hostility to Family Allowances was replaced by strong approval, with a recommendation in favour of payment to the mother.

the difficulties of family adjustment and the Association's workers prepared to improve their skills to meet them.

These new demands, however, were not matched by new sources of income. On the contrary, donations and subscriptions were precarious: finance was a constant source of anxiety. At the same time the Association recognised that its administrative machinery was in drastic need of overhaul.* Yet it was during this period that the Central Committees showed considerable vitality. The Marriage Welfare Committee, for example, promoted experimental centres which developed into the Family Discussion Bureau, which was to transform casework for disturbed families. At the same time the F.W.A. embarked on a series of 'research projects' and successfully applied to a number of Trusts to sponsor them. These projects merit separate consideration.† They could not have been carried through without the enthusiasm of Astbury and the vigorous support of the honorary officers and chairmen of committees.

The Association also continued its function 'to gather evidence of the effects of social legislation on the lives of ordinary people'; it drew the attention of local authorities to any failures it had discovered in the exercise of statutory powers and duties. After the Second World War there were acute housing problems, both the shortage of houses in relation to need, and the overcrowding of older houses which raised even more difficult social questions: they were responsible for a large proportion of the problems brought to F.W.A. family social workers for solution. Some of the practical questions met in the Districts by families who were rehoused were sent on to the General Purposes Committee for guidance.‡ In 1954 the Districts were reporting that the bedding sold by the L.C.C. 'Half-way Houses' was so poor that it sometimes wore out before payments were completed. The following year the F.W.A. was regretting that the L.C.C. would only house a family from a rehabilitation centre if £60 worth of furniture could be provided. The Districts had to consider how far they could themselves help, when rehousing meant the health and stability of a homeless family. The F.W.A. continued to hold a

---

* See Chapter 11   † See Chapter 10
‡ One instance of pressing need was revealed in 1950 when Astbury asked the L.C.C. Housing Director whether it had adopted any scheme for the sale of furniture to tenants on hire-purchase terms (as it was legally entitled to do). The result was negative.

watching brief on the subject as it affected family life, from time to time approaching local M.P.s on questions of policy in relation to rehousing.[13]

Meanwhile Astbury had tried to extend the influence of the F.W.A. both nationally and internationally. He had always been closely interested in co-operation with the 'kindred' or 'associated' societies from his early days, when he was a frequent speaker at their conferences in various parts of the country. Much of the Society's war work was national in scope. In 1943–44 Astbury was negotiating for still closer alliance whereby one National Family Welfare Association might be established. But the suggested name was not acceptable to the majority. The suspicion that the F.W.A. was seeking to become the dominant partner roused the natural pride of other societies in their own traditions and achievements and their determination to preserve their identity. The F.W.A. did not reach the national status to which it had aspired, although its own National Casework Department continued, as in past years, to be concerned with a wide range of problems.*

When, after much negotiation, the National Council of Family Casework Agencies was formed, the F.W.A. was only one among a number, but it made a valuable contribution in providing a meeting place and secretarial services. With the departure of Astbury's successor in 1960, the National Council tried unsuccessfully to get a grant to carry on; it had, therefore, to come to an end. It had done some useful work since it was set up in the late 40s including an investigation, sponsored by the Carnegie United Kingdom Trust, into 'Family Casework and the Country Dweller'.† (The report was published by the Family Welfare Association.) The National Council's annual conferences, with excellent speakers and lively discussions, had been among its most valuable activities.

Astbury was always intensely interested in overseas developments‡[14] and was a member of the Executive Board of the International Conference of Social Work. With the F.W.A. National

* The number helped in this way was limited, amounting to some 2,000 cases annually.

† An investigation carried out in 1950–51 in Northumberland, County Durham and Oxfordshire by W. P. Smith and H. A. Bate edited by A. V. S. Lochhead. The Chairman, Eileen Younghusband, contributed a Foreword.

‡ He also much enjoyed a 'Thank you' tour to the United States in 1946 and visited it again in 1948 to attend three conferences.

Casework Secretary he also attended meetings of International Social Service in Geneva, and was able to report, with considerable satisfaction, in 1953, that 'the F.W.A. undertook to become, in name as well as in practice, the British Branch of International Social Service'.*[15]

Although much constructive work was undertaken in this transition period,† the 1950s seemed to be dominated by the domestic problems which accompanied planning and re-organisation within the Association. These involved not only the administrators but busy caseworkers who were called to innumerable meetings. The conflict between the older professional workers and the newly-trained became more apparent. Voluntary workers were also divided—on whether case committees should be lay or professional.‡ Tensions between Districts and 'Central' became more acute. There could be no compromise between 'the old' and 'the new'. Financially, too, the Association had reached a low ebb. It was finding it difficult to recruit newly-trained university students.

It was an unhappy period as Astbury neared the end of his tenure of office.§ The social and economic upheavals of the war and post-war years affected social institutions and ways of life throughout the country. A new generation of young professional social workers were demanding new attitudes to social problems and a new approach to administration within their Association. Some societies were irritated by Astbury's tendency to present a ready-made plan instead of bringing them into consultation at an earlier stage. Yet he was remembered by others as 'most tolerant and progressive'.[16]

The twenty-five years of Astbury's secretaryship had seen important developments within the Society. His great oppor-

* F.W.A. Annual Report, 1954–55. 'The international work having increased beyond the capacity of the Casework Department to deal with it, the Council had decided to break off this section of the work as an entity of its own in separate accommodation in Denison House.'

† See 'The Projects', Chapter 10.

‡ E.g. the Chairman of the Islington Committee strongly supported the continuation of the lay case committee while the Chairman of Fulham supported the new professional case committee.

§ Astbury gave a lively address at his last Annual General Meeting in 1956, when he reflected on 'twenty-five years with the Family Welfare Association'. He had always shown a saving sense of humour to carry him, and others, through difficult situations.

tunity had come during the war when his practical ability and
flair for organisation had full scope. The award of the C.B.E.
brought some recognition of his contribution to family welfare.
Sir George Haynes, director of the National Council of Social
Service, paying tribute to Astbury on his retirement, testified to
'his many gifts and qualities which have won him the regard of so
many people. His readiness to enter into problems of other
organisations, his ability to appreciate new situations, his un-
rivalled knowledge of the sources of help, and his unfailing
humour which, so often, both on and off the platform, has
relieved the atmosphere of tedious meetings and, above all, the
gift of friendship which has endeared him to people in all walks
of life—these are some of the qualities which marked him out as
a leader of exceptional influence during the past twenty-five
years'.[17]

3. *Example of an Experiment in Cooperation*

It seems a fitting appendix to an account of the Society's work
during the Second World War to refer to 'An Islington Experiment',[18] a record of a co-operative effort to meet the needs of
refugees, just before Dunkirk, and of families 'bombed-out' in the
first air-raid in East London. It gives a good idea of the spirit
behind so much of the work, and of the flexibility of mind and
action brought to bear on new and very demanding situations. It
also illustrates how readily the statutory and voluntary bodies
worked together in areas where a good relationship had already
been established. The writers report:

The contribution of the C.O.S. . . . was the organisation . . .
and the enrolment of volunteers. The trained worker is used
to dealing with people and should know when to listen, and
what to look for, how to get at the real trouble without
offence and what sources are available for help for any real
need. And a trained worker can make the most of the volunteer
who may not have that type of experience or knowledge but
has invaluable gifts of friendliness, personal interest, un-
professionalism and common-sense. There were all types of
volunteers: married women, retired civil servants, borough
councillors, church workers, working men, club girls,

musicians, office girls, boy scouts, Toc H members, a young solicitor who was turned into a Poor Man's Lawyer, and even a very professional hairdresser who bobbed one of the secretaries on the spot.

In the early days information had to be collected by the Secretary by direct enquiry to the Ministry concerned, or by newspaper cuttings, etc., then indexed and made accessible and brought rapidly up-to-date for the ready use of new workers: this 'doubles the secretary's work, but it is worth it'. The intensity of demand and the type of help needed followed events closely. The practical good sense of the workers comes out clearly in the face of the inability of certain officials to take responsibility. The family social workers, in spite of the pressure of immediate needs, attempted to deal with personal problems as they became apparent. They were also able to draw attention to needs hitherto unrecognised; for example, their request to the Mayor for small sums to enable exhausted women to get a cup of tea, or to get a train back to their centre or billet, led to the distribution of the Lord Mayor's Fund: 'which occupied, almost immediately, the biggest place in our work'. Similarly, they understood the feelings of those families who, rejoicing in the safety of their shelters during weeks of intermittent bombing, suddenly saw 'their home streets devastated and their Anderson shelters hanging on the chimney tops or lifted into the next field. 'If only', they said, 'we could get out of this for even a week.' The result was a house in the country outside Oxford with ten bedrooms, taken over and furnished (it had been shut up for years) by the C.O.S. with help from the Mayor's Fund, gifts of Canadian blankets and American baby-clothes, the use of the Borough Council car, with personal help from a Senior Clerk, one of the bombed-out families, a C.O.S. member and local Oxford friends. Within a week negotiations were completed, the place roofed and decorated, fires lit and some 'black out' put up and the first group of bombed-out families were enjoying the peace of the countryside. Week by week more people were sent and a warden and a cook were found (Oxford friends had managed hitherto: other work was done by the visitors). A nursery school was started in the stables; while the families were in the country other billets or jobs were found for them. The C.O.S. had the strong support throughout of local Oxford friends and of the Mayor of Islington. The Refugees of England Committee adopted the house and gave it furniture and various comforts. The C.O.S. Secretary summed up the work: 'It has now an Oxford committee, a proper nursery school, a regular Sunday party, visitors at the weekends, and snowdrops coming up along the drive.' The work was altogether rewarding.

The final comment is of special interest in view of later developments in statutory responsibility and professional social work:

> It has shown among other things that social workers can double their usefulness by working for an official body with public funds behind it, without impairing the flexibility of the voluntary society, while, conversely, the welfare work of an official body ought to be planned and managed by the trained social worker. Efficiency in this work lies with the professional not with the official. And we hope that after the war particularly, when social reconstruction of all kinds will be attempted, this principle will be remembered by those in power.

CHAPTER TEN

Special Services, Projects and Enquiries

1. The Advisory Services

(a) Citizens Advice Bureaux

An advisory service had long been a recognised part of day-to-day C.O.S. work. During 'Munich Week', 1938, the Society and District offices had been inundated with anxious enquiries: How can I get Granny away to a safe area if there is a war? Will my son have to go when he's the only one to keep the shop running? or What shall I do with my tortoise?

The idea of having special advisory centres had already been under consideration by voluntary organisations.*[1] Astbury could speak from experience of a pioneer experiment in 1924 when he was Secretary to the Chester Council of Social Welfare.†[2] When, after the International crisis in the autumn of 1938, a conference was held of leading voluntary societies, these early centres provided a useful pattern. Negotiations in the ensuing months led to a national plan which could be operated immediately, should war break out. Advisory bureaux were to be autonomous, each with a local management committee, the link to be provided nationally by a Central Committee.‡ It was agreed that the National Council of Social Service should be responsible for the central office and secretariate.§

* The question was raised in the annual report of the N.C.S.S. for 1935–36.

† As the result of a suggestion by the Town Clerk, the 'Citizen's Friend' had been set up by the Chester Council of Social Welfare, with the co-operation of other organisations, to give advice on domestic, industrial and legal questions: the local Law Society arranged a rota of solicitors to give free legal advice. A similar experiment was later carried out in Halifax.

‡ The Central Committee was set up with R. C. Norman as the first chairman and Dorothy Keeling as secretary.

§ Later it was the N.C.S.S. which produced the valuable 'Citizens Advice Notes' for the distribution of up-to-date information to all Bureaux.

In London the C.O.S. took responsibility for the Central or Inner London area, the London Council of Social Service for Outer London.[3] The ability of experienced family social workers to meet emergencies had been frequently demonstrated. When war broke out C.A.B.x were established by twenty-eight C.O.S. District offices in most of the Metropolitan Boroughs* and, in September 1939, they were thronged with enquirers. The first rush died down when the immediate expectation of bombing was not realised but there was a steady stream of citizens seeking advice, men and women with every kind of educational and social background.

In November 1939 the C.O.S. was asked by the International Red Cross to receive and transmit messages from persons in England who had relations in enemy and enemy-occupied countries. They passed on some 16,000 messages in the first thirteen months and paid some 13,000 visits. When, in September 1940, the 'Blitz' came, both the C.O.S. and C.A.B. offices were overwhelmed with enquiries, particularly about 'priority classes' for evacuation. 'Not only the C.A.B.x but the C.O.S. committees were working long hours dealing with applications, chiefly from those who obviously ought to leave London—the sick, the aged, the mentally unstable—but for whom Government provision did not then exist. It was impossible to find billets for them, but we could, and did, thanks to the most generous grants made by the Red Cross Society, pay fares and other expenses for a very large number who had friends to go to but could not otherwise have got away.'[4] The writer adds: 'Some of our critics would be surprised to see the flexibility of a Society which is thought to confine itself strictly to the most orthodox principles of relief. . . . We were being asked not to help people to replan their lives, or even their budgets, but to come to their rescue in sudden or urgent necessity.'

It was difficult to keep accurate statistics under the prevailing conditions.† While the C.A.B.x tried to unravel the many tangles, the C.O.S. workers were ready to help by taking over problems

---

* The exceptions were in the Districts of Poplar and Whitechapel. Bethnal Green C.A.B. was set up in connection with St Margaret's House.

† In the inner London C.A.B.x some 111,000 interviews were recorded for the thirteen months, September 1939 to September 30th 1940, requiring correspondence and telephone enquiries for some 45,000.

where further constructive plans were necessary.* Willing co-operation from other agencies, both statutory and voluntary, was also a
feature of the emergency work, and C.O.S. experience in organising
such assistance was a valuable asset in its C.A.B. activities.

In some areas the work of the C.O.S. and of the C.A.B.x was
carried out at the request of the Borough Council in association
with the Council's Information Services, sometimes in the
Administrative Centre (Town Hall or Library).†

Some of the problems could only be dealt with by experts; legal
difficulties, income tax problems, questions of valuation were
referred to Poor Man's Lawyers,‡ Income Tax Advisers, and Poor
Man's Valuers,§ all of whom gave voluntary service. Sometimes
they attended sessions at the C.A.B.x, sometimes (for example,
many of the solicitors and barristers), at the Legal Advice Centres.
The Cambridge House Settlement Legal Advice Centre was
opened in September 1939, the Mary Ward Settlement Centre,
in 1942; ‖ both of these were carried on under the aegis of the
Association through whom L.C.C. grants were later negotiated.
A C.O.S. worker was often in attendance at an evening session of
a C.A.B. to prepare material for the expert concerned. A voluntary
typist very often accompanied her.

The C.O.S. was very fortunate in its voluntary workers, many
of them with earlier experience of C.O.S. work, all of them
prepared to undergo training to equip themselves for their
exacting task.¶ Lecture courses were arranged, as well as in-
service-training with experienced staff. It was the policy of the
Society to appoint only trained officers to be in charge of its
C.A.B.x. Later, preference was given to candidates with a basic
social science qualification, and twelve months' in-service training
was required of all recruits. In 1964, the F.W.A. C.A.B. enquiries

* A nice illustration of the expectation of impartiality was a request that the
C.A.B. should try to get a C.O.S. committee to reverse its decision, this at a
time when many C.A.B.x were sited in C.O.S. offices.

† See Chapter 9, 3, for example of such co-operation.

‡ In association with the Bentham Committee.

§ Through the efforts of John Watson, F.S.I., and the Poor Man's Valuer
Association, they gave advice on claims for compensation under the War
Damage Act.

‖ Docklands Centre opened later (1945).

¶ One of the influential workers, Mrs Enid Eichholz, who had had experience
in the Oxford C.A.B. before training with the C.O.S., stressed the value of
trained workers 'to carry out interpretation in C.A.B. work'.

represented some ten per cent of problems dealt with throughout the country. As more professional C.A.B. officers were appointed the F.W.A. had fewer volunteers. The stringent requirement of a minimum of three days per week reduced the number offering service until, today, the proportion of voluntary workers compared with those in the rest of the country is small.*

C.A.B.x played an essential part in the war years. In the F.W.A. Inner London Centres, the peak was reached in 1943–44 with 184,438 callers.† The only service which disappeared with the cessation of hostilities was the transmission of Red Cross messages. It was inevitable that some C.A.B.x should close when the war ended: for example, there were six closures amongst the Inner London C.A.B.x in the year 1945–46. After March 1946 there there was a big reduction in grants through the Ministry of Health, but at the same time local authorities were empowered and encouraged to aid the Bureaux.‡⁵ Financial uncertainty gave the Family Welfare Association some anxiety but they had increasing support from the Borough Councils, many of whom provided both premises and generous grants. In the year 1947–48 two Metropolitan Boroughs asked the F.W.A. to open a C.A.B.§ The continuance of the two Legal Advice Centres was also in the balance since they had been largely financed during the war by the British War Relief Society of the U.S.A., the Pilgrim Trust and the City Parochial Foundation; this aid was due to end in 1947. Legal Advice was still much in demand and it was hoped to keep these centres open, at least until the Rushcliffe Report's recommendations on Legal Aid to Poor Persons was implemented.⁶ Fortunately the L.C.C. came to the rescue while solicitors, barristers and other helpers continued to give their services. The G.L.C. followed the practice of channelling grants through the F.W.A. (By 1970, when rising costs were causing anxiety, agreement was reached that the Association should operate the Legal Advice scheme: payment could then be made from the Legal Aid Fund.)

---

* The C.A.B.x throughout the country had a generous response from volunteers.

† See Diagram 2.

‡ After the end of March 1946, Exchequer grants were limited to £8,000 annually towards headquarters and regional expenditure. This permissive section was embodied in the Local Government Act, 1948.

§ Lewisham asked for one in its Town Hall premises. Westminister City asked for a C.A.B. to serve Pimlico.

The social and economic developments since 1945 have assured
the survival of the Citizens Advice Bureaux and the need for
guidance through the complexities of modern society has justified
the expenditure of public money.* In 1948 Beveridge had foreseen
their value: 'They (the bureaux) cannot solve all the problems
brought to them, but they can do something to lighten every
problem by bringing understanding of it.' Beveridge pointed to
three general services: 'First, the bureaux explain the working of
public authority to the citizen . . . he comes to regard it as something not alien and hostile to himself but something for which he
may be responsible. . . . Second, the bureaux help to protect the
citizen against public authority, when the latter through mistake
or stupidity is acting wrongly. . . . Third, the bureaux make the
world appear to many citizens in distress to contain some element
of reason and friendship.'[7]

Since 1948 there has been little change in the organisation and
methods of the bureaux. There have been, however, some refine-
ments in the classification of problems and the presentation of
statistics since 1949. This has given a useful indication of the
trends: in London, the long continuance of housing problems as
first in the cause of anxiety and distress, with personal and family
problems as a close second.† As each new piece of social legislation
was passed, more enquiries followed, e.g. the passing of the National
Insurance Acts‡ and the various Housing and Rent Acts§ brought
many more citizens seeking information. The Hire Purchase Act
and Post-War Credit arrangements brought further problems. In
the 1960s the C.A.B.x noted a further increase in trading problems.
(This followed the C.A.B.x evidence to the Maloney Committee
and the Government decision in 1963 to invite C.A.B.x to take part
in 'Consumer Protection' and 'Consumer Education'. For this
service the Board of Trade gave financial help.)

Another post-war development, in line with F.W.A. traditional

* The F.W.A. received from local authorities hundred per cent grants for its
Bureaux which included salaries of central C.A.B. staff, relief staff, and trainees;
other administrative expenses are borne by the F.W.A.

† In 1970 housing problems were still the largest single item.

‡ In 1948 many citizens from all ranks, from directors to self-employed,
were included for the first time, while other groups, like variety actors, went
into new categories. The C.A.B.x had callers from every class.

§ The Housing Repairs and Rent Act was responsible for a marked increase
in housing and tenancy problems during 1954–55. Another large increase
followed the Rent Act, 1957.

policy,[8] was the training of students. The universities and other institutions recognised the Association's stress on the need for skilled interviewing: 'Labelling a problem with a name is perhaps a statistical necessity ... but it omits the bulk of the work done by the Bureaux—the need to clarify the problem before advising ... even though it turns out to be a familiar question there is the personality of the questioner to be taken into account in making the reply.'[9] There we see the influence of the psychological approach, already prominent in the training given in F.W.A. District Offices. The places offered to students who were given practical work under the supervision of the trained secretary in charge of the bureau were used to capacity.* The F.W.A. arranged a series of refresher courses for established workers. The emphasis on training in a succession of official reports, particularly the Younghusband and Curtis Reports, gave national perspective to the discussion. The increase in salaries during 1963–64, and again in 1967, considerably improved the recruitment of trained workers.

Meanwhile, the F.W.A. kept in touch with the London Council of Social Service which was responsible for the Outer London Bureaux.† The difference in organisation made closer contact difficult since each of the Inner London Bureaux was linked directly with the F.W.A. central C.A.B. Advisory Committee with its Liaison Officer, while each of the Outer London Bureaux was autonomous, with responsibility to its own local committee. A strong link was, however, provided by the London Regional C.A.B. Advisory Committee, whose Chairman, Sir Parker Morris,‡ had co-operation very much at heart. In the 1960s there was a determined effort to strengthen the partnership and to secure greater unification of the London Bureaux which would fit more readily into the new London structure of local government. However, as with other voluntary groups, there were difficulties; there was greater success in the sharing of training schemes. By 1970 a joint full-time training officer to serve the whole of London was appointed and a new course was held at the North Western Polytechnic for experienced C.A.B. workers.

* In addition to university students and others in this country, the C.A.B.x were constantly welcoming overseas visitors for periods of observation.

† It is interesting to note that in 1966–67 the total number of enquiries in nineteen C.A.B.x operating in inner London almost equalled those in the sixty-two C.A.B.x operating in the outer London service.

‡ Sir Parker Morris was for many years Town Clerk of Westminster.

The F.W.A. C.A.B. Officer has a duty to keep abreast of National developments, to strengthen the link with the National C.A.B. Council. The close relationship between the F.W.A. and the N.C.S.S. in several fields of social service has offered a channel of communication. Like other C.A.B.x the F.W.A. sends a supply of information regularly to C.A.B. headquarters. It also contributes useful evidence for official committees of enquiry (e.g. evidence to the Milner Holland Committee.)

The continued confidence of the public and of the statutory authorities in the work of the London C.A.B.x has been demonstrated by new requests for more centres. As Sir Parker Morris wrote:[10] 'The C.A.B. service . . . is now recognised as a permanent part of the social machinery of the country. Its great value lies in the confidence and respect in which its work is held by the public, in its close relationship with both Central and Local Government and in its independence, which enables bureaux to advise with a sense of responsibility, but with impartiality, on problems affecting relationships between citizens and authority.'*

Lord Denning had put the work of the C.A.B.x in perspective and recognised the significance of their role in 'the social revolution of modern times' when he spoke in 1957 at the National Standing Conference of Citizens Advice Bureaux. 'In this revolution', he said, 'the Citizens Advice Bureaux have played an important part. They have helped to smooth out friction and to oil the bearings of the whole machine. It has been done within the short space of twenty years; a free service, free to those who receive, voluntary for the most part by those who give; supported indeed by the State but not controlled by it; supported by local authorities but not controlled by them; and, I hope, like the law, never to be controlled by any public authority.'[11]

(b) Family Discussion Bureaux

The problems brought to the Citizens Advice Bureaux had shown that many people sought advice about marital difficulties. The District Offices of the F.W.A. had had similar experience.

---

* The F.W.A. illustrated this in their special contribution to the Silver Jubilee Celebrations in 1964. Their documentary film 'Advice to All', with the C.A.B. liaison officer, Mrs Hawkins, as technical adviser, was made possible by a grant from a private charity.

Diagram 2

Chart Showing the Total Number of CALLS at the Family Welfare Association
Citizens' Advice Bureaux October 1939 to April 1969

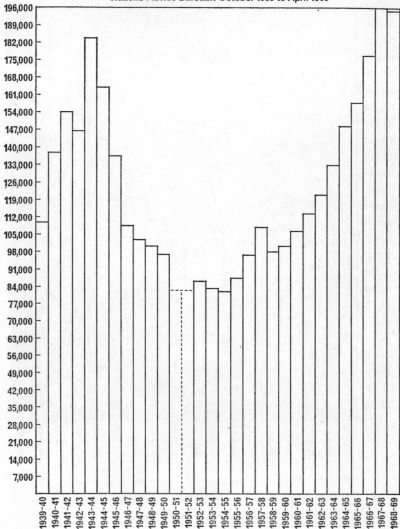

Notes: (1) 1950–52 Change in date of financial year. Statistics for 18 months
adjusted.
(2) The post-1960 figures include incoming telephone calls and letters,
as well as personal calls at the bureaux.
(3) This chart shows the number of visits paid to Bureaux, and is larger
than the number of enquiries, as, if an enquirer has a complex
problem necessitating several visits to the Bureaux each of these
visits is recorded under "Calls" but the problem is recorded only
once under "Enquiries".

G

Diagram 3

Chart Showing the Number of ENQUIRIES Made at the Family Welfare
Association Citizens Advice Bureaux from 1951-52 to 1968-69

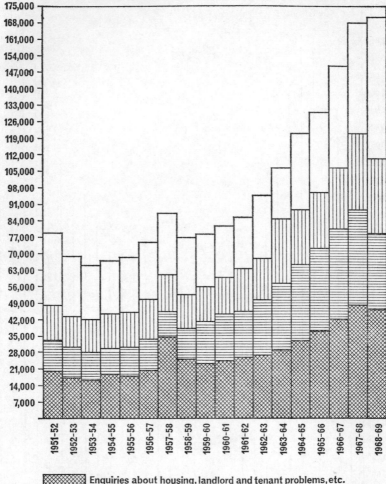

Enquiries about housing, landlord and tenant problems, etc.

Enquiries about family and personal problems.

General Information enquiries.

Other enquiries.

Note: The category of ENQUIRIES shows the total number of problems
coming to the Bureaux in the London Region. Some are by letter or telephone, the majority by personal visit of the enquirer.

The Association therefore gave special thought to the question of prevention: would it be possible to help families threatened with the breakdown of marriage at an earlier stage in their difficulties? If so, family social workers would want to improve their skills in marriage counselling. Preliminary discussions were held with the Marriage Guidance Council and in 1944-45 a joint experiment was carried out: six Marriage Guidance Centres were opened, each in charge of a fully trained social worker with the assistance of others specially qualified. An advisory panel was provided by the Marriage Guidance Council. During that winter thirty F.W.A. workers attended lectures organised by the M.G.C. It was soon felt that more expert help was necessary. Moreover, the experience of trying to combine this extra work with their ordinary family casework showed that too heavy a burden was being put upon the family caseworkers.

There seemed no doubt about the need, which was confirmed in the reports of the Denning Committee[12] (and, later, of the Harris Committee[13] who recommended statutory aid for marriage counselling). The Association therefore decided, in principle, to set up special centres and to seek expert help.* With its usual thoroughness the F.W.A. secured experienced advisers as members of its planning committee, two from the Peckham Health Centre and two from the Tavistock Institute of Human Relations.† A scheme was submitted to the Goldsmiths Company for an experimental project. It was successful and the Trust supported it to the extent of a £2,000 grant. In 1947-48, two centres were opened each in the neighbourhood of a psychiatric unit which had promised to help.‡

The interesting feature of this early stage of development was the effort made by the workers at the two centres to discover the real need and to explore the possibility of preventive work. For six months they talked to individuals and groups who might be considered to be a cross section of the population. They met doctors, social workers, clergy, leaders of community organisations

* Mrs Enid Eichholz (later Balint) was the inspiration behind the more professional approach to this service. She was strongly supported by Mrs Pincus who succeeded her as secretary.

† Drs Scott Williamson and Innes Pearce of the Peckham Health Centre and Dr Wilson and Miss Menzies of the Tavistock Institute.

‡ Fulham had the promise of help from Dr Main of the Cassel Hospital and Hendon that of Dr Bowlby of the Tavistock Clinic.

and others who would have experience of family needs and who might later wish to refer families to the centres. At the same time they had discussions with mothers attending maternity and child welfare clinics, with staffs of fire stations, members of various social clubs and centres, groups from the staffs of factories and parent-teacher associations. The informal group discussions in this pilot investigation seemed to be welcomed. It was noted that many were ready to talk about problems and difficulties said to be typical of friends and relations; some still thought of consultation as 'giving advice', or as 'interference'; others thought it would be 'a confession of failure'. The term 'family discussion' seemed to be more acceptable than 'marriage welfare' and gave its name to the project launched in 1948. Some workers continued to meet, for example health visitors, hospital almoners and probation officers, as well as F.W.A. and C.A.B. secretaries. Two 'therapeutic groups' also continued, one in a maternity and child welfare clinic and one in a school.

The Family Discussion Bureau decided that it could make its own best contribution by concentrating on casework. The workers had found in the community discussions a feeling of despair about finding a solution to these complex emotional problems. At this point advice was sought from the Tavistock Institute. The application of psycho-analytic concepts to family casework was carefully considered. Dr Balint's suggestion of discussion by means of the case-conference was welcomed. The development of training now reached a crucial stage. The decision to run training concurrently with casework and the use of the case conference in this process influenced not only the work of the F.D.B. but that of the F.W.A. as a whole. It was felt that two valuable results were the conception of the group of workers as a team and the integration of consultants into the unit.

The training, started in September 1948, was held both at the Tavistock Institute and the Tavistock Clinic.*[14] The centres, shortly to be renamed Family Discussion Bureaux, were now recognised by the Home Office. Representatives of the F.W.A. Marriage Welfare Committee, a very strong and active group, together with the National Marriage Guidance Council and the

---

* Much of the material for this chapter is based on an article by Mrs Eichholz and supplemented by an interview later, and by reference to 'Social Casework in Marital Problems' (see source notes 14 and 15).

Catholic Marriage Advisory Council, were members of the Joint
Training Board set up by the Home Office who paid the Association's administration expenses. The cost of running the Family
Discussion Bureaux was met by a further grant from the Goldsmiths Company.

The F.W.A. looked upon its two Bureaux as experimental
centres which would make a contribution to research while
carrying on the work of counselling.* The Association therefore
applied, in 1949, to the Nuffield Foundation for support for
research into patterns of family relationship. They hoped to
complete a three-year study (1950–52) of 100 families in Fulham
to see how they could best be helped to meet the strain of family
life. The pressure of work forced the postponement of research,
but the experience gained led to 'improvement of social casework techniques'.

The L.C.C. looked sympathetically on the work of the Bureaux
and gave an interim grant towards the increase of the work in
London. An application to Middlesex, however, failed and the
F.W.A. was forced to close its Hendon Bureau in 1951. Clients
were now seen at Denison House as well as at Fulham.

The next step in development followed the decision to centralise
the work in one Bureau† and to continue the research. It necessitated four additions to staff which included two experienced
clinicians for casework supervision. 'Referrals' were now more
selective‡. A grant from the Carnegie United Kingdom Trust
enabled the Bureau to plan a five-year scheme. In 1953–54 a
report was prepared on a study of 1,250 families: 'Social Casework
in Marital Problems'.[15] It is significant that the sub-title was 'The
Development of a Psychodynamic Approach'—significant of the
interest in this aspect of training and of casework, evident not
only in the F.W.A. but in other professional social work bodies.§

* Mrs Eichholz reported that by 1949 it was felt that the workers undertaking individual casework were in need of clinical help. Four psychoanalysts
at the Tavistock Institute, Dr Balint, Dr Kelnar, Miss Joseph and Dr Wilson,
took seminars, helped later by a psychiatric social worker, Miss Hunnybun of
the Tavistock Clinic.

† At Chandos Street, Cavendish Square. It later moved to Beaumont St., then
to Belsize Lane where it is at the present time, in spacious modern quarters in
the Tavistock Centre.

‡ The current cases averaged 75 but this gives no indication of the number
of new cases, which were over 200, but only of the number at any given moment.

§ The Institute of Almoners was particularly interested.

The F.W.A. comment is worth quoting: 'The . . . important feature has been the stabilisation and development of the Family Discussion Bureau's function as a training agency. The organisation of the Bureau as a working group, of which the psychoanalytic consultants are members, is of unique value for continuous group training and the Bureau provides a setting in which the operation of dynamic principles, both in family and casework relationships, can be observed particularly clearly.'[16] The Home Office who inspected the work of the F.D.B. and thought well of the venture, paid three-quarters of the salary of a caseworker who undertook supervision, in addition to the grant already recorded for administration and training. It was now the turn of the Marriage Guidance Council, the original agency to offer training, to seek the help of the Bureau for training a group of senior counsellors. The recognition of the Bureau's standing as a training centre was now more general, as clinical psychologists and others came voluntarily to gain experience in marital casework.

By April 1956 the experimental period was ending with the cessation of Trust grants.* The F.D.B. workers felt that clients were now coming to them with a greater feeling of hope: the despair of a solution noted in the early community discussions seemed to be passing. The F.W.A. took stock of the developments, noting particularly the contribution to 'preventive mental health'. The use of the Bureau for training had extended to probation officers, health visitors and mental health workers. Both voluntary and statutory bodies were making demands on the training facilities, some for short courses, e.g. three-weeks' seminars, some for a year's 'apprenticeship' training.† The training of supervisors in casework was considered to be specially valuable, since it would lead to a wider understanding of the new methods.‡ The F.W.A. noted with satisfaction that some thirty per cent of those who came to the Bureau in 1955–56 were referred by doctors for therapeutic help. 'The Bureau look forward to a close working relationship with psychiatrists under the National Health Service.'

* The Eley Trust gave a grant for the year 1955–56 and the C.U.K.T. added a final substantial grant (£3,000) to its already generous support over five years.

† E.g. two experienced Probation Officers who attended for three days a week for twelve months.

‡ E.g. a number of the young F.W.A. family caseworkers.

The F.W.A. now decided that the pilot experimental stage had passed and that the Bureau could go forward to further development under the Tavistock Institute of Human Relations which had co-operated from the beginning. The transfer to the Institute was accomplished smoothly, without change of premises and without interruption of work. The current grants gave stability, and all the sponsoring bodies approved (particularly the Home Office, the L.C.C. and the C.U.K.T.). The last report issued on the Bureau's work by the F.W.A. (1956–57) noted the increasing use of the Bureau both by clients seeking help, and by social workers seeking training. General practitioners, specialised hospital departments and psychiatric social workers sent more patients. Middlesex County Council now sent its community psychiatric social worker for a course of weekly discussions, while West Ham Public Health Department formed a discussion group (health visitors and medical staff) with the help of the Bureau. The Institute of Almoners* was increasingly interested in the training offered. The F.W.A. itself planned a close association of the Bureau with two of its area offices. Its Marriage Welfare Committee had cause for satisfaction as it looked back on the eight years' work of the Bureau. The first paragraph of the F.W.A. report reads: 'The Association is parting from the Family Discussion Bureau with best wishes for its future and with pride, mixed with regret, that this flourishing concern should go to another sponsoring body.'[17]

The Bureau had been fortunate in its two outstanding secretaries. They, in turn, were fortunate in the support they received from the F.W.A. Secretary and from the Marriage Welfare Committee whose chairmen took an active interest in this pioneer experiment. The F.D.B. was fortunate, too, in securing the close co-operation of psychologists and psychoanalysts from the Tavistock Clinic and the Tavistock Institute, both in planning the venture and in carrying it through

There is no doubt that the experience gained in establishing the F.D.B. had a strong influence on the Association's increasing concern for disturbed and unhappy families. It has been said that 'the Family Discussion Bureau was, perhaps, the most important development in casework inaugurated by the Family Welfare

* The Institute was renamed Institute of Medical Social Workers in 1964.

Association'.* Today the F.D.B. is established as a well-known section of the Tavistock Centre.

2. *The Problem Families Project*

The idea of studying families, then being labelled 'problem families' by Medical Officers of Health, was discussed by the F.W.A. Administrative Committee in 1948. A strong sub-committee was set up in 1950 with representatives from the universities,† two hospital almoners, one Medical Officer of Health, two from the Family Service Units, of whom one was their research worker, two experienced lay members and several F.W.A. representatives who were most closely concerned. This committee put forward a plan for research 'with emphasis on the aetiology of the problem family, with casework treatment as the secondary goal', and applied to the Carnegie United Kingdom Trust for a five-year grant. They were successful and proceeded with the appointment of a full-time psychiatric social worker, with a part-time research worker as adviser. The committee had already suggested the aims, scope and method of enquiry. After some six months, the part-time adviser left and a full-time research worker and a secretary were added. The actual field work occupied a period of four-and-a-half years. The report was presented to the Carnegie United Kingdom Trust in 1956. The Trust was not, however, prepared to publish it. It was hoped that the University Social Science Departments might welcome the case studies for student training, but the Joint University Council were not willing to publish and the report remained for private use by the Family Welfare Association. The intensive study of a few families (there were some twenty families included in the project) where the casework is highly confidential does not lend itself easily to presentation in a form suitable for publication.

The workers had stated their aims in modest terms: 'to do intensive casework with a limited number of families and so to work out and provide for social workers an approach, a way of regarding families that are seriously out of adjustment with their surround-

---

* Successive chairmen were the Reverend Michael Clarke, and Mrs Godfrey who made this statement.

† One a tutor in the Institute of Psychiatry at the Maudsley Hospital, another a tutor of practical work in a Social Science Department.

ings, so that treatment can follow; and to indicate the aim and activities which it is unwise to pursue in this field.' The workers found themselves concentrating on questions relating to the structure of the family; they became absorbed in the actual case-work. By the nature of the case they had to work at the clients' pace. They had to deal with a multiplicity of problems and to discover how to secure the co-operation of a family, often in the face of indifference. Contrary to the original plan, they found it impossible to give any indication of causes. In fact, as they stated, 'the report has a therapeutic rather than a scientific function. . . . The approach we outline does not establish any new facts or generalisation. What it does do is to indicate how one should best approach actual cases, what one should look for in analysing a complex situation, what precautions one should bear in mind and what implicit assumptions one should be aware of, which objectives it is reasonable to aim at and which objectives, hopes, policies, or demands it is in principle or in practice impossible to entertain. All these questions are more methodological than empirical, and they will provide relatively little help in the actual treatment of a case at a given moment. The conclusions aim at self-therapy of the caseworker in the first instance, rather than therapy of the family by the worker. . . . We have tried to develop a suitable approach or attitude of mind which caseworkers and others may find effective in dealing with difficult families.'

The report included some useful assessments of the kinds of problems met with, and an apt summary of the assumptions implicit in casework with difficult families. Much of what was said would apply to families anywhere and to casework in any situation; for example: 'For the purposes of case study it is essential to begin with the client's viewpoint.' A reading of the case studies shows that some twenty families, who would most likely be looked down upon and rejected by their fellow citizens, had been treated courteously, given continuous support through many difficulties and consequently had begun to look to the workers for help to the point of dependency. It was at this stage that the F.W.A. had misgivings. Few of the 'project families' could stand alone; very little improvement in standards could be discerned. The workers had to plan carefully, in the last stages of the project, to withdraw.

The F.W.A. had, from its early days, declared its intention of

G*

strengthening those families who were struggling to regain their independence. They had required the active co-operation of such families in planning the future management of their own affairs. They recognised that the Family Service Units had made work amongst families with many problems their special concern. In future the F.W.A. was to select its clients with greater care, concentrating on those families where preventive casework could more hopefully be carried through—although, for some years yet, certain Districts continued to give 'supportive long-term help' to 'difficult families'.

3. The Family—Patients or Clients?

The subtitle of the study, 'Co-operation in Social Casework by Almoners and Family Caseworkers', gives the setting for this project.

The initial steps were taken, in July 1956, by the hospital almoners (to be known as Medical Social Workers after 1964). They had always worked very closely with the F.W.A. but they were apt, in their own words, 'to refer patients with a multitude of long-standing personal and material difficulties who had failed to make use of the many statutory services available to them'. With the current emphasis, in various fields of social work, on 'prevention' the almoners re-examined their use of other resources to see whether patients might not be more appropriately helped, perhaps at an earlier stage, in a setting away from the hospital atmosphere. They felt that they were often in a position to detect early signs of social breakdown, and that the F.W.A. might welcome more of such patients and fewer of those with chronic problems. They therefore invited the Association to joint discussions which led to the agreement by the F.W.A. to sponsor a combined casework and research project. Once more they were fortunate in getting the support of charitable Trusts—in this instance four Trusts financed the project.* A steering committee was set up under a widely experienced Chairman† and a special worker was appointed who began work on the project in June 1958, and completed it two years later. The Report was published for the

* The Joseph Rowntree Charitable Trust, the Sir Halley Stewart Trust, the Thomas Wall Trust and the Noël Buxton Trust.

† Margaret Godfrey who had long served the F.W.A. as a voluntary worker and represented the Association on several statutory and voluntary bodies. She had been Chairman of the Family Discussion Bureau.

F.W.A. in 1961. In addition to the workers engaged on the project, the Association was in touch with Advisers who gave their help in individual problems.

Although the project was a small one, run in conjunction with an Almoners' Department of one hospital, it was thought that the results might give useful pointers for future extended action. There were, in all, thirty-nine patients referred by the almoners, of whom thirty-one accepted the offer of help. Nine of these did not persevere after the first interview. Those who had continuing casework help were thought to have gained considerably in their ability to face their troubles and to live happier and more useful lives. The workers hoped, too, that they had come nearer to an understanding of the meaning of 'preventive casework', and that they had identified some of the main problems, both in the selection of clients likely to benefit and in the process of 'referral' from one caseworker to another. In fact, it was realised that these were different aspects of one problem: how best to prevent social distress or how best to help an individual to solve problems of social living. These were indeed restatements of the first principles of the F.W.A.—'Its methods encourage him to recognise and use the strengths and to moderate the weaknesses in himself, his family and the community in which he lives'[18] might have been written by Helen Dendy (Bosanquet) in the 1890s.

The modern writers went on to recognise the limitations: 'the total prevention of social distress by casework, or any other process, is obviously impossible. . . the preventive element in casework lies in its effect in preventing the prolongation or worsening of existing conditions, or their repetition over the years'.[19] The recognition by the patient or the client of the real nature of his difficulties, an important part of the caseworker's objective, and his acceptance of help, were in themselves active steps towards his capacity to meet his problems.

Some tentative conclusions, drawn from this necessarily limited study, would be generally accepted by caseworkers in all fields; firstly, that the client must see that the proffered help is appropriate to his need and that it must be offered in such a way that he sees its value; also that it must be offered at a time when he is ready to use it. The workers claimed that the high proportion of success in those families who accepted and continued 'treatment', was due largely to the fact that help was offered before the problems became chronic and that the process of referral was carefully studied and skilfully carried out.[20] Secondly, it was concluded that important elements in the success of referral were the workers' skill in assessing, not only the nature and extent of the problems, but the client's ability to use casework help. This, too, goes back to the nineteenth century caseworkers' offer to 'the helpable', although at that time the term was often misinterpreted and had subsequently to be dropped. The selection of 'appropriate clients', to use the modern terminology, and the ability to transfer them skilfully to whichever agency could best meet their needs were only possible when professional confidence existed between the organisations concerned. Another finding, now generally accepted by caseworkers, was illustrated during the project: that 'the separation of clients' needs' into material and non-material is not valid. Clients' tolerance of material hardship varied. 'Improvement in personal relationships was usually reflected in greater ability to manage material problems.'

The workers considered what service the F.W.A. could offer for which there was no statutory provision. Looking at the question from the point of view of the hospital patients 'who were beginning to move away from illness towards a fuller life in society', they concluded that the 'permissive' setting of the Association was more acceptable after the more authoritative atmosphere of a hospital. 'Having no statutory framework, the F.W.A. caseworkers can be flexible both as to the types of clients they try to help and their method of working. . . . The workers can select clients for continuing help and determine the period of casework offered in a way that is not possible for workers in many statutory settings.' As has been said before, 'They can be discriminating', both in those they decide to help and in the kind of service they offer. This is not possible in a statutory service.

Bearing in mind the intention to produce a study which could offer 'good teaching material',[21] the report contained a substantial section giving a description and analysis of the 'cases' dealt with in the course of the two-year project.[22]

4. *The West Indian Project*

The F.W.A. has been fortunate in the support given by charitable trusts to its various projects where field work and research were combined. In its 'Project for the Welfare of Coloured People in London' it had a very generous grant from the City Parochial Foundation for a three-year pioneer experiment, 1955–58, to see what were the problems of assimilation and how they could be minimised or prevented if help and advice were given at an early stage. According to its customary procedure, the F.W.A. set up a strong steering committee representative of those most knowledgeable in the field of enquiry.* As with so many of its special committees, the Association invited an eminent member of another organisation to act as Chairman, in this case Miss O. Cram, L.C.C. Principal Organiser of Children's Care. The project was served by West Indian as well as other trained social workers, and close touch was kept with the Migrant Services Division of the Committee in the United Kingdom for the West Indies, British Guiana and British Honduras (formerly the British Caribbean Welfare Service). The report was published in 1960.[23]

The first step was the opening by the F.W.A. of a special Citizens Advice Bureau in Lambeth where there was some concentration of West Indian families; the C.A.B. was, as usual, open to all citizens in the Borough. A West Indian and an English family social worker were appointed. A second West Indian family caseworker was attached to an F.W.A. area office in North London, while a third was appointed as Liaison Officer and supervisor, working as a member of the Central staff.†

A study of family problems was made possible by the ability of the workers to give 'long term casework help' to some four hundred families. The detailed report of the main problems met with by this immigrant group, together with suggestions for ways in which they might be tackled, form an important part of the analysis made by the Liaison Officer, Mr Hyndman.[24] The special difficulties are closely linked with the cultural and family background of these new settlers. He shows how ready the West Indians are to adapt to new customs, and what effect these changes have, in turn, upon family patterns. When the Report was pre-

* The Steering Committee included representatives from statutory bodies, e.g. the Colonial Office, National Assistance Board, L.C.C., as well as from voluntary societies, e.g. British Red Cross, Institute of Almoners and Family Service Units.

† The project suffered some sad reverses with the death of the West Indian C.A.B. worker and the withdrawal of the area family caseworker before the project terminated.

pared it was decided that, as a knowledge of the West Indian background was so important for a real understanding of the problems, a section should be given to this. Another section was included to show what were the reception problems of arrival in England and what was the organisation to meet these. To give some comparative material a short section was added on West Indian welfare in three provincial cities.* When the report was published in 1960 the foreword by Sir Arthur Howard, Chairman of the Board of Trustees of the City Parochial Foundation, left no doubt that the Trust had had every confidence in asking the F.W.A. to undertake this 'limited pioneering experiment'. The enquiry was completed when the tragic 'Notting Hill Riots' showed the urgent need for a deeper understanding of race relations in this country. It was hoped that the F.W.A. report would offer a basis for further analysis.

In combining field work with research, the F.W.A. not only gave an advisory and casework service to a proportion of the West Indian families in two London areas, but it saw and met other needs. For example it recognised the necessity for an education policy 'firstly for the new migrant, who had to be taught how best to react to the social environment in which he was placed, and secondly for the members of the host country, who, because unaccustomed to any large numbers of colonials in their midst, developed fears which had to be dispelled. Trade Unions, the Workers' Educational Association, Townswomen's Guilds, professional and lay bodies, were among the groups where courses of lectures or general discussions were inaugurated to help place the West Indian migration in proper perspective.'[25]

The second educational venture was the arrangement of special classes in basic English. A certain number of West Indians were 'unlettered and semi-literate' and the F.W.A. made enquiries to see whether the L.C.C. Education Department could meet their special needs. This was found not to be possible; the Institutes and the evening departments of Day Colleges did not offer what was wanted. There were wide differences in the background and education of the students enrolling in the F.W.A. classes and their ages ranged from sixteen to fifty-nine. Only two instructors were available; consequently teaching had to be limited to very small groups and the total number of students

* Bristol, Liverpool and Nottingham.

could not exceed about forty-five. This pioneer work merely touched the surface, but it pointed to a very real need, and it encouraged some of the students to go on to the L.C.C. classes when they had passed the first laborious stage. The experiment had shown that special encouragement and help were needed, particularly in areas where West Indians had settled in substantial numbers.

5. *The Family Centre Project*

During the 1950s both voluntary and statutory bodies were showing increasing interest in the preventive aspects of the social services. A series of official enquiries and reports—on Housing,* on Mental Illness and Mental Deficiency, on the Rehabilitation Training and Resettlement of Disabled Persons, on Maladjusted Children, on Health Visiting, and finally, in 1960, the long-awaited Ingleby Report on 'The Prevention or Forestalling of Suffering of Children through Neglect in their own Homes'—were all concerned at some point with the prevention of family breakdown. A valuable circular issued by the Ministry of Health was headed: 'On the Prevention of Break-up of Families'.[26] The Younghusband Report, 1959, emphasised the importance of 'Liaison with workers in related statutory services' if preventive work was to be effective.†

Many of the Voluntary Organisations already had a tradition of preventive work. The Family Welfare Association, in particular, had always stressed this aspect of its efforts 'to strengthen the family'. In 1951 there was considerable concern within the Association at 'the increasing degree of overlapping both in function and visiting', and their effect on family life. In October, 1951, Astbury submitted a memorandum on the question, pointing out that some of the 'Case Conferences' had disclosed as many as fifteen agencies in touch with one family at one time.[27] He suggested setting up a 'Composite Case-Work Unit' in which the Family Welfare Association, Invalid Children's Aid Association, National Association for Mental Health, Association of Psychiatric Social Workers, the Institute of Almoners, School Care

---

* E.g. 'Unsatisfactory Tenants' issued by the Central Housing Advisory Committee in 1955.

† See especially Chapter 10.

Committees (L.C.C.) and the F.W.A. Problem Family Project Group should participate. In addition there should be a panel of consultants to include the F.W.A. Family Discussion Bureau, the Children's Officer, the N.S.P.C.C., the Medical Officer of the L.C.C., the Probation Officer and the National Assistance Board Area Officer. A detailed plan was attached, giving the practical administrative procedures to be adopted towards discovering the most appropriate agency in the Unit to deal with the applications and the subsequent methods to be adopted. The characteristic feature of this first scheme was the sharing by a number of casework agencies of one building and one central register, with one 'intake department'.

A second scheme was considered soon after, submitted by Miss A. B. Read, Head Almoner, St Thomas's Hospital, who was also the chairman of the F.W.A. Training Committee. The main emphasis in Miss Read's memorandum was on a combined unit, i.e. a merger.[28] During 1952 there were frequent discussions between the authors of the two schemes and Miss Rattenbury of the I.C.A.A., together with informal approaches to the L.C.C. and to the Carnegie United Kingdom Trust, both of whom were interested. The idea of a single composite unit rather than a centre for a number of co-operating agencies was gradually accepted.

During 1952 negotiations between the voluntary agencies concerned led to agreement in principle to the formation of a 'composite unit' by the F.W.A. and the I.C.A.A. The Institute of Almoners were sympathetic but felt that it was 'difficult for a medico-social worker to be a fully integrated member of the unit': 1953 gave promise of further practical steps, and possible districts appropriate for the experiment were considered.

Unfortunately, in each of the two agencies most involved, domestic problems of re-organisation, changes of staff and other difficulties delayed action. The subject was not allowed to drop, however, and informal meetings were called in 1955 to consider where the emphasis should lie in casework in a combined unit. Attention was focused, as in current discussions in related fields, on the family as a whole, and on the importance of family relationships.

The impetus for renewed endeavour came from the City Parochial Foundation. Early in 1959 a meeting, representative of voluntary and statutory bodies concerned with family social work, was convened by Sir Donald Allen, the Clerk to the Foundation, and a committee was appointed 'to explore the possibility of setting up a combined family casework unit and to prepare a scheme for an experiment in this field supported in the first instance by the Family Welfare Association, Family Service Units, and the Invalid Children's Aid Association. The report and the subsequent memoranda prepared by the three agencies were considered during 1960. The emphasis was on an experimental project combining the provision of a comprehensive casework service and research into the needs of families. (The question of the 'Prevention of Overlapping' no longer arose.)

In 1961 the City Parochial Foundation made a substantial grant to cover a five-year project. A representative Committee of Management was in action by the end of 1961* and a Director of the Unit was appointed in July 1962† to begin work in August of that year. The unit, established in Hackney,‡ was known as The Hackney Family Centre and it was generously staffed. In addition to the Director there were seven caseworkers, one seconded from each of the participating organisations and four others recruited for the purpose. It was immediately busy, as statutory and voluntary agencies began at once to refer families in need of skilled help. The health services, in particular hospitals and clinics, local authority health departments and doctors, were a constant source of referral. The Centre was well used by other charitable organisations and the C.A.B.x also sent on clients. The Centre evidently filled a need felt by a wide range of other workers within and on the fringe of social work who from time to time referred families. As it became known, people in need of such help applied directly.§[29]

* It consisted of representatives of each of the organisations concerned in the early discussions, with a co-opted member of the L.C.C., who had also taken an active part, and an independent Chairman.

† The Director, Miss Boselli, had been an experienced F.W.A. family caseworker. I am indebted to her, and to others concerned, for discussing the Project with me.

‡ At 41 Boleyn Road, Stoke Newington, with Mrs Hilary Halpin, J.P., as Chairman. She was followed later by Miss Robina Addis of the N.A.M.H. In 1966 the Centre extended its service to cover Shoreditch, which became part of the London Borough of Hackney with the re-organisation of Local Government.

§ In 1967 the F.W.A. reported that about one-quarter of all applications were of this kind. Statutory and voluntary agencies referred almost equal numbers.

The participating agencies followed the work of the Centre with close interest. As the F.W.A. reported: 'The combined casework unit is a most important and possibly far-reaching experiment.'[30] The Director and her staff tried to combine the two-fold purpose of the experiment; while they carried on their casework service they were in close consultation with the officers of statutory and voluntary agencies, and with representatives of the local community, trying to discover what were the unmet needs in the area, and what kind of service the Centre could best give.

It was hoped that the report, which was expected to be published at about the same time as that of the Seebohm committee, would make a useful contribution to the study of family needs and to the function of family-centred social work in relation to other voluntary and statutory services. There was no doubt that the workers within the Hackney Family Centre derived considerable benefit from sharing the experience of work in a different setting. In the I.C.A.A. the emphasis on the family with an invalid child had given the workers particular understanding of the effects of illness or disability and the kind of help and support needed by the family in such circumstances. The F.S.U. workers had seen the need to reach out to families with many problems, with the offer of help and with immediate practical assistance as an earnest of goodwill. The F.W.A. had shown how a client could be helped to take responsibility for solving his own problems. The Centre's casework service as a whole was enriched by the different skills brought in by the team.

When the five-year experimental period was drawing to a close, the question of the financial future of the Centre was urgent. The Borough of Hackney had already made a contribution when work was extended as a result of the reorganisation of the London boroughs. It was anxious that the Centre's work should not come to an end with the last payment from the City Parochial Foundation. As the Authority considered a large increase in its own grant it also looked for the support of the three sponsoring agencies. Unfortunately I.C.A.A. and F.S.U. did not feel able to divert money from work in their own fields. There was also the feeling that their specialised contribution had become obscured as general family casework predominated. The F.W.A. agreed to consider continuing its interest if it could raise a special fund. The Sembal

Trust offered a conditional grant,* but a substantial sum had still to be raised annually if the Centre was to continue on the same scale. Unfortunately other demands made it difficult for the F.W.A. to finance it and the Centre became part of the general pattern of family social work.

It would have been in line with F.W.A. tradition to make this venture: to look upon the Hackney Family Centre not simply as one amongst others of its family casework offices, but as offering a special opportunity for trying out new methods of counselling. One suggestion already made was to combine group work with other forms of help. There is no doubt that one of the most appreciated of the Centre's assets had been its friendly, welcoming atmosphere, akin, in many respects, to that of the settlements. Its spaciousness gave room for mothers and children to enjoy the company, not only of one another, but of students and staff.

The Centre in its five-year experimental period made a useful contribution to the education and training of students. Those doing their practical work there evidently found it a rewarding experience. They had a room of their own and thought the supervision given by the family caseworkers excellent. They particularly enjoyed the friendly informal meetings with the families who so obviously found that the Centre met their needs. It is not possible to say whether any contribution has been made to research as the report has not been published.

6. *Other Projects*

From time to time the Association made other special studies which were sometimes called 'projects', but which were mainly for internal use. Such was the 'Administrative Officer Project' carried out in Area 4, over a period of two years, 1958–60. The account of this small experiment in casework administration[31] shows how an attempt was made to draw in the whole staff and the students, as small changes were introduced at the same time as casework went on during a very busy period. The writer adds, 'Perhaps in time it will be possible to help social workers to learn how to work as administrators, as one learns nowadays how to

---

* The Sembal Trust offered £500 a year, provided a similar sum was raised elsewhere. The total sum needed annually to supplement the Borough grant was estimated as £3,000–£4,000 a year.

become a caseworker'*.[32] The project was carried through when the whole administrative machinery of the Association was under review (see the Cunliffe Report, Chapter 11). It was important that social workers and administrators should have a better understanding of each other's roles at a time when the statutory social services were rapidly expanding. Any contribution to a discussion of administration related to social work, however small, was worth making.

* Six years later *New Society* noted: 'Most social workers are uninterested in administration.' By the end of the decade the Seebohm Committee's report and the Local Authorities Social Services Act, 1970, had drastically altered the situation. (See Conclusion, pages 358 and 364.)

Part IV

SOME ASPECTS OF PERSISTENCE AND CHANGE

CHAPTER ELEVEN

Problems of Administration and Related Matters: 1869–1969

1. Early Difficulties and Recurrent Problems

Problems of administration are such an integral part of the Association's history that the present writer found it impossible to leave them aside (as C. L. Mowat chose to do in *The Charity Organisation Society, 1869–1913*). It is interesting to find that other organisations, including educational establishments, have recently experienced similar tensions to those recorded by the F.W.A. during the process of reorganisation.

The F.W.A. from its earliest days had been concerned with problems which grew directly from its structure—a federation of some thirty to forty District Committees, with a representative Central Council. As in all democratic institutions, there were bound to be tensions: the Society had to solve the perennial conflict between greater control at the centre, in the interests of uniformity and efficiency, and freedom in the Districts, to encourage experiment and local participation. Loch was constantly reflecting on the need to tolerate certain weaknesses, whether of excess of zeal or of indifferent work, in order to maintain freedom of action for local groups; at the same time 'Central' must pass on to the Districts suggestions for improvement in a form acceptable to the heterogeneous committees.

As with many other institutions the question of communication was the vital factor. In spite of the representative composition of the Central Council, contained in the 'Provisional Rules' of 1869, the Districts tended to feel themselves out of touch, sometimes out of sympathy, with policy at the centre. This was natural in view of the rapidity with which Districts were started. Loch set himself to strengthen the lines of communication; there was a considerable flow of ideas through 'visitations', meetings, conferences, the Society's journals, and the issue of a stream of pamphlets with local as well as Central contributors. Special Committees were set up from time to time to consider problems of relationship. Loch's ability as an administrator was proved largely by the success he achieved in getting a smooth-working machinery.

If there were bound to be tensions in internal administration, arising from the structure of the organisation, there were also bound to be tensions of another sort, arising from the nature of a voluntary Society. For a great part of its history the majority of workers, both in the field and in the District offices, were volunteers. When, in the twentieth century, trained and salaried workers played an increasingly important part, the relationship between 'lay' and 'professional' workers became a question of great importance for the well-being of the Society. Membership of Central committees was an issue which focused attention on the differences between those who shaped social policy and those who organised the practical work in the Districts. 'Professionalism' was for a time suspect, until the trained workers were strong enough to demand discussion of the relation between policy-making and casework practice. They were later to challenge the competence of lay committees to advise on casework principles and practice.

Questions of efficiency, of communication and of the relationship of volunteers and professionals were from time to time dominated by problems of finance. The trend towards centralisation was speeded up under financial pressure, after the Second World War, and brought to a head in the reorganisation of 'areas' in the late 1940s. The new machinery of administration after the *Cunliffe Report* of 1960 owed much to professional influence, but the pressure of financial need gave final weight to the argument for the concentration of the advisory service and of fund-raising at the centre.

The early structure of the Central Council, preserved for a great part of the Society's history, consisted primarily of elected representatives of the District Committees. Chairmen and Honorary Secretaries of District Committees were *ex officio* members. In addition, there were a small number of representatives of the larger Metropolitan Charities and a few 'additional members' elected by Council. The Council appointed sub-committees as needs were recognised. The Medical Sub-Committee and the Districts Sub-Committee were amongst the earlier of the standing committees. In addition *ad hoc* committees were set up to enquire into and report on special problems. As committees proliferated and business grew heavier, a smaller Executive Committee was set up, later to be known as the Administrative Committee, which, by the beginning of the twentieth century, was the executive body dealing with a mass of miscellaneous business and receiving reports from a number of sub-committees.[1] These committees give some indication of the interests of the Society and of the organisation of its work. They included:

The Districts Sub-Committee: This is concerned with the supervision of the Districts, the appointment and training of paid workers, and grants to the Districts for general expenses. The Medical and Convalescent Sub-Committee. The Emigration Sub-Committee, acting jointly with the East-End Fund. The Provincial Sub-Committee. The Special Committee on Social Education (i.e. the education of future workers, etc.). The Committee on the Assistance of Schoolchildren. The Thrift Sub-Committee.

In later years, in addition to Districts and Medical, Training, Research, and Social Policy were amongst the special interests; Emigration and The Assistance of Schoolchildren no longer needed special consideration.

The tendency to multiply Standing Committees, as well as to set up numerous *ad hoc* committees, meant increasing the work of the staff at 'Central' and of the representatives of other organisations who were members; it also called for sustained interest and much time from the additional or co-opted members, many of whom were experts in their own fields. During and after the Second World War the burden of these meetings was increasingly felt; for example, questions thrashed out at one meeting (e.g. the District Meeting of the Association) were considered by the General Purposes Committee, sent on to the Administrative Committee (later known as Administrative Council) and then often considered again at all levels.* Much time was spent discussing

---

* It was no wonder that, in 1958, at a Domestic Meeting of the Association, it was resolved that 'no confidential matters relating to individual members of staff should come to the General Purposes Committee and that the personal

the composition and jurisdiction of committees. When the *Cunliffe Report* was issued in 1960 it was not surprising to find a strong recommendation for revision of the Administrative Structure. One observation of general interest on the issue of 'relationship' may be quoted: 'There are too many channels by which matters may be transmitted to the final policy-making body from the field-workers. . . . This results in uncertainty in making decisions, lack of discipline . . . waste of time in referring issues to and from . . . committees and general sense of frustration for everyone.'[2] Since so much of the administrative process persisted until the 1960s it is worth looking more closely at the earlier organisation and means of communication.

The most prominent Department in the first five years seems to have been the Enquiry Department, in line with the Society's special interest in 'repressing mendicity' and in detecting fraudulent practices in charitable organisations. It became a useful source of information on Charities and, in modern times, has been more appropriately named 'The Information Department'. The production of *The Charities Register and Digest* (later *Charities Digest*), and of *How to Help Cases of Distress* (later, *Guide to the Social Services*) has been amongst the most useful of the Society's activities. In the early days the cheapness of printing made easy the wide distribution of pamphlets and tracts. *Occasional Papers* became one of the best-known methods for disseminating the Society's views. The Districts sent in *Annual Reports* to 'Central', which added a comprehensive review and bound them all together year by year in a substantial volume. The Society sent many of its early articles to *The Parochial Critic*, but, in 1872, it started its own weekly journal *The Charity Organisation Reporter*. This ran for some years at a loss and was replaced, in 1885, by a monthly journal *The Charity Organisation Review*, which became a quarterly in 1922. This was renamed *Social Work* in 1939.

Full and careful documentation was characteristic of the Society's organisation and administration, both at Central and at District level. An administrative activity, begun with the foundation of the Society and continued with great energy, was the issue

affairs and movement of Staff are executive matters and not for discussion at any Committee—lay or professional—but should be dealt with by the appropriate Executive Officer, in conjunction with the Chairman and/or Vice-Chairman of the Administrative Committee'.

of *Forms and Papers*, mostly for the use of District Committees; these covered every contingency: e.g. application forms, agendas, accounts (ledgers, receipt books, loan forms, etc.), announcement of meetings, reports, minute books, day entry books, warning notices and mendicity tickets (these were discontinued after a few years). The Society took the greatest pride in its case-papers, which were uniformly kept by all its Districts and by many affiliated societies. The C.O.S. system of case-recording and indexing was watched with interest by other voluntary societies and by Government Departments. It was with great satisfaction that the Society reported[3] that the Local Government Board had ordered the general adoption of case-papers by Boards of Guardians.

In spite of the many efforts to establish efficient administrative machinery, the rapid expansion in the early years in both the poorer and the better-off Districts led to difficulties. Friction was first evident over a financial issue in 1870 when St George's[4] objected to the tone of the request for 'a considerable grant of money without being properly authorised'. This Committee took the opportunity of stating the 'grounds for dissatisfaction', asking for a reconstruction of Council which 'should consist entirely of representatives from the District Committees'. They noted that 'St George's has not received so much benefit as it had hoped from the conferences at Council'. This District was to act as 'gadfly' on a number of occasions, challenging, amongst other things, the payment 'of large sums' to the Secretaries at 'Central'. Its fear that 'Central' might make too great a demand on the resources of the Districts for its own expenses led it to make the suggestion, which was not, however, followed up: 'that District Societies . . . should pay a small percentage on their receipts to defray office expenses, thus rendering needless any canvass by the Council for direct expenses'.

A greater area of conflict arose in 1875 and 1876 with the formation of the Districts Sub-Committee and the proposal for the greater supervision by Central of the Districts, in order to improve standards. Lord Lichfield resigned from the Chairmanship of the Council on the issue of the greater control by Central over District Committees, and the centralisation of funds. The advocates of local independence won the day, although Central could still admonish the weaker Districts as it administered grant-aid. One criticism was specially noted: that 'it would remove a good deal of latent opposition to the proposed Districts Committee if the work of the sub-committee to be appointed could be clearly defined'. Attempts to define clearly the function of committees were a feature of the Society's administration in subsequent years: they did not always succeed.

In the same way the Society considered carefully the functions of its officers as it experimented in new forms of organisation. For example, in the *Annual Report* for 1897–98 we have an account of the newly appointed 'Organising Secretaries' each one of whom was to advise a group of Districts: 'they act as advisers to the local Committees, help them in the training of volunteers and aid them generally in strengthening their position and influence in the Districts'.[5] By 1912–13, needs had changed and this general account no longer sufficed. The Society therefore set up a special committee 'to consider and report upon the work of organising secretaries with a view to a clearer definition of their function and the most profitable distribution of their services'. This type of enquiry has modern parallels as the Association once again felt the need for a review of the work of its committees and of its officers, in the light of changing needs.

'How much control' was a recurrent issue between 'Central' and the Districts. From time to time a break occurred either through the action of a dissatisfied District, as when Sydenham seceded from membership, and changed its name,* or of 'Central' who instigated the resignation of a committee and encouraged the formation of another to replace it, as in Shoreditch and Clapham.† Occasionally 'Central' took action on particular issues, for example when it called to order a District Committee which had appointed as its Honorary Secretary 'one who had been retired by the C.O.S. as paid District Secretary because he had not adequately represented the Society's views'. 'Central' could only go so far as to disapprove of such action, while recognising that 'according to general practice, . . . District Committees are free to appoint any person as Honorary Secretary, whom they select'.

District Committees were to continue, from time to time, to resent 'interference', and 'Central' was sometimes inclined to be

* In 1890–91. Similar action was taken by Cambridge later when it changed its name to the Cambridge Aid Society.

† Shoreditch Committee, said to be 'half-dormant', was persuaded to resign, 1890–91. Clapham Committee, said 'not to be very satisfactory', was replaced by the Clapham and East Battersea Committee, 1892–93.

high-handed with District Committees. The relation between the Districts Sub-Committee and the Administrative Committee illustrates this tension.* Some bitterness was apparent when, in 1940, the Administrative Committee requested the District Sub-Committee to consider the attitude of certain District secretaries 'as to the inviolability of their recommendations', and to report back.

But few exchanges were as acid as that. In fact, many requests were sent from the District Committees asking for guidance from 'Central'. There were pleas for easier channels of communication. Could not deputations from District Committees attend meetings of the Districts Sub-Committee to discuss problems? (1914) or could there not be more informal visits from Central to the Districts? Sometimes the request suggested a more serious failure of communication: 'when special enquiries were made by the District Committees for the Administrative Committee, with suggestions', then 'the committee should be informed of the purpose and result' (1916).[6] Was this, perhaps, the reason why, in 1936, 'Central' was complaining that District offices had failed to reply to enquiries from Headquarters?

Following the upheavals of the First World War there was an increasing desire for a better understanding: 'Surely in these days there can be no two opinions about the desirability of real closeness of touch between the Executive of the Society and its officers', wrote Woollcombe on behalf of the Secretaries and Registrars,[7] in 1919. The Registrars had already made a bid for representation on the Council in 1914, but had lost. Now, in 1919, it was decided that they might attend but not vote. There was discussion in the 1920s about the representation of paid secretaries, but in 1925 the Council came down firmly against voting rights for secretaries. In 1932 it was resolved that 'no paid member of Council or of District Committees shall be a member of any Committee or Sub-Committee except Training and Propaganda'. In 1944, however, 'additional members' of Council *could be* paid secretaries. By

---

* In the early 1920s, for example, the procedure for friendly visiting on behalf of other organisations was minuted by the Administrative Committee; a letter was subsequently sent by the Districts Sub-Committee suggesting the addition of the phrase 'at the discretion of the local committee', and the substitution of 'it would be well to make reference to "Central"' for 'a reference should be made to the Central Office'. The Administrative Committee accepted the first suggested amendment to the Minute but not the second.

1950 paid secretaries were included as '*essential members* of Council'.* But the right of representation did not give the secretaries the 'closeness of touch' for which Woollcombe had pleaded. In 1953 the complaint was voiced: 'District Committees should be informed of work done by 'Central', including the use made of the Society by Government Departments and officials'.

Sometimes lack of communication, and confusion concerning function, occurred within the Central Administrative machinery. In 1949, for example, the Establishment Committee 'regret not having been afforded the opportunity of making a contribution in regard to the suggested reorganisation of the District Committees, and ask the Administrative Committee to allow the committee to examine and comment on the final draft of the sub-committee before it is submitted to the Administrative Committee for consideration'. It is not surprising that the 1950s were unhappy years for the Association.

A serious attempt to renew its public image was made during these years when a decision was reached to take more positive action on publicity. So far, reliance had been placed on the Appeals Committee to bring the Association to public notice. In 1953 a special Press and Publicity Committee was set up with an active Press Department at 'Central'. This was followed by a vigorous advertising campaign. (In 1960 'Appeals' and 'Press and Publicity' were amalgamated to become the Appeals and Public Relations Committee.) It is a measure of the changed attitude of the Association, as well as of its standing in the community (so different from Loch's day), that it now decided to employ a part-time press officer 'to keep the name of the Association constantly in the public eye so that its name and purpose were familiar to those who might support it'.

In the years between the two world wars few administrative changes of importance to the Districts had taken place. There were closures of some offices in years of stringency, and re-opening when the Society's financial position was stronger. There had been some extension into new areas such as Hendon and the great housing estates like Downham. Occasionally voices were heard suggesting more help to hard-pressed secretaries by the assump-

* Four paid secretaries had already been co-opted on to the active Social Policy Committee. In 1960 Cunliffe was to look upon staff representation as a mistake.

tion of full responsibility for fund-raising at 'Central'. But any suggestion of greater central control continued to be resisted by the District committees.

The pressure for reorganisation had come mainly as a result of the financial extremity of the late 1940s. A firm of business consultants advised concentration of resources, and the first big step towards centralisation was taken when the Districts, reduced by 1948 to nineteen, were grouped into eight areas; some of the less well-trained workers, recruited in the difficult post-war years, now disappeared. Regional organisation did not at once lead to a happier or closer relationship between District Committees and 'Central'. But the professional social workers were in a stronger position. Not only had they secured representation on the important Central Committees, but their own secretaries' meetings had become more forceful. They sent in suggestions and prepared memoranda with considerable success, particularly in their onslaught on 'traditional theory and out-of-date methods'.*

One strong feature of the Society's history had been its readiness to re-examine principles and practice in the light of changing needs. Its Reorganisation Committee, reporting in 1949, considered, once more, the relationship between Central and the Districts. Although there were some members who argued plaintively that 'there seemed to be strange forgetfulness . . . these (i.e. the Districts) *are* the Association' yet the committee as a whole was aware of the tensions. They noted that there was a lack of confidence between the two. At the same time they re-affirmed that the Association was, in fact, a federation of Districts, and they upheld the status of the Districts. The General Purposes Committee also kept a sharp eye on relationships: when the newly-formed Areas sent in a protest, the Committee supported them and affirmed, 'they cannot recommend the intervention by Council in the domestic arrangements of an area committee'. Tensions mounted as Area Committees and 'New Centres' were formed; and professional caseworkers sought for clearer guidance, and for further opportunity to improve their skills.

How these aims were secured is discussed elsewhere.† The real

* The change of name and the reversal of social policy in the 1940s owed much to their hard preparatory work and the care with which they presented their case.

† Chapters 12 and 13.

development in Administration followed the recommendations of the *Cunliffe Report* of 1960.*

2. *Forward to Cunliffe. John S. Burt, 1960–68, and Reorganisation*

When Astbury left, a firm lead was needed at the centre both in administration and in casework. Durham was appointed in 1956. During his four years' service the event of importance was the setting-up of a full-scale review, financed by the Gulbenkian Foundation and directed by Muriel Cunliffe of the University of British Columbia School of Social Work.† She had the aid of strong steering and advisory committees. That the Association had, still, a large fund of goodwill is evident from the composition of these committees. The 'Working Panels' on Function, on Structure and Organisation, on Standards of Practice and on Personnel Practices were representative of a wide variety of interests in the field of social work, while the Steering Committee had some distinguished and authoritative members.‡

The determination of the Association to undertake so large and fundamental a review had been, in fact, a last resort, in the face of many problems. The Steering Committee, at Muriel Cunliffe's request, prepared the way for the *Report* by engaging Dr Willoughby§ for six months during 1958–59 to make analyses of the records of current cases in all the Area offices.

The *Cunliffe Report* was an able and comprehensive document. It put the Association's work in historical perspective; it did not hesitate to call attention to shortcomings; it brought together clearly those features of its past which were worth preserving. It

---

* The Steering Committee held its first meeting in November 1957. The report was presented in April 1960.

† Miss Cunliffe had secured release from the University of British Columbia for a year.

‡ Sir George Haynes, C.B.E., Director of the N.C.S.S., Chairman. Miss Robina Addis, P.S.W. of the N.A.M.H. Mrs Margaret Godfrey, Chairman, Area I, F.W.A. Miss M. Roxburgh, O.B.E., M.A., A.M.I.A. H. Whitbread, Esq., T.D., M.A., Chairman, Administrative Council and General Purposes Committee. Miss Eileen Younghusband, C.B.E., LL.D., J.P. (later D.B.E.), with H. R. Durham, M.A., General Secretary, F.W.A.

§ Dr Gertrude Willoughby of the London School of Economics. These records were, unfortunately, destroyed. The Association's early emphasis on the preservation of documents as a contribution to social history was, alas, no longer understood.

set a high standard for future development. The value of the *Report* was not that it was revolutionary in its recommendations but that it gave clarity of view. The proposals were all directed towards greater simplicity of structure, towards the abolition of obstacles to communication, towards more effective use of resources. There was a more adequate alignment of functions. The focus was on the promotion of a high standard of family casework service.*

In 1960, when the *Report* was presented, Cunliffe found 'a general sense of discouragement within the Association'. However well designed the F.W.A. had been to meet the circumstances of an earlier age, there was now urgent need for revision. Recommendations were made with a view to making the Family Welfare Association 'once more a force to be reckoned with among the social services of London'. The following *Annual Report* of the Association caught 'the unmistakable glow of infectious optimism which . . . appears to radiate from the Review'.[8]

The new secretary John Burt, renamed Director, was appointed when the *Report* was almost completed. He was charged with the immediate duty of reorganisation on the lines of the *Cunliffe Report*. Burt had had valuable experience with the City Parochial Foundation,† although he was unfamiliar with casework. He had the willing co-operation of F.W.A. staff and committee members and was able to carry out his task promptly and efficiently.

Cunliffe had directed attention to the causes of the current difficulties: 'The present administrative structure of the Association is in great need of revision. It has come into being according to the demands of a period in history no longer effective, and was devised to serve clients presenting a different set of circumstances from the current caseloads. Perhaps even more significant, it was designed—if one can use that word in this context—to utilise the services of a group of volunteers who had started and executed the work and therefore had a strong interest in retaining control over

---

* References to specific recommendations will be found in relevant sections of this study (e.g. casework, volunteers and administration).

† There had always been a close association between the F.W.A. and the City Parochial Foundation since the C.O.S. had been instrumental in securing the appointment of a Royal Commission which led to the passing of the London Parochial Charities Act, 1883. The C.P.F. had, over the years, given generous financial support to the F.W.A.; in the modern period their clerk, Sir Donald Allen, had been a very good friend. (The Hackney Family Centre owed much to his inspiration.)

H

performance of duties, planning and policy-making at every level of administration. Currently the difficulties which have resulted from this situation are expressed in both functional and structural problems.'

Some of the more acute problems were examined, at both 'Central' and Area level, and detailed recommendations were made, most of which were closely followed. The *Report* stressed the need for sound, vigorous, and imaginative leadership, suggesting that the title 'Director' was more in keeping with his duties. It was suggested, too, that such a Director should be able to delegate departmental responsibility. Only so, could there be the much needed team-work between committees and staff.

Reorganisation during the months following the acceptance of the *Report* resulted in structural division at the centre into five main departments—Accountancy, Appeals and Public Relations, Casework, Citizens Advice Bureaux, and Information, each with its Chief Officer and Advisory Committee.

The principal departure from the recommendations was the lack of provision for a Research Department,* with a research worker qualified in the field of social research (preferably one who was also a caseworker). There was, in fact, a change of emphasis in the new administration. The F.W.A. had, in the past, been research-minded. Research, as one of its functions, had been written into the Constitution. As we have seen, the preservation of documents was, in part, a conscious effort to provide material for future historians;† a Research Committee had been set up in the years between the two world wars,‡ and a number of experimental projects, as a contribution to research, had been carried out under Astbury in the 1950s. (The Family Centre, discussed in Astbury's time was not, in fact, begun until the 60s.)

However, a new idea of research emerged. In the 1960s an efficient, largely centralised organisation was built up and the Association kept abreast of new managerial and administrative

* It should be noted that Cunliffe's suggestions for topics for research were largely concerned with casework, and casework research was later considered within the casework department.

† In the early 1960s the Association seems to have made a break with history. Area reports were no longer bound with the Council's annual reports as part of the archives. However, the area reports were subsequently collected and bound separately and there was no loss of continuity in the records.

‡ Under the leadership of Alexander Farquharson of the Institute of Sociology.

methods. The Casework Department* was particularly active and the new Casework Consultant and the Casework Administrative Officer were soon planning modern methods of collecting and recording material which should be available for research. They were in touch with qualified research workers in the universities and elsewhere. 'On-going research by practitioners' was held to be important in the new era. As the Casework Consultant wrote, 'I think that practitioners now need to place much greater emphasis on reflective consideration of their own situation and functioning within it, and then communicate their findings to others.'[9]

The new structure facilitated the trend towards centralisation. Professional family caseworkers in the areas were responsible directly to the Case Consultant at 'Central' and not to the Area Committees. Regular meetings at 'Central' by the workers and frequent visits to the areas by the Consultant meant ease of communication and a two-way flow of ideas. Caseworkers were gradually shedding all responsibilities save that of casework. Fund-raising and accountancy were largely centralised.

The new problems were the relationship with the Area Committees and the use of volunteers. 'Public relations' in the areas, particularly with the local authorities who were now giving much increased 'grant aid', was also under discussion. For example, should 'Central' in future be responsible for all public relations? This, indeed, would be a break with the old tradition. The idea seemed to be much in favour with the professional social workers: they could then give all their time to casework.

Meanwhile, the Association had extended its other services. A summary of a Five-year Review of Developments following upon the 1960 reorganisation was given by the Director to the Representative Council in October 1965. The following selected items will give some idea of the main changes and the new trends:

Accounting was mechanised, entailing a major reorganisation of the system: the first step was taken towards centralisation of Area accounting. There was clarification of the Trustee function of the Association. (The Executive Committee were

---

* Cunliffe had suggested the appointment of two senior officers of comparable status, a head of department and a consultant. Funds were insufficient, however, and the functions were combined in a 'Casework Consultant' who was also head of the Casework Department. An Administrative Officer was appointed to whom she could delegate some of the work of the Department.

now Trustees of assets and funds and this was recognised by the Charity Commissioners.)

Following the Trustee Investment Act, there was a complete review of investments, with provision for periodical review by the Finance sub-committee. Notable financial changes in five years were reported:

Total Income	1959–60	£74,996
Total Income	1964–65	£116,355
Total Expenditure	1959–60	£69,592
Total Expenditure	1964–65	£107,262
Income from Special Funds	1959–60	£44,572*
	1964–65	£54,679*

* Excluding new funds.

In the Appeals and Public Relations Department the process of collecting subscriptions and donations, recovering tax on covenanted subscriptions, and finding new subscribers continued. A Family Welfare Year was launched by the Chairman when he was Lord Mayor and, although the Association did little more than recover the cost of the campaign, it was felt that 'a number of valuable lessons were learned'. The Department decided that, as a London Charity, the F.W.A. could not expect to raise large sums from a widespread public. 'The raising of money for family casework was a difficult problem. It had to be explained to those who would take the time to listen.' An important decision was now reached: funds for day-to-day work must come increasingly from borough councils in whose areas the work was done. Funds for development and research must still be sought from voluntary sources.

The Association was now definitely committed to a financial policy in direct opposition to that of Loch's and Pringle's day. Would dependence for so large a proportion of its income on statutory bodies affect the nature of its free choice as a voluntary society or would the selection of clients be made with a view to the expectation of local authorities and their statutory social workers? The answer remained in the future. Meanwhile the Director zealously pursued the new policy and local authorities generously responded.

There had been considerable development in the Information Department. One of the most important was The Educational

Grants Advisory Service* which started as a three-year experimental scheme in 1962 and assumed such proportions that it was decided to run it as a separate Department in 1965. The scheme provided a liaison service for the educational grant-making charities and had links with the Department of Education and Science, Local Education Authorities and the British Council. The Association offered help and advice to students (and sometimes to parents) of whom about a third were from overseas—students for whom adequate provision could not be made from statutory sources. The service was welcomed by the educational charities since it was able to deal effectively with enquiries and applications and to prevent overlapping.

The Department was also concerned about the effect of the Charities Act, 1960, and the compulsory registration of charities with the Charity Commissioners. The work of the Department was considerably increased as, carrying on the traditions of the Enquiry Department of former days, it examined the results of the 'general assumption that anything registered under the Act was reputable'.† Subsequently 'an approach was made to have the matter raised in the House of Lords'. Discussions were held with the National Council of Social Service by whom a Working Party was set up at the instigation of the Charity Commissioners to consider a Code of Conduct for fund raising by charities. The Director accepted an invitation to join the Working Party and the Association suspended its own enquiries pending the report.

The Department's production of the annual *Charities Digest*‡ continued and demand reached some 2,500 copies. Its sale of *Guide to the Social Services* rose steeply from 1,500 in 1960 to 6,250 five years later. Sales continued to rise steadily as it became a recognised textbook, with local authorities amongst the buyers. (As we have seen, the information and advisory work was not confined to the Information Department; the F.W.A. Citizens Advice Bureaux continued to flourish, see Chapter 10 (I)).

* The service was financed mainly by the Goldsmiths and Drapers Companies.

† The Department's suspicion of one registered charity led to discussion with the Charity Commission; subsequently the promoter of the charity was prosecuted and convicted on four charges of fraudulent conversion and five of false pretences. He had a three-year sentence and the charity was struck off the register.

‡ *Register* was dropped from the original title to prevent confusion with the *Charities Register* maintained by the Charity Commissioners.

In contrast to the development of these long-established activities, the Association gave up two others. They handed over the publication of *Social Work* to the Association of Family Caseworkers* and they gave up their Library. The reason was largely lack of money to run them efficiently. *Social Work* had been costing the Association some £500 a year.† The Library, with its very fine collection of books and historical documents, was housed in the basement and had for some years been neglected and little used. It had no librarian. The *Cunliffe Report* made a number of useful suggestions, mostly related to the development of the Library in relation to a research department. It would have been necessary to secure large funds for the purpose and the Association did not feel that this was a priority. It was thought, too, that the collection should be more accessible to other readers. In 1965 wisely, in the circumstances, the greater part of the contents of the Library was handed over on permanent loan to the London University Library (Goldsmiths)‡ and to the National Institute for Social Work Training, the former accepting most of the books, the Parliamentary Papers and similar documents, the latter taking the journals and some duplicate copies of books. Minute books, *Occasional Papers* and some old case-papers were retained by the F.W.A. until in the year 1967–68 an offer was received from the Greater London Council to house all the remaining documents in their Library.

The F.W.A. had often 'hived off' its work once the pioneer stage had been passed. The Invalid Children's Aid Association had been an early example. The Family Discussion Bureau was a later instance. More recently the Association had decided that the time had come to merge the Old People's Homes Department with the Elderly Invalids' Fund.

Two areas of work had remained much as before, namely National Casework and Pensions. Although, administratively, they came within the Casework Department, for historical reasons they

* For some years the Association of Family Caseworkers had co-operated in its production and, as they had no journal of their own, they were glad to take it over.

† A grant by the Sembal Trust to subsidise it for two years was received and handed over to the A.F.C.W.

‡ The University agreed to house them with others of a like nature and to give access to the University Library to persons authorised by the F.W.A. The University also undertook to renovate the books.

continued to function almost as separate entities; the number of applicants dealt with was limited by the available funds and staff.* National Casework had to be conducted by post on behalf of clients outside London where no casework service was available. Some organisations and trusts also delegated their responsibilities to the F.W.A. where casework help was thought desirable but where they themselves were not equipped to give it. In discharging these duties the national casework secretary keeps an up-to-date list of experienced volunteers and a panel of trained workers (e.g. married women with family responsibilities or those recently retired) who do voluntary work as required. The London secretary receives reports on each case and acts as 'go-between', making full use of the statutory social services in various parts of the country and of grants from charitable sources. When the National Casework Department acts as agent for a national society there is an agreed payment, related to the numbers helped and varying with the societies. The Association acts as trustee for a number of bequests and trust funds, for example The Musicians' Benevolent Fund and the Women's Land Army, providing the necessary organisation and amenities for effective help.† The Pensions Department administers small pensions to those in various parts of the country who are in need, usually those ineligible for statutory pensions. The pension almoners are asked to watch carefully for any signs of need for casework help. It is often a social worker who takes the initiative in applying for the pension on behalf of a client. The nature of the work has hardly changed from that of a generation earlier.

The most fundamental changes in the 1960s occurred in the relationship of the Society with Local Authorities, largely consequent upon the London Government Act and the Children and Young Persons Act, 1963. The new responsibilities for preventive work placed upon the statutory bodies, particularly on the Children's Departments, made it essential that every source of family social work should be tapped. The long experience of the

* The Pensions Department has been run for many years by an Honorary Pensions Officer, Miss Collins, The National Casework Department by Miss Twentyman.

† The F.W.A. has been asked from time to time by the Charity Commissioners to act as trustees, or to appoint trustees, to small charities where difficulty had been found in ensuring continuity of management. There is close consultation with the Commissioners in any problems of management.

F.W.A. made it a welcome ally. The size of the grants from the London Boroughs in 1959–60 compared with those after 1965 is some indication of the changed relationship:

L.A. Grants to the F.W.A.	1959–60	£1,800
for Casework Service*	1965–66	£25,000
	1966–67	£36,423
	1969–70	£49,695

As the Director reported in 1965, 'It is in the work of this (Casework) Department that the future of the Association lies, and in this Department where the problems do and will arise.'

Postscript

In the Centenary year, 1969, the Association was full of hope for expansion.† It planned new schemes, closely related to its experience of casework. It gave priority to 'The Development of Group Treatment' which would require the reconstruction of one of its existing centres and the addition of specially trained staff. Secondly, the Association hoped to meet the increased demands for training students from the Universities and the Colleges of Further Education by appointing extra staff in each of its seven Area Offices. Thirdly, it planned to expand its services by establishing three new Area Centres in Greater London. A tentative start was made to introduce some of the family social workers and some selected clients to the group therapy method.‡

Unfortunately the special Centenary Appeal did not bring in the hoped-for increase in financial resources. The fortunes of the Association reached a new low ebb as several senior officers resigned (including Burt's successor§ and the Casework Consultant). When Janet Lacey's appointment as Director was confirmed the F.W.A. was facing a critical situation. In the Foreword

* Grants from Local Authorities for C.A.B.x were separately recorded. In 1969–70 they totalled £88,931.

† A souvenir programme was issued which set out a programme of expansion and development for 'The Next Ten Years'.

‡ Patricia Daniel, F.W.A. Casework Consultant, discussed the problems very frankly at the Centenary Conference. An edited version of her paper was published in *New Society*, 17th July, 1969.

§ Mr Burt had resigned in November 1968 and was followed as Director by Mr Malcolm Ford, appointed in February, 1969.

to the *Annual Report*, 1969–70, the Chairman, Sir Charles Trinder, wrote: 'This has been a year of crisis for the Association. At a special meeting of members in July 1970 . . . it was decided to take drastic action. . . . In consequence a Board of Management was appointed to take full responsibility for the affairs of F.W.A. The Board is required to report to the members every six months.'

The Association has met severe crises in the past and overcome them. It remains to be seen whether the new pattern of administration will be workable and whether the final appeal of the Chairman will bring the hoped-for response: 'I hope we can rely on the support of the members of the Association as we tackle the difficult but eminently worthwhile task of helping the F.W.A. to survive for another century.'

CHAPTER TWELVE

Education and Training

The Family Welfare Association can justly claim to have been a pioneer in the field of education and training for social work. It was also one of the first voluntary societies to appoint trained salaried workers in all its Districts. Another justifiable claim is its early recognition of its function to train not only its own voluntary workers but those who wished to go on to other fields of work. Another characteristic of the Association, which has persisted throughout its history, was its readiness to seek expert help both in its preliminary deliberations, and in carrying through its schemes for education and training. The experience of informed members of other organisations and the knowledge of university teachers were sought, and generously given. The Society was itself to offer 'practical work' to university students from all parts of the British Isles, and from overseas.

Most of the ideas and experiments of the productive years of the late nineteenth and early twentieth century were derived from three C.O.S. pioneers, Octavia Hill, C. S. Loch and Helen Bosanquet, and from the Warden of the Women's University Settlement, Margaret Sewell. They were also based on the cumulative experience of the first generation of family social workers. Their value lay in the combination of theory and practice.

The C.O.S. was fortunate in having Octavia Hill, practised in teaching her methods of housing management to her own recruits. As a keen C.O.S. working member, she was a strong advocate of 'apprenticeship training'. When the London settlements were established the Society had close links with each in turn, but particularly with Toynbee Hall and the Women's University Settlement in Southwark. Miss Sewell,* Warden of the latter, was

* Miss Sewell was not only Settlement Warden and a pioneer lecturer, but also the writer of a number of *Occasional Papers* for the C.O.S. It is interesting to find Miranda Hill, sister of Octavia, joining Miss Sewell in giving the Joint Committee series of lectures (curriculum 1896–98).

one of the first to organise group discussions and lectures, side by side with practical experience of settlement work. When Octavia Hill and Margaret Sewell joined forces in the 1890s to establish a combined course of practice and theory for their volunteers, as well as for the paid workers, the educational value of such a course was immediately apparent. That each student should gain experience in more than one field of work was an essential element; that lectures and discussions should be planned in close relationship to practice was another. Meanwhile, District Secretaries of C.O.S. offices in various parts of London were considering the training of volunteers to be a necessary part of their work, and the Council was giving serious thought to the whole question of 'social education'. In accordance with established practice, papers were read to the Council and published for discussion in the *Charity Organisation Review*. One such, by Mrs Dunn Gardner, was of sufficient general interest to be published as an Occasional Paper.[1] It showed both practical knowledge and an insight into sound educational method. University tutors have since had occasion to echo Mrs Dunn Gardner's plea that students should be regarded always as learners, not as additional workers in a busy office. The stress on the importance of giving thought to the introduction of the newcomer to unfamiliar work is also noteworthy: that she should be *interested* from the start is sound educational method in any setting.

It was characteristic of C.O.S. principles in general that Mrs Gardner should stress the importance of training the student to see the work for individuals in relation to the total situation: the individual in relation to his family and neighbourhood: the resources available in relation to the need. Success in training depended upon whether the student had been able to grow in knowledge of the relation of the part to the whole. Another valuable lesson, relevant today, is the recognition of the necessity for wise supervision, remembering that 'our workers have quite as varied natures as our applicants, and require to be dealt with in quite as varied a manner'.

The C.O.S. followed up the increasing interest in training by long articles in successive annual reports.[2] The need was recognised for training the volunteers, the 'bona-fide doers' within the organisation, side by side with 'the future co-operators', 'the natural allies' of the Society. 'Happily the number of those who come to the Society with a view to working elsewhere ultimately is on the increase.' At the same time the C.O.S. was concerned to train 'those who will continue to work for the Society, and may become its leaders, as Honorary Secretaries, Chairmen, or members of Committee'.

The year 1896 was memorable for the formation of the Joint Lectures Committee. Representation from the National Union of Women Workers was secured, as well as from the Women's University Settlement and the C.O.S. The lectures organised by the Committee were well attended and were closely related to the practical experience gained in the agencies. Professor Smith,[3] in considering the curriculum arranged by the Joint Committee, concludes that 'there is a continuity and visible integration of content much in line with modern professional social work education'. The C.O.S. in June 1897 set up its own training committee to consider the 'in-training' of its probationary District Secretaries. It should be noted that the committee considered it important that opportunities should be given, both to these District Secretaries and to Honorary Secretaries, to spend some time at the Central Office 'to obtain an insight into the general work of the Society'. A knowledge of administration, as well as of casework principles and practice, was an accepted part of training. The visit to 'Central' became an established practice.*[4]

In the following years Mrs Helen Bosanquet's influence is seen in the greater interest in 'social economics' in the training curriculum. Not only was she now taking part in lecturing, but her book, *Rich and Poor*, was on the recommended reading list, side by side with Loch's *Charity Organisation* and Octavia Hill's *Our Common Land*. In 1901 she produced her lengthy pamphlet on *Methods of Training*[5] which became the blueprint for C.O.S. training in subsequent years. Much of what she said re-emphasised points made by Mrs Dunn Gardner earlier. But Helen Bosanquet brought out more vividly certain problems of training which are of particular interest in view of discussions in recent years. One of these was 'specialisation':† 'though this is an age of specialisa-

---

* The Report of the Special Committee on Training is an interesting document. This is discussed later. Its stress is on the importance of a wide view, 'beyond casework'.

† Titmuss, in his introduction to M. Smith's study, drew attention to the dangers of specialisation, both specialisation in function and specialisation at the wrong time in the processes of learning. Eileen Younghusband discussed a

tion, the student must be made to see that he cannot afford to neglect any of the influences affecting the lives in which he is interested; that specialisation indeed means learning more, not less'. 'A man is not a specialist because he knows only one theory, but because he knows one thing better than others.' Contrary to the image held by later generations of Helen Bosanquet as a rigid traditionalist, we find her, in this paper, arguing against conventional ways of thinking: 'conventional ways of classifying cases, conventional modes of help, conventional rules for making enquiries, all are dangerous, and especially dangerous in our work. . . . every case is unique and individual'. Like Loch, she insists on the need to base 'social education' upon social philosophy; principles and attitudes are of first importance. On these can be built the appropriate skills, techniques and methods. Like Loch, too, she considers that social reform must march with plans for helping the individual: 'the contradiction which sometimes appears between the two is only apparent or at most temporary'.*

The next phase in the pioneer stage came with the suggestion that the C.O.S. training schemes would benefit from a closer alliance with University teachers. Several University professors responded to an invitation to become members of a General Committee to consider a C.O.S. scheme which was to include Settlements as well as Charity Organisation Societies in various towns. Elizabeth Macadam points out that it was through a suggestion of C. S. Loch to his friend, Professor Gonner, that the School of Social Science was established in Liverpool in 1904, in association with the Victoria Settlement for Women and the Liverpool Central Relief and Charity Organisation Society.[6]†

With the extension of the schemes of training to centres outside London, the Joint Committee had broken up‡ and had been

similar issue in *Social Work in Britain*, 1951. Soon after, the universities were planning their 'Generic' courses, although the Carnegie Grant for the first course was not given until 1953.

* In later years the Society was not entirely successful in relating the two. The pull between the Reformers and the Caseworkers was apparent after Loch's retirement.

† The School became fully incorporated in the University in 1917. The University of Birmingham was the first actually to register Social Science students as internal students in 1908. Bristol, Leeds and Manchester followed.

‡ The Women's University Settlement withdrew since their Articles of Association confined their work to London. The official connection with the N.U.W.W. was also discontinued.

replaced by a Special Committee of the C.O.S. on Social Education. There was considerable debate in the London C.O.S. on the desirability or not of creating an independent body which should use university teaching but provide its own realistic knowledge for the application of theory to practice. In the end the decision was reached to establish the School of Sociology, and Mr Urwick (later Professor) became its first Lecturer and Tutor in 1903.*[7] (The Honorary Secretary of the Joint Committee, Mrs G. F. Hill, continued to devote herself to the work as Secretary of the new School of Sociology.) The schemes planned for the School of Sociology were followed in essence by social science departments in later years. Social education, Loch pointed out in 1907,[8] included three groups of studies. (1) Social theory and administration (a comprehensive curriculum taking in history, politics and economics) (2) Sociology (including analyses of social structures, theory of social growth and change, etc.), and (3) Practical instruction. The practical work was organised through the co-operation of various agencies, and included several months in a C.O.S. office. A point of special interest in these early experiments is that plans were made,† and in part carried out, to extend the opportunities for social education to the general public; it was hoped, in particular, to reach teachers in elementary and secondary schools.

By 1910 the School was considering extending its lecturing and teaching to local centres. The C.O.S. was already offering its newly appointed staff the opportunity of attending lectures at the School of Sociology while receiving 'in-training' in the District Office. As M. Smith has pointed out, by this time several levels and kinds of social education were thought necessary to meet the various demands: full-time professional education, part-time study extension classes, and in-service training.[9]

It is clear that the School had been hampered by financial difficulties. The Special Committee had made efforts to raise funds, a special grant had been made by the C.O.S. and some income was derived from fees. In 1912 Professor Bernard Bosanquet, who was Chairman of the School, as well as an Honorary Officer of the

* In July 1903 the C.O.S. special Committee was established as 'a separate and independent committee'.

† The *C.O. Reviews* of 1904 and 1905 make several references to such plans. Several papers on the subject were read and published.

C.O.S., reported that finances and accommodation were inadequate, and that the London School of Economics had proposed taking over the School of Sociology, as a nucleus for a Department of Social Science and Administration, and that he recommended acceptance. An agreement was reached that Urwick should continue to direct the Department and that other staff would also remain. The general plan of professional education would also continue for two years. On this understanding the transfer took place in July 1912. The C.O.S. was to continue its association through the provision of practical training for L.S.E. students in its District Offices. (It was one of several such agencies.)*

In the early years after the amalgamation of the School of Sociology with the Social Science Department of L.S.E., Urwick, now Professor, continued to make clear that the course was equally divided between practical and academic work. In the session 1917–18 the Ratan Tata Foundation undertook complete financial responsibility (the Department became the Ratan Tata Department of Social Science and Social Administration). The Charity Organisation Society had never been completely satisfied with the training after the amalgamation and, in co-operation with other institutions and agencies, had tried out various schemes. It showed its vigour, during the pressure of war, by promoting its own twelve month training course, in which it co-operated closely with other agencies (its first students were awarded the C.O.S. certificate in 1916). It was now looking to Bedford College as the more sympathetic Institution to provide courses of lectures in Social Economics and Social Ethics. The success of the efforts of the Joint Social Studies Committee which had promoted these lecture courses led to the decision by Bedford College to establish a Department of Social Studies. By 1919 a permanent director was appointed, Mrs Helena Reid, who had gained much of her practical experience with the Charity Organisation Society. Mrs Reid fulfilled the early C.O.S. expectations that a Director of a University Social Studies Department should combine academic scholarship with practical experience.†10 But the students had no formal teaching in method in the University Department. There

* There were some misgivings in the Society about the influence of the Webbs and of socialist theories on the School's teaching, and on the attitude of its students.

† That she still thought C.O.S. principles and practice of value in the post-war years is shown in her reasoned paper published by the C.O.S. in July 1923.

was, as yet, no body of accepted methodology of practice related to theory. The gap was filled by general discussion with students in tutorial sessions.

Recognition of the importance of training for social work was given officially during the First World War when first, the Ministry of Munitions and, later, the Home Office sponsored students to take an intensive course of training in University Social Science Departments.* The general interest in Reconstruction after the war encouraged the universities to offer extramural courses in the social sciences;† but these were unrelated to practical work. The universities, meanwhile, stimulated by the interest of the Home Office, had formed a Joint University Council for Social Studies‡ to co-ordinate and develop the work of Social Studies Departments in universities. One of its concerns was the consideration of the relationship with statutory and voluntary agencies.§ The only outstanding change in the organisation of university courses in social studies between the two world wars was the establishment in 1929 of the Mental Health Course at the London School of Economics, the first professional course within the universities.[11] Though the psychiatric social workers were a small proportion of the total number of trained social workers, their influence was important in the subsequent development of training in all fields. The American Commonwealth Fund had generously financed the Mental Health Course (as well as the Child Guidance Council and the Canonbury Clinic) and there was a renewal of interest in this country in the development of social work in the United States. The C.O.S. was sufficiently aware of its importance for training to send one of its workers, under the sponsorship of The Commonwealth Foundation, to study developments in the United States.|| The Society also kept abreast of current discussions as it sent representatives to the International Conferences of Social Work which were a feature of

* The purpose was 'welfare' in factories.

† E.g. the 'Extension Courses' of London University.

‡ The first meeting was held in April 1918. In 1935 it added 'and Public Administration', a title in keeping with the expanded interests of the Council.

§ Later most of the departments sent their tutor, responsible for co-ordinating academic and practical work, as one of their representatives on the J.U.C.

|| Miss Olive Crosse who, as Training Secretary, afterwards became responsible for organising the practical work offered to students. She worked closely with the tutors in university departments.

the late 1920s and the 1930s.* It was also much involved with the formation of the British Federation of Social Workers in 1935. Like other organisations it had high hopes of the work of the League of Nations Advisory Committee on Social Questions when, in 1938, a sub-committee was asked to report on training.† How much sooner this country would have worked out an effective plan for the employment of trained social workers in the statutory services had not war intervened can never be known. As it was, the lessons of the First World War were forgotten at the outbreak of the Second. After initial failures, full recognition was given to the need for skilled help in solving many of the social problems inevitable in the upheavals of large-scale war.‡

The contribution to the welfare of the community made by trained social workers became apparent during the Second World War. The publication of the first *Younghusband Report*,[12] 1947, sponsored by the Carnegie United Kingdom Trust, made the need more widely known. A supplementary *Report* four years later[13] showed the demand to be more urgent. The third *Younghusband Report*, that of the official Working Party on Social Workers in the Local Authority Health and Welfare Services, 1959, left no doubt that social policy must include greater support for the employment and training of social workers. New statutory provisions in child care,§ mental health and probation gave the impetus for more 'preventive' social work which demanded skilled and experienced workers, already in short supply. The establishment of the Council for Social Work Training and the recognition of Colleges of Further Education offering the 'Younghusband Courses' gave new opportunities which encouraged recruitment from a wider field. Eileen Younghusband's influence on social work training and casework practice in this country has been incalculable. The F.W.A. was fortunate in having her enlightened help in many of its activities.‖

There were other trends which had a marked effect on education

* In Paris in 1928, London, 1932, and Frankfurt, 1936.
† The rapporteur was to have been S. W. Harris of the Home Office.
‡ See Chapter 9.
§ Particularly the important section 1 of the Children and Young Persons Act, 1963.
‖ Her wide experience was specially valuable as she had kept in close touch with developments overseas. Many of her published papers were those read at international conferences.

and training. The casework agencies, of which the largest single voluntary organisation was still the F.W.A., and the lecturers who, since the war, were taking a closer interest in the relation between theory and practice, had become more aware of the changing attitudes of clients.*[14] A greater measure of social security, a comprehensive health service and a policy of full employment brought higher standards, which, in turn, led to higher expectations. At the same time a more widespread, popular knowledge through radio, television and the Press, of 'stress situations' encouraged men and women to seek new kinds of help; parents anxious about their children, husbands and wives with marital problems, tended to seek aid at an earlier stage of their difficulties. The F.W.A., sensitive to these demands, responded, as in the past, by seeking expert help. The resulting project, the 'Family Discussion Bureau', which contributed so much to the psychodynamic approach to casework, has been fully discussed above (Chapter 10, 1(b)).

Higher standards were bringing into prominence the families who failed to reach the norm. 'Problem families' came into the field of debate, as Medical Officers of Health wrote urgent reports on the low standards of these families and the consequent demands on a variety of services. At the same time social workers were writing sympathetically of the need to understand the multiple causes of the problems and to give such families long-term support†[15] (see Chapter 10, 2.)

Meanwhile greater knowledge of population trends threw into prominence the need for more thought on the care of the elderly, both geriatric care in hospitals and welfare work and housing provision within the community. Later still came the challenge to the complacency engendered by the concept of 'The Welfare State'; attention was drawn to families where the weekly income was insufficient, widows, especially those with children, and the lower paid wage earners who were shown by the 'Child Poverty Action Group' to be living below standard. Social workers would have to be on their guard against the assumption that financial

---

* Yet, as Noel Timms has pointed out, little valid evidence had so far been gained of the reaction of clients to casework. Some research in this field was started in 1967 with the active co-operation of the F.W.A. It has since been published.

† The F.W.A. was not to continue its detailed work for such families. The Family Service Units were concentrating their efforts in this field.

need was of secondary importance as a cause of distress, or—as the modern caseworker would say—that it was merely 'the presenting problem'.

There had, meanwhile, been significant advances in the social sciences which helped to balance the more extreme forms of the psycho-therapeutic approach. Sociologists, in particular, had stressed the effects of culture on values and attitudes and, consequently, on behaviour; they had shown the closeness of family and kinship ties in some urban areas; they had drawn attention to the importance of 'the role concept' in understanding the individual within the community.

The post-war years had been years of ferment in thought and practice throughout the field of social work, both in this country and overseas. Successive United Nations seminars had helped to spread new ideas. More young social workers went to Canada and the United States to supplement their training.

One of the chief weaknesses in education for social work in this country was the almost entire dependence upon American publications.* It is doubtful how far practising social workers took note of the British publication, in 1939, of *The Study of Society*,[16] which sought to put methods and problems into perspective. It was a serious attempt to relate the specifically human sciences of psychology, social anthropology and sociology to social problems; it was interesting that, in a discussion of some methods of sociology, it was the tutor of the L.S.E. Mental Health Course who was asked to contribute a section on 'The Methods of Social Case Workers'.† The first substantial publication by a group of professional social workers in this country appeared soon after the first *Younghusband Report*. Edited by an experienced hospital almoner, Cherry Morris, *Social Casework in Great Britain* brought together accounts of casework in all the varied fields, thereby throwing light on the role of the caseworker as it was seen by the practitioners themselves in 1950. Studies in a more specialised field were issued by Tavistock Publications Ltd. That by the Family Discussion Bureau, *Social Casework in Marital Problems*, 1955, recorded a pilot scheme in this country to throw light on

* E. Macadam had published *The Equipment of the Social Worker* in 1925, but it was a general study, reflecting the views of the period, and no longer met the new needs.

† It was unfortunate that it was published in the year of the outbreak of the Second World War, 1939.

family relationships. It was a product of fruitful co-operation between the F.W.A. and the Tavistock Clinic and Tavistock Institute.* The F.W.A. also made a useful contribution by publishing the results of other investigations,† e.g. *The West Indian Comes to England*;[17] and *The Family: Patients or Clients?*[18] It had already published *Family Casework and the Country Dweller*,[19] on behalf of the National Council of Family Casework Agencies, and *Professional Education for Social Work in Britain*, for the Pringle Memorial Fund.[20]

The revival of interest was marked by the issue of a new journal, *Case Conference*, devoted to Casework.[21] There was also a noticeable increase in the proportion of articles relating to casework in the older journals such as *Social Work*. The professional journals of the Psychiatric Social Workers and of the Hospital Almoners were already committed to such discussions. In 1964, with the publication of the works of Noel Timms[22] a fundamental study of social casework was undertaken.

In 1964 the time was also thought ripe for the publication of a series of papers and articles written over the years by Eileen Younghusband under the title, *Social Work and Social Change*. As the author says: 'It (social work) has been profoundly affected by social change in general and has also begun to be more articulate, precise and objective about its own methods and aims.'‡

In this country the established pattern of training had been maintained with little change until the Second World War. The F.W.A. continued to offer opportunities for practical work to the universities and other institutions in spite of war-time difficulties, though the number of students was necessarily reduced. Much rearrangement of timing and placing was necessary when Bedford College and the London School of Economics were evacuated to Cambridge. During the war an average of some 200 students each year gained experience in practical work with the C.O.S.§

With a view to preparing for the anticipated demand for professional social workers in both statutory and voluntary services

---

* See Chapter 10, 1(b).   † See Chapter 10, 3 and 4.

‡ This book was one of an excellent series designed for the use of students, practising social workers and others, and published by The National Institute for Social Work Training.

§ Many of them also made a distinct contribution in very demanding circumstances.

after the war, the Society joined in consultations with universities and government departments to consider schemes to attract men and women with war-time experience. The mature student needed more carefully thought out 'concentrated' training courses if he or she were to be drawn into social work as a career. (Meanwhile C.O.S. staff joined with others to give lectures to such groups as British Red Cross Detachments, the Queen's Institute of District Nursing and Ministry of Labour Resettlement Officers—particularly on casework methods and the work of voluntary organisations.) It was at this time that the Society looked sympathetically at the desire of its own workers to improve their professional skills. They anticipated the need to give help in the readjustments necessary when ex-servicemen and women returned to civilian life and evacuated mothers came home.* It was noted with satisfaction that several Social Science Departments of universities were planning courses with the psychological aspects of casework in view.

Apart from the F.W.A.'s own in-training course, there was no recognised professional training for family casework.† Students with a basic university social science qualification were recruited by the F.W.A. and taught 'on the job'. After the war, in response to new demands, the universities rapidly increased the number of basic courses‡ [23] and added to the professional courses. Child Care was added in 1947 to the already established Mental Health courses, but there was no radical change until 1954.

This year saw a real breakthrough as new ideas and methods were tried out in the 'Applied Social Studies' or 'Generic' Course at the London School of Economics. This proved its worth and spread, in time, to other universities. 'Family Casework' now appeared as one of the options for professional training, and organisations like the F.W.A. had to re-examine their facilities, in order to co-operate fully in the new schemes which were carefully planned to relate theory and practice more closely. The increased demands for training, together with the stimulus of new ideas in theory and practice, deeply affected the Family Welfare

* A refresher course on marriage problems was organised with Dr Mace of the Marriage Guidance Council as leader. The F.W.A. was later to develop its work in this field through its Family Discussion Bureau (see Chapter 10, 1(b)).

† E.g. there was nothing comparable to the professional training for psychiatric social work or hospital almoning.

‡ The average pre-war number of students was 540. The total for 1945 was approximately 930.

Association. The young workers, in particular, were striving to improve their skills. Astbury had given strong support for the starting of the Applied Social Studies Course at L.S.E. The Association re-deployed its staff so that two centres might be able to offer facilities, under the supervision of two well-qualified F.W.A. secretaries, for the practical training of students on the new Applied Social Studies Course.* Supervisors from North America were invited to conduct seminars and to act as Consultants to family social workers in all the Districts so that standards in general might be raised.

At the same time the Tavistock Institute of Human Relations continued to offer the 'Advanced Courses' in Casework,† which it had started after the Second World War. The Family Discussion Bureau was already training groups of workers from various fields of social work.

The weak point, so far, had been the lack of success in integrating theory and practice in the basic courses. Some efforts had been made early in the war to improve the quality of training by a combined effort of the universities and the casework agencies. In 1941 a Joint Committee on Family Casework Training had been set up. The somewhat *ad hoc* nature of the Committee gave place two years later to a formal body with representatives from the Joint University Council and various casework agencies. It also included the Association of Family Caseworkers. The object was to bring together all those concerned with the family casework training of students in order to set up agreed standards of practice. Part of the function of the Joint Committee was to send representatives to the family casework agencies taking students to see whether required standards were reached. These agencies were listed as offering 'training' or 'experience', depending on the qualifications of their staff and the quality and nature of their work. Such 'visiting' was a time-consuming and sometimes thankless task,‡ but it helped to improve standards, and was a useful guide to university tutors.

* The F.W.A. now discontinued its own special 'in-training' course.

† The supervisor of the F.W.A. 'New Centre', Miss Keenleyside, had taken one of these courses.

‡ The writer was involved in these activities and recognised the difficulties of agencies who felt themselves to be 'down-graded', if they were listed as offering 'experience' only and not 'training'. Yet this was a service of considerable value for students at different stages of experience and maturity.

Two developments changed the emphasis of the Committee's proceedings. One was the greatly increased demand for training places after the war, the other was the development in casework theory. The Committee's representatives who visited agencies now regarded themselves as advisers, rather than as inspectors. They sought to encourage agencies to increase their skills and to give thought to methods of training. The Family Welfare Association, as the largest family casework agency offering training, had taken an active part in the work of the Joint Committee (it later provided both the meeting place, Denison House, and, for many years, the Secretary of the Committee).*

Meanwhile the interest of the Home Office in the training of probation and child care officers, and of the Ministry of Health in that of medical social workers and psychiatric social workers, encouraged the universities to establish other professional courses as well as the generic courses, while many of the 'basic' social studies courses continued to need 'placements'.† The University of London Extra-Mural Department also organised a new course, the External Diploma in Social Studies, which included practical work.‡ The demand for training places increased further when Health and Welfare Authorities sought training for their established officers, as well as for their recruits. The Joint Committee on Family Casework Training was aware of the strain on Agencies offering practical training, when so many and varied demands were made upon them. It was particularly concerned to preserve the opportunities for family casework training for the 'pre-professional' student. For this reason it emphasised the contribution to be made by the Agencies in laying the foundations of basic training. The emphasis would change at the professional stage when 'the learning of skills' would be paramount. In 1964 the

* The Joint Committee had first met at the headquarters of the Institute of Almoners. When applied social studies courses and other professional courses made still further demands on agencies, the Joint Committee widened its scope; it included, not only agencies offering general and family casework training, but others doing specialised work, like the Family Service Units and the Invalid Children's Aid Association.

† Later, special 18-month courses for graduates in non-social science subjects combined basic and professional training.

‡ This was taken by students busy during the day either in paid employment, often related to social work, or as housewives. Those in jobs had to get leave of absence for some six months for their practical work. It was an exacting and worthwhile course.

Joint Committee summed up the purposes of 'practical casework' as a basic course under seven headings which would have been acceptable to supervisors from the beginning of the century: '(1) The illumination of theory; (2) Philosophy of Social Work (to be 'caught' rather than 'taught'; (3) Professional Ethics; (4) The Opportunity for Students to test out their own aptitude for social work; (5) The Development of those qualities which are essential in a social worker (this included 'the foundation' for the development of skills and competence, later to be emphasised in the professional course); (6) Understanding the function of different social agencies; and (7) Reports and Records.'[24]

The Family Welfare Association decided to accept students with a variety of background training. In 1967, for example, they took twenty-four from the professional social work courses and thirty-seven from the pre-professional courses and the Home Office Course (probation and after care).* In each case the F.W.A. made a special effort to plan each student's work to suit his needs.

The students from the Applied Social Studies Courses would be given greater opportunity to learn and to practise casework skills. The basic course students would be given general insight into the work as a whole, carrying some responsibility, but of a more limited nature. Supervision of students, in whichever category, was recognised as a very important duty and time was set aside regularly for consultation and discussion. An example of the readiness to cooperate with university tutors in planning the work of students was given in the F.W.A. Annual Report for 1967, when two students with a special interest in Social Administration had a short 'placement' at 'Central'. This, too, recalls the earlier training when knowledge of administration was thought to be essential for the equipment of the social worker. One difference in the 1960s was that the Casework Consultant had a full-time Casework Administrative Officer to help organise the placement of students. This was a development which, together with the frequent consultations with the principal family social workers who supervised the students, added to the value of training.

---

* It is interesting that area IV, which at first had been thought of as the special centre for the new 'generic' training, accepted students from various courses; in 1967 they included six basic course students, eight from Applied Social Studies, and two from the National Institute for Social Work Training.

In the long run the quality of the practical training depends on the quality of the caseworkers. Some further study of their record, of how they saw their role and what problems they felt needed discussion, will be considered in Chapter 13.

CHAPTER THIRTEEN

Casework*: How the Association saw its Function and the Caseworkers their Role

N.B. This Chapter should be read in the context of that on Education and Training (Chapter 12) and amplified by reference to the illustrations (Appendix). 'National Casework' is noted in Chapter 11.

Although, from their foundation, C.O.S. District Committees were helping families in distress, the term 'casework' did not appear in the records until a decade later. It was 1913 before casework was acknowledged to be the Society's chief function. Until then the emphasis lay on charity organisation. The C.O.S. only gradually played down its early role as a detector of fraudulent practices in the charitable field. It had frequently to refute the suggestion that the Society was only another relief organisation. But in spite of the C.O.S. claim to be offering a special service the pressure of events compelled it from time to time to modify its practice. For example, in the first few years poverty in some parts of London was so great that the workers were distributing, without enquiry, 'bread to be then and there eaten'. In consequence, the Council . . . 'felt themselves obliged by the nature of the case to advise committees to give relief themselves, in the last resort'.† The first manual,[1] *Suggestions for Systematic Enquiry into Cases of Distress*, had very little in common with later 'casework'.

Yet, already, in many Districts, there were elements of casework: there was, for instance, considerable concern about the quality of 'visiting'. Most contacts with distressed people were made in the applicants' own homes by the paid, untrained agents

* Until the term 'casework ' became well established it was written as a hyphenated word or as two separate words. The various forms continued side by side for many years.

† See Chapter 3, 3.

who reported to the District Committee. Many of the Committees who considered these reports had representatives from the Society for the Relief of Distress, already practised in visiting; S.R.D. visitors were willing to give experience to C.O.S. volunteers. Most Districts could also count on the active support of the local clergy. One, St Maylebone, had Octavia Hill with her experienced band of helpers. The question of visiting the homes of those in need of help became a subject of increasing importance in the Society's deliberations. Sir Charles Trevelyan advocated 'a thorough system of house-to-house visitation'.[2] This was agreed in principle by the C.O.S. and suggestions were issued to District Committees on how to organise it. It was recognised that no comprehensive scheme could be carried through until the number of volunteers had been greatly increased.

By 1877 the Society decided that the whole question must be reconsidered. The original scheme was unrealistic in view of the large numbers for whom 'house-to-house visitation might be wise and useful'. There were also dissident voices within the Society on the propriety of such visiting. Alsager Hay Hill, for example, 'feared the injury which the invasion of these lady brigades from the West End would do to the East; it should be left to neighbours to help each other'.[3] As a result, a strong Committee was appointed which included Octavia Hill and Alsager Hay Hill. Two of their suggestions are strikingly enlightened in view of current charitable practice.

That poor persons shall not be visited unless on some definite errand, or unless acquaintance has been previously made with them; or, lastly, unless there is some special reason for believing that the visit will be acceptable. There are, perhaps, few things that would tend more directly to the development of a healthy tone between all the classes than for it to be recognised that well-to-do strangers should no more knock at the door of a working man without some distinct object or introduction than they should at the door of one in their own rank in life. The second condition of sound visitation is that relief should not be directly connected with it unless under very exceptional circumstances. The whole intercourse will be spoilt if the question of giving and receiving be suffered to intrude into it.[4]

By 1882, when Loch issued his guide, *How to Help Cases of Distress*, the cruder forms of relief had ended and Districts were building up their 'case'* experience. About the same time the term 'case-work'† was used to describe the kind of charitable work done: directed mainly towards supporting deserving families who had fallen upon hard times and helping them to regain their independence. The term gradually acquired new meaning as 'case-workers' gained in knowledge and understanding, and as new needs were identified.‡

Until the Charity Organisation Society as a whole had agreed upon the place of casework in the organisation of charity, there was little chance of development in this field. Although by the end of the nineteenth century most of the Districts thought of casework as their chief function, they often found themselves at variance with the Central Council on this issue.

The declared object of the C.O.S. was 'to improve the condition of the poor by the organisation of charitable relief'. Under C. S. Loch's secretaryship there were repeated efforts to educate the District committees in the wider conception of their function. The division between the 'reformers' and the 'caseworkers' continued to influence policy for another generation. The issue came to the fore in a discussion on Training in the 1890s: 'The district offices of the C.O.S. exist, not to get their own special office work well done, nor to assist a certain number of cases every year, but to improve the general condition of the poor.'[5] The Training Committee put the point even more forcibly as they considered the education of the learner. Their 'First Report' urged that, 'to offset the danger of too great absorption in lesser matters, it must be impressed upon the learner' that 'casework is mainly to be used as a means of organisation, and that "the

* It was unfortunate that the term 'case', long known to law as 'the instance of things occurring', or 'the statement of facts', should so often have been applied in social work to the individual, or family. The Family Welfare Association, for a great part of its history, had found it difficult to convince its critics that it did not treat persons as 'cases'.

† It was used in the C.O.S. *Annual Report*, 1882, in the account of the experiment of sending to some of the Districts paid 'officers well acquainted with the principles and methods of the Society and able to form a centre of charitable workers and to ensure the thorough execution of case-work'.

‡ Few attempts had, so far, been made in this country to examine the structure and processes of casework or to offer a definition, although American writing on the subject was of increasing interest to British social workers after the 1920s.

improvement of the condition of the poor" as a whole is a much nobler and more far-reaching object than the relief of a certain number of cases of distress'.[6]

Some attempt was made to reconcile ultimate aims and District practice in a paper written in 1912:[7] 'This paper is written in the old-fashioned belief that through casework we may organise . . . if we cannot "co-ordinate" charities as we wish, let us be thankful that we do ultimately help them to co-operate.' The following year the Society admitted openly: 'All Committees find a common ground in casework. Many, of course, do much besides but it is casework which forms the bulk of the work of the Society throughout London.'[8] Yet, in 1919, there was still some difference of opinion amongst practising secretaries upon the future of casework. Norah Hill, who was to serve the Society with distinction for many years, thought at that time that 'casework is a thing of the past'.[9]

In the years between the two world wars, the practice of casework was affected by the new economic and social conditions. Demand became so urgent during the depression that District workers were involved in an increasing number of 'short-term cases', many of them applications for practical help. New sources of aid from statutory bodies and new money available from Service Funds made it easier for the Society to get help on behalf of their applicants. The Districts pointed out, from time to time, that they were driven to give relief when they found that others failed to meet the needs, or were not meeting them adequately. The term 'relief', once shunned by the Society, was now in frequent use. A re-statement for 1922*[10] referred to 'our aims and objects in relation to the special needs of this very difficult time' as follows: 'Our work is two-fold. The best known and most popular side of it is the work of relief on individual cases.' The writer added, 'The other side is, perhaps, less recognised, but it may be briefly summarised as the co-ordination of effort and the linking together of the various forms of help available. . . .'

When Astbury, then an assistant to Pringle, made his *Restatement of Case Work*, in 1930,†[11] he asked what had led caseworkers astray since 1918. He called for critical awareness of the trend

---

* Written by a much respected professional worker, Miss E. F. Bolton.

† 'the stage . . . reached where casework was being confused with the granting or securing of financial aid'.

towards relief as distinct from casework. However, the pressure was too great, and the Society was claiming in 1937–38 'First aid casework shows flexibility'.* It should be added that some 'long-term casework' continued throughout the period as 'the Turner' and other cases, summarised in the Appendix, will illustrate. Pringle's reference, in 1925, to 'good casework' as 'the antidote to Bolshevism', must be counted as an aberration from the main lines of development.

Casework, for the greater part of the Society's history, was family-centred. This was interpreted in various ways, in accordance with changing views on the extent of family responsibility. When the Poor Law dominated public opinion on assistance to the needy, the extended family was under an obligation, as far as they were able, to come to the support of any member in distress.† With the break-up of the Poor Law and the development of the statutory social services the 'extended family' no longer had legal obligations, but the C.O.S. still saw the family as the rallying point, as it considered all sources of available help. 'The prevention of family breakdown' through timely casework was a guiding principle at all periods. The Society was also concerned to restore 'the whole family', the 'family as a unit' if treatment was to be 'remedial'.‡ In the late 1950s the F.W.A. was still stating its 'fundamental aim' to be 'to work for social improvement in and through the family: to seek, with every means at its disposal, to restore the family as the true basis of civilised society'.[12] In contemporary casework the family is again the point of reference even when, as sometimes happens, 'the client' is an individual isolated within the community. His 'family history' is sought, to throw light on his present difficulties. In line with the new pattern of family responsibility, accepted by the community in its statutory provision for those in need, the F.W.A. would not necessarily expect adult members of a family to come to one another's aid. They might well, however, consider, with the client, how far the family could willingly give appropriate support—both practical and otherwise.

---

* It is significant that during these years the Society's accounts, unlike those of subsequent years, gave considerable publicity to 'The Sources of Income (Relief Only)'. (See Diagrams 4 and 5.)

† This included the responsibility of grandparents for grandchildren.

‡ The terms 'remedial' and 'treatment' are to be found in early C.O.S. records.

Another ingredient of good casework, demanded throughout the Society's history, was knowledge. Knowledge of character and knowledge of the sources of available help came high on the list of requirements in the pioneer phase. The early thinkers and writers, who helped to shape the pattern of social work, went further: they had in embryo, a sociological approach to the problem of the individual in relation to his family and to his environment. They were concerned with the effects of their work on the neighbourhood and the community at large. Knowledge must include these wider aspects. This was put clearly by Helen Dendy (later Bosanquet) in a paper printed in 1893.

> Now this thoroughness of knowledge at which we aim will take two directions. It will involve, first, a careful study of the characters and circumstances of the individual men and women with whom we come in contact in the first instance; and it will involve, further, a full acquaintance with the wider social conditions and tendencies within the limits of which we work, and without knowledge of which our efforts are likely to be self-destructive.
> ... Then the man, with his character such as his temperament and surroundings have made it, can only act within the community of which he is a fraction. His every movement is influenced by relations of innumerable kinds. . .[13]

Caseworkers were able, in later years, to include the knowledge resulting from the development of the social sciences, particularly psychology and sociology.

There is no doubt that much modern casework can be traced to the principles and practice worked out by the pioneers. As we have seen, two outstanding women, Octavia Hill and Helen Bosanquet, who were also experienced District workers, had considerable influence on early developments in casework. (The influence of Octavia Hill was thought by Mary Richmond to have been considerably greater in America than in England.)[14] They had the breadth of vision which led them to anticipate some of the problems still facing us today. Octavia Hill was writing, as early as 1873, that lack of communication was one of the problems to be faced by the community; she pointed out that there were 'the statesmen, philanthropists and political economists' on one side and, on the other, 'the workers in the field who came face to face with those in trouble'; there were 'the studious generalising thinkers and the loving individualising doers who need to be brought into communication'.[15] The language may be antiquated but the thought is modern.

Helen Bosanquet was also much concerned with the idea of failure in communication: '. . . in as much as no two people ever have just the same experience, or receive just the same answers to their questions, it is probable that no two people ever really understand one another, or are at all times able to communicate intelligently'. She asks, '. . . is it not safe to assume that in a considerable number of cases opinions from which we differ require interpretation rather than refutation?'[16] Helen Bosanquet has most often been remembered for her failure to appreciate the force of economic pressure in her analysis of the causes of poverty and unemployment. She deserves closer attention for her thoughtful contribution to casework theory.* Octavia Hill has been recognised for her pioneer work in housing. She is less well known for her contribution to casework. A modern writer goes so far as to credit Octavia Hill with 'as good a description of social casework as any we can give today',[17] namely: 'Each man has had his own view of life and must be free to fulfil it. . . . In many ways he is a far better judge of it than we, as he has lived through himself what we have only seen. Our work is rather to bring him to the point of considering and to the spirit of judging rightly than to consider and judge for him.'

Octavia Hill wrote much, and spoke often, on the theme of friendship in social work—'the friendship which has little to do with outward gifts, and much to do with human sympathy'.†[18] The importance of friendship in social work was a noticeable feature of the many appeals made from time to time by the C.O.S. for volunteers. It was a quality much stressed in later obituary notices.‡[19] 'Friendship' and 'human sympathy' were early statements on relationship.

As we have seen, the pioneers were much concerned with

* She also made some very useful suggestions in the discussion of training. Cf. Chapter 12.

† Modern caseworkers would still agree that sympathy is a necessary quality, although they would now use the wider term 'empathy'.

‡ Cf. Mr Mocatta, a voluntary worker: 'He considered the obligation of charity as a definite personal duty to be fulfilled with the care and solicitude that a friend would have towards a friend'. See Chapter 14.

ethical questions, particularly with the interpretation of 'obligation': of the rich and better educated towards the poor and deprived. It was the mainspring of their desire to make sound decisions on how to 'select and discriminate, when to help and when to step aside'.[20] In any case, the Family Welfare Association has at no time had the resources, either in money or in personnel, to accept all the cases referred to them. In the first phase of development the general standards of morality, and the wide acceptance of the virtue of self-help,* alike combined to determine the C.O.S. to limit assistance to 'the deserving': those who had proved their strength of character by past effort to meet adversity. As C.O.S. workers gained in experience and understanding, the censorious attitude was less pronounced. Selection was now applied to 'the helpable'. Districts varied considerably in the emphasis placed on 'moral character' as a factor in assessing how far a family was helpable.† Some Districts in the 1890s were already suggesting that they should do more to help the 'undeserving'. Helen Dendy was asking for an 'impartial' approach:

> Human beings cannot be treated as simple units, as if they were all of one kind, and entirely independent of each other. In the first place there is the man himself and his character; to handle these without a proper understanding is like experimenting with chemicals of which we do not know the properties—the results are more likely to be disastrous than beneficial. Perhaps it is because we have so habituated ourselves to regarding character from the point of view of merit only that we rarely attempt to approach it as impartial students of cause and effect.[21]

The question was openly discussed in 1914: 'Those who deserve least sympathy sometimes need it most.'[22] During and after the First World War the community at large took a less stern view of morality and many C.O.S. workers were more tolerant. Workers in the years between the wars were expressing some embarrassment that Service Charities, asking the C.O.S. for reports, insisted that 'marriage lines' should be seen. By the end of the 1930s the main test in C.O.S. selection was the need of the client and the

* Samuel Smiles' writings on this subject were very popular.
† See Chapter 3, 3 for a more detailed account of persistence and change in the Districts.

I

ability of the agency to meet it. Character, or personality, were still important in determining how far the client was likely to co-operate in the casework 'treatment'. But old attitudes died hard and some committee members were reluctant to approve of any suggestion to help those who did not conform to strict standards of morality as they understood the term.*

In spite of variations in practice there had been considerable agreement on the essential elements of casework. The pioneers had a clear conception of their objects in helping families in distress, and they gave careful thought to the qualities needed by those who carried out the work. Loch summed up two funda-mental components of casework in his 'Principles of Charity'.† First Principle: 'No work of charity is complete which does not leave behind it an increased power, moral, physical or economical.' Second Principle: 'The family, not the individual, must be treated as the unit.' It was emphasised that 'social bonds must be maintained and utilised'. District workers were under a strong obligation, once they had made a decision to help, to be thorough, both in discovering the full extent of the need, and in seeing that the help given was 'suitable in kind and adequate in quantity'. The ethical content of casework was emphasised from the begin-ning. Respect for each person was the basic principle: it was grounded in the belief in human brotherhood.‡ Belief in the responsibility and worth of the individual demanded that case-work should strengthen the ability of the applicant to help himself. It meant, too, that any information given to the worker should be treated with respect and accepted in confidence. 'Confidentiality' has been a cardinal principle of casework throughout.

When new influences and new knowledge led the social workers of the 1950s and 1960s to examine their casework afresh, con-temporary attitudes to morality coincided with the detached view brought by professional caseworkers to their assessment of personal behaviour. Moral questions were often posed, but the emphasis was, now, on the client's attitude, on the way in which he viewed his relationship with others. The situation being what it was, could the client use casework help satisfactorily? Problems of morality were now one category amongst the many complex

---

* See, for example, 'The Dane Case', Appendix.

† These were repeated in successive editions of *How to Help Cases of Distress*, until the mid-1930s.

‡ E.g. the teaching of Octavia Hill, Loch and the Bosanquets.

social and personal problems brought by clients to the Family Social Workers (the term later replacing Family Caseworkers).

Meanwhile the family caseworkers had been much concerned with the more general question of the ethics of social work. Conferences and numerous articles in professional journals reflected this interest: for example, the residential conferences organised by the Association of Social Workers in 1952, followed by the much-discussed *Notes on the Ethics of Social Work*, and that of 1959, on *Morals and the Social Worker*. Students in the Social Science Departments of universities had already had an introduction to ethics. Some university professors had long taken a direct interest in social questions.* An example of the widespread interest in the question was the invitation, given by the Joint University Council for Public and Social Administration to Dorothy Emmet to address them on *Ethics and the Social Worker*, in 1962. The Paper, together with comments by Noel Timms, was published by *The British Journal of Psychiatric Social Work*,[23] and F.W.A. workers were deeply involved in the discussion as it affected their professional approach to casework.

Who did the casework and what was its quality?

As we saw earlier, by the mid-1870s, voluntary committee members were taking part in the interviewing and visiting, while the agent did the routine enquiry work. By the 1880s 'Central' decided to employ some 'well-paid officers' to ensure greater continuity and higher standards, particularly in areas where it was difficult to recruit regular volunteers. Some Districts continued as late as the 1920s to rely on Honorary Secretaries and Treasurers, with some paid clerical help and an agent. Women were always welcome recruits to the band of friendly visitors.† Until the Second World War the Society still depended largely on volunteers for much of its personal work with families. New volunteers were given 'in-training' by the District secretaries, who looked upon this duty as an important responsibility.

Several attempts had been made to set out more precisely the

* Loch had already shown the strong influence of T. H. Green on his thought and practice. In 1911 MacCunn had published *Liverpool Addresses* on the Ethics of Social Work. (I am indebted to Timms for this last reference.)

† The visiting of pensioners was a well-established activity, continued into the 1970s.

organising, training and casework functions of the District secretary. One of these read: 'It is quite wrong . . . to expect that the Secretary of any Committee should do the bulk of the case-work; though he must be cognisant of all that goes on in the office, he should himself . . . only carry just enough of it to keep the work up to that high standard of efficiency on which he must depend for an illustration of the truth of those principles which have called the Charity Organisation Society into existence.'[24] After the First World War, as more Districts had trained secre-taries, it was no longer possible to deny these young professional workers the right to consider themselves caseworkers. But the work of a busy office left little time for much direct personal intervention in family casework by the secretary. If she was very fortunate in her volunteers, or in her students, she might do more. This situation was not always acceptable, either to the University Social Science Departments, or to the C.O.S. itself. In 1928 the Administrative Committee were recommending that 'the C.O.S should consider how far its casework is carried on by students . . .'.[25]

It was not until the burden of 'relief work' or 'First Aid Case Work' was lifted in the late 1940s, by the greatly increased responsibilities of statutory authorities, that family social workers could be free to give more time to casework 'in depth'.

The study of work in the Districts has shown how varied was the practice of casework until after the Second World War; its quality was dependent largely upon the composition of the com-mittee, the support of voluntary workers, and the personality of the secretary. While constructive and thoughtful work was done in some Districts, others showed weaknesses which gave the Society's hostile critics good cause for complaint. Some within the C.O.S. were equally critical.* Rules made for the general guidance of District Committees had, in some areas, been rigidly applied;† yet, in theory, 'flexibility' was the distinguishing mark of a voluntary organisation. The willing co-operation of the client,

* Loch had pointed out that some workers were 'altogether too detective'. More than a generation later a C.O.S. worker was observing: 'that certain C.O.S. committees were chiefly concerned in the task of finding out how *not* to help their applicants'.[26]

† The writer, as a student in the late 1920s, was concerned when strict adherence to a 'negative rule' prevented a hospital patient in urgent need of convalescence from being offered a place in one of the Homes supported by the Society, solely on the grounds that the applicant had been treated in 'a Poor Law Hospital' (where she had been most unhappy).

'a unique person whose self-respect and independence must be upheld', was still a cardinal principle of casework; in practice, some of the more autocratic members of 'decision committees' could with difficulty be persuaded that it was not the task of the committee to impose their plans, and their standards, on applicants for help.*[27] Trained social workers sometimes had considerable anxiety in 'steering cases through committee'.

Various devices were used to reduce the influence of reactionary elements and to use professional skill more effectively. One method widely used was to form a smaller case committee to consider 'difficult cases', leaving the more straightforward applications for the larger lay group. The select small committee had, in fact, been advocated many years earlier by C. S. Loch, who had deprecated the waste of time and inefficiency of detailed discussion of cases by a full committee. It was not until 1953 that the Re-organisation Committee of the F.W.A. recommended all Districts to consider replacing lay case committees by 'internal staff conferences'. It was some ten years later that the professional staff became fully responsible and the Society could expect greater uniformity in the practice of casework in all the centres.

We have seen from earlier sections how much thought had been given by the Association to the improvement of skills in interviewing, visiting, counselling and assisting. Noel Timms has reminded us of 'the difficulty of making precise and detailed statements about interventions in the life of one human being by another'.[28] It is significant that he quotes an American, H. Perlman, as giving 'one of the most succinct and lucid statements' about casework, namely, that it 'is complex by virtue of the varied knowledges which feed it, the critical commitments which infuse it, the special auspices and conditions of its practice, the objectives and ends which guide it, the skills which empower it'.[29] Although the English usage may not be entirely satisfactory, it will be helpful to bear this statement in mind as we examine the development of casework within the Family Welfare Association.

It was the caseworkers themselves who, out of their experience of changing needs, questioned existing practice and threw out new ideas. The 1890s had been such a fruitful period. The ferment of thought during and after the First World War challenged the

* This was shown starkly in the controversy arising from the Elliott article *Who shall scape Whipping?* (See Appendix.)

workers, once more, to think afresh about traditional methods of casework. On their behalf the C.O.S. Secretary had written to Dr Cyril Burt in 1918:

> 'Social workers are deeply anxious to know whether they can improve their efforts by a study of psychology in a technical and specific way.' Dr Burt answered 'no', if was meant the study of standard textbooks and attendance at certain lecture courses.*[30] His reason: 'Psychology is yet in its infancy . . . it has not reached the mature stage of an applied science.' But he held out great hope for the future in 'the science of individual psychology'. 'Where character or personality is in question there psychology—were it in any way a complete or well-established discipline—should be the master science.' Modern caseworkers might like to note Dr Burt's prophecy, made in 1918: 'the future solution of problems will largely depend on the social worker'.

In spite of the new interest in psychology in the early 1930s, it was a long time before it affected, consciously, the day-to-day practice of family caseworkers. The older, experienced secretaries continued, as before, to try to understand the nature of the problem, and to assess the need. They made allowances for differences of character and circumstances. They appreciated the emotional effects of distress, and gave compassionate service to the best of their ability, following the teaching of C. S. Loch. They knew that the 'right relationship' with the man or woman in need of help was essential if they were to win confidence. They were aware of the need to guard against their own prejudices. But, in the 1930s, with their heavy 'case-loads' they were usually too much engaged in the work in hand to give overmuch thought to psychology. The psychological approach was thought to be more appropriate to psychiatric social workers who had taken the mental health course.

In training students, F.W.A. secretaries were careful to warn them of the pitfalls of prejudice, and of ill-informed and hasty judgment, but they were not expected to go further into 'this soul-searching and exacting aspect of casework'.†[31] University tutors

---

* Dr Burt accepted the C.O.S. invitation to give an address on the question.

† Few would go so far in the expression of horror of casework in the United States as did Mrs Milnes in 1931 (see p. 132).

in general would, in the mid-1940s, have shared with Una
Cormack some misgivings if 'ordinary students', sent for a short
period (some eight to twelve weeks) of practical training, were
subjected to 'psychologically orientated casework'.

> The relationship of the ordinary caseworker to the client is
> that of one citizen to another, and the main business of the
> ordinary caseworker is, by duly appreciating the other man's
> circumstances and individuality, to give him every facility for
> taking or leaving the particular service the caseworker's
> employer, statutory or voluntary, has to offer, whether it be
> hospital treatment, vocational guidance or a loan to set up
> shop. Need the relationship between student and supervisor
> go further? (Barbara Wootton would surely sympathise with
> this view).[32]
>
> Again, with all respect to the venerable maxim: 'Know
> Thyself', is not the period of practical training particularly
> the time set aside for Knowing Other People? Knowing other
> people and administering a social service are in themselves
> such intricate processes that it seems unwise to complicate
> them gratuitously by amateur psycho-therapeutics. And the
> ordinary caseworker is no more than an amateur in this field.[33]

But some of the young social workers were no longer satisfied
with traditional methods. Those who had trained with older
secretaries began to question the need for so much investigation.
They were impatient with irksome methods carried over from the
past. They found some of the Committee's decisions harsh. They
felt that they had been insufficiently prepared for the interviewing
and visiting expected of them. They were concerned that so much
casework was little more than relief work. They wanted to have
greater opportunities for understanding human behaviour, and
analytical psychology seemed to point the way.*[34]

The late 1940s and the 1950s were years of discussion, experiment and questioning, with the professional workers taking a
prominent part. There is an interesting parallel with 1918 when
F.W.A. workers had asked Dr Burt what they could learn from
the new psychology. In 1948 the F.W.A. caseworkers taking part
in the Family Discussion Bureau scheme (see Chapter 10, 1(b))

* E.g. an article by Mary Keenleyside in *Social Work* October 1958 gave
rise to much discussion.

asked Dr Balint of the Tavistock Institute of Human Relations whether he would teach them the psycho-dynamics of the family. He, too, said 'No' to formal teaching. He did, however, give active help by introducing, and himself participating in, a series of case conferences. This method was to have considerable influence on the development of casework throughout the Association.

The various projects undertaken by the F.W.A. in the 1950s reflected the increasing concern with emotional conflicts in family relationships. The development of 'a psycho-dynamic approach', worked out during the experimental period of the Family Discussion Bureau scheme, led to greater concentration on therapeutic work with individuals and married couples. This was thought to be 'a contribution to the mental health of families'. One disappointing feature of the early phase of the F.D.B. project was the disinclination of individuals or married couples to come forward spontaneously, at an early stage of their difficulties, to seek skilled help. They were usually referred by other social workers or by doctors when breakdown seemed imminent.

The F.W.A. now paid increasing attention to the question of referral. How could a troubled and possibly nervous client be encouraged to accept the proferred help from a hitherto unknown worker? The joint project undertaken by the Institute of Almoners and the F.W.A. (see Chapter 10, 3) drew special attention to preventive casework and the art of referral. It also, incidentally, threw light on the way in which caseworkers saw their role, both in relation to their clients and to other social workers. 'Successful referral is at all times a skilled process. It depends on the worker achieving a sound judgment of the nature of the problem out of what is a complicated and confusing experience for the client, conveying the substance of this to him and assessing his ability to use casework help.'*[35] The psychological knowledge which caseworkers found particularly useful at this stage is reflected in the following passages:

> This can only be achieved on the basis of sound knowledge of the ways in which people behave under strain or in the face of grave distress and difficulty. The caseworker must have

---

* Cf. Malcolm Ford: 'referring a client to the appropriate agency is a very skilled job. . . .'

some understanding of the defences people put up to protect themselves against suffering and failure and be able to interpret the complex feelings which may be hidden by a barrage of words or a hostile attitude. She must be able to assimilate the information given by the client and to assess how far it is factually correct or how far distorted by distress, fear or poor intelligence. And she must begin, even in the early stages of a contact, to form a tentative plan for working towards solving the difficulty. . . .

When she has some understanding of the situation the next stage is for the worker to convey it to the client in such a way that it is intelligible to him. Only by sharing fully in clarifying his problem is the client helped to feel that it is manageable and is encouraged to want to work on it. At the same time, he can see the worker as a sympathetic and knowledgeable person and can experience casework as a helpful process.

Once the problem is recognised, the way of solving it can be discussed and the possibility of being helped by another worker introduced. This must be done in a way that demonstrates that such a transfer is a purposeful thing, aimed at helping him. He must be assured of the worker's understanding and goodwill, but not so much involved in a relationship with her that he sees referral as a rejection. It is a difficult balance for the worker to maintain. It requires nice judgment and quick thinking so that it does not appear to the client that the first worker heard enough to alarm her and cause her to send him elsewhere. Rather the client should be quite sure that the worker understands the difficulty sufficiently to send him to a place which will certainly accept him for help.

It should be remembered that the choice of accepting the offered service lay with the client.

The hospital almoners and family caseworkers co-operating in this small experimental project concluded that the casework was successful to the extent that there was

. . . evidence of increased ability in clients to understand themselves and the effect of their attitudes and actions on their families, friends, and colleagues. Signs have been noted of their increased capacity to modify their behaviour in such a way that difficulties can be seen more realistically and

I*

tackled, or prevented from happening. Evidence has been sought in practical demonstration that couples threatening separation were actively planning to live together; in increased ability to discuss points of difference instead of retreating into silence or flight; in increased ability to obtain and keep work; in ability to plan expenditure and co-operate in plans for their children's education, and in the will to play a greater part in the life of the community.

Those family caseworkers who participated in the projects were stimulated by the new opportunities for shared experience; those taking part in the Family Discussion Bureau project had welcomed, in particular, working in a team which included skilled consultants. But other caseworkers in the F.W.A. areas had not all acquired the new feeling of confidence. Although it was now the policy of the Association to encourage all their caseworkers to learn 'the application of psycho-therapy to casework practice', some found it difficult to get the insight expected. The appointment of consultants and supervisors trained in the more advanced methods followed in North America did not meet all the demands from the areas. For some of the older F.W.A. family caseworkers the 1950s were a testing, often a frustrating, period.*[36]

As we review the influences which affected the development of family casework after the Second World War we see that the new thinking had been given an impetus from two sources: firstly, the attempt to help the many clients with emotional problems arising from the difficulty of adjustment to post-war conditions (see Chapter 10, 1(b)); secondly, the development of new methods of social work education and training (see Chapter 10 and 12). Each of these added to the knowledge and 'technical ability' of the family caseworker.[37] Caseworkers felt better prepared to meet the demands for preventive social work. This demand was stimulated by important official reports which resulted in new social legislation and expanding social services.† The workers were encouraged, too, by the *Younghusband Reports* which had played a large part in calling attention to the need for many more trained and skilled social workers (see Chapter 12).

---

* Cf. David Donnison for a detailed discussion of the problem as it affected one F.W.A. area.

† Especially the National Health Service, Child Care, and greatly improved Social Security Measures.

Changed social and economic conditions after the Second
World War had demanded fresh thinking on the role of the
F.W.A. The Council set up various *ad hoc* committees, including
a Reorganisation Committee,* which stated the purpose unmistakably in casework terms.[38] The opening sentence reads:
'Family casework agencies exist today to render a casework
service to individuals and families, who, because of personality or
environmental difficulties, find it impossible either to achieve a
measure of personal satisfaction, or to fulfil their responsibilities
as members of the family and of the community.'

By 1957 the Administrative Council of the F.W.A. decided that
a full-scale review of policy and procedure was necessary 'in the
light of the far-reaching social changes of recent years'. As we
have seen,† the Cunliffe recommendations led to substantial
reorganisation.[39] Regular meetings of the consultant and the
principal family social workers followed the transference of
responsibility for casework from the area committees to the Head
of the Casework Department. The new development gave the
caseworkers some release from the tensions which had been
building up during the 1950s.[40] It gave them an opportunity to
share their experiences and to discuss their problems; they gained
in self-assurance as they endeavoured to improve their skills. It
seemed to the caseworkers that a larger proportion of their clients
needed help to solve stresses within the family circle: they found,
as before, that psychological problems were often associated with
economic difficulties.

When the Boroughs agreed to give aid to the F.W.A. for its
family social work, regular reports were submitted, prefaced by a
summary of casework as follows:

> The broad aim of social casework treatment is to strengthen
> the person's own capacity to resolve, ameliorate, or tolerate
> his social difficulties and to effect some improvement in his
> social functioning.

This is in direct line with the purpose of the pioneers of C. S.
Loch's day, but the language has changed. The following account

* To review the functions of a Family Casework Agency in the light of
present day social conditions and to consider the closely related problem of the
best way to perform these functions with the limited staff and financial resources
available.'

† This was discussed more fully in Chapter 11.

of the methods of social caseworkers would certainly have surprised earlier workers:

Social casework is a method of helping people and its major therapeutic tool is the use of the relationship between a person needing help and the social worker. The method is appropriately employed in any kind of situation which involves personal distress and the inability of a person or family to deal unaided with their interpersonal and social problems.

Some accompanying statements show clearly how the F.W.A. family caseworkers saw their role in the late 1960s:

... a professionally qualified social work staff ... which offers help to all, whatever their problems in social and family life. Skilled counselling is given to families, couples and individuals, whose troubles and anxieties prevent them from leading happy and satisfactory lives. Londoners make use of our services in marriage difficulties, debts, and money management problems, trouble between parents and children, bereavement, desertion, loneliness or fear of growing isolation, lack of employment, difficulties in how to use official sources of help, and many other problems.

It is interesting to compare casework past and present to see what has persisted amidst the vast social and economic changes of a century. By and large, the above account would have satisfied social workers of an older generation. Many of the Districts were helping to solve just such problems throughout the present century. Some, even in the 1880s and 1890s, were discussing how best to help families in these or similar situations. F.W.A. reports in the first half of the twentieth century leave no doubt that much support was given to relieve anxiety and to bring hope to many families whose problems had seemed overwhelming. This was often done under conditions far below modern standards, in drab, often noisy rooms, with inadequate office equipment and clerical help. It was done, too, in face of constant demand for services which, since 1948, have been the responsibility of the State. We must remember also the extent to which other social workers had come to expect the F.W.A. to supplement their efforts. Probation officers, moral welfare workers, health visitors and hospital almoners in London had turned to the Society, often at a moment's notice. The Public Assistance Committees and the National Assistance Board's officers knew that the F.W.A. would co-operate to support some of their families with special needs.

Older workers would have agreed with the current view that the 'essential qualifications of a social worker seeking to help a person to sort out personal and social difficulties' were 'a willingness and an ability to understand and enter into the feelings that have influenced particular attitudes and behaviour'. But whereas older workers, at their best, relied on their natural sympathy and intuition, and their long experience, modern professional social workers had the advantage of the 'advance in the science of individual psychology' foretold by Dr Cyril Burt in 1918. They were also freed from the obligation to fill in the old 'casefront'; they could concentrate on asking 'the right questions'; they were trained in the observation and interpretation of the behaviour of persons under stress; they learned to take more account of their own reactions and to pay particular attention to 'the relationship' between the worker and the person in need of help. The care with which the family social worker passed on the client to a new worker was one of the distinctive features of the new approach.

The 1967 report sums up 'the qualifications of a social worker' as follows: 'Above all, we adapt our casework service to individual needs by encouraging people to work on their problems in their own characteristic way. This calls for patience and effort on both sides.' An older generation of social workers were often apt to make a plan and expect or persuade their clients to fit into it, although there were remarkable exceptions. The best of the workers, from early in the century, were urging their students to work *with* and not *for* their clients. Had not Octavia Hill, in the nineteenth century, striven hard for the acceptance of this approach? Charles Loch certainly supported it, though some of his followers failed to put his teaching into practice. In 'the exercise of patience' the professional social workers of today have a great advantage over their predecessors. 'We give a great deal of time to listening to people talk and think aloud, to working things out with our clients and to supporting them while they try out new ways of behaving.' The modern worker has a very much smaller 'case-load'; she sees all her 'clients' by appointment and each worker has a separate interviewing room, made as attractive as possible. She is also relieved of a great deal of administrative work, for example, fund-raising is now largely centralised. The emphasis is on family casework as her proper function. Although it is still thought advisable for the family social worker to keep in close touch with statutory and voluntary services in the area, far less time is spent outside her own office.*

There is also considerable resemblance to earlier work in the 'main area of difficulty' or 'the nature of the problem' which has prompted the client to seek help, or which is found by the social worker to be the chief need. There is no doubt from past records that economic difficulties were often the chief single cause of distress, although the immediate need may have been for medical, surgical or convalescent aid, or for help to get better housing, etc. At the same time, as we have seen, the need for support through emotional stress of various kinds was often recognised and met. From time to time, particularly after the First World War, Districts were reporting: 'problems are now more complex'. Past analyses of the kind of help given showed a range of practical help and 'Other Forms of Help' without specifying relationship problems. In the 1960s greater refinement of analysis was introduced to include: Marriage Difficulties, Problems in Parent-Child Relationships, Economic Difficulties, One-Parent families, Physical Handicap or Illness, Old Age, Housing, Mental Disorder, Social Isolation, Other Problems.

In spite of the increased provision for social security and the wider recognition of the social workers as 'skilled in relationship problems', the greatest single 'area of difficulty' brought in the late 1960s was still economic. In the three years for which such analyses were made in the 'Returns to the grant-giving London Boroughs', economic difficulties headed the list, although marriage difficulties were fast catching up.† Some families had more than

---

* Whereas many of the older secretaries took a large and active part in such work, sometimes acting as Chairman of kindred societies, the workers of today select and limit their outside work, often sharing representation on other bodies between the various social workers attached to an office. The contrast is clearly seen if we compare the vast amount of outside work undertaken by Miss Malleson in the past, in what is now Area IV, with that of each of the recent family social workers.

† In 1965–66 of some 2,000 families helped, 498 of the problems were economic, 445 were marital, and 248 were housing difficulties. Parent-child relationships, physical handicap or illness, social isolation, mental disorder, one-parent family (in that order) accounted each for over 100. Old age followed with 85.

one problem. If we look at the total number of problems, economic problems can be seen in perspective as one only of the many difficulties. Faulty relationships of various kinds—between husband and wife, parents and children, between one individual and the community in which he feels isolated—these together account for the largest proportion. Social workers believed that professional skill would help clients to understand and come to terms with their problems. They regarded family casework as a preventive service, undertaken in the early stages to avoid a final breakdown. The F.W.A. considered that, as a voluntary organisation, offering a casework service to anyone who wanted help with personal problems, they gave a choice to citizens who were not necessarily in touch with a relevant statutory service. The Association was encouraged by the fact that an increasing number of clients were 'self-referred'. (This is in contrast to the early experience of the Family Discussion Bureau.) The family social workers welcomed, too, the greater opportunity to co-operate with professional colleagues in the statutory services.

In a study of the development of the Family Welfare Association it seems relevant to discover what the Society itself regarded as typical of its casework and what special problems called for discussion at various times. The examples in the Appendix are selected from the period during and after the First World War, that is, since casework was thought of as forming 'the bulk of the Society's work'. They were all published by the F.W.A. As far as possible I have used the writers' own words, since the language current at the time in itself throws light on 'How caseworkers saw their role'.*

* Some examples of earlier casework are to be found in the general considera- tion of work in the Districts before 1914 (e.g. Chapter 3, 3).

CHAPTER FOURTEEN

The Volunteers: Variety and Length of Service

'Those who show an evangelistic enthusiasm to save people in distress or reform the world' tend, according to a contemporary family caseworker, 'to be unsuitable as volunteers in a social welfare service.'[1] Had this criterion been applied for the greater part of the history of the Family Welfare Association, the society could hardly have survived, and many social reformers would have been deprived of valuable experience before going on to serve in wider fields. C. S. Loch himself would have agreed that excess of zeal is likely to impair judgment. He claimed that charity must be scientifically based. The Society was a pioneer in requiring its voluntary workers to have supervision and training. But if enthusiasm was not enough, it was held to be a very desirable quality, if linked with a willingness to learn.

No one can read the annual reports of the Family Welfare Association without amazement at the records of long service by volunteers, for twenty, thirty, forty years and, in a number of cases, for over half a century. There were many others who gave valued service for lesser periods. As one District reported in 1880, 'As nearly every member of the committee is either a professional, official, or businessman, time is to them what money is to many others.'[2]

It is impossible to include a statistical account of the volunteers, or a full description of the many kinds of service, since voluntary work was not recorded in like form by the various District Committees. Even the actual numbers of volunteers working in each office were seldom reported.*[3] One return made in 1895

---

* The only attempt by the Society to give the total number of 'visitors' was not satisfactory since they tried to ascertain the numbers engaged in social work throughout London. The returns were not complete, but there was enough information to suggest that the number totalled about 10,000. Unfortunately, for our purpose, they did not say what proportion of these were attached to the C.O.S.

gave the membership of District Committees as about 1,200; an estimate of the number who took an active part in the work of the Society was from eight to nine hundred.[4] A very useful list of opportunities open to voluntary workers is given in the *C.O.S. Annual Report*, 1885, entitled *What Workers Can Do for the Poor in Connection with the C.O.S.* Some volunteers came for half a day a week only, to do a specific job, others came every day, ready to take part in any branch of the work.

A large number of committee members in the early days were 'working members'. It was usual to find the Chairman ready to give personal service, for example, by approaching employers on behalf of an applicant. When a District formed a Skilled Employment Committee, one of the voluntary workers acted as Honorary Secretary. Most committees had an Honorary Medical Officer who was prepared to advise on particular cases;* sometimes a doctor, occasionally the Local Medical Officer of Health,† was so interested that he became a regular committee member. Some Committees also had a lawyer as a member, while others called for voluntary legal aid as the need arose. Most secretaries could rely upon a local businessman, a bank manager, an accountant, or, sometimes, 'a leisured woman skilled in accounts', to act as Honorary Treasurer.‡ This was an important role in a Society dependent upon charitable funds; so was the work of a volunteer 'who had an unfailing skill in securing new subscribers'. Others were adept at publicity, writing to the Press or preparing appeals.

In most Districts, fund raising, by means of special efforts, including the inevitable jumble sale as well as the occasional concert, etc., was in the hands of volunteers. The clothing store or 'shop' was run, not so much to acquire funds, since articles were sold at a nominal sum, as to help applicants in times of need;§ volunteers

---

* E.g. before and after convalescent treatment arranged by the Society.

† One of the most distinguished was Sir William Hamer who had, as Chief Medical Officer of Health for the L.C.C., taken a keen interest in the Society, and on his retirement served on the Medical Sub-Committee.

‡ In the year 1890, the Central Council appointed a firm of auditors to audit the accounts of all the Districts. Many of the Honorary Auditors who retired had given service over a long period. In thanking these volunteers the Society added: 'It is thus hoped to obtain greater uniformity, security and method in the keeping of accounts throughout the many District Committees.'

§ In the 1890s and other crisis years, the clothing store was a stand-by in times of severe unemployment. In the years between the two world wars, and

gave regular service in collecting, storing and distributing the goods. In addition, they organised savings schemes and thrift clubs 'to encourage self-help and sounder budgeting', and 'to promote habits of industry and temperance'. Voluntary workers also took upon themselves the important task of maintaining good 'public relations'. They travelled all over the country lecturing to the general public on the aims and methods of the Society, held 'drawing rooms' for the same purpose, and sought to ensure the adequate representation of the C.O.S. wherever relief, statutory or voluntary, was being administered. To this end, many volunteers served on the committee of other voluntary bodies, while others sought office as Poor Law Guardians.

Some workers showed particular interest in certain specialised aspects of the Society's activities. The annual reports record the 'devoted service' of individual members in furthering, for example, the welfare of elementary schoolchildren, ex-service men and their families, or the homeless, or in assisting emigrants, or promoting housing reform. Occasionally, this deep interest and concern would culminate in specific schemes for improvement, such as 'the erection of public washing houses, and the conversion of a graveyard into a quiet and beautiful space'.[5]

Amongst the most welcome volunteers were 'those who found joy in friendly visiting', particularly those who acted as 'almoners to the elderly' for whom pensions had been raised by the Society; or those experienced voluntary workers who could be relied upon to visit a 'difficult family' and to 'follow up' until confidence was gained and co-operation assured; or the volunteer who was available to accompany a nervous patient to hospital, or to see the children off to a holiday or convalescent home.

Particular instances of readiness to spend time and money on enquiries and experiments are recorded throughout the Society's history, though the first period under C. S. Loch was the most fruitful in pioneer ventures subsidised by private individuals.* Sometimes the money was provided by someone in close touch with the work, though not a serving member. Such was Mr Peek, a member of the London School Board, who provided a sub-

---

later, when rationing was in force, the 'shop' was a boon to mothers trying to clothe their growing boys and girls. One or two were still in existence in the late 1960s.

* Later pioneer work was generally sponsored by Charitable Trusts.

stantial sum for a three-year test of C.O.S. methods of enquiry into the needs of schoolchildren.* A generous member of the Society was Mr Allen D. Graham who financed the scheme he and Colonel Montefiore had proposed for helping sick children, which led to the foundation of the Invalid Children's Aid Association.† There was the enquiry into the likelihood of work in the industrial North for unemployed London men, when all expenses were paid by a C.O.S. Council member.‡ The furnishing of an office, the replacement of goods not covered by insurance after a burglary, the refunding of money stolen by a fraudulent agent, the offer of a rent-free building as headquarters for the Society (in this instance refused by Loch)§ were other examples of generous help by volunteers. As was customary in other charitable organisations, members regularly opened their homes or their gardens to groups of pensioners and others, where a tea-party was a feature of the occasion. Not many Associations could count on their members to guarantee the payment of 'a gentleman to assist the secretary' for some two years, as Deptford did in 1880, or to make good a deficit in the Society's accounts, as was done in Loch's early years as Secretary.‖

The early work of the Society for emigration gave considerable scope to volunteers, who spent both time and money in discovering suitable areas and in aiding the organisation of effective schemes. Long years of service given by distinguished specialists and others to the Medical and Convalescent Committee were amongst the most valuable contributions made by volunteers. In this field it is of interest to note the reference, in the Society's annual report for 1884, to 'the energy and devotion of the Honorary Secretary and of the lady secretary . . . who between them have visited nearly all the Homes to which patients are sent'. Considering there were some seventy convalescent homes, this was no mean achievement: in each case the best home to suit the needs of individual patients was carefully selected. In 1908 a member of Islington Committee opened a Cottage Convalescent Home to take six patients at a time. A widow, with her delicate child, was installed there as housekeeper.

From time to time we read of volunteers who took full responsibility while their colleagues went on holiday. In the first

* In 1875—£1,000 per year for three years.   † In 1886. See p. 101.
‡ See pp. 85–6.   § See p. 50.   ‖ See p. 50.

summer of the Society's history two of the Honorary Secretaries 'kept office' at 'Central' during the holiday months of August and September. It was a quiet period and one of the secretaries, Mr Alsager Hay Hill, who was to give valuable service, wrote a memorandum* which gave an excellent summary of the problems of the time and how he saw the needs of the future.† Such leisurely deputising was in great contrast to that of later years.‡

A major role for volunteers was claimed by Miss Norah Hill§[8] when, in 1919, she described the C.O.S. as 'mainly a stable centre of volunteers to serve on statutory bodies and to run welfare work'. This was in line with the current suggestion that, if the Society changed its name, a suitable title would be 'Society for the Organisation of Voluntary Assistance and the Encouragement of Social Service'.[9]

One of the services valuable to the Society, but often little noticed, was that of 'extended influence', as Mrs MacIver called it in 1932.‖[10] She drew attention to the important function of volunteers in keeping the name of the C.O.S. before the public. They not only kept alive interest in the Society, but also had considerable influence on subscriptions.

Weaknesses of the Voluntary System

If volunteers gave some valuable service to the Society there were also inherent weaknesses in the system. The C.O.S. was often in two minds on the question; when, for example, in 1879 it was proposed to appoint paid secretaries, there was considerable

---

* Work was slack during the holiday months and many District Offices closed down, e.g. in 1872 St Marylebone reported that the Office closed for three weeks during August, and the Committee adjourned for six weeks. The reason given was that there was an abundance of employment for the poor, and as the rich were away there were fewer professional beggars preying on them.

† Years later it was published under the title, *The C.O.S. in its Infancy*.

‡ For example, in one instance the Honorary Secretary took over, at a moment's notice, at a very busy period, when the salaried worker was taken ill: in another, during the Second World War, the worker left unexpectedly to go as sociological adviser to the A.T.S.[7] and the Honorary Secretary came to the rescue for two months until a new Secretary could be appointed.

§ Miss Hill gave some fifty years of valuable service, doing a great deal of voluntary work before she became one of the Society's paid Secretaries.

‖ Mrs MacIver was one of the experienced family social workers who gave long service to the Society, mostly before the psychological influence permeated casework.

opposition. However, Mr Alsager Hay Hill, himself a voluntary worker, won support as he argued, 'The Society had undertaken certain definite functions and that these could not be discharged if these offices, which ought to be armouries, were turned into toy-shops where men of leisure might find amusement.'[11] The C.O.S. was to raise the question of the voluntary worker repeatedly, in discussions at 'Central' and at Conferences, in District Reports and in their journal. A fair sample is taken from *The Training of Volunteers*[12] written in 1895:

> The training of volunteers must go very much further, if the Society's aims are to be accomplished . . . It is manifest that the comparatively small number of persons of leisure that are available can only form a nucleus of workers in large areas, often very far distant from their homes. They can but initiate changes, and extend that influence which as an educated class they ought to possess: and it must be admitted that among the ranks of volunteers are many who do not care to work seriously, of whose help a fair show may be made, but on whose regularity and conscientiousness little reliance can be placed. By degrees, therefore, the District Committees should become centres for interesting and training those men of ability and insight who, belonging to the trading and working classes and resident in the neighbourhood, ought, by reason of these qualities to have a chief place in the administration of local charity in many parts of London.

Unfortunately for the Society, able men 'of the trading and working classes', who were prepared to give of their scanty leisure, preferred to work for Trade Unions and Friendly Societies, or for their political organisations or, later, as Borough Councillors. There was considerable suspicion and dislike of the old C.O.S., and few from the working class or the lower-middle class could be persuaded to respond to the repeated efforts of the Society to recruit them. It was one of the weaknesses of the Society that its volunteers were drawn almost entirely from the upper-middle class, even though many did their best to enter sympathetically into the troubles and problems of families of whatever class.

A Southwark report put another point in 1900:

Training new workers is a recognised duty of the Secretaries, and they are glad to have so many fresh helpers—chiefly from the Women's University Settlement—who come with great regularity on their appointed day or days, and are always ready to be of use in every possible way; but it must be remembered that beginners are an anxiety rather than an assistance just at first, and too often leave us when they have become really useful volunteers.[13]

In the same year, Hampstead District, drawing attention to the success of the 'lady Secretary' in gathering round her an enthusiastic band of friends, also noted that:

it must be remembered that it is just those who join most actively with us who are oftenest called away either by other public interests or by home duties.[14]

Already the Central Council was concerned that:

the thought of the younger generation of the middle class is turned to new problems. In part, but only to a small extent, are its members active in poor law or in municipal work.*[15]

However, the Council took comfort from the fact that:

. . . the number of women who train themselves with a view to undertaking systematic charitable work in London and elsewhere, in connection with, or apart from the Society, has increased, so much so . . . that 'training' forms a large part of the daily business of the secretarial staff of several District Committees, especially St Olave's, Camberwell and Brixton. All of this represents a comparatively new departure. . . .[16]

The Society soon learned to select its recruits more carefully and to train them for the work in which they seemed most interested, and for which therefore, they were most suited.† Secretaries gave much time and thought to the task of deploying and 'briefing' their voluntary workers.

In a difficult area, where few local volunteers were available, when the District had to rely on helpers from outside, some of

---

* In the same year an enquiry showed that fifty-seven members of the C.O.S. were serving on L.C.C. Committees.

† A number of *Occasional Papers* and articles on training referred to the importance of discovering and keeping the interest of the volunteers.

whom travelled long distances, the Secretary could not often expect more than half a day's work from each. She had to use her ingenuity to find the appropriate job and to dovetail it with that of other part-time workers. In more fortunate areas, where volunteers were local residents, the Secretary had to plan carefully to keep some busy in an office with limited accommodation, while others went out visiting. It was common practice for several voluntary workers to share a table for letter-writing and recording. In one District, until the 1940s, where experienced volunteers shared in the casework, several interviews took place at the same time, in the same room, round the same large oval table. Privacy was possible only because the babel was sufficient to prevent over-hearing a neighbouring conversation. Lack of suitable and sufficient accommodation for responsible work was a very real weakness which affected the efficiency of the work, not only of the volunteers, but also of the professional family caseworkers.

An additional weakness in having to rely so heavily on voluntary workers was due to the 'holiday habits'*[17] of the class from which they came. Volunteers from the leisured class had been accustomed to taking long and fairly frequent holidays. This middle class pattern had probably influenced the Society in giving generous holidays to its salaried workers who were, after all, 'quasi-volunteers.† In the years between the two world wars, university students in Social Science Departments were often offered holiday jobs in the C.O.S. Districts. These partly-trained young workers had sometimes to take considerable responsibility while the Secretary was away. This, too, must be regarded as a weakness.

Perhaps one of the greatest difficulties in using volunteers was that of influencing them, even worse, of removing them, if their views became set. It is the obverse of the long-service pattern. C. S. Loch was himself aware of one aspect of this difficulty when he addressed the Council on the question in 1903:[18] 'Districts where indifferent work was done could only be dealt with slowly, as the group of people interested in them changed and opportunity for reform occurred.' In the 1930s and 1940s, some, at

---

* Some Committees felt so frustrated that they reported testily to the First Committee on Training, 1898, 'volunteers are away all the summer and ill all the winter'.

† The long holidays were certainly an attraction which offset, in part, the low salaries.

least, of the younger trained members saw the older volunteers
as barriers to change. It is possible that the increasing difficulty
in getting young volunteers, and the long service of those trained
in other ways, perpetuated older methods. Loch himself would no
doubt have been ready to change.* In 1919, Miss Edith Neville
had urged the Administrative Council 'to let the younger members
take on their full share in guiding the Society'. The Society must
get out of its groove.[19] Another view was expressed by Mr Woollcombe who reminded the meeting that when he joined the
Society† the responsible officers of *all Committees* were the
Honorary Secretaries; the change, in his view, had discouraged
volunteers.

But the pattern of social and economic life had changed. When,
in 1908, an appeal in *The Times* had launched the Personal
Service Association,‡[20] to meet the demands of a period of heavy
unemployment, there had been a very large response.§ As a result,
the C.O.S. and other organisations recruited many volunteers in
every District. After the 1914–18 war, far fewer volunteers
offered their services, and the results of special appeals were poor.
The C.O.S. gave considerable thought to the whole question,
discussing reasons, and suggesting remedies. They were particularly anxious that the promising system of Mutual Registration
should not suffer: before the war most of this very laborious work
had been done by volunteers. The Society lamented, in 1920,
'the war and its after effects have made the voluntary trained
worker almost non-existent'. The offer of the Young Conservatives in 1924 to do social work was considered but, although not
refused, was not too cordially welcomed. 'It must be made clear',
the Administrative Committee ruled, 'that such work was not
made a cloak for political propaganda.'

An appeal by the C.O.S. a few years later was more hopeful.

* Cf. Chapter 2.

† He had been Secretary of Battersea in 1887, and became Secretary to the
Council from 1919–23.

‡ The recruitment took shape under the leadership of the Hon. Mrs Alfred
Lyttleton as Chairman and Miss Violet Markham as Hon. Sec. Miss Markham,
writing her autobiography, many years later, gives the date of the formation of
the Personal Service Association as 1911: but C.O.S. 1908–09 Reports were
giving an account of the recruits who came to the various Districts.

§ Similarly, a special appeal in the year 1913–14 brought in some 10,500
names in three months. The C.O.S. reported that volunteers worked daily
from 10 a.m. to 6 or 7 p.m. to register them.

Sir Charles Mallet wrote to *The Times* on 24th October, 1928, putting forward the idea that 'men retiring from various services and avocations beyond the seas might find satisfactory scope for their activities in the work of this Society'. Fourteen replies to this letter were received. 'From among the number we are sanguine of securing several voluntary workers of first-class value.'

The Society had also to consider the financial aspects of the reduction in the voluntary force. An Honorary Secretary who worked full time with the help of other volunteers,* or two Honorary Secretaries who shared the work of a District Office, would save the salary of a professional worker.† It was also noted by the Society that the volunteers who gave regular help to a paid Secretary, sometimes for two or three days a week, considerably reduced the strain of her work. The C.O.S. was under no illusions about the very low salaries they paid their Secretaries. As they said in 1919,[21] referring to the 'devoted and efficient salaried secretaries', 'to the extent that the salaries the C.O.S. can afford to offer do not represent the full market value of the work done, and a C.O.S. Secretary makes sacrifices to the cause, (she) is in that sense *a volunteer*'.

In some cases, the new economic conditions had made it impossible for workers to dispense entirely with a salary. Some experienced voluntary workers later came on to the staff as salaried workers.‡ The Society was to find, in more than one instance, that these 'devoted and efficient Secretaries' were willing to go on half pay—nominally half-time—but in fact working as hard as before when a financial crisis threatened. In 1927–28 the paid Secretary of Chelsea District Office offered her services free of salary until times were more propitious; this was gratefully accepted. The weakness of this dependence on voluntary help,

---

* E.g. the *Holloway and N. Islington Report* of 1900 states 'Our Hon. Sec. acts entirely in an Honorary capacity and is at the office every day (Sundays excepted) seeing applicants in the mornings and carrying out the office work of the Society during the rest of the day. She is assisted by the daughters of a clergyman, and twelve other volunteer workers.'

† Chapter 15 for salary structure.

‡ E.g. Miss N. Hill and Miss O. Crosse. Some started as paid Secretaries, and then gave long service as volunteers, e.g. Miss Hugh-Smith, who served the Association in a variety of ways, both at 'Central' and in the Districts. She represented the F.W.A. on numerous Committees and was also known to be an excellent writer of reports. For some years she edited *Social Work*.

however it was interpreted, was apparent in the strain on workers.* Several broke down and had to take a long period of sick-leave. Until the Society was able to offer salaries 'at market value', and could cease to rely on a haphazard structure of uncertain voluntary help for the more responsible work, they could not expect to develop a forward policy to meet the changes in the economic and social life of the community. Already there were fewer leisured, moneyed, middle-class men and women available. Younger women were seeking training to equip themselves to earn an independent income. There was now a wider choice of posts open to them.

There were many who, a few years earlier, might have agreed that 'there must be a certain sacrifice of personal interest', or that 'they are doing the work of their desire in the help of those who suffer and are distressed. (This) . . . must be their compensation'.[22] There was a difference of opinion in the Society about whether 'the unwonted delights of earning money . . . might not unfairly be labelled selfishness',[23] or, whether 'there are a good many young men and women who feel that it is not right to be supported by their parents longer than is necessary'.[24] After the 1914–18 war thoughtful young people were themselves questioning many of the traditional attitudes of voluntary organisations. While continuing to gain useful experience in C.O.S. District Offices, many social science students were, indeed, looking to the State to provide basic social security for families in need. Other students who decided to take up family social work as a career continued to ask awkward questions, sometimes rousing the older workers to defend the past with burning zeal. In some Districts there was considerable resistance to any suggestion that the responsibility of lay members should be lessened.† There was a growing fear that 'professionalism' was encroaching. T. E. Lloyd, in discussing *Ideals of Social Service*, voiced this fear openly in 1930:

> With the increase in professionalism there is a tendency which has been fully developed in America, where, I understand,

---

* As a result of cuts in Council grants in 1921, many Districts cut back on staff, including the Agents, the Clerk, the Collecting Officer, etc., the extra work often being thrown on to the volunteers.

† Such opposition continued into the 1960s. The *Cunliffe Report* drew attention to the strong interest of volunteers in retaining control at every level of administration.

there is no longer any place in social service for those not professionally trained.

In a later address to Chairmen and Representatives of District Committees, Lloyd himself indicated a weakness of volunteers, connected with the class from which they were drawn:

> I have said once before that the C.O.S. is like a club; but it is a club which is sometimes apt to be a little exclusive, a little jealous of new members . . . there is far more than one would believe in the attraction of good fellowship.

There spoke the representative of the old school—the volunteers of the C. S. Loch and Pringle period. In 1932 the C.O.S. was still reporting: 'Apart from a nucleus of paid officers the Society depends upon unpaid service.'

On the whole, the F.W.A. was fortunate in having many volunteers and salaried social workers who respected one another, each valuing the other's contribution. In general, they worked well together, but here and there a volunteer of the 'old guard' could be obstructive on a committee. Until the early 1950s,* the 'Case Committee' was generally composed of lay members and representatives from other organisations in the District. Some of these were themselves trained social workers, but the majority, though experienced, were not professionally trained. The argument for keeping lay members on an F.W.A. Committee was often similar to that for having lay magistrates on the Bench: they brought a variety of mature experience to their task. They also gave considerable support to the social worker, and it was often helpful, as in 'The Dane Case'† to be able to say to a client, 'I will put this before my Committee'.

As new knowledge and professional training gave social workers greater assurance, they were ready to take greater responsibility. In some instances, the lay committee themselves felt that the time had come for all casework to be in charge of professional workers. Area I‡ was one of the first to experiment with the new District 'Case Conference'§ during the year 1953–54. It consisted entirely

---

* The Reorganisation Committee of the F.W.A. encouraged the setting up of internal staff 'case conferences' to replace the old case committees in 1953.

† See Appendix.   ‡ Hammersmith and Fulham.

§ The terms 'case conference' or 'case Committee' were interchangeable at first, but 'case Committee' was later adopted to describe the internal staff committee.

of professional workers. The experienced and very sympathetic voluntary members continued to take a close interest in casework policy. They heard reports from the case committees, kept abreast of developments, and were able to initiate or join in discussions on a variety of social questions.* They also formed a very valuable link between the community and family social work.

In two other Districts, the Society itself decided to reorganise the whole structure and to set up 'New Centres' as an experiment in the fully professional approach to casework practice. There was some resistance by the active lay committee in Area IV whose experienced social worker was to be sent to another District to make way for a younger, highly trained caseworker and her team of specially selected colleagues. However, the Society announced that it was not going to impose this policy on every District: the method was to be flexible, each District being left free to decide for itself to what extent lay committees should take a responsible part in case decisions. The experiment made a good start but some Districts, like Islington, decided that their Committees, consisting of widely experienced members of the community, still had much to give in helping to solve some of the difficult problems arising from casework. The Organising Secretary, herself a trained, experienced worker, valued the help they gave, not only in an advisory capacity, but in their activities on behalf of particular families.†

It was not until the 1960s, after the *Cunliffe Report*,‡ that the new policy was generally accepted. The lay area committees were to continue to be the link with the community: they served in an advisory capacity and could initiate discussions on questions of general interest. They were to be kept informed of developments in professional casework, but they were no longer to be personally involved. In the reshuffle which followed the reorganisation of the London boroughs, Islington was amalgamated with

---

* I am indebted to both Mrs Torr and Mrs Godfrey for much of this account.

† The Chairman, who, as the daughter of the former British Ambassador to France had lived in Paris, and travelled widely, was able to do most valuable work for refugees during and after the war. Her sympathetic approach and practical grasp of needs were matched by her ability to organise help from many quarters. Another member was a friend of a Q.C. whom she was able to interest in a number of cases where legal advice was essential. The Organising Secretary was Miss H. Morris.

‡ See Chapter 11.

Area IV and its lay committee was dispersed, not without bitterness. Although volunteers no longer took any part in casework as such, many were still welcomed as 'pension almoners'. Some volunteers kept up 'friendly visits' on their own account with individuals or families they had known for many years past, but such activities, in the nature of the case, were declining.

All Districts were able to keep together their representative Area Committees, 'to be their link with the community' and 'to advise on general questions'. Some for a while had volunteers to issue appeals and raise funds. Their Honorary Treasurer was still available, although for some years consolidated accounts were presented by the Central Council. Soon, however, fund-raising was largely centralised and Districts were relieved of much of this responsibility. The Central Council itself continued to have distinguished honorary officers as chairmen of the Association and of the several committees. For example, Lord Sandon, as Honorary Treasurer, guided the financial affairs of the Association for seventeen years; the Honorary Pensions Secretary, Miss Collins, and the Assistant Honorary Treasurer, the late Mr Blunden, long experienced as voluntary workers, gave regular help on the old scale. But it was a sign of the times that, in 1967, Mrs Godfrey, the Chairman of the Casework Advisory Committee,* who had had over twenty years' experience as a volunteer in responsible work both in the District and at 'Central' and in representing the Association on several important public committees, resigned so that this Advisory Committee could have a professional social worker as its Chairman.

Before going on to consider some of the reasons for the changing pattern of voluntary assistance, and to see what volunteers still have to offer, it is worth looking more closely at the contribution of some of those who helped to shape the Society's history. All in all, it is an impressive record since many of the Society's volunteers were also actively concerned with other forms of social service, many as Guardians, some as Councillors, most as representatives on the committees of other voluntary organisations; some were active in wider fields.

---

* Mrs M. Godfrey had been Chairman in Hammersmith before it amalgamated with Fulham, when she became Chairman of Area I. She was herself experienced in casework, but, while she supported the policy of professionalism, was confident of the continued need for the voluntary society.

Frederic David Mocatta (1828–1905) was one of the best known of the early supporters of the C.O.S. A great Anglo-Jewish banker and philanthropist, he combined a wide variety of interests in charitable enterprises of Jewish and non-Jewish origin. His staunch support of the C.O.S. had much in common with his outstanding work for the Jewish Board of Guardians. Each body put the organisation of charity high among its objects. Each made thorough investigation, adequate relief and business-like case-recording essential elements of their method. Mocatta not only gave generously of his time and money, serving on innumerable committees, but took a personal interest in individuals and their problems. It was said of him in a C.O.S. obituary:

> He considered the obligation of charity as a definite personal duty to be fulfilled with the care and solicitude that a friend would use towards a friend. He never spared himself: he would inquire and assist, and write and advise and take counsel in order that his help might be given to the best purpose . . . in the same spirit he discussed the general questions of charity and charitable administration . . . to him it seemed that any system of relief that led away from independence could not be right . . . many years week after week he came to the meetings of the Medical and Convalescent Sub-Committee and of the Council of the Society.[25]

He kept in close touch with Loch, sometimes arguing on problems of policy, sometimes challenging orthodox views, always concerned with basic questions of poverty. 'Things must not be allowed to remain as they are.' He suggested a measure of graded income tax; he contemplated State interference 'for the care of suffering'[26] and advocated a more aggressive intervention in public health questions, 'knowing that my (C.O.S.) friends, . . . think me a little unsafe and crotchety on these points.[27] Yet, like Loch, Mocatta could not shake off the economic theory and the social philosophy in which he had been nurtured. His attitude towards State pensions and 'other threats to family responsibility and individual self-respect', were those of the C.O.S. He was a product of the age, but one of the finest representatives of English philanthropy of the Victorian era.

Octavia Hill was the outstanding woman amongst the early

C.O.S. voluntary workers.[28] By the time Loch was appointed as a young secretary in 1875 Octavia Hill was thirty-seven years old, and already experienced in various forms of charitable work. Her most famous contribution was in the field of housing, as a result of which she had been invited to co-operate with Lord Shuttleworth on a Special Committee on Working Class Housing, leading to the Artisans Dwellings Act of 1875. She became a member of the first District Committee of the C.O.S. in 1869 (St Marylebone) and was a member of the Central Council from its foundation in 1869. Her friendship with Loch, and her many papers, prepared for meetings and conferences all over the country, made her one of the best known and most highly respected of the pioneers of the Society. Mary Richmond paid tribute to her influence on developments in North America. Loch wrote of her:

> She was to many as a light, a strong personality, a rare and beautiful character, moved by sympathy and guided by a very direct and discerning sagacity.

Remembering the times when he and his wife Sophie visited her, he added:

> How much was read in the days we spent with her. To read to her was delightful. Would that there were a chronicle of those days and talks, and of the stories she used to tell so amusingly and vividly . . . In telling these the sympathy, observation, humour, and originality which penetrated all her work came to life and told the tale.*[29]

There were a number of other women, less well known, who did valuable work of a lasting character. Such was Mrs Rose Dunn Gardner who, with her husband, worked for the Society in Lambeth and at 'Central' from the 1880s. She gave particular attention to the training of volunteers and read a very sensible paper on the question to the Central Council in 1894.†[30] The width of her interests made her a valuable counsellor. Amongst other things, she was a Justice of the Peace and a member of the After Care Committee for young prisoners from Wormwood Scrubs.

* This very short note on Octavia Hill bears no relation to her importance in the history of the Association. Her biographer, E. Moberly Bell, shows how much Octavia was stimulated by her connection with the C.O.S.

† See Chapter 12.

Miss Sophia Lonsdale, a contemporary of Mrs Dunn Gardner was another outstanding voluntary worker. Her early work was done as Honorary Secretary of the Lichfield Society, founded in the 1880s, a C.O.S. office affiliated to the London Charity Organisation Society. She was the daughter of Canon Lonsdale who was Chairman of the Committee. She proved to be a staunch and somewhat formidable exponent of C.O.S. principles. She, too, attached great importance to the training of volunteers, one of whom was to become one of the most valued of the London C.O.S. Secretaries.[*][31] As late as 1924, Miss Lonsdale was writing an *Occasional Paper* on the work of the C.O.S. which was in essence a recruiting pamphlet: 'You will not find our office a dull place' was most certainly true in her case.[32] After her father's death, Sophia Lonsdale came to London 'where she was at once placed on many of the most important committees'. Miss Lonsdale was said to have a sense of humour and a ready wit and to have a richly stored and cultivated mind, but when abuses had to be remedied and reforms taken in hand, no one could be sterner or more courageous in seeing the remedy through to a conclusion.

Some examples of Miss Lonsdale's practical achievements, in addition to the personal work for the Lichfield Society, are given below:

Firstly, as a Poor Law Guardian, she found that in one of the Poor Law Schools the children were unhappy and neglected. After persistent effort she revolutionised the whole school, under new staff. One of the reforms she introduced was to provide suitable attendants for the toddlers in a small house in the grounds, to replace the former practice of getting some of the inmates to look after the children in the workhouse; mothers in the workhouse could have access to their children, under happier conditions. In another workhouse she discovered an unsatisfactory master and matron who were falsifying the accounts, and saw that they were replaced. It was noted that she never spared herself, although she often had to visit outlying workhouses by slow and tedious train journeys: it was before the days of the motor car. Secondly, she reported to the Local Government Board the bad conditions of the drainage system and the sewers. The heavy cost

---

* Miss E. F. Bolton was herself the daughter of a Lichfield Vicar, and 'had first-hand knowledge of the troubles and problems of her father's parishioners when she was appointed as paid Secretary to the Lichfield Society'.

of the new system made her very unpopular with the ratepayers, but she was not deterred. Thirdly, she was responsible for the foundation of the High School for Girls which was much needed in the City of Lichfield. These by no means exhaust the list of good works carried through by this determined but much loved lady who was said by Mr Pringle to be

> remembered as one of the personalities which gave to the C.O.S. movement the quality of greatness, without which it would not have risen above the ranks of the useful.[33]

Miss Edith Neville's active life spanned more than half a century of voluntary work with the C.O.S./F.W.A. and other societies. Her response to the needs of her time was in direct line with the teaching of Loch: her casework reflected the principles and practice of the 'old guard' before 1920: her contribution to the 'the betterment of the condition of the poor' would have satisfied the high hopes of the pioneers, but it was also in accord with many of the demands being made today for better social and cultural provision within the community.

Edith Neville joined the C.O.S. South St Pancras Committee in 1900, serving it as Honorary Secretary until 1920, and later as Vice-Chairman. She remained a member of the District Committee until 1946, and was still its representative on the Central Council when she died in 1951. She had long been a valued member of the Central Administrative Committee. She had something in common with the redoubtable Miss Lonsdale, both in her very active work for the C.O.S. and in her involvement in social work in wider fields. It was said of her that 'her business-like and often alarming manner was known to intimidate students and committee members alike, but she was held in deep affection by those who really knew her and had learnt that the manner concealed a very deep concern for conditions in St Pancras'.[34] She was, apparently, far less alarming to applicants. She was also very successful in recruiting, before the First World War, a large number of volunteers who were then thoroughly trained.

As Honorary Secretary, she also welcomed other social workers in the District. For some years before the First World War regular meetings of St Pancras social workers were held in the C.O.S. Office to discuss local problems. Other work undertaken in this first decade in close co-operation with the C.O.S. was the

K

formation of the first Invalid Children's Aid Committee in the District, the promotion of a Skilled Employment Committee and the development of the new School Care Committee. She was the Chairman of the Group Care Committee, and later of the Local Association of Care Committees. It was she who impressed the Borough Council with the need for trained volunteers to undertake the visiting of infants. This was in 1905 before the establishment of statutory Maternity and Child Welfare Services. It was Edith Neville, too, who brought together volunteers for the first St Pancras Council of Social Service. She became its Honorary Secretary and, 'from that position, adventured in many different fields of social work'.[35]

The improvement of housing conditions was one of Miss Neville's greatest interests. She maintained that better housing policy would have been far more worthwhile than sanatorium treatment. She helped to found the St Pancras Housing Society,* as one of a group representing the Council of Social Service, the C.O.S., and Magdalen College Mission, under the inspiration of Father Jellicoe and his enthusiastic band of helpers. Miss Neville later became the Chairman of the St Pancras Housing Society, and it was said of her that she helped to balance the enthusiasm of its supporters by her firm belief in sound management. A row of Cottages for Old People in Somers Town has been named in her honour 'the Edith Neville Cottages'.

> At the outbreak of the First World War Miss Neville worked literally night and day for about six weeks with the South St Pancras S.S.A.F.A. at a time when Government provision for the wives and families of Reservists was non-existent.[36]

After the war, her thoughts turned to discharged servicemen and she combined work for S.S.H.S. and membership of the War Pensions Committee with her C.O.S. work till 1920.

She had become a member of the Council of the Mary Ward Settlement in 1915 and remained a member till her death. She was twice Honorary Warden and, during the Second World War, gave much personal help to the Citizens Advice Bureau there. As Norah Hill recalled, it was while Miss Neville was Warden that she gathered together the

* It was known originally as the St Pancras House Improvement Society.

remarkable band of amateur actors who, first in the Settlement theatre, and then in Somers Town, delighted St Pancras
audiences for years with thirty different plays annually, at
entrance fees no higher than cinema charges. The Second
World War and incendiary bombs closed and destroyed the
St Pancras Peoples' theatre, of which Edith Neville had been
first Honorary Secretary and then Honorary Director, but
Miss Neville kept in touch with her company and they played
together occasionally after the war. Her strong belief in the
cultural value of good drama was equalled by her belief in that
of pictures and sculpture. For years she has taken groups of
people round our permanent collections, loan exhibitions or
to the Academy, helping them to understand how to look at
objects of art. In recent years she had been working with
a Committee she brought together to develop this idea and
extend it to include famous buildings.[37]

In her desire to bring beauty into drab surroundings Edith
Neville turned to small as well as large ventures, such as the
encouragement of window-boxes and children's gardens. She also
helped to found, in 1923, the Restaurant Public Houses Association, and, later, became its Chairman.

Those who knew Miss Neville paid her the great tribute that
she never allowed her wider interests to detract from her very
personal concern with the troubles and problems of individuals.
She continued to receive letters from old C.O.S. 'clients', one of
whom, shortly before Edith Neville's death, enclosed a gift of
money to help others as he had been helped some twenty years
earlier. Miss Neville, in her earlier days, contributed articles,
some of which were published by the C.O.S. as *Occasional
Papers;* e.g. in 1911, *The Assistance of Schoolchildren,*[38] and in
1916, *Some Suggestions for the Care of Widows and Their Children.*[39]

The life and work of Edith Neville illustrate the reciprocal
nature of voluntary work. Volunteers gained their experience of
personal work with the Society, gave of this knowledge in wider
fields of public service, and, in turn, brought back much of value
to the Society.

Miss Winifred Locket was, in many ways, a contrast to Miss
Lonsdale and Miss Neville. She is nearer to our own time,
though her long life of service overlapped with theirs. When notice

of her death was being prepared in January, 1967, by a social
worker who had known her well, it was with astonishment that it
was discovered that she had gone as a volunteer to Lewisham as
far back as 1902. She was still visiting 'her pensioners' in 1960.
Her vigour and *joie de vivre* made her chronological age seem
irrelevant. Within a year of going to Lewisham, Miss Locket was
its Honorary Secretary, carrying considerable responsibility for
family social work in the District. She lived for many years at the
Lady Margaret Hall Settlement when she moved on to work in
North Lambeth. She never lost her deep affection for the Lambeth
citizens whom she always regarded as her friends, keeping in
touch with many of them long after she had left the Borough.

In 1927 she moved, unwillingly at first,* back to Lewisham, at
the urgent request of C.O.S. Central who felt they needed an
experienced worker to help families on the great new housing
estates of Downham and Bellingham. Miss Locket understood at
once how much the tenants missed the neighbourliness of the
homes they had had to leave under slum clearance schemes. She
co-operated wholeheartedly with the London County Council in
the provision of community services, and was said to have been
the inspiration behind the Centre activities. She thought nothing
of attending Community Centre and other meetings on two or
three evenings a week after spending all day at the District Office.

In 1928, she returned to Lambeth to help organise the Relief
Fund for families flooded out when the Thames overflowed its
banks. Then she was back at Lewisham, immersed once more in
the personal work with the families for whom she had so great
an affection.

Miss Locket was never one of the orderly and business-like
volunteers so highly prized by the pioneers: her case papers had
often to be searched for—but this weakness was recognised by her
colleagues, and willingly dealt with, for she was one of the most
welcome of the Honorary Secretaries who served the Family
Welfare Association. As one of her younger colleagues said,
recently, 'Her sense of humour and her loving-kindness made it
great fun to work with her'. Another recalled: 'She could be

* Her first reaction was: 'Nothing would persuade me to go.' She seems to
have combined work for the two Districts as she did not resign finally from
Lambeth until 1932, when she was elected a Vice-Chairman. She also, at
various times, acted as Hon. Sec. in both East and West Lewisham.

critical, and show indignation, but it was a kind, righteous indignation, balanced by her care to praise good work'. For Miss Locket was a good teacher. She delighted to take newcomers on a 'whistle-stop' tour of the neighbourhood in her dilapidated car, to meet some of her families and to get a general idea of the area.* The spontaneous welcome she received reflected her own warm-heartedness.

During Miss Locket's long life of service as Honorary Secretary, she represented her District on the Central Council and was an outspoken member of a number of their Committees. She was also much in demand as a speaker, not only in London, but in many provincial towns where there were 'kindred societies'. Miss Locket wrote from time to time in the Society's journals. One of the most interesting articles gave the point of view of 'the client' who wrote to Miss Locket in 1925 about his problem 'which she helped him to solve.' Her comment, in 1949, showed her true humility as she reflected on 'the terrifying responsibility of handling other people's lives'.†

It was not only the Family Welfare Association who recognised the quality of Winifred Locket. During the Second World War, when a Lewisham school received a direct hit and many children were killed, the Mayor asked her to comfort and help their parents and surviving children, many of whom were injured. The friends made at this time were writing to her a generation later. It was long remembered that, though nearly seventy years of age, Miss Locket was one of the fire-watchers on the roof of Southwark Cathedral, after she had spent the day in her District looking after 'bombed out' people. In 1957, Miss Locket was awarded the M.B.E. for services to Lewisham.

Miss Katharine Lawrance was born in November 1863 and died in September 1954.[40] A great part of her long life was given to voluntary work for the C.O.S./F.W.A. She was noted in her own day for 'her devotion to casework', for her readiness to go

---

* I am particularly indebted to Miss Luce for her reminiscences, and I have incorporated some of her phrases used in a short paper, which she read to the F.W.A. Council. Miss Morris and Miss Renall have also given me first-hand information. I am glad, too, to be able to write from personal experience since, as tutor to some of the students in Miss Lockett's District, I met her from time to time, and was once taken on just such a 'whistle-stop' tour.

† I referred to this in Chapter 13 as it also belongs to the account of the development of casework.

'on loan' to other Committees during holidays, or to fill a gap caused by illness, and for her great interest in the well-being of her professional colleagues. It was said to be largely due to her efforts that the staff owed the improvement in the conditions of service and of salary. When we read her statement on 'the importance of good casework',[41] made as long ago as 1912, we find a sympathic and perceptive approach by one still convinced of the soundness of the method accepted at that time, but critical of those who thought of a family in need of help as 'a case'. Miss Lawrance thought it an important part of her duty as Honorary Secretary to take a close interest in other social work in the District, and she represented the Society on many outside bodies. She was also an active member of various Central Committees, and Chairman of the old Districts Sub-Committee. When she died, at the age of ninety-one, her biographer wrote:

> Daughter of a Judge of the High Court, Katharine Lawrance brought a fine mind, a great sense of justice and a humility of spirit to bear on everything she did.

The Family Welfare Association was indeed fortunate in recruiting a great many volunteers who devoted their considerable gifts to family social service. A study of the Society through its 100 years of development shows that the above examples of service were not isolated cases. Until the 1960s, every District annual report had references to the variety of work done by its experienced volunteers. Not all were as widely known as the Edith Nevilles or the Winifred Lockets, but they were much valued in their own Districts. Some of them preferred to remain unknown except to the regular workers at the District Office. They were 'the unobtrusive workers' so much admired by Octavia Hill.[42] There were, for example, the two Misses Barber, Ann and Margaret, who were glad to do much of the routine work at Islington District Office but had no wish to be nominated for membership of the Central Committees. The following notes provided by the Islington District family social worker,[43] who knew them for a great many years and valued their help very highly, will give some idea of the extent of such voluntary service.

Margaret Barber became a member of the Holloway Executive Committee in 1900, Honorary Secretary in 1907 and Honorary Pensions Secretary from 1909 until her death during the year

1945–46. She had been a regular member of the Islington Committee, and went to the office every morning to write individual appeals for funds to help particular families, and to provide pensions for the old and sick. It was due to her efforts that a friend left the residue of his estate to the Islington Committee, to be used for pensions.

Ann Barber became an associate member of the Holloway Committee in 1900, Assistant Honorary Treasurer in 1905 and Honorary Registrar in 1910. She also came to the office regularly every morning, and was Assistant Honorary Treasurer until she resigned in 1961. She preferred not to attend Committee meetings except once a year when the finances were considered. Both sisters had strong personalities and decided views on the function of the C.O.S. They were devoted to the work in Islington, and lived in the Borough for many years.

The opportunity to recruit volunteers varied considerably from District to District. Some, like parts of the East End of London, had few middle-class leisured residents and had to rely on the goodwill of those who were prepared to travel to give regular part-time help. If the Districts were lucky enough to be within reach of a settlement such as Toynbee Hall,* they could generally rely on the residents to give regular personal service. The Settlements usually sent a representative to the local C.O.S. Committee; sometimes the Warden became Chairman or Vice-Chairman. Some Districts, like Hammersmith, Chelsea and Fulham, were fortunately placed to attract voluntary workers (such as Miss Duff)† who lived in the area. In 1946–47, the Chelsea and Fulham Report described 'the quite irreplaceable loss in the death at the age of eighty-eight of Mr Frank Weber who had been connected with Fulham since 1911, and its Chairman since 1919', He never missed a Committee if he could avoid it, and took the

* Some thirty residential settlements were founded in many of the poorer Districts of London in the following years and many workers there found useful experience and opportunities for service with the Society. As Poplar reported in 1895, 'New life has been infused into our work'.

† Miss A. Duff had a very long record of service: it was said of her in the 1950s 'in addition to all her other work (she) has written endless telling appeals for Chelsea and Fulham. She still takes a keen interest in the Society although no longer able to play an active part'. See the article signed 'A.D.' in *Area I Annual Report*, 1956, where there is an interesting comparison with 'forty years ago' in Fulham. She continued into the 1960s as Chairman of the Grants Committee.

Chair for the last time only three weeks before he died. He was said to have given most wise and sympathetic attention to every case, and understanding support to the staff. In fact 'throughout the Society Mr Weber was accepted as the "star" Chairman, and less experienced officers came to see how the job ought to be done'.[44] This area, like Islington, had two sisters, the Misses Cree,* who gave regular and efficient help as Honorary Secretary, and as Pensions Secretary respectively, and in several other spheres such as the organisation of the Free Legal Advice Centre. They were, also, both almoners for the Society for the Relief of Distress.

Such examples of help from several members of a family, sisters, or husband and wife, were features of voluntary work in several Districts.† There were instances where a salaried worker married one of the voluntary workers and then served in a voluntary capacity. One of the most famous in the history of the Society was that of Miss Helen Dendy, a District Secretary in Shoreditch before she married Professor Bosanquet. Helen Dendy had taken a 1st Class in the Moral Tripos at Cambridge, specialising in Political Economy. She did some lecturing at Oxford and then decided to do social work. After a period of C.O.S. training in South London she was appointed to the Shoreditch District in 1890. She became an active member, with Loch, of the Royal Commission on the Poor Laws. She wrote many papers,‡[45] and articles for C.O.S. journals, and edited the *Charity Organisation Review* from 1909–21. But she is best known for her books on economic and social questions and for her early history of the Society under the title *Social Work in London*. E. P. Price, who wrote her obituary notice,[46] remembered her best for her tolerance, quoting her statement: 'Is it not safe to assume that in far the greater number of cases opinions from which we differ require interpretation rather than refutation?'

Dr Bernard Bosanquet,[47] the Idealist Philosopher, had been a friend of C. S. Loch at Balliol, and was his close neighbour at Oxshott. He took an active part in social work in Chelsea and Shoreditch, and served on the C.O.S. District Committees there

* Miss E. W. Cree and Miss A. M. Cree who served during, and after, the Second World War.

† E.g. the two Misses Humphrey of the Holborn, Finsbury and City District, whose membership 'went back to the early days'. They retired in 1930.

‡ She had read a paper at the first meeting of the Charity Organisation Conference in 1893, on *Thorough Charity*.

for thirteen years. He was a member of the C.O.S. Administrative Committee for eighteen years and its Chairman from 1896–97. He was closely associated with the School of Sociology. From 1898 until his death he was an additional member of Council, becoming Vice-Chairman from 1901–15, and Chairman from 1916–17, resigning on account of ill-health. Professor Bosanquet was always ready to champion the Society, contributing a number of letters to the Press, etc.*[48]

Less famous, but very good friends to Islington District were Mr and Mrs Blyth. Miss Percival was the first paid Secretary of Islington in the mid-1880s, when she married Mr Blyth, a member of the Committee. Mr Blyth seved in various Honorary offices, for most of the time as Chairman, for some forty years. He had a wide range of interests, especially in connection with the Whitechapel Gallery. Mrs Blyth, who survived her husband by a few years, had been noted for her special interest in housing and thrift.[49]

The period between the two world wars saw the end of the years of service of many who had worked during the C. S. Loch era. Obituary notices and notices of resignations in the *C.O.S. Reports* of the 1920s and 1930s pay tribute not only to the many tasks undertaken, regularly, over a long period, but to the personal qualities of the voluntary workers. It is evident that many volunteers enjoyed their work and that others enjoyed working with them. To take some examples from the year 1925:

Miss Catherine Davies, whose 'in memoriam' notice appears in the *C.O.S. Annual Report* for that year, had been a friend of Sir Charles Loch and joined the South Lambeth Committee in the mid-1880s.

> She took a leading part in our work for the next 30 years as Hon. Sec. and gave, by her personal influence, a friendly tone to our discussions, which made our meetings quite a pleasure.†

It was noted that she had 'by her tact' maintained very good relations with the local authorities, etc. Other personal qualities referred to were her wise counsels, and considerate treatment of

---

* E.g. 'A necessary Social Function'. He claimed that the C.O.S. 'stands now as the no-class representative of trained neighbourly assistance and wise and efficiently organised administration'.

† The personal tribute was paid by a former Chairman of South Lambeth, Mr Gurney Salter.

K*

applicants. She seems to have been able to combine both 'zeal and self-denying activities'.

There was also the Reverend C. H. Chard,[50] whose connection with the Whitechapel Committees had stretched back for more than half a century. He was Vice-Chairman when he died. It was reported of him that

> his active help was always at our disposal . . . of his personal kindness and devotion to East London it would be pre-sumptuous to speak.

His generous financial help was also noted.

Mentioned in the same year was Mr Crowder, the Honorary Secretary of the Stepney and Mile End with St George's-in-the-East Committee, who

> throughout his long lifetime gave himself with devotion and self-sacrifice not only to the service of the Society, but to that of the entire District.

Among the various practical activities to his credit were the erection of public washing houses, and the conversion of the St George's-in-the-East graveyard into a public garden (mentioned earlier). Mr Foulger of the same District was also remembered with gratitude for his work for the welfare of sailors, in which he was especially interested.

Hampstead reported the death of its 'brilliant, lovable and beloved Chairman of the Executive Committee',[51] Mr Harold Spender, who was also renowned for his literary and political work (he had recently been honoured by the University of Athens as Doctor of Laws), and for his keen interest in the welfare of Londoners who went annually to the hop fields in Kent: he and others had been concerned to secure improvements in the scandalous accommodation available at that time. Hampstead also regretted the loss of Dr Henry Rayner, who had been for many years Chairman of the Infant Welfare Committee,

> and for many more our helper and adviser in those medical matters in which he was an acknowledged expert.

In 1925, too, the C.O.S. reported the loss of Sir William Acworth, the railway expert, for many years Chairman of the

Camberwell Committee, and of the Central Administrative Committee.

> He had served on many boards and committees and acquired a knowledge and experience of local administration which found expression in letters and articles published in *The Times* and other journals.[52]

Another distinguished member, Sir Athelstan Bains, joined the Paddington Committee after his retirement from a career in public service in India. He became Chairman of the Committee and retained his interest in the Society and its work after his retirement from London.

Continuing with the year 1925, the *Annual Report* also included the notice of Colonel M. Slater 'whose benign disposition made him equally valuable and welcome'. His special interest had been in the well-being of ex-servicemen and their dependants. His work for the C.O.S. after his retirement from active service had been connected with the South Lambeth Committee and with the Associated Societies Committee.

Finally, for that same year, 1925, the C.O.S. reported the death of Dr Burge, Bishop of Oxford, a Vice-President of the Society:

> ... it was during his tenure of office as the Bishop of Southwark that we reaped the greatest benefit from his friendship. When in charge of that Diocese he was equally ready to take a hand in promoting the plans of our Committee and officers, and to call them into counsel in furthering his own.

The year 1925 has been taken as a sample of the value the Society placed on the service of its volunteers. A study was made of a series of such notices in the *Annual Reports*, at five-yearly intervals between the 1870s and 1960s. This gave a comprehensive picture of the many kinds of help, of the special knowledge and experience brought to the Society by its volunteers, and of their wide interests in other charitable activities. It also showed the contrast between the emphasis on voluntary help in the earlier periods and the gradual diminution in the number and quality of 'the notices' in the reports of the 1950s and 1960s.*

* It is significant that when Winifred Locket died in 1967, after some sixty years of outstanding service as a volunteer, there was not even a mention, let alone an obituary notice, in the following F.W.A. *Annual Report* or issues of *Social Work*.

After the Second World War the total number of volunteers declined, their strength varying from District to District. Some family caseworkers continued to welcome the mature public-spirited men and women who could be relied on to give a variety of personal service. Others, anxious to promote a professional casework service, found it difficult to combine this with the use of volunteers, however experienced. The Areas had their voluntary committees, but many of the members were professional social workers; others represented the local authorities. A few only were 'lay members'; an honorary appeals organiser was always welcome; so were the volunteers who visited F.W.A. pensioners. (They seldom distributed pensions, as did the 'almoners' of the past, since pensions were now often sent by post.) By the mid-1960s the old pattern of voluntary help had been drastically changed. Direct personal help to people in distress was in the hands of the professional workers.

Had the diminution in the number of volunteers giving personal help to families come about, as Lloyd suggested in 1930, because they were discouraged by the growth of professionalism? Was it true that, as the Association was asked to take an increasing number of trainees from Social Science Departments and from other organisations, the family social workers found it more difficult to spare time for the supervision of volunteers? Did they even prefer the students, with their greater theoretical knowledge? Was this preference influenced by the fact that, as one university lecturer put it:

> It is . . . obviously easier for professional social workers to manage and impress young students in training than to cope with older volunteers of determined views and independent resources.

In fairness to the Association it must be added that great pressure was put upon it to accept students for practical work as Social Science Departments expanded and new courses were started in other Institutions. As students from the 'Applied Social Studies' courses came along, there is no doubt that their training and experience often made them welcome in a busy office.

As the middle-aged and elderly volunteers departed, there were fewer to take their place. The middle-class young woman has her career. When she marries and has a family, she often looks to the possibility of taking up professional work again when her children are older. The demand for qualified family social workers has intensified. There are also fewer men and women of leisure on the old middle-class pattern, who, with ample domestic help, were free to devote what time they wished to voluntary work.

But is there, after all, something in Lloyd's prophecy of the 1930s? In 1950, one District reported:

> Now the class line no longer exists, the attitude of the philanthropic Lady Bountiful, which Octavia Hill was even then combating (1869), has given way entirely to the trained social workers using their specialist skills to enable families and individuals to overcome their difficulties.[53]

Has professionalism driven out amateurism in family social work in this country, as was said to be true a generation ago in America?

In this connection it is important to be rid of the too glib description of the volunteer as 'the frustrated spinster' or the 'maiden aunt' or as 'someone with a guilt complex', or, most contemptuous of all, as 'the do-gooder'. Even here Helen Bosanquet, while recognising the dangers, had something positive to say which had more insight than many of the facile dismissals heard today:

> Perhaps the lesson which of all others we are most slow to learn is that in order to do well it is not enough to mean well. . . . Nowhere is this discrepancy so grave as when we come to take up charitable work, to 'do good' as it is so often mis-called. . . . it is comparatively seldom that we find anyone who can give an account of the good he wishes to do, and can show in what way he proposes to bring it about.
>
> . . . by thorough charity, . . . we mean charity that is *thoroughly thought out;* we want people to work with their eyes open, to know, so far as it is given to men to know, what the results of their action will be. . . .

If some modern writers 'cannot love a philanthropist',* there is no doubt that many philanthropists knew how to love their neighbours. They may not all, by any means, have lived up to the

---

* E.g. D. Macrae, cf. Chapter 2. But, as Loch said, 'It is consoling to find how similarly good people act who hold different views'. (*Diary:* 12th September 1877.)

principle accepted by the Society in 1870, that a visitor must have permission to call, since the poor had rights as friends. But the Society set a high standard, and courtesy and respect are always essential requirements in a family social worker, whether she be a professional caseworker or a volunteer.

How can we reconcile this with the charge of 'arrogance' which was so often levelled against C.O.S. workers in the past? An example given by Owen in *English Philanthropy* may in part, though not wholly, explain this. He quotes Henrietta Barnett who recalls the Hill 'At Homes' for old tenants who 'entered shyly by the back door', and uses this as an example of the 'patron-client' relationship, with its arrogant assumption that 'the superior virtue of the rich entitled them to regulate the lives of the poor'. There is sufficient truth in this to make it a plausible deduction, and it might well have been applied to many workers in the Society. Yet no one considering the work of Octavia Hill as a whole, and reading some of her writings, already quoted, can doubt her genuine concern and friendship for each family, and each individual. The 'shy entrance' at the back door was certainly customary behaviour in England at that period; it was expected by the old tenants themselves and was probably less embarrassing for them than entry at the front. Henrietta Barnett's experience of a vicarage in Whitechapel or our own experience of a more democratic society cannot be applied without imagination to nineteenth century class relationships.

The C.O.S. made conscious efforts to bridge the gulf between the middle class, from which the majority of volunteers were drawn, and the working class, from whom came the majority of the applicants for help. This was often unsuccessful, and their failures were sometimes bitterly publicised. The charges of arrogance lessened as the class structure weakened. In the period between the wars, changed conditions made for better communication; when Barbara Wootton revived the charge in recent years professional family social workers were highly indignant. Some of the younger workers themselves had a working class background. Many of the local authority representatives on F.W.A. area committees were working people.

With greater knowledge has come a higher expectation of skilled work in all branches of social work. The increase in the statutory social services has reinforced the desire for high standards of personal service. The need to 'individualise the social services', so strongly urged by the Association throughout its history and vigorously acted upon by its volunteers, is now generally accepted by public bodies. The resulting demand for the trained, full-time social worker considerably outstrips supply. Re-deployment of skilled workers to fill supervisory posts, to advise and train others with less experience, or less skill, is now recognised as one of the chief needs. It may be that insufficient thought has been given in the recent past by the voluntary organisations, including the F.W.A., to the possibility of attracting, once more, responsible voluntary part-time workers, who are prepared to give regular, dependable personal service. Or, more might be done to use the occasional volunteer, who is ready to be called upon as need arises, for a special visit, or to accompany someone to a dreaded hospital consultation, or to do some extra work in the office. Kensington, in the past, had a list of such 'occasional' volunteers, known as 'Associates'.[54] Sometimes the F.W.A. successfully co-operated with other voluntary organisations for occasional help, for example, from Red Cross workers who would visit sick and aged persons.[55]

Social workers, in the past, were well aware that it required care and patience for the effective use of volunteers, but it often brought rich rewards, not only to the families in need, but to the volunteers and to the family social workers themselves. Now that 'community care', whether of the elderly, the physically handicapped, the socially isolated, or the mentally disturbed, is officially recognised, there is need for the encouragement of volunteers, who can be helped to give the kind of personal service which is most appropriate in each case.* Several such cases were reported from Islington in the early 1960s, when eviction was averted at the last moment. The kind of help given might often be no more than straightforward, neighbourly service, but it might also lead to more constructive, permanent results when the need for skilled help was recognised. Volunteers and professional social workers could have valuable complementary roles.

It is often difficult to sustain the interest of volunteers in purely

---

* The voluntary worker in the not-so-distant past who offered to collect week by week the rent of the family threatened with eviction because the mother had been unable to save from wages which were paid fortnightly, spared the family much misery, and the community considerable expense.

administrative office work, though some have a flair for this. More
are ready to do the less spectacular, routine jobs if some thought
is given to showing the link between such work and the welfare of
the individuals concerned. The F.W.A. in the past put great
emphasis on the value of these personal links.* Now that much of
the administration in the F.W.A. has been modernised and
centralised, there is not scope for the same variety of voluntary
help in the areas. But volunteers may be found useful in this
sphere, too, to supplement the efforts of the salaried staff, if they
can offer efficient help, especially if they can be called upon in
time of crisis.

As we have seen, the Association continued to rely on volunteers
for its strong Central committees; many members took an active
part, especially the chairmen, honorary secretaries and honorary
treasurers.† (We find among the ordinary members many who
served on various committees over a long period.)

The F.W.A. has always required its volunteers to equip themselves for intelligent service. This policy was maintained when
Citizens Advice Bureaux were set up.‡ Although a trained
salaried worker is in charge of each C.A.B. run by the F.W.A.,
some voluntary workers are still welcomed to help advise on the
many problems brought to the Bureaux. Volunteers must be
trained and carefully briefed and must be prepared to find their
way amongst the intricacies of Local and Central Government
regulations. But they must also have many qualities of the older
volunteers; sympathy and understanding, together with some
insight into whether or not further help might be needed and
where it might best be found, are still essential qualities in personal
service of this kind.

The present generation has learned how important are good
relations between the statutory and voluntary bodies. It was also
well known to their predecessors in the F.W.A., who counted this
a necessary part of 'charity organisation'. Volunteers contributed
greatly to such understanding as they combined service to the

---

* E.g. its laborious efforts to raise funds for the cost of helping each family
were consciously made in order to keep the personal link between the giver
and the receiver.

† Reference is made in relevant sections to some of the long-service volunteers active at 'Central'. The selection of particular periods for illustration has
meant the exclusion by name of many other outstanding voluntary workers.'

‡ See Chapter 10(1).

Association with a vigorous part in public life. Family social workers today are more aware of the role of administrators in the complex structure of voluntary and statutory social services. Now that statutory authorities as well as voluntary associations employ professional social workers, the bridges between statutory and voluntary organisations are likely to be strengthened. Will this be equally true of the professional workers and the volunteers? As the *Cunliffe Report* suggested, 'it is an interesting challenge to determine whether professional use can be made of a non-professional worker'.[56] Cunliffe, in spite of certain reservations, had no doubt that the F.W.A. still needed voluntary workers since:

(1) there are families on the caseload of every Area which could benefit from the interest, resources and skills which some volunteers can offer; and, (2) the Association needs the enthusiasm and support which adequately prepared volunteers can give to the whole organisation.

The F.W.A. maintains its status as a voluntary society, although it receives an increasing proportion of its funds from statutory sources. It still relies largely on voluntary direction of policy, although it has a strong team of professional advisers. There is a valuable tradition in the F.W.A.* of the co-operation of the professional and the layman in the service of the community.†[57] The Association has also shown that careful selection applies both to volunteers and to professionals. 'We can individualise treatment, provided we can get the right individuals to act as the agents.'[58] Both volunteers and professionals need preparation for their particular role. It remains to be seen whether the consultant and the principal family social workers are sufficiently convinced of the responsible contribution which might be made by the volunteers to be willing to replan their timetable to include supervision and consultation for the voluntary workers as well as for the students and the junior professional caseworkers. Cunliffe's ideas on this question are worth further consideration.‡[59]

* It was not always appreciated that the F.W.A., though a voluntary society, had employed an increasing number of trained, salaried workers, from the 1880s onwards.

† Cf. article by The Lady Norman: *The Lay Committees and the Professional Worker*.

‡ A comparison with the ideas set out more than three quarters of a century ago (*What Workers can do for the Poor in Connection with the C.O.S* —C.O.S. *Annual Report*, 1885), gives a telling illustration of change and persistence.

CHAPTER FIFTEEN

Finance

For a Society which was soon to become known for its strict and business-like methods and for its keen detection of fraudulent practices in charitable organisations, its own unfortunate financial beginnings come as something of a shock. During the first few months, when the nature and objects of the proposed new society were being hammered out, two successive assistant secretaries misappropriated the funds; the first quarrelled with the Honorary Secretary and refused to hand over the subscriptions or to give up the Society's books and papers; the second drew cheques for £40, as well as keeping for his own use £4 in subscriptions and £4 advanced by one of the founder-members.* The first meeting of the Executive Council of the new Society on 22nd April, 1869, was, in fact, concerned solely with a review of the financial situation in the period since 1st March when Mr H. Solly had resigned as Secretary. 'Up to the 1st March', we learn, 'so far as the Committee are able to judge, a due check was kept upon the accounts, and the receipts and expenditure nearly balance' [*sic*].[1] Since then 'a lax system seems to have prevailed'. After discussing the misappropriation of funds they conclude that 'no responsible person seems to have been nominated to supervise the expenditure', nor were vouchers produced. At a second meeting, three days later, it was resolved to request General Cavanagh to become Honorary Treasurer. A strict watch was, thereafter, kept on accounts, with Honorary Treasurers playing an important part at District and 'Central' level. This continued throughout the history of the Association.

Expenses were incurred in the preliminary planning months and during the first year of the Society's establishment, without any firm source of income. An early subscribers' list shows a total

* It was noted that after his six weeks' salary was deducted, the Society stood defrauded of £42. This would leave £1 a week as his salary.

of £154 2s. 0d., of which Ruskin had contributed two-thirds. The Society evidently ran into difficulties, for we find Ruskin again coming to the rescue with a gift of £100 in January, 1869.*2 In the autumn of the same year Hicks, one of the Honorary Secretaries, offered an advance of £20 'to enable the business of the Society to be carried on'. At Michaelmas, Lord Lichfield made a special donation of £20 for rent.

Lord Lichfield had already guaranteed the rent of the Central Office for the first year, and he seems to have been called upon to pay. The Marquess of Westminster now took the 'guarantor' idea further; in June, 1870, he called a meeting of wealthy landowners and established a 'Guarantee Fund'. Amounts drawn in the next four years were £800, £1,000, £1,000 and £559 15s. 11d. Gradually a 'Donors and Subscribers' list† was built up, the total rising from £659 in 1870, £900 in 1871, £1,653 in 1872 to £3,153 in 1874.

In Loch's early years the financial position of the Society still caused anxiety. We find him suggesting, for example, that Council members might be asked to contribute to a fund to which he himself would also subscribe.

In its first year it is clear that the Society had not come anywhere near financial stability and its accounts were amateurish. By the end of 1869, it was reviewing its financial position. A sub-committee reported in December that the estimated 'fixed income' from regular subscriptions might be put at £100 per annum. There was a bank balance of £180. Present expenses, they reported, reached £395—rent £80, assistant secretary £140, clerk £52, boy £13, office £110. The sub-committee set its sights higher: 'The expenses really necessary in order to [secure] the efficient carrying out of the work may be estimated as follows: rent £80; secretary £250; clerk £100; boy £26; query office expenses £150; query £95; total £701.'3 The upgrading of the secretary is worth noting since the sub-committee was recommending that Ribton-Turner should be appointed as a salaried organising secretary. His work so far had been on an honorary basis. In fact, the expenses in 1870 reached £1,665; by 1874

* Its acceptance was debated, but eventually it was resolved that it was 'not to be entirely devoted to liquidation of arrears but only a proportion'.

† Provisional Rules of 10th June, 1869, had provided that any subscriber of not less than £1 1s 0d. would be a member of the Society.

they had risen to £3,653 with salaries, £975, as the largest item.

Considerable hesitation was expressed about making a public appeal, for a variety of reasons, chiefly that the Society had stressed that it was not another relief society. The Districts, meanwhile, were raising their own funds to meet administrative expenses. Any money given to individual applicants must be raised 'case by case' by direct appeal 'from person to person', or, in special circumstances, through the use of 'The Golden Book'.* The Society continued to stress throughout its history that its Districts had no relief funds of their own: they only channelled existing resources, each committee acting as a clearing house for other charitable organisations or individuals.

The wealthy Districts, like St George's, Hanover Square,† had no difficulty in getting funds to set up their District offices. Others in the poorer areas could not hope to raise sufficient to cover expenses. Consequently the Society soon decided that if offices were to be established in the Districts where they were most needed there must be a central fund. On 14th February, 1870, it was resolved to form 'The Central Districts Aid Fund'; contributions were received from the wealthy Districts, and from individual donors, and 'Central' applied them in aid of the organisation of committees in poor Districts. After 1872 a separate account was kept and later annual reports showed which Districts gave and which received.‡

By this time the finances of the Society were in good order; the accounts were audited from 1872 onwards by two members of H.M. Exchequer Audit Department. District Committees continued to make their own arrangements, until the decision by 'Central' in 1889 that accounts of District Committees also should be professionally audited.§

After considerable discussion, the C.O.S. had decided in the 1870s to appeal for funds, not only for general administration but for special purposes. One of the largest of these was the Convalescent Cases Fund, and, for a time, the Emigration Fund. The

---

* Donors who allowed their names to be inscribed could be called upon when special difficulty in raising money from other sources had been experienced.

† See p. 317.

‡ By the end of 1873 six Districts contributed a total of £1,696, of which £1,000 was from St George's, Hanover Square.

§ Messrs van de Linde were appointed in 1890.

year 1887, selected by C. L. Mowat as an illustration of the financial position of 'the C.O.S. at the zenith',* illustrates the Society's growth during Loch's secretaryship. The Council summarised its expenditure and that of the District Committees[5] (I have given the figures to the nearest £):

	Organisation	Relief†
Council	£4,662	£3,986
District Committees	£10,391	£22,261

Special funds varied as demands changed. The Districts increased their work for needy old people until, by 1908, they were spending some £20,687 on pensions alone. After the introduction of the statutory Non-Contributory Old Age Pension Scheme in 1908, there was less demand, but the Society still spent considerable sums to help 'respectable old people' for whom a 5/– weekly pension was inadequate, or who felt it less a blow to their self-respect to accept charitable aid. In 1913 the Districts spent over £22,000 on 'Special Cases', and a little under £15,000 on Pensions. The General Expenses of the Districts were still near the 1887 level at £10,956. 'Central' paid some £5,300 for salaries and training expenses for the Districts and contributed £2,105 by way of grants. Donations and subscriptions had risen by 1913 to £10,614.

In the year before the First World War, the summary given by Council[6] of the Expenditure of 'Central' and of the Districts showed:

1913–14	Organisation		Relief
Council	£8,297	Special Cases	£1,347
		Emigration	£497
Districts General Expenses	£11,830		
District secretaries and agents in training	£5,456	Special Cases and Pensions	£36,760

* Some £7,455, from 1,450 persons, was received from subscriptions and donations. A Relief Fund brought in £1,092; the Convalescent Cases Fund reached £2,977; the Surgical Appliances Fund £525; and the Special Cases Fund £1,353; the Emigration Fund totalled £1,065. The District Committee Fund was small, namely £108. The Council's expenses included some £3,855 for District grants and District secretaries' salaries. 'Central' had also to meet the cost of its own greatly increased salaries to a total of £1,579.[4]

† The Council points out that besides the sums entered for relief, many other sums, often of considerable amount, have passed direct from the donor to the recipient, after consultation with the District Committee concerned.

In 1913–14 donations and subscriptions had fallen to £8,881, but legacies, always an uncertain item, were up to nearly £13,000. There were still a number of Special Funds, but the only one of any substance was that for convalescent and sanatoria cases which totalled £2,239. The Emigration Fund had fallen to £680. A small fund, £144, of some interest, was that to augment the salaries of travelling secretaries. A final statement on balances at 30th September, 1914, gives a total of approximately £58,570.

The Society had been noting for several years before the First World War that its obligations and expenditure had increased at a greater rate than its income. After the war the C.O.S. made great efforts to increase its income from voluntary sources and the Districts were constantly being urged to arouse greater local interest and support.

Diagram 4

Charity Organization Society. London (England)
Sources of Income (Relief Only) Ten Years
28 Offices 1925-1934

	1925	1926	1927	1928	1929	1930	1931	1932	1933	1934
Total	£40837	40283	39467	41070	42514	40921	40038	38602	35557	35582
Charitable Sources	20795	20587	18921	19635	20383	19946	20531	20321	19501	20070
Private Appeal	12433	11604	11969	12536	13285	12001	11148	11000	9886	9385
Applicants Payments	7609	8092	8577	8899	8846	8974	8359	7281	6170	6127

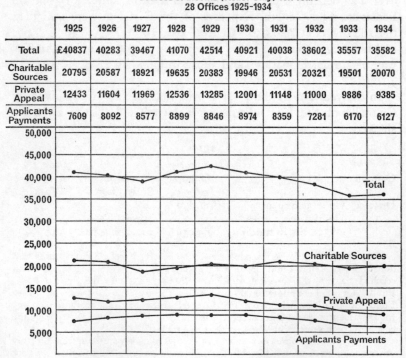

Note: Extracted from C.O.S. Annual Report, 1935

Diagram 5

Charity Organization Society London. (England)
Percentages of Sources of Income (Relief Only) on Totals of
10 Years 1925-1934 District Offices

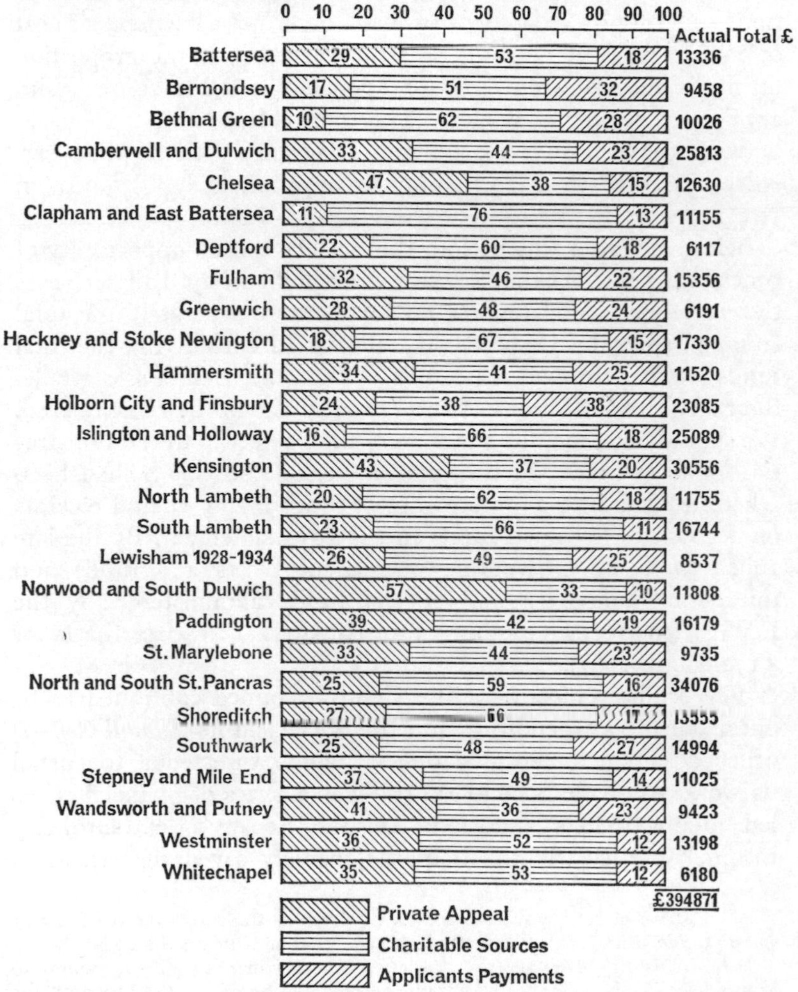

District	Private Appeal	Charitable Sources	Applicants Payments	Actual Total £
Battersea	29	53	18	13336
Bermondsey	17	51	32	9458
Bethnal Green	10	62	28	10026
Camberwell and Dulwich	33	44	23	25813
Chelsea	47	38	15	12630
Clapham and East Battersea	11	76	13	11155
Deptford	22	60	18	6117
Fulham	32	46	22	15356
Greenwich	28	48	24	6191
Hackney and Stoke Newington	18	67	15	17330
Hammersmith	34	41	25	11520
Holborn City and Finsbury	24	38	38	23085
Islington and Holloway	16	66	18	25089
Kensington	43	37	20	30556
North Lambeth	20	62	18	11755
South Lambeth	23	66	11	16744
Lewisham 1928-1934	26	49	25	8537
Norwood and South Dulwich	57	33	10	11808
Paddington	39	42	19	16179
St. Marylebone	33	44	23	9735
North and South St.Pancras	25	59	16	34076
Shoreditch	27	56	17	13555
Southwark	25	48	27	14994
Stepney and Mile End	37	49	14	11025
Wandsworth and Putney	41	36	23	9423
Westminster	36	52	12	13198
Whitechapel	35	53	12	6180
				£394871

Private Appeal
Charitable Sources
Applicants Payments

Note: Extracted from C.O.S. Annual Report, 1935

In the mid-1930s the Society did much to encourage the Districts and to help them with their local propaganda. For this purpose 'Central' produced a series of graphs and diagrams which, quite unashamedly, stressed the 'Relief' work typical of the years between the wars.

Diagram 5 is of special interest in showing applicants' contributions—usually by repayment of loans or, in part payment of cost of equipment (e.g. surgical). District variation, in the proportion of funds derived from private appeal, charitable sources and applicants' payments, is clear. The total volume and the sources between 1925 and 1934 are shown in Diagram 4 with the peak year, some £42,500, in 1929 falling to approximately £36,000 in 1933.

Before and after this period, the Society lost no opportunity of proclaiming the fact that it was not a relief society. In later years the Society's annual reports no longer gave separately the total amounts spent by Districts on 'relief'.* In considering the total funds passing through the hands of the organisation as a whole, the financial transactions of the Districts should be remembered. We should note, too, the function of the Society in the administration of trust funds. In the pioneer period the C.O.S. had been asked to administer a few small trust funds†[7] and we find receipts on account of five such funds in the 1914 statement. By the late 1960s there were fifty-nine permanent trusts and funds and thirty-four temporary and special funds administered by the F.W.A. (the former totalling approximately £193,000, the latter £172,600 in 1967).

The ordinary income of the Central Council continued to be outmatched by expenditure and the Society in its *Annual Reports* called attention to repeated deficits which threatened to curtail its work. After the Second World War a series of financial crises led to drastic reorganisation. Yet the Society's 'extraordinary income', particularly the bequests, usually saved the situation.

---

* To arrive at comparable figures with those of the inter-war years, every District *Annual Report* would have to be analysed and the results collated.

† An interesting discussion, in 1891, on whether or not a gift of money 'to be used for C. of E. cases only' should be accepted by one of the Districts was favourably decided with only a very small majority, 'so long as membership of a religious body is not made in any way a consideration in the granting of relief'. One of the arguments used in favour of acceptance was that the C.O.S. would be acting as Trustee for the fund.

Although such a financial position was far from satisfactory, since legacies are unpredictable, it will be seen from Table 6 below that from the beginning of the century the Society's income, in general, kept pace with the increased costs.* From the 1930s training fees from the universities and other bodies were another source of income;† so were administration charges, as responsibility for additional trust funds was accepted. The financial hazards of voluntary societies are, in a sense, increased when they accept substantial aid from local authorities whose services they supplement. Grants can only be made from year to year for the current year and may, at any time, cease abruptly. In some cases it is not known until a year is far advanced whether or not a grant will be made for the current year by a particular borough. The Association, however, must incur long-term commitments in connection with its casework service and it is a matter of vital necessity that funds should be available in reserve to meet these commitments.[8]

In spite of a satisfactory increase in income from voluntary sources (43 per cent between 1957 and 1967) it had not kept pace with the increase in expenditure (100 per cent). The chief anxiety was the drain on the Association's reserves. The following passage from the F.W.A. report for 1967 expresses this concern:

> In 1957 the resources available amounted to the cost of one year's working and were regarded as an acceptable margin. At the rate expenditure is now running the resources at the moment represent the cost of only four months' working. . . . It is felt that the absolute minimum at which available reserves must be maintained should not be less than the cost of six months' working.

Voluntary societies have a long tradition of living dangerously. The Family Welfare Association has also a tradition as a pioneer in the field of social service. Fortunately the charitable trusts have generously supported F.W.A. experimental projects. Fortunately,

---

* Between the 1940s and 1960s nearly every Income and Expenditure Account published in the annual reports showed a deficit. The setting up of a Legacies Equalisation Fund helped to compensate for the amount overspent. Reserves, nevertheless, sometimes reached a dangerously low level.

† Till then the practical training of students had been carried out by the Society without charge.

too, the value of the Association's work has been officially acknowledged by statutory authorities, both Central and Local.*

It will be noted that subscriptions today are nominally the same as sixty years ago but, taking into account present-day monetary values, they contribute far less. There is also a considerable element of tax recovery included in today's subscriptions.

The unpredictable nature of legacies is brought out clearly in Table 6. Taking the average of the seven items quoted in Column 3, £4,740, this sum is not far from the average allocated each year from the equalisation fund. The trend in nominal value is slightly upwards but the purchasing power today is considerably less.

The year 1967 is added to the table giving a comparison over seven decades, since it shows the full effects of the Council grants (two-thirds costs). The very marked increase in Cost of Area Offices (Column 9) is accounted for largely by the increase in area salaries.†

Summary of Salary Structure

Before 1900, the District Committees employed very few paid workers. Most required the services of an agent, who drew between £45 and £95 per annum, according to the District, a collector who received 'poundage' (a fixed percentage of the amount he brought in), and, occasionally, an accountant, a house-keeper, a messenger or office-boy, and perhaps temporary help during a difficult period. When paid secretaries were appointed after 1881 in some of the Districts, their salaries varied between £100 and £150 a year. The bulk of the work still fell on volunteers, which kept administrative expenses low.

This situation changed when, in the early years of the twentieth century, the number of paid Secretaries began to increase. In 1911 the C.O.S. introduced changes in an attempt to attract more men and women into the Society to cope with an increasing case-load and, it was hoped, to give the work of charity organisation higher

---

* So far, statutory support of the F.W.A. has been by way of grants. It was open to Local Authorities to give financial support on an agency basis. (See my discussion of this in *Voluntary Societies and Social Policy*, 1957.)

† I am much indebted to the late Mr Blunden for Table 6 together with material for the notes and comments.

standing in the community. A new salary scale was introduced as follows:

	Male	Female
District Committee Secretary	£150	£100–£130
District Secretary	£170–£200	?
Organising Secretary	£250	£200

By 1915, thirty-three District Committees were receiving grants from 'Central' to defray the cost of a paid Secretary; four bore this expense themselves. There was considerable disparity between the salaries of District Secretaries, which ranged from £103 to £195. This financial burden was further increased when, in 1920, 'The Council was obliged by the steadily increasing cost of living to revise the scale of salaries paid to all classes of its staff'. Until now secretaries were still thought of as 'quasi-volunteers' and, until after the Second World War, most of those who became family caseworkers had either a private income or received a 'hidden subsidy' by living at home.

In 1920 the highest paid District Committee Secretary received £258. By 1940 this upper limit had risen to £350, while the lower limit was £250. By 1945, when there were twenty-two Districts, all of them had secretaries paid for by 'Central' but the cost of additional clerical assistance had to be borne by the Districts themselves. Since the Second World War the Association has been reticent about disclosing individual salaries, even to members of its own Administrative Committee. When, in 1948–49, Districts were reorganised into nine main areas (and Hendon), only the total cost of the salaries of secretaries and assistants for each area was given. By 1950 the cost of the ten areas' salaries (including Hendon) was £12,513. It was generally known that salaries of F.W.A. workers lagged behind those of comparable workers in other professions. By the 1960s the F.W.A. tried to bring them nearer those being offered to trained social workers by local authorities.

In 1964 the areas, now reduced to seven, cost 'Central' £23,989. The following year the areas were reorganised 'to meet the circumstances created by the Local Government Act, 1963'. It was not until substantial grants were received from the boroughs that the Association could at last, in 1967, keep salaries level with those paid by local authorities. Reference to Table 6, Column 9, will indicate the trends since the 1930s (cost of Area Office to 'Central' reflects the cost of salaries).

TABLE 6. RECEIPTS AND PAYMENTS, CENTRAL OFFICE, 1904–1964, and 1967
(Excluding self-supporting projects)

Financial Year	RECEIPTS						PAYMENTS				
	Donations (1) £	Subscriptions (2) £	Legacies (3) £	Interest (Incl. Rent from Properties) (4) £	Other Receipts (5) £	TOTAL (6) £	Salaries (Central) (7) £	General Office Expenses (8) £	Cost of Area Offices to Central (inc. salaries) (9) £	Cost of Other Items (10) £	TOTAL (11) £
1904	3,514	4,737	1,624	309		10,184	2,724	1,724			4,448
1914	4,078	4,803	12,866	1,927		23,704	2,238	2,085			4,322
1924	7,077	4,076	775	1,158		13,086	1,975	2,196			4,171
1934	3,557	4,041	4,205	3,386	Admin. 423; Training Fees 240	15,852	3,992	2,335	10,404		16,731
1944	6,684; Gift 100 {*}; Special Don. 12,000	3,730	100	1,869	Admin. 1,856; Training Fees 341	26,680	3,875	1,835	14,782		20,492
1954	13,103	4,840	4,330	1,693	Admin. 2,564; Training Fees 1,939; Special Effort 1,752	30,221	7,348	2,201	15,836		25,185
1964	21,263 Includes Spec. Donation	4,414	9,174	4,980†	Admin. 3,028; Training Fees 1,898; Special Effort 2,136	46,893	12,395	4,828	30,780	Projects Costs 2,565	50,568
1967	20,952	4,431	8,101	6,714	Admin. 3,838; Training Fees 1,708; Publications 1,984; Special Effort 361; Borough Grants 36,423 ‡	84,602	15,103	8,533	59,432	1,600	84,668

(*) The figures from 1944 onwards included the Special Grants from various Charitable Trusts.
(†) The increase is due to the large capital increase in Special Funds between 1954 and 1964.
(‡) Before 1967 Borough Grants were much smaller and were negotiated by area offices and appeared in their accounts.

Notes on District Finance, 1871–1914

All the District accounts were regularly audited, and presented according to C.O.S. Council requirements: but the form changed with the years and it is not possible to compare them. In the first few years the returns show that a high proportion of the receipts comes from donations and subscriptions, and a great part of the expenditure is on administration. The wealthier committees are contributing to the poorer, and most of them show repayment of loans by applicants (loans were always free of interest). Items from some of the established Districts' accounts in 1872 show some interesting features:

St George's Hanover Square, one of the wealthier Districts, out of its total receipts for the year of £2,407, lists £1,364 from subscribers and £305 from repayment of loans. Amongst the items of expenditure we find £380 as subsidies to other committees and £217 to the Migration Fund, 'Aid' accounts for £717 (gifts £419, loans £298).

Islington, one of the poorer Districts, has a total for fifteen months of £391, of which £93 was a grant from 'Central' and £297 from subscriptions and donations. Its expenditure on 'Aid' was only £32: the separate items show grants 'in kind' of £26, in money £5 and 'bread to tramps' 14s.

Paddington was sufficiently well-off, with total receipts for the year of £1,338 to make a £25 grant to Shoreditch. Its expenditure on administration came very close to that on 'Aid' (£419 and £417). An item for the loan of sewing-machine and mangles throws some light on the human situation, when many of the poor took in washing to help make ends meet.

By the 1880s it had been decided that Districts should separate the General Fund and the Relief Account. This was more satisfactory as each District could now show clearly how the money was raised and spent for the specific purpose of assistance, whether for convalescence or for special cases, or for more general relief.

For example, St George's in 1884 had a General Fund of £922 and a Relief Account of £1,041. The latter showed that 'private persons' had contributed £654 and Institutions £46 for special cases. Others had contributed £32 for convalescent cases. Details of expenditure show not only grants to patients but subscriptions to five Convalescent Homes. Paddington

Table 7

SUMMARY OF EXPENDITURE OF THE SOCIETY.
1912–13 AND 1913–14.

	Organisation 1912-13 (£ s. d.)			Organisation 1913-14 (£ s. d.)			Relief 1912-13 (£ s. d.)			Relief 1913-14 (£ s. d.)		
Expenditure of the Council:												
General Expenses	5,309	3	2	4,063	12	2	—			—		
Publications	181	8	3	201	8	5	—			—		
Medical Working Account	424	0	3	489	14	5	—			—		
Emigration Working	142	7	5	198	14	5	—			—		
Thrift and Saving	164	13	6	170	17	3	—			—		
Expenses at Central Office — Registration	761	19	4	795	9	0	—			—		
District Committee Account	172	12	6	75	0	0	—			—		
Library	75	14	9	65	4	0	—			—		
Provincial Committee	301	19	9	338	4	11	—			—		
City Office	458	9	2	1,817	17	2	—			—		
Propaganda				81	3	8	—			—		
	7,992	8	1	8,297	5	5						
Special Cases, &c.	—			—			1,590	3	11	1,347	6	4
Emigration Cases	—			—			821	0	2	496	12	9
							2,420	4	1	1,843	19	1
Expenditure of District Committees:												
General Expenses	10,956	10	11	11,830	8	8	—			—		
District Committees' Audit	21	0	0	50	8	0	—			—		
District Secretaries and Agents in training	5,357	1	6	5,456	7	3	—			—		
Special Cases and Pensions							37,037	11	3	36,759	13	7
	16,334	12	5	17,337	3	11	37,037	11	3	36,759	13	7
	24,327	0	6	25,634	9	4	39,457	15	4	38,603	12	8

The above table gives as far as practicable a summary of the expenditure incurred by the Council and the forty-two separate District Committees federated with it. Subject to an annual estimate and audit, each of the District Committees conducts its own financial work and publishes separate statements of accounts. Besides the sums entered for relief, many other sums, often of considerable amount, have passed direct from the donor to the recipient, after consultation with the District Committee. Of these, obviously, it is not possible to give any statement

had a General Fund of £771 and a Relief Account of £747. In both Districts a substantial sum was transferred from the General Fund to subsidise the Relief Account. Not all the money could be raised by special appeal to individuals on each 'case'. Islington in the same year had a General Fund of £381 and a Relief Account of £252. Here, as in the other Relief Accounts, the largest single item was 'contributions for special cases of distress' from 'private persons and Institutions'.

A useful change in the presentation of accounts made at 'Central' showed the total expenditure of District Committees together with that of the Council. A summary of two years given in the 1914 *Annual Report* of the Society is reproduced in Table 7.

CHAPTER SIXTEEN

Some Criticisms of the C.O.S./F.W.A.

In the nineteenth century C.O.S. adherence to Individualism and 'the fierce gospel of self-reliance' roused considerable hostility. The first fifty years of the Society's history were turbulent. Not only was its social theory provocative, but its methods often roused bitter protest. It ran foul of charitable organisations like Dr Barnardo's and the Salvation Army and its stern rules in the selection of applicants caused considerable bitterness. Helen Bosanquet, writing the first *History*, sought to vindicate the policies of the C.O.S., as 'a fighting society': 'Unlike most benevolent institutions it has not pursued its work with the comforting assurance of general approbation, but has been forced to till its fields and gather its harvests with the weapons of attack and defence always close at hand.'[1] Lord Shaftesbury put the same point in rather different language: 'I am happy to say that this Society has taken the very able and very unpopular course of ferreting out what is wrong and exposing it.'[2]

When, in the year 1884, there was a resurgence of hostility, the C.O.S. started a file endorsed 'Complaint, Criticism and Abuse'. Some of the Districts had felt the full force of criticism as they tried to carry out orthodox principles and methods: sometimes the local Press took up the cause of a rejected applicant.*[3] As Helen Bosanquet herself admitted, 'a certain number of cases—a very small proportion of the whole—are inadequately treated by the District Committees'. Sometimes 'scurrilous statements' were issued to the Press or printed as letters or pamphlets, by 'persons whose interests the Society had interfered with'. Helen Bosanquet added: 'those attacks have been strengthened in their effect upon

---

* H. Bosanquet reports an 'even more ambitious attack' by the Suburban Press in 1875, when 'one of the most ingenuous caricatures of the Society' was widely circulated.

the public mind by the fact that there is a class of thoroughly respectable and even admirable persons who genuinely dislike and disapprove the fundamental principles of the Society'.

George Lansbury must have been an extreme example of 'this class of person', as he looked back in his old age to the C.O.S. of his childhood. Lansbury was a harsh critic. He recalled his early life in Whitechapel where the Board of Guardians and the C.O.S. together pursued a policy which Lansbury saw as 'heartless and brutal in its effects on the lives of the poor'. It made Lansbury 'a bitter enemy of the Charity Organisation Society and all its works'.*[4] His attitude was in sympathy with those who cried 'curse your charity'.†[5] The C.O.S. nickname, 'Cringe-Or-Starve', may not have been appropriate to a Society committed to upholding the self-respect of the individual struggling to maintain his independence, but it expressed the bitterness of those who rejected its methods of investigation. Perhaps Lord Attlee fitted Helen Bosanquet's description rather better.‡[6] He appreciated many of the good points in the C.O.S. 'positive contribution': their investigations were thorough, a certain number of individual cases of misfortune were relieved, and a certain amount of co-operation between charities secured. He praised their work for 'the family as a whole', but he thought many of their methods harsh and tactless. He disliked their 'bourgeois code of morals and lack of sympathy'. Above all he disliked their social theory, 'their rigid adherence to early ideas as to the sphere of the State and voluntary action'. Lord Snell was another socialist critic who later recorded 'the weaknesses of C.O.S. principles' but he went further than many in his appreciation of some of the excellent family social work done in the Districts.[7]

Beatrice Webb was one of the most vocal critics among the intelligentsia. She and Loch were implacable opponents on the Royal Commission on the Poor Laws.§ She had begun her

* Lansbury wrote his autobiography in 1928. It was, he said, written from memory.

† This was reported as having been shouted at a meeting of the unemployed in West Ham in 1909.

‡ When Attlee was working as a young man in the East End of London, he examined the work of the C.O.S. His analysis was given later in less impassioned terms than those of Lansbury.

§ It was she who organised the campaign to popularise the Minority Report. Loch was said to have made a substantial contribution to the Majority Report.

L

'apprenticeship' to the study of social problems with the C.O.S. in Soho. Commenting later on her experiences from the 1880s onwards, she notes how, at first, she had thought them honest but mistaken, and how later 'when the latter-day leaders of Charity Organisation and I had become respectively propagandists of rival political and economic theories, we fought each other's views to the death'.[8] By then Beatrice Webb was referring to 'the subversive character of the movement, alike in thought and feeling'. After dealing forthrightly with its mistaken social theory, she records her dislike of its earlier assumption 'of social and mental superiority', of 'its self-complacent harshness', of 'its rigid voluntary idea', and of its 'detective visiting'. She concluded that it had 'little effect either on poverty or on the lives of the poor'.

The C.O.S. was much given to self-criticism. Loch himself was one of the most severe; so were some of the honorary secretaries.* Some of the Society's most outspoken questioners were to be heard at the Provincial Meetings; for example, Mr Grisewood at the Winter Conference of 1904 who, quoting an American writer, charged the C.O.S. with wrong thinking on the Poor Law; or J. Pearson Bush,[9] an Australian, who, at the Annual Conference at Edinburgh, accused the C.O.S. of failing to achieve anything. 'Are the opinions of the members of the Charity Organisation Society in touch with public opinion?' he asks, and replies, 'in my opinion they are not.' One, a Canadian, accused the Society of taking too comprehensive a view of their role,† while another thought it gave too great attention to details, losing sight of wider issues. The summer and winter conferences continued to give many opportunities to a variety of speakers to challenge policy and practice, and the papers were published later in the Society's journal. The letters and discussions which followed were, no doubt, a healthy growth in the main body of C.O.S. membership, although they sometimes strengthened the ultra-conservatives in their traditional beliefs. This was true of Pringle who rejoiced that the Society changed 'not one jot or tittle'. In general, the C.O.S. members' saving grace was their ability to recognise their failings,

---

* E.g. Mr G. Elliott. See p. 333.

† E.g. Mr T. H. Falk in 1924, who spoke of 'not wholly condemning the State and of not assuming for all time the responsibility of co-ordinating the whole social programme of a country'.

even to call public attention to them, and, from time to time, to do something about it.

It was many years before the C.O.S. accepted criticism of its social theory. There had been much discussion when the C.O.S. opposed the social legislation of the Liberal régime of the early twentieth century, especially the feeding of schoolchildren and the provision of old age pensions. The provisions affected the family at crucial points and some of the District and Provincial members showed their dissatisfaction with official C.O.S. policy. It took the Society some forty years to live down this episode in its history. It was noted at the time that young men coming down from Oxford and Cambridge were critical and disinclined to offer voluntary service as in the past.[10] Loch promised a full-scale discussion in his address to the Council in 1907. The following year the Council set up a Special Committee to report on organisation and methods, one of its main studies being concerned with the reasons for the unpopularity of the C.O.S. In view of Canon Barnett's earlier outspoken 'Friendly Criticism', which gained such publicity in the 1890s, it is interesting to find him submitting a memorandum to the Committee, advising the Council 'to be silent for a time as to C.O.S. principles', and to concentrate on fostering the enthusiasm of the District Committees. The first suggestion did not meet with approval: the fear of unpopularity would never deter the Society from being outspoken in a righteous cause. Yet the report, though printed,* was marked 'Private and Confidential, for the use of members of Council and of District Committees only'. Was the C.O.S., in fact, becoming more sensitive to outside criticism? Some thirty-eight members gave evidence to the Committee, stating the chief reasons for C.O.S. unpopularity to be 'that the Society favoured Individualism as opposed to Socialism', and that 'it was disliked by the working class as being largely representative of a class which they feel to be injuring them and doing them a great injustice'.†

The C.O.S. had repeatedly tried, and generally failed, to win over the more thoughtful of the working class. They had hoped, with little success, to persuade them to become members of

---

* Printed in 1909 and, until recently, to be found in the Library of F.W.A.

† Criticisms by applicants (or clients, as they were called later) were not often recorded, nor was it known why applications were withdrawn, since there was no 'follow-up'. In the late 1960s a special enquiry was undertaken for the first time in the Association's history (see p. 354, note*).

C.O.S. committees. They had invited Trade Unionists, officers of Friendly Societies and members of the Workers Educational Association to speak at their meetings, but such occasional contacts had little permanent effect. The gulf remained.

There was, in the early twentieth century, growing hostility from Socialist thinkers and writers. The *New Statesman* became one of the C.O.S.'s bitterest critics. The Fabian Society thought it worthwhile to bring out a Tract in 1911 devoted to *The Case against the Charity Organisation Society*.[11] As the writer, Mrs Townshend, explained, 'those of us who are keen that the public sense of responsibility should be awakened with regard to destitution must feel that this opposition on the part of "charity experts" is of the utmost importance'. As the points discussed represented the view of the opponents of the C.O.S., and as some of the arguments have been repeated at intervals till recent times, the Tract is worth further examination. Mrs Townshend asks why it was that 'the most strenuous opposition to almost every scheme for social betterment comes from a body of people who are devoting their lives to that very purpose'. She attempts to set out fairly the aims of the C.O.S. She concludes that it started with some useful suggestions from Solly, Hicks and Hawksley in 1868, that it did some valuable early work after its foundation in 'spreading sound views on charitable work', in 'promoting due investigation and fitting action in all cases' and 'in repressing mendicity' (three of the objects set out in the C.O.S. *Manual*). She found excellence in its work in training the public in the responsibilities of alms-giving and in initiating orderly and efficient methods of social work. More surprisingly, in view of later criticisms, she adds that the Society 'has taught how to sift helpable cases, and how to choose right modes of help'. She noted that many of the paid investigators for Royal Commissions and for the L.C.C. owed their efficiency to its training.

The Society's want of success as an organiser might be accounted for by the fact that it also became occupied with the bestowal of relief. Its principles, worked out in practice, then became a creed: 'This creed . . . which arose out of temporary conditions, many of them badly needing alteration, has gradually assumed a kind of sacred character and a strange structure of social theory has been built upon it.' Mrs Townshend's comment explains something of the Fabian attitude to the C.O.S. 'The very excellence of the Society's work has served to make this theory more mischievous for it comes before the public backed by the honoured names of devoted workers.'

The Fabian Tract selects certain fundamental errors for special notice: that the C.O.S. traced the increase of pauperism and of destitution to one source—relaxation in the principles of the 1834 Poor Law; that they looked upon State 'interference' as a necessary evil; that they assumed that unearned income injured the poor but not the rich; that they accepted human arrangements as if they were heaven-sent and unchangeable, e.g. a competitive wage system. Most of the political and economic argument had sufficient force to make the Tract a telling piece of criticism. Other strictures on class divisions followed: the self-satisfaction of the upper and middle classes with their easy and sheltered lives, their privileges paid for by the contribution of the poor or from public money. The writer makes clear the fundamental cleavage of social theory between the C.O.S. Individualists, and the Fabian Socialists. Her belief that C.O.S. theory was 'insidious' and 'mischievous' colours the presentation of certain other facts. Although she quotes from the Bosanquets and from Loch, she deals less than adequately with Loch's ideas of charity and underrates C.O.S. views on the importance of the total environment in an assessment of family needs. The Fabian Society was more concerned with the fundamental issue of replacing charity and poverty by a new social order. It paid little attention subsequently to the C.O.S. The C.O.S. discussed the Tract in its *Journal* but nothing much emerged from the encounter. As with Loch and the Webbs, the points of view were so divergent that there could be little or no communication.

A more friendly discussion in the following year, 1912, arose from letters from Violet Markham,*[12] who admired some of the practical work of the C.O.S., but was critical of its theory. She wrote both to the *Spectator* and to the *Charity Organisation Review* urging the C.O.S. to find a middle way, to accept the need for collective responsibility and 'to re-state the whole of our social formulae in the light of new conditions and new experience'.[13] Loch had little time left to make so fundamental a change.† The

* In later years Violet Markham contrasted the spirit of the Chesterfield Settlement with the 'odious spirit of patronage . . .' and rejoiced that the idea of 'charity' of fifty years earlier had changed. 'Some good people can have a vested interest in the poor.'

† He was taken seriously ill in 1913 and resigned in 1914.

Society missed its opportunity to go forward with greater insight into the new era precipitated by the First World War.

One of the most widespread criticisms levelled against the Association throughout its history was that of arrogance. Some of those most friendly to the C.O.S. had disliked its 'autocratic' and 'ambitious' claims (for example, Lord Shaftesbury). Alfred Marshall was another who, while holding the Society in high regard ('It is difficult to overrate the debt that the nation owes to the C.O.S.' he had stated in 1893),[14] acknowledged that 'they have some weaknesses': one of these was its 'oligarchic' character. He suggested to the Royal Commission on the Aged Poor that its basis was 'people who used to be the governing classes but are not the governing classes now'.

One of the classic examples of 'Friendly Criticism' was that of Canon Barnett, a great supporter of the C.O.S. who became one of its sternest critics in the mid-1890s.*[15] He had already written to his brother in 1888 on his return from a meeting: 'I went to meet a lot of C.O.S. folk re a proposed Training Farm. They were just impossible—refusing to do anything except to clothe themselves in the dirty rags of their own righteousness.'[16] Barnett was less fierce in *Christianity and the Charity Organisation Society*— 'the thoroughness with which they enquire into causes has not always been undertaken in Christ's spirit of tenderness'.[17] Another criticism made in 1897 by a well-known High Church clergyman of the Christian Social Union brings home the point: 'theories which on the lips of Canon Barnett are spiritual, if mistaken; and from the pen of Mr Loch are able, though fallacious, become in the practice of meaner men merely the gospel of the buttoned pocket'.[18]

The C.O.S. tendency to arrogance persisted. A voluntary worker who gave long and valuable service to the Society recently recalled being chided by her supervisor in the 1920s because as a student she had bracketed the C.O.S. with the British Empire as 'two of the most arrogant institutions in the world'. She spoke for other thoughtful and increasingly critical students. Sometimes a member of staff found the situation intolerable, as, for instance, one of the men who, when it was learned that he was about to marry one of the women social workers, was called to Central and

* A full account of his paper, given in July 1895 at the invitation of the C.O.S., is found in his wife's biography.

asked how he proposed to live on one C.O.S. salary.* His indignation led him to resign immediately.

As late as the 1940s the Administrative Committee considered
the charge: 'that the C.O.S. was autocratic and dictatorial'; they
decided that there was 'some truth in this': they recommended
that 'Secretaries should interpret the Committee's decision to
other agencies tactfully', and added with some circumspection,
'especially when their financial help is required'. Much later
Barbara Wootton suggested that it was 'largely under the influence
of the American cult of psycho-analysis' that social workers had
presented such an 'appallingly arrogant image of themselves'.†[19]

Finally, it is worth noting the attitude of the universities. After
the First World War the University Social Science Departments
were more closely concerned with the C.O.S. as they sent an
increasing number of students for periods of practical work.
From time to time criticism was outspoken as, for example, that
by Mrs Milnes.‡ Her main criticisms were: that the C.O.S. had
a distorted view of the effects of State action because their work
was chiefly among the failures, that C.O.S. methods were rigid
and that the Society was stagnating. (She added that she believed
greatly in the value of family casework.) The general attitude was
probably expressed by Miss Elisabeth Macadam, who, as honorary
secretary for many years of the Joint University Council for
Social Studies and Public Administration, was aware of the
tensions which sometimes arose: 'Whatever views may be held
about its past social philosophy', she wrote, 'the unbiased person
must admit that the C.O.S. represents, and always has represented,
thorough and scientific work and that its offices provide an
admirable and indispensable training ground.'[20] Mrs Reid of
Bedford College had been a strong supporter of the Society (she
had written a persuasive and reasoned article on *The Application
of C.O.S. Principles to Present Day Conditions*,[21] but the London
School of Economics had a different reputation with the Society.
Many District secretaries were convinced that L.S.E. students
arrived with a biased view, determined to be critical. The Webbs'

---

* It should be noted that, as late as the 1940s, it was customary to require the
resignation of professional women upon marriage, e.g. teachers and health
visitors in the Local Authority Services.

† Barbara Wootton added:'the admirable work that social workers do bears no
relation to the silly things they are apt to say'.

‡ See p. 132.

early influence at L.S.E. was thought still to infuse the School's teaching. But the C.O.S. Secretary at 'Central' found the students 'guileless'. The charge that the Society was stagnating was rejected.

In general, criticism died down as the Society withdrew from the limelight. The Districts no longer complained year by year that they were 'so misunderstood'. Such criticism as there was received little publicity, since it arose largely within its own membership. Some of the unpopularity complained of in the 1920s reappeared briefly in the 1930s with the changed political complexion of the L.C.C.,* but the close co-operation of the Society with Local Authorities and Government Departments during the Second World War broke down all barriers.

The *New Statesman* kept up a desultory attack with an occasional article, letter, or review,†[22] but compared with the vehemence of earlier invective, when 'C.O.S.' was an emotive title, later critics were mild indeed. After the Second World War the new title Family Welfare Association coincided with the general acceptance of family social work by public and private agencies alike. The F.W.A. had now discarded out-dated methods together with the old social theory which had evoked such bitter hostility.

The Association's tradition of frank self-criticism continued until the 1960s. The *Cunliffe Report* did not hesitate to show up weaknesses, whether of casework practice or of administration. It is to the credit of the F.W.A. that it had for the greater part of its history been ready to examine its work in the light of informed criticism.

* See p. 141.
† The C.O.S. Administrative Committee in 1941 agreed that a letter should be sent to the *New Statesman* denying 'statements made with reference to our declared views'.

Casework Problems at various periods submitted by Members for Discussion: Examples and Comments

N.B. The following 'case studies' are all taken from published articles. The Association always gives fictitious names. Apart from the 'Turner case', the accounts which follow are given, for the most part, in the words used at the time, as an indication of the way in which the workers thought of their role. I have added comments.

Casework during and after the First World War is illustrated by a C.O.S. official publication known as 'The Turner Case'. It is a long document,[1] itself a summary of records extending over three years of intensive work and some ten years of occasional friendly visiting. The following outline (reduced to note form), will give some idea of the thoroughness and variety of the practical help given to a family with a very poor medical record. Here and there we have indications of the support given by the worker to the mother as she faces a series of crises within the family. The record also indicates the nature of the statutory and voluntary help available at that time and the efforts made by the C.O.S. to 'organise' it on behalf of the family.

1. *The Turner Case. Printed as 'a specimen of the Case Work of the London (England) Charity Organisation Society', 1915–28.* Father, Mother and two young children. (Father referred to as Mr T, or T., Mother as Mrs T.)

Medical History
Mr T. tuberculous, children always ailing. Sent by hospital almoner when T. to have yet another operation (tuberculosis glands in neck). Surgeon recommended patient, a printer's machinist, to have out-of-door work in the country. Mrs T. near time for third confinement.

L*

Help Given by the C.O.S.

Advanced loans until insurance benefits came through. Asked hospital to keep open Mrs T.'s work (kitchen work under housekeeper). Kept in touch with Church Sister who was helping and with I.C.A.A. Mr T. and eldest child sent away to convalescent homes; Mrs T. tries to get younger child into nursery and to get work, although she herself in poor health (after child birth and influenza). C.O.S. supports Mrs T. with small money gifts and loans. Mrs T. always returns loans when benefits come through.

Enquiries, meanwhile, about possible country work. Younger boy now ailing and after medical report is referred to I.C.A.A. Mrs T. urged by hospital not to find work but to look after her children at home. Mr T. agreed, as he was anxious about the children. C.O.S. decided that as this was likely to be 'a long term case' the Turners should apply to the Relieving Officer. C.O.S. consulted the Ts. about the application to R.O. and 'T. did not seem at all annoyed at the proposal'. An allowance greater than that by C.O.S. is made by the Guardians.

Records show that Mrs T. was glad to be able to talk to the C.O.S. Secretary about her difficulties.

C.O.S. suggested T. seek work through Employment Exchange but T. was sent to unsuitable job. Re-application to R.O., who would not increase allowance; Mrs T. had to pawn many household articles. C.O.S. decided to take case off Poor Law and increase allowance. Medical interest continued. C.O.S. inserted advertisements for suitable work. Meanwhile, T. got himself a job with long hours and un-suitable work (carting undressed skins at Docks).

C.O.S. now tried a personal approach: i.e. C.O.S. worker recommended T. to a relative of hers in the country. As T. was happy in country work and gave satisfaction, C.O.S. arranged to pay removal expenses for family to join him. C.O.S. also redeemed articles from pawn and paid week's rent (total cost £7 5s. 9d.).

(C.O.S. informed relieving officer of results and the Guardians expressed approval of constructive work of the C.O.S. The Secretary continued to visit the family in the country from time to time.)

Mr T. again ill—T.B. dispensary and sanatorium treatment. Mrs T. carried on his work. When Mr T. able to return to work Mrs T. got a job in a munitions factory, putting the two youngest children in a nursery. She did night work, with very little sleep for months. She immediately began paying back to C.O.S. 5/– per week.

Continued story of misfortune
Two boys now found to be T.B. Mr T. got a thorn in his eye and lost sight of one eye—operated on in his old hospital in London. Mrs T. had to give up job to be with Mr T. and was very near a nervous break-down. Later returned to work (and beat record in shell-making). Mr T. returned to country and got job in munitions. Mrs T. taken ill and sent for convalescence by C.O.S., but returned early because worried about children.

The T.s received compensation for loss of T.'s eye—they sent it immediately to C.O.S. C.O.S. said 'it was much too much' and when T. still wanted to repay in full, C.O.S. opened a banking account for them, 'against further contingencies'.

Each of their later children (twins) had T.B. joints, but the ex-C.O.S. Secretary who saw them from time to time reported that 'they were delightful children'. She added some reflection on whether the fact that Mr T. was only kept alive through C.O.S. help was in fact eugenic (viz. three more children—delicate) but concluded that 'one feels the world must be better for their existence'. The Secretary was full of hope for the family who seemed to be happily settled in Worcestershire.

Comment
The records contain little more than the bare facts of the needs as they occur and the help sanctioned by the Committee. But, here and there, it is obvious that the C.O.S. was giving more than material assistance. Support for Mrs T. during the various family crises when misfortune followed misfortune was an important

part of the service; so were respect for Mr and Mrs T.'s courage, satisfaction at the happiness of the children and at the close-knit family bond (this included Mrs T.'s mother who was reported to be hard-working and poor). The respect of the worker for the family was matched by the family's confidence in the worker. The family also had the continued interest of the doctor, the hospital and the T.B. dispensaries.

The 'Turner Case' illustrates some of the weaknesses and deficiences of the social services. In spite of the great increase in the number of social services, they were disconnected and dilatory. The hospital almoner and the C.O.S. workers tried to provide the link and give interim aid.

Statutory Benefits used by the Turner Family included:	Sickness Benefit, Disablement Benefit, Poor Relief, Services of the Ministry of Labour, Workmen's Compensation, T.B. Dispensary Services (partly voluntary).
Voluntary Services included:	The Voluntary Hospitals, Convalescent Homes, Invalid Children's Aid Society and the Church. (The C.O.S. was in constant touch with each group and with the statutory authorities, especially the Relieving Officer and the Employment Exchange.)
The Pawnshop:	Mrs Turner had sometimes to turn to this source for immediate financial aid, but the C.O.S. helped to redeem the articles from pawn (they included the sewing-machine, wedding-ring, and clothes).

C.O.S. thoroughness to the last detail is apparent in the help given for the family removal from London to the country. (Not only were the removal arranged and train tickets purchased, but an extra 2/– awarded 'for labels and string'.)

Nowhere in the records do we find specific reference to the 'relationship between worker and client'. But the overall impression is one of a very warm relationship between the family (especially the mother) and the social worker. It is significant that after her retirement the Secretary kept in friendly touch with the family and visited from time to time for some ten years after the last official entry in the records.

2. The 1920s showed some questioning of current case work, although the majority of workers seemed still to be convinced that the methods of the past had proved their worth and must be maintained. A much discussed article was published in 1927 in the *Charity Organisation Quarterly*;[2] the writer, Mr Elliott, had been a District Secretary as far back as the early 1890s and a voluntary worker since 1923.* He pointed out that his misgivings were shared by a number of well-disposed persons and he referred to an example of certain decisions of his Committee which he could not approve. The following account, though lengthy, is given in his own words.

A man had been paralysed from the waist down since 1923. With his wife and one child he lived in one room in a slum, and, before his illness, had been a newsvendor. In 1925 application was made to provide him with an invalid self-propelling tricycle to enable him to escape from his prison cell of a room, and possibly to resume his work as newspaper seller and become once more independent of parish relief. Omitting points that for the purpose of this argument may be considered irrelevant, the unexpected tidiness of his home, the extremely favourable impression made by his wife, and so forth, it is suggested that we should concentrate our attention on the two points that have an important bearing on the question under dispute, that question being what considerations may justly be taken into account by a Committee in dealing with such a case and what may not.

(1) The medical evidence, not very clear and not, as it turned out, justified by the event, seemed to indicate that the man's illness was likely to get worse rather than better.

(2) The man—a rough sort of fellow—was unwilling or unable to give references as to character, got surly and complained of what he professed to consider the inquisitional methods of the Society, and more particularly refused to give

* Although he had some misgivings he thought that much of the adverse criticism of the C.O.S. was misplaced. He prefaced his article by a eulogy of 'the wisdom, the self devotion, the patience, the tireless industry, and, above all, the wide charity with which . . . they (members and secretaries) discharge their difficult task'.

Army details, though he claimed to have served from 1915 to
1919. He said that he had been 'crimed'. He was told that
that might not necessarily make any difference, and that in
any case no appeal for money should be made to his regiment
without his express permission. But he refused as obstinately
as before to give details.

The application was turned down. To one at least of the
Committee the only possible justification for this decision
was the medical evidence; if the man was to die or if the
paralysis was to spread to the rest of his body, it was obvious
waste of money to buy him the tricycle. Otherwise he ought
in common humanity to be given it; whatever he had done,
in or out of the Army, he did not deserve that fate. In other
words, *in such a case the question of character was utterly and
entirely irrelevant, and ought not therefore to have been introduced at all.*

But, as regards the other members of Committee, it is only
too certain that to the great majority of them the question of
character was of prime importance. The proof of this is that
two years later, in this very year of grace, the case came up
again, sent by a rich man to whom the paralytic had written,
begging still for the tricycle, and who asked for a report. The
man was once more visited. His disease was certainly no
worse. Except for his paralysed legs he was a strong, hefty
fellow, good for another thirty years of life, so far as one
could judge; the doctors had been unduly pessimistic. But
he refused to answer questions as stubbornly as ever. The
report sent to the rich man told the bare facts of the case,
fairly and impartially enough. But it was *not* said that the
Committee recommended the gift: on that point care was
taken to refrain from the expression of any opinion. The rich
man interpreted this as he was almost bound to interpret it,
and replied that *in view of the report received* he had decided
to take no further action in the matter. Once more the man
lost his case; and this time there could be no question as to
the reason: it was his character that condemned him.

(Mr Elliott continues):

Here let it be made quite clear that the position taken up in
this paper is not that character should never be taken into

account, nor yet that investigation is needless. Investigation will be necessary in every case. But investigation about what? Not, as the writer would contend, the same sort of investigation for each and every case. When the question of character is relevant, character should be investigated; and in a vast number of cases the question of character is all-important, just because lack of character in the distressed man would render any help that we could give utterly valueless. Not 'undeserving' but 'unhelpable' is the word we want. The Society is very right in insisting and continuing to insist on this vital truth. All this the writer steadfastly believes. The Society appears to be wrong, in practice at all events if not in theory, in failing to recognise that this truth, important as it is, is only a subordinate one. Surely the wider truth is that *help should only be given where and when it can be shown that the applicant (a) will really (and, as a rule, permanently) benefit by the assistance asked for, and (b) is unable to obtain what he needs by his own unaided efforts; but when proof can be given of these two conditions, then help should be given.* Can it be shown that in the case of our paralytic (a case only taken as typical of many others) the tricycle would not have been of real and permanent value, whatever faults of character he might have? If so, on what grounds should it have been refused? . . . It were to be wished that the words, 'desert' and 'deserving', so detestable in this connection, should be expunged from the social worker's vocabulary, or, better still, the very ideas from his mind.

If there is truth in what has been said, there follows a corollary, important and practical. *A vast amount of investigation, as at present carried on, is quite superfluous; and if superfluous, then not merely and negatively useless, but positively harmful and mischievous.* . . . The best argument in its favour is that inquiries which appear at first to be irrelevant sometimes lead incidentally to the discovery of useful information; to the discovery, it may be, of a way of helping the applicant which he himself had not suggested but which is likely to prove of more permanent benefit than what he had originally asked for. This argument, as contrasted with those previously considered, is at least respectable (which they are not), but has to bear more on its shoulders than it has the strength to carry.

Mr Elliott goes on to consider other reasons for 'this lust for undiscriminate investigation' which, he thinks, are really psychological rather than logical.

One is professional zeal, that potent and subtle source of evil as well as good. By this is here meant not merely the crude and unintelligent adherence to formula, known as red-tape, but the laudable desire of the functionary to do his job well, to be *thorough*. District Secretaries want to have their casework up to the highest standard. Unfortunately the inspection of casework which is carried on from headquarters tends to encourage the belief that casework can only err in the direction of omission and not of commission. It is a matter for regret that committees should not occasionally be warned against asking too many questions as well as against asking too few. The agents of the Society are especially liable to excess of zeal in this particular form. . . . The Society is justly critical of what it describes as 'mass action'. Is there not something that might be called 'mass investigation'?

Mr Elliott had sent this article to the editor of the C.O.S. *Journal* with a note that, although it contained adverse criticism, he hoped it would be published since 'it was at least honest and . . . not meant in any unfriendly spirit. If I did not in the main admire and respect the work that the Society is doing, I should not give so much of my time, as I do, towards furthering it'.

Like the 'Dane Case'* a generation later, this example was used by the Society to arouse discussion amongst its members and a good deal of correspondence followed in subsequent issues of the *Quarterly*. Many of the letters strongly upheld the relevance and the value of assessing character. Might not the tricycle have found its way to the pawnshop the day after its arrival and its proceeds to the betting tout or the publican?[3] Yet it was agreed that some committees let their zeal outrun their discretion—Committees should take warning.

The article and the correspondence which followed gave a revealing picture, not only of the assumptions behind much of the casework of that period, but of the various approaches in District Offices. It also challenged the quality of 'Central' inspection of District work.

* See p. 342.

3. A second example of work in the same period shows how much depended on the policy of the District Committee, even more, on the quality of the family social worker. This example has another interest since the account was written by the client and sent some years later to the Honorary Secretary concerned.*[4] The following is a brief summary of his own version:

> He had been sent by a Regimental Agency for help in 1925, an ex-prisoner, anti-social and bitter, and rejected by society. Yet he was warmly welcomed and treated with the respect due to a human being in need. He remembered not only the practical help he received and the understanding and sympathy, but the joy and vitality and humour of his rescuer.

Few details are given of what was done to 'rehabilitate' this young man who was on the verge of despair. That it was effective 'seemed obvious' to him. It is worth noting the comment of the social worker herself as she looks back on 'this long-term case': 'I draw no conclusions from this document beyond one which is not new: the terrifying responsibility we take on ourselves when we attempt, with the very best motives, to handle other people's lives.'†

4. During the 1930s, 'casework' was still thought of by many of the workers as 'the organisation of charity' on behalf of individuals in need, though the emphasis was always on personal service. As a highly respected secretary reported in 1938,‡[5] 'The Charity Organisation Society is a Society for organising charity. Nothing more nor less'. Throughout the decade this committee cited cases for the benefit of subscribers to show how actively the social workers had laboured on behalf of individuals and families, sometimes asked to help by the relieving officer, sometimes by the medical officer, or by a hospital almoner; always co-operating

---

* The client was then engaged in writing his 'Life'; the F.W.A. published extracts in *Social Work*.

† See 'Winfred Locket', Chapter 14.

‡ Miss E. F. Bolton was Organising Secretary. She was long remembered as a woman of great humanity and as a 'wonderful trainer of students'.

with other organisations to secure the appropriate service. An example quoted as 'a success story' will illustrate the kind of services given, the friendly listening expected, and the detailed word picture typical of the case summaries of the period. Is there not also a touch of patronage in the almost Victorian atmosphere evoked by the writer?

Mrs G. was badly burned in the terrible air raid near Drury Lane, and was a sufferer and unable to work for the rest of her life. We undertook to administer her weekly allowance, and, as it was not enough for her and her little nine-year-old daughter Jessie, we raised money from other sources and took it to her regularly for fifteen years. Convalescence and holidays were arranged for both of them from time to time. There were gifts of coal and help to get clothing and teeth and spectacles were secured, but chiefly it involved a weekly visit to bring her her money, to listen to her complaints and to share her interests.

Thus we heard not only about her health in considerable detail, but also about her neighbours, her praises of the Vicar and her criticisms of his successor (of whom, however, she came to speak much more favourably), about her cats and their numerous families, her new chest of drawers, her sewing machine, which she could work with her one practicable foot, her linoleum, her fear of thunderstorms, her conservative club and its meetings, but, above all, the doings of Jessie; her school, her work, her Girl Guides and Sunday School in which she taught, her becoming 'difficult', and her 'definite young man', till finally she had to be taken to the infirmary, where, as her pension ceased, we were able to provide her with a small sum for extra comforts till she died. Jessie was left alone, but was engaged to the very satisfactory young man (though he *was* only 5 ft. 7 ins.), who had long before written to Mrs G. to ask 'permission in good set terms, as a gentleman should, to pay his addresses', and soon after was married in a 'periwinkle blue dress, the gift of her employers'; she wrote to thank us for our wedding present and for always being 'so kind and understanding'. All this involved the writing and receiving of letters, and the paying of visits, to the number of 984!

5. There were other Districts where the emphasis was different: East Lewisham stressed the fact that the Society

> is emphatically not merely another Relief Society for doling out miscellaneous charity. It is mainly an Advice Bureau, a nerve centre for all kinds of social effort, a liaison office for putting people in touch with each other.[6]

Some of the examples given in the published reports indicate that the anxiety of the applicant was the factor which the worker usually noted and set out to relieve. One illustration makes this clear:

> Mr South, an equally harassed but older man, was sent by his doctor for help to get to a Convalescent Home. He had been with one firm for many years, but owing to re-organisation, had been obliged to take different work in another department where he found himself among men of very different standards and tastes. This had resulted in a nervous condition that made him quite unfit for work of any kind. A prolonged period of convalescence did much to restore his confidence, but other work was of the utmost importance and through the interest of the Employment Officer of the Public Assistance Committee an excellent post was found for him, where among congenial surroundings he can gain his self-confidence and self-respect.

6. Another feature of the 1930 District Reports is the satisfaction the committees have in helping individuals and families who 'struggle to maintain respectability'. Students are invited to note not only this trait in so many of the C.O.S. applicants but also 'the readiness to co-operate shown by employers, doctors and clergy, hospitals, public and private societies and kindhearted individuals'.[7] Of four examples given by Islington in 1933 two are quoted where there is persistent struggle against ill-health of one or more members of the family who prize their independence. In the other two examples we have people 'of refined stock' whose piteous condition is relieved by the 'untiring effort of the Society and the courage of the clients'. One of these illustrates this aspect of the Society's casework:

Mrs X. is a widow of seventy-six, of whom it may certainly be said that she has seen better days; now, with the exception of a devoted daughter-in-law (cf. Ruth and Naomi), she is alone in the world with the old-age pension as her sole income. Three years ago her husband died of cancer in Charing Cross Hospital, but owing to mental trouble he had become obliged to give up his work a year previously and when he died Mrs X. was found to be left penniless. We cannot give the story of the struggle for independence from that time till the Church Army, in October last, referred her to us for general help; it is a more pleasing task to relate how help was afforded when the Committee had resolved to respond to the request.

The line of attack, or rather, of persuasion, in this case, was clearly in the direction of sea-farers' charities, for Capt. X. and his family for generations had been sailors and who could resist the appeal of one whose ancestor was Master Shipwright of the Navy in the time of Charles II and whose portrait is in the National Portrait Gallery? Moreover, Capt. X. was well-known as a marine inventor, and through his boat-disengaging gear—the standard fitting for the Royal Indian Marine and alternative fitting for H.M. Navy—he claimed to have saved some hundreds of lives during the war. The appeal was successful and in April a pension of £20 a year was granted by Trinity House to Mrs X. The old lady now lives in some degree of comfort; she is fond of reading, her eye-sight is good; she is able to do beautiful crochet work, and is full of gratitude to all who have helped to save her from the dreaded 'institution'. (In this case, forty-two letters written from our office appear on the file.)

7. Islington's report for 1938–39 was written when the Second World War had broken out. The year's work was summed up in an opening paragraph:

We were busier than ever with the usual needs and the usual problems. And in the usual way there were convalescence to arrange, surgical appliances to supply, removals to finance, tools for work to be bought, and individual difficulties to be solved.

The comment on the needs and how they were met is worth noting as an indication of the constant awareness that casework involves much more than the giving of practical help, important though that was:

Some needed very heavy financial help, some needed none; but all needed time, thought and sympathetic handling. For instance, among the surgical appliances supplied were spectacles for an elderly spinster, a backbrace for a butcher's boy and contact lenses for the mother of a family. The need in each instance was equally urgent for the patient, although the spectacles cost only 5s. 3d. a pair and the contact lenses twelve guineas.

Again, it cost a good deal to send a couple back to the north, so that the sick wife could be looked after by relatives and the man freed to go to work. And it was a heavy expense to send a hearty young widow and three delicate but mischievous children to their old home in Devonshire, where Granny could look after the children while their mother went to work.

On the other hand, it cost very little money to befriend and re-establish a very forlorn woman, who had lost husband and daughter in one year and was spending her time either weeping in her bedroom or trying to bring lawsuits against her fellow tenants for imaginary nuisances. This woman was gradually restored to a better frame of mind through the friendship of one of our workers, and through the kindness of another we got her a post as caretaker. Yet a third young volunteer now visits her regularly. Needs and problems of this type have in no way diminished since the outbreak of war, but under new conditions further new problems have arisen.

8. The late 1940s and the 1950s may be seen as a transition period in family casework as practised by F.W.A. workers. The new, younger, trained workers were highly critical of the older 'charity organisation' approach. In their view, a professional attitude demanded an awareness of the insight which psycho-analytical theory might offer to the practising caseworker. As we have seen,

they were determined to improve their own powers to help their clients by seeking opportunities for further training, e.g. by a course with the Tavistock Institute of Human Relations,* or by a period in one of the North American Schools of Social Work or by supervision of their own work by an experienced professional caseworker, usually from America or Canada, or by access to a consultant for difficult cases.

'The Dane Case', reported in the late 1940s,[8] seems to have been used as a cautionary tale by the F.W.A. It is worth considering at greater length since it shows the uncertainty during the transition stage in F.W.A. casework. The discussion which followed reflected some of the new 'professional' attitudes. 'The Dane Case' was introduced to readers as 'a basis for discussion' since it 'throws up problems which may often confront a visitor in the F.W.A.' The case, described in some detail in an article in *Social Work*, is headed 'A Study in Family Life'. A much-shortened version with quotations from the original, will illustrate the issues under discussion.

It is 'an irregular family': Gladys, aged twenty-four, had left her husband four years before, for alleged cruelty, and was living with Jack Dane, the father of her eleven weeks' old baby, Roy, in one very overcrowded room. Gladys' brother-in-law, in whose house the Danes are living, resents his wife's action in taking in the Danes. Gladys' mother, who lives within pram-walking distance, and a married sister are in close touch with the family and speak well of Jack. The mother would mind Roy, if a pram could be got for him, so that Gladys could return to her clerical work. The first application (its nature was unspecified) for help had been made to the Mayor who had sent Jack on to the F.W.A. Gladys 'felt badly about asking for things'. Jack had only gone 'as a last resort' as there was a slump in the building trade and he was out of work; unemployment benefit was insufficient for them to buy the special milk needed by the baby and to pay for Jack's shoe repairs, worn out through continually tramping in search of work. (Gladys had not asked for special supplies of milk at the Infant Welfare Centre.)

* Miss Keenleyside, in charge of the 'New Centre', Area IV, took this course.

The F.W.A. worker made a number of calls: she was allowed to discuss the situation with Gladys' mother, but tried unavailingly to get permission to get in touch with Jack's parents in the West Country. Throughout the reported interviews, Gladys showed herself to be spirited and independent.

The worker made it clear that the result of the application was dependent upon the decision of the Committee. She had already told Gladys' mother that she was uncertain about the Committee being willing to help 'in view of there being no marriage'. Later, Gladys showed the worker a very nice new pram which had been offered through a friend for a bargain price of £10. She asked whether a loan could be arranged for this sum; Jack had just got a job and once she had the pram she could start earning and soon pay back the amount. On the morning of the Committee meeting, fifteen days after the first application, the worker called again to say that there was a second-hand pram available at the office for £5. She thought the committee might more easily make a grant for this, and invited Gladys to come and see it. Gladys did not react favourably to the suggestion and ended an unwelcome visit by expressing some resentment about 'the impossibility of getting help in trouble, . . . even though you have told all your business'.

When the Committee met there was some opposition to making a grant, as the worker had feared, but only two members objected on account of the unmarried status; the majority were concerned with the needs of the baby for fresh air, but the second-hand pram was thought to be adequate; the F.W.A. should not sponsor a sum of £10, nor was it advisable for the Danes to start with such a large debt. The Committee offered a grant of £5 for the second-hand pram. The worker felt so disturbed that she took her record to a caseworkers' discussion group 'to strengthen her loyalty to the decision'. The case ended in an unorthodox fashion. As expected, Gladys would not give way about the new pram which she had used for a week, and the worker did her best, in various ways, to break down hostility, finally going to the length of putting a personal gift by the sleeping baby of £2 (with a nice little story of her own indebtedness to a former helper, etc.).

It is interesting to find that when the worker had asked for support from her colleagues to help her face the difficult final visit (to give the committee's decision) the group discussed the issues almost entirely in terms of the feelings of both the client and the worker. This was in marked contrast to the committee's concentration on the material aspects (including the baby's need for fresh air).

The Dane case was widely discussed in F.W.A. groups; for a considerable period *Social Work*[9] carried letters offering criticism and suggestions—ending with a final assessment of the deficiencies of English casework by a notable American caseworker.

A great many questions had been raised by the report of 'The Dane Case' and in some of the subsequent replies we find not only criticism of the worker's lack of skill, but criticism of the procedure and policy of the F.W.A. which still asked for 'references', which still paid 'home visits' without appointment,* and which was still dependent on a lay committee's decision. The F.W.A. was asked to look again at the principles or ethics which guided them. The letters are revealing.

> One letter was concerned with the sociological effects of such 'mishandling': it would seem to be an example of 'charity' in its perverted meaning: it disregarded the changes in attitude which thought of assistance as a duty owed by the community to the individual. Another letter, written by an F.W.A. Secretary who had become a psychiatric social worker, reflected the new psychological approach and used the vocabulary already familiar in American casework literature. The first interview should enable the client 'to orientate himself to the worker and to her agency'. Possibly the worker's decision to visit again the same afternoon was 'motivated by a desire' to get a second impression, etc. We soon find that 'it is less important to discover what is the exact nature of the problem than to learn what is the client's attitude to it'. The next steps are designed to enable 'all parties to the application to orientate themselves correctly before any action is taken'.

> A number of cases reflecting the caseworkers' new psychological

---

* Few realised that some of these practices had been condemned a half century earlier by Octavia Hill and Helen Dendy (Bosanquet).

approach were reported at some length in District annual reports, for example, 'the Kirk case'.[10] It shows the appalling difficulties resulting from the acute housing shortage after the Second World War and the years of effort to reach a solution. The report is too long and detailed to be included here, but it is interesting to note that the work for and with the family might have been matched by that of many of the earlier family social workers; by contrast, the awareness of the processes of casework method is new: 'the slow building up . . . of a relationship with the client which will bear the strain of sharing the cost of re-adjustment on the deeper levels of the human personality'.*[11]

9. *Social work* in the 1950s welcomed discussion of problems raised by the new developments of casework. One of these is considerably outspoken as it shows the worker seeking re-assurance, as well as increased skill, in meeting needs which she 'senses' but of which 'the client is not always fully aware'.

A Case History from a Family Agency[12]
In submitting this article the caseworker 'hoped that it will illustrate how the caseworker moves from the outward problem presented by the client to the underlying factors which need to be handled if a real solution is to be achieved. In dealing with the client's needs at this level the caseworker needs guidance from a worker suitably equipped to give supervisory or consultative help. This case material is intended to show the use made of group consultation'.

The account which followed this statement of purpose opened with a letter from:

Mr Jones asking for help with a housing problem. There were only a bedroom and a combined kitchen-living room, and he and his wife shared their double bed with 'a daughter who was rising five'. The first interviewer, who was inexperienced, saw the situation simply in terms of trying to help Mr Jones to get more suitable accommodation. Her senior, who took over when the chances of rehousing were seen to be small, 'sensing a problem which went deeper than bad housing',

* New language matched the new approach.

offered a series of appointments which were at first used by
Mr Jones to reinforce his assertion that 'rows at home' were
due entirely to housing conditions. The worker gradually
changed the focus from a new flat to Mr Jones' feelings. A
little later she 'openly placed the focus of interviews on
Mr Jones' marriage difficulties'. The worker had only one
interview with Mrs Jones, which was enough to assure her
that the sexual estrangement was due to Mr Jones' inhibitions
and not to Mrs Jones' refusal. Further interviews with
Mr Jones revealed anxiety not only about his own feelings
but about his small daughter who, to his embarrassment,
asked awkward questions.

At this point, after about six interviews, 'the worker felt
she would need help in handling' Mr Jones' difficulties; she
talked them over in a case conference with a consultant and
other members of staff '. . . the discussion helped the worker
to see Mr Jones' problems more clearly'. The article proceeds
with a case history, relating Mr Jones' childhood experiences
to his guilt feelings about his daughter and also about his
mother. However 'The consultant did not feel that Mr Jones
would need to work through these underlying feelings of
guilt but that help could be given on a more superficial
level. . . . It was decided that the worker could go on to help
Mr Jones consciously to see the treatment goal as enabling
him to resume sexual relations with his wife.'

Several following interviews were much concerned with
Mr Jones' anxieties about his small daughter sleeping with
her parents and the need to give her sex information. 'The
focus was now placed on the need for Mr Jones to work
through his own feelings with the goal of making it possible
for him to give information to his daughter.' Once more 'the
worker felt she would need support in her next step'. Another
group consultation was held.

There seems to have been some difference of opinion about
whether the father, rather than the mother, should give such
information, or whether both parents should share. 'The
consultant thought that the worker could help Mr Jones
through the process of preparing to give information . . . ;
getting ready to impart knowledge would be a means of
gaining it himself'. After further interviews, 'when the

worker had helped him to reach the point where he could accept them, she lent him some books on giving sex information to children. . . . Eventually the little girl was given a new single bed in the kitchen and Mr Jones went back to sleep with his wife. . . . He now felt less frustrated and the tensions at home relaxed. The quarrels subsided and Mr Jones seemed better able to tolerate outside stresses. This was shown specially in relation to the housing difficulty; he was able to accept quite calmly that he would have to wait until the Council made him an offer of a larger flat'.

10. The Family Welfare Association had always hoped that some of their records would offer good teaching material for students. With this in mind they published in 1961, *A Study of Co-operation in Social Casework by Almoners and Family Caseworkers*,* in the hope that the Project 'would make a valuable contribution to current thought on various aspects of casework practice'.†[13] The study was designed, in part, to see how far casework could be used in the preventive field: 'whether clients who were only in the early stages of difficulty could be helped by casework to avert extensive breakdowns'. The Introduction to the Report states clearly the purpose of the F.W.A. in the early 1960s and may be said to sum up the main objectives of the family social workers.

The Family Welfare Association exists to help people at times when they are unable to deal effectively with the problems confronting them and their families. . . . The F.W.A. aims to understand the significance of the problem to the individual, and bases help on this personal approach.

The F.W.A. hoped that its role as a society offering a preventive service would be generally recognised by other social workers. Its own decisions to select cases with great care were an important step in this emphasis on a preventive casework service.

The comments of the caseworker on one of the families, with whom they felt some success had been achieved, will serve to illustrate how the Association saw its role at this time.[14]

Mr and Mrs A. in their 30s, had three children of school age,

* See Chapter 10.
† Mrs M. Godfrey, Chairman of the Steering Committee.

the youngest of whom, aged six, had just left the hospital, since no medical treatment had been thought useful for her attacks of *petit mal*. The family was referred to the F.W.A. and became one of those studied in the 'Project'. It had been thought by the doctor and the almoner that Mrs A.'s anxiety was a potent factor in aggravating the child's illness. In the course of interviews over a period of nine months, Mrs A. had shown herself angry and resentful, full of complaints about the quarrelling of her children, the unreliability of her husband, overwork and money (he was a house painter and his work was irregular), and her own physical health (she had various minor disabilities). Mrs A. also discussed the family history with the worker, showing her own closely-knit family and the bond she felt with her mother, and by contrast, the 'deprived' childhood of Mr A. who had been illegitimate, and, until the age of twelve, an epileptic. The interviews with Mr A. had shown him at first antagonistic, and then willing to discuss his worry at his inability to keep his work and his knowledge that he was an inadequate parent. Summing up, the caseworker notes:

'Both Mr and Mrs A. used the caseworker to unburden their feelings of failure and anger with themselves. They came to see in some measure how the problems of their early life had always been disabling for them. As they understood more clearly their own part in creating their problems and how the members of their family reacted on each other, they began to think of ways of living more happily. At one point Mrs A. took steps towards separation but decided against it; they were able to accept the recommendation that Ann should attend an E.S.N. school, and they made their own plans for rehousing in their old area. Mr A. lost his job as a result of this, but soon found and retained one in which he felt more confident.

'It seemed that they could now see themselves and each other more realistically, and could discuss differences instead of quarrelling. Mrs A. began to see that she needed her mother as a support, but was less dependent on her and therefore less resentful about her. The family is by no means a consolidated group, but they see themselves as working towards staying together.'

11. The kind of casework practised by the family social workers in the late 1960s did not lend itself to open discussion of the kind practised in the 1940s and 50s.* Problems were now discussed at the professional level. However, the F.W.A. gave two examples of family casework in their annual report for 1967 to show the kind of skilled help they were giving and to illustrate how other services, both statutory and voluntary, made use of the F.W.A.[15]

(A.) Referred to the F.W.A. through the Children's Department:

. . . a young couple with three small children were referred to us through the Children's Department; they were in heavy arrears with their rent, faced possible eviction and the reception of the children into care. Our caseworker found on her first visit there had been a violent argument between the parents because the father had not been told of the mounting debts. Sickness had kept him out of work and he was drinking heavily when he was at work. He gave his wife insufficient money for housekeeping and she, fearing his wrath, had been secretly borrowing from money-lenders at an exorbitant rate of interest and was getting ever more deeply into debt.

During regular weekly interviews at their home, the F.W.A. social worker helped this couple to start being more honest with each other jointly and to face the responsibility for what was happening. The father began to see how irresponsible he was in relation to his family and his wife began to recognise that by refusing to trust him she was only making the situation worse. Through successful applications to various charitable funds we helped this family to pay off some of their debts until their remaining commitments were just within their weekly income. As the mother gradually became less upset and anxious she was able to take a part-time job to ease the financial difficulties. With our help and support the parents were able to pay off the arrears of rent gradually but steadily, so that the threat of eviction passed. There is now a much

* The writer was allowed to see casepapers showing 'typical work' in 1967, but not allowed to use them for the purpose of illustration. In 1970, when this section was in draft, the Association published *The Voice of the Social Workers* in which members of staff discussed how the work was done in relation to selected cases.

warmer, happier family atmosphere at home and the father, in consequence, no longer drinks so heavily.*

(B.) Referred to the F.W.A. through one of their Citizens Advice Bureaux:

. . . the father of two teenage boys and a girl of six came to us on the advice of one of our Citizens Advice Bureaux. In grief over the death of a favourite sister, his wife had attempted suicide and had subsequently left him for another man. Her husband, our client, was shocked, hurt and humiliated. He managed to look after his home and children with the help of neighbours and kept his job although he became very depressed. He heard occasionally from his wife and knew that she was ill and still suffering from suicidal tendencies, but dared not ask her to return in case she rebuffed him. His health deteriorated and so, inevitably, did his ability to hold his job. The little girl had started walking in her sleep; the boy of twelve was having severe bouts of asthma that necessitated hospitalisation; the eldest boy's schoolwork was becoming unsatisfactory. It was clear that the whole family was involved in a worsening situation due to the absence of the wife and mother. In desperation the husband went to the C.A.B.

When the father saw his F.W.A. social worker he poured out his pent-up feelings and found relief in sharing them with someone who set aside time to listen, not once, but many times. He began to be aware of some of the reasons for his wife's desertion, including her feelings about her sister's death. He still felt resentful at her desertion of him for somebody else, but he faced the fact that she might have been seeking the sympathy and comfort that he had been unable to offer. After many interviews, he began to feel less anger and more pity for his wife, acknowledging his own failure in his behaviour to her. Eventually he brought her home. When the F.W.A. caseworker first saw her she was still very distressed but relieved to be with her family again. She is now under the care of a psychiatrist, although living at home

---

* This example, in its essential features, might have belonged to almost any period in the Association's history.

and trying to rebuild her family life. At the beginning of this family's tragedy, while the father felt hurt and resentful, he could not talk to his wife without increasing their hostile feelings to each other. His gradual change of feeling led to a change in behaviour.

In the account of the successful work with this second family we see the professional caseworkers giving both practical and psycho-therapeutic help, as they co-operate with other social workers or supplement the treatment of the psychiatrist. No longer do we hear the cry of the older volunteer as she reflected on 'the terrifying responsibility of handling other people's lives'. The trained family social worker today may well be in a better position to understand some of the underlying causes of distress and to have greater confidence in helping disturbed people. Yet, at both periods of casework practice at its best, the person in distress who sought

TABLE 8

FLUCTUATIONS IN CASEWORK

Applications in Selected Years, 1874–1946
Selected from C.O.S./F.W.A. Annual Reports

Date	I Made	II Decided*	III Assisted	IV Not assisted	V % assisted (based on number 'decided')
1874	(omitted)	12,656	4,755	4,738	37·5
1884	(omitted)	20,409	9,637	10,772	47
1895	(omitted)	23,603	10,656	10,593	45
1910	22,320	(omitted)	8,463	(omitted)	
1911–14 (average)	18,493	17,587	7,439	(omitted)	42
1914–18 (average)	12,255	11,263	6,329	(omitted)	56
1919	10,851	9,734	5,946	2,293	61
1929	15,355	15,214	8,186	4,479	54
1939	16,488	15,711	8,492	3,766	54
1946	15,261	15,025	10,664	1,941	71

Note: Post-war figures do not distinguish between 'assisted' and 'unassisted'. New classification prevents further comparison.
  I have added column V.

  * 'Decided' means considered by the Committee, dealt with and 'closed'.

TABLE 9

Applications 1919–1946

from C.O.S./F.W.A. *Annual Reports*

I	II	III	IV	V	VI	VII†
Year	Made	Decided*	Assisted	Not assisted	Withdrawn	%
1919	10,851	9,734	5,946	2,293	1,991	61
1920	13,240	12,560	7,169	3,391	2,403	57
1921	14,714	14,001	7,253	4,578	2,586	52
1922	13,982	13,657	7,113	4,311	2,233	52
1923	14,315	13,662	7,359	4,128	2,175	54
1924	15,026	14,421	7,814	4,112	2,495	54
1925	14,574	14,186	7,840	3,862	2,484	55
1926	15,090	14,632	8,019	4,185	2,428	55
1927	15,713	15,464	8,296	4,744	2,424	54
1928	16,836	15,759	8,567	4,627	2,565	54
1929	15,355	15,214	8,186	4,479	2,549	54
1930	14,876	14,735	8,010	4,275	2,450	54
1931	15,646	15,259	7,565	5,188	2,506	50
1932	17,191	16,804	8,016	6,293	2,495	50
1933	17,187	16,588	8,099	5,819	2,670	49
1934	17,722	17,496	9,169	5,450	2,877	52
1935	15,856	15,435	8,114	3,943	3,378	52
1936	15,560	14,970	7,841	3,704	3,425	52
1937	14,299	14,344	7,958	3,329	3,057	55
1938	15,524	15,111	8,286	3,600	3,225	54
1939	16,488	15,711	8,492	3,766	3,453	54
1940	16,352	16,430	10,101	3,397	2,932	61
1941	18,801	18,806	12,823	2,863	3,137	68
1942	15,895	15,158	9,860	2,684	2,614	61
1943	16,238	15,123	9,783	2,607	2,733	65
1944	17,335	16,806	11,424	2,206	3,176	68
1945	15,163	14,265	9,988	1,777	2,500	70
1946	15,261	15,025	10,664	1,941	2,420	71

New Classification after 1946 prevents further comparison.

* 'Decided' means considered by the Committee, dealt with and 'closed'.
† Column VII shows the relation between IV and III.
I have added this column to show changes in the proportion assisted.

DIAGRAM 6

Total Number of Applications to the C.O.S./F.W.A. Compared in Two Periods

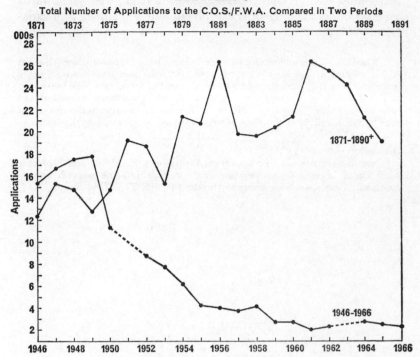

† The annual figures for this series are subject to periodic changes in classification, but the overall trend is not affected. This applies also to 1961–66.

N.B. After 1950 there was a change over in presentation of accounts from September to March. The 1950–52 Report covers the period September 1950 to March 1952. Owing to this change, total applications for 1952 relate to an 18 month period. The line between 1950 and 1952 has therefore been adjusted to an annual basis. A similar adjustment has been made for 1963.

The above graph gives an indication of the overall trends. A comparison is made between recent years (some twenty years preceding the Centenary) and the first twenty years for which figures were available (1871–90). The early figures show an ascending curve, with periodic fluctuations, from approximately 12,000 applications in 1871 to some 26,000 in 1881 and 1886. The troughs and peaks reflect London trade fluctuations, depending often on the severity of the weather and its effect on work in the Docks and the building trades.

The later figures ascend from 15,000 to nearly 18,000 for the immediate post-war years until 1949 and then drop sharply to 11,000 in 1950 followed by a steady decline to 4,000 in 1955. This reflects not only the general improvement in the standard of living and the new social security provisions, but the reorganisation within the Association. In the 1960s the F.W.A. settled down to an average of approximately 2,000 applications annually, in accordance with the new casework policy.

M

help found a sympathetic hearing. This, in itself, went far towards
a better understanding of the problem and sometimes to a satisfactory solution.*

* The F.W.A. was seldom in a position to know what the client himself thought
of his treatment, nor why an application for help was withdrawn. Even a
successful outcome, from the social worker's point of view, gave little indication
of the client's ideas on how the interviews went. Occasionally a reaction was
recorded, as in the 'Dane Case'. Not many felt moved to write, as did the young
man 'rehabilitated' after the First World War (see pp. 342 and 337).

Addendum
   When this section was in preparation Professor J. E. Mayer and Professor
Noel Timms secured the cooperation of the F.W.A. in some research on this
question. It has since been published under the title *The Client Speaks*.[16]

Conclusion

The study of the Family Welfare Association has an interest and importance which go far beyond its role as a London charitable society. Its history and its work are interwoven with the development of new patterns of family life in this country as industrial and social changes gathered force.

Adaptation to a rapidly changing society has created a host of problems for the family, while it has offered fresh challenges and opportunities. The uncertainties of economic growth, together with the devastating effects of war, have introduced elements of instability beyond personal control. Families have fallen victim to economic depression and unemployment and the war-time loss or disablement of the chief bread-winner, as well as to the long-standing problems of sickness, infant mortality, old age, etc. which bore particularly hard on the low wage-earners and the fatherless families.

The increasing complexity of modern society with its higher expectation of civilised living has imposed standards beyond the capacity of some to reach. Psychological stresses, no less than financial ones, have been more than some families could bear. Recognising these problems—albeit slowly and unevenly—society has gradually organised auxiliary services, both voluntary and statutory, which today we know as family social work.

As a pioneer body the Association helped to lay the foundations of family social work not only in this country but overseas. North America, in particular, traces the origin of its extensive casework service to the old Charity Organisation Society. The F.W.A. in turn, acknowledged its own debt when some of its members went to Schools of Social Work in the United States and Canada, and

North American caseworkers were invited as consultants to the London Districts. It was a Canadian from the University of British Columbia who was asked to undertake the Association's full-scale review in 1960.

The relation between family social work and social and economic change clearly emerges as we look back one hundred years (1869–1969) in the life of the Family Welfare Association. Growth or stagnation in the Association's development can be traced in relation to three periods—pre-war (1869–1914), inter-war (1918–39) and post-war (1945–69).

For most of the first period wage-earners stood at risk at predictable stages of their lives, for example, during parenthood and in old age; their marginal income left them most vulnerable during crises such as sickness or unemployment. Mutual aid schemes were necessarily limited to a minority of the better paid. In hard times there remained only the dreaded Poor Law or charity. The C.O.S., in the pioneer period, pursued a vigorous policy of charity organisation and agitation for Poor Law reform on behalf of families in distress. Unfortunately, it did this under the inspiration of Individualism, showing active hostility to the new radical thinking.

In this period the C.O.S. was inclined to make extravagant claims ('equal to a Department of State'). It was one of its own supporters who pointed out that its attack on 'pauperism' had made very little difference to the serious problem of poverty in London. It sometimes failed to recognise that it dealt with only a small minority of working people; it tried hard, but most often failed, to get industrial workers to serve as members of its committees. Yet, in spite of its shortcomings, it made a lasting contribution to the development of family social work: the principles laid down by Loch are, by and large, valid today. The Society took an active part in promoting legislation (e.g. on housing) and encouraged C.O.S. District participation in local efforts to improve social conditions. It campaigned relentlessly for the replacement of doles by adequate Poor Law relief and for the organisation of charitable effort to eliminate wasteful duplication amongst the many Victorian charities. Above all it did outstanding pioneer work which pointed the way to the development of some of the later social services.

In the second period, between the two world wars, unprecedented economic depressions were followed by considerable expansion of the Social Insurance and Assistance services. But the C.O.S. found that, in practice, these services were too fragmented and not universally available, leaving much to be done for 'the family as a whole'. Although this period has often been described as one of stagnation for the Society, the C.O.S. carried out a useful 'holding operation' during the uneasy, inter-war years. An increasing number of agencies both public and private—hospital almoners, probation officers, Assistance Board officers, health visitors, etc.—were glad to call upon trained social workers for further help and the C.O.S. took pride in its role as 'handmaid'. That it was no longer in the limelight and failed to embark on any pioneer experiments, was due, in part, to Pringle's misunderstanding of the growth of Collectivism (which he dismissed as 'an aberration').* This might have been disastrous for the C.O.S. had not the hard-pressed District secretaries continued to offer a much-valued family service, which counter balanced the Victorian individualistic philosophy emanating from Central.

In the third period the Society had to make considerable adjustments to changed conditions. The Second World War, with its challenge and opportunities, shook the C.O.S. out of its nineteenth century philosophical groove. Under Astbury the Society welcomed the Beveridge proposals and the new Social Security schemes and marked the reversal of its social theory by a change of name. 'Family Welfare' now more fittingly described the Association's function. 'Charity Organisation', as Loch conceived it, had, in any case, failed. In the mid-1940s it was hoped that full employment and the new social security measures would remove the last traces of grinding poverty; the F.W.A. realised that the National Health Service would make much of its former work unnecessary; to meet the new needs it was generally thought that charitable organisations might concentrate on counselling and 'supportive help'. They were soon to find that, although the standard of living had risen in the community at large, there were certain sections who still bore the burden of poverty and dependency. Financial problems continued to rank high among the

* His reference to Sir James Barrie's *Wintry Tale* is pathetic in its *naïveté*: 'Collectivism was a phantasm . . . which, like Miss Julie Logan . . . has vanished' (C.O.S. *Annual Report*, 1931). In fairness to Pringle it should be remembered that he was greatly respected by the District secretaries and was able to inspire them to renewed effort in difficult times.

difficulties brought by clients to the F.W.A. By the late 1960s family social workers were increasingly concerned with those coming from disturbed or unhappy homes, whether or not there was associated poverty.

As we examine the achievements and failures of the Association throughout its long history we should ask whether it made any distinctive contribution to family welfare. The constant demand for a high standard of service, whether by volunteers or by salaried workers, should come high in the assessment. It led to the early foundation of training schemes which were open not only to their own social workers but to others in related fields. The demand for training continued to grow until it became a recognised qualification in all branches of social work.*

Inseparable from this pioneer work was the gradual development of casework theory. There is a remarkable similarity between some of the problems discussed by the early social workers and those of today: not surprisingly, when we consider that they are human problems which persist while conditions change. Helen Bosanquet wrote vividly of 'the difficulties of communication' in social work; Octavia Hill was surely making an early statement on 'relationship' when she wrote of friendship and sympathy as the fundamental requirements of a visitor. All the pioneers held 'knowledge', both of the individual and of his environment, to be indispensable.

The family social workers continually sought to improve their knowledge and their methods. In 1918 they were asking Dr Cyril Burt whether a study of psychology would help. They were advised to wait. A generation later they were asking Dr Balint whether the new dynamic psychology would give them a better understanding of their own and their clients' behaviour. In the 1950s there was some division within the Association as the older members continued to stress the need to see the individual as a member of the community, while the younger ones were seeking a psychotherapeutic approach to each client.† In the 1960s family

* When the Local Authority Social Services Act, 1970, came into force the most responsible posts in the new Social Service Departments required social work qualifications.

† In the late 1950s caseworkers received some devastating criticism from those who were hostile to the new approach. Barbara Wootton, in particular, poured ridicule on the search for 'something deeper underneath'. She deplored the 'all-pervading mystique of "the relationship" '.[1]

social workers, undeterred in their exploration of the uses of dynamic psychology, gave, at the same time, greater attention to sociology. They took note of the criticism from North America that casework might be ineffective in meeting social needs.[2] The casework journals, far from claiming authority for their methods, were now showing awareness of the danger of 'erecting a theory into a belief'. By the end of the 1960s the F.W.A. family social workers were, with many others in related fields, taking a lively interest in the development of social work under rapidly changing conditions.

It is interesting to recall earlier discussions when Loch had urged District secretaries to take preventive action: to combine work for individuals with a concern for the reform of local conditions. As a result the old C.O.S. had carried out some useful schemes in some of the 'Bad Areas' which they renamed 'Improvement Areas'. This two-fold approach has an echo today when a writer describes the need for 'new thinking' about social work practice: 'personal casework on the one-to-one basis must be provided within the same framework as the other supportive and preventive community services if the circumstances which lead to the breakdown and crises are to be removed'.[3]

Closely related to the development of casework was the growth of a professional attitude. From Loch onwards there had been concern for a responsible approach, both to the client and to the community. An essential element was 'confidentiality'. In the training of students and of volunteers the Association has made a valuable contribution to the ethics of social work. As advances in the social sciences and the expansion of the social services widened the area of choice, and as many more workers were brought in as 'auxiliaries' in family welfare, so new questions of professional conduct were raised. The F.W.A. family social workers achieved a new professional confidence. Their status now corresponded to that of other comparable professional groups. There was an active professional association and salaries were brought into line. This reflects not only the fight within the Association to break down the old 'quasi-volunteer' standing of the salaried worker, but also the changed attitude towards women professional workers in general. It reflects, too, the demand for trained workers as the statutory social services expanded and the need for skilled family social workers received public recognition.

One consequence of this new professionalism was the demand for a reduction in the number of clients accepted. This was essential for improvement in quality. Prolonged sessions for each client in an attractive room were required for sound casework. Many families who in the past had sought counsel and short-term help had now to look elsewhere and one of the most significant changes in F.W.A. family social work after the 1950s was the large drop in the numbers helped. Fortunately the Association's C.A.Bx., staffed by trained social workers, were able to offer an advisory service which, in part, offset the drop in counselling once offered more extensively in the F.W.A. District offices.

There is one facet of the Association's method which has been severely criticised in the past, but which is now better understood, namely, that of selection of clients. Its procedure in the early days of selecting 'the helpable' (sometimes called 'the deserving') aroused widespread hostility. Yet those who were in close contact with District work, including some socialist critics, realised that 'discrimination, properly exercised', brought help where it was most needed. Moreover, when resources are limited, a family social work agency must decide where it can best use its skill; and, as Loch pointed out, in the best interests of the client the worker must know 'when to stand aside'. Today 'work discrimination'[4] is also thought to be necessary for the protection of the social workers: 'It is important to know how to say "no".' Loch had already said something similar when he claimed that cases must be limited 'according to visiting power after selection by enquiry'.

Of the multiple effects of social and economic change upon the F.W.A., one of the most outstanding is the altered position of the voluntary worker. Not only has the supply of volunteers greatly diminished, owing to changes in the social class structure of Britain (reducing the size of the leisured class with their command of domestic help) but, advancing professionalism has deprived them of their former status. The F.W.A. has continued to welcome volunteers for some essential activities, as members of committees, as friendly visitors to pensioners, sometimes as 'aides' in routine administrative tasks, or as helpers in Citizens Advice Bureaux. 'Central' and 'the Areas' have been fortunate in having distinguished Chairmen, Treasurers and other honorary officers who have given generously of their time. But voluntary workers no longer have 'a unique, inalienable function of their own' in family social work. The account of the impressive contribution made by volunteers in the past may suggest other ways in which widely experienced men and women might again help in giving responsible personal service to families. It would need careful thought and planning in relation to professional workers' other obligations, in particular, the commitment of the F.W.A. to the training of students.*

The main justification for a voluntary society is generally thought to be its ability to experiment and pioneer. That the Family Welfare Association has fully justified its existence on these grounds is evident from its history. The following brief summary will recall some of its main achievements. The F.W.A. record in the field of health and family welfare is outstanding. We saw how the old C.O.S. discovered through its work in the Districts how close is the relation between health and social conditions. The Association also identified many unmet medical and social needs: surgical and convalescent aid were early examples. In this field the C.O.S. had been able to evoke considerable charitable support. The lack of dentures as a bar both to health and self-respect, and sometimes to employment, was generally less well understood. The Districts recognised the need and strove to meet it in the period between the two world wars, long before the National Health Service was established. But though they held the view that the supply of teeth was no trivial matter in family welfare, they were almost overwhelmed by its implications. We saw that one overworked family social worker wryly reported: 'We cannot always remodel the outlook of the entire family because one member of it requires teeth.'

The Society also gave valuable service as it drew attention to the plight of the disabled and established the principle of rehabilitation. (This was done to good effect on behalf of sufferers from tuberculosis.) In all these ventures it secured expert help and advice from doctors who served on its committees and acted as honorary consultants. It also co-operated wherever possible with other interested charitable organisations (the welfare of the blind and of the mentally handicapped are good examples). Not only

---

* Volunteers did not always respond to the offer of formal training: e.g. when an excellent course was organised and widely publicised, following a suggestion in the *Cunliffe Report*, the attendance was so small that the lectures were discontinued.

M*

did 'Central' organise valuable hospital and convalescent home schemes, surgical aid schemes, etc., but the Districts co-operated with enterprising medical officers of health in a number of boroughs to establish health visiting, infant welfare centres, tuberculosis after-care, etc. Many C.O.S. workers gave generously of their time in serving these new ventures. Similarly they helped to set up, and to man, some of the first school care committees. The F.W.A. continued, throughout its history, to work closely with the health services and with local doctors. Such co-operation is proving useful today when emotionally disturbed people seek help.

Among the Association's outstanding pioneer efforts for the health and social welfare of families was the foundation of two organisations which continue to do valuable work. The Institute of Medical Social Workers (formerly the Institute of Hospital Almoners) and the Invalid Children's Aid Association owe their origin to the foresight of F.W.A. pioneers. In more recent times the Family Discussion Bureau was established within the Association and then transferred to the Institute of Human Relations with whom it had co-operated from its early days. An even later venture was the founding of the Family Centre, Hackney, the result of co-operation between the F.W.A., the Family Service Units and the I.C.A.A.*

Another early experiment worthy of notice was the establishment of Skilled Employment Committees. These were often the outcome of efforts to rehabilitate a member of a family. The old C.O.S. failed to recognise the nature of economic forces but it constantly sought new ways to mitigate some of the effects of adverse industrial conditions. It was a C.O.S. worker who opened the first Employment Enquiry Office in Soho in 1870 and it was the C.O.S. Committee on Unskilled Labour which gave William Beveridge much of the material for his discussion of the 'Reserve of Labour' in his seminal book, *Unemployment: a Problem of Industry.*[5]

One of the most impressive facts emerging from the study of the F.W.A. is the thoroughness with which investigations were made and projects undertaken. The Association has shown great aptitude for securing the service of expert men and women on its

* This has since taken its place among other family social work offices run by the F.W.A.

'select committees'. It instituted a number of social enquiries and published the results, often acting as 'gadfly' to the Government Departments concerned. For a great part of its history the F.W.A. took every opportunity to co-operate with others in getting amendments to existing legislation or, in some cases, in initiating the processes leading to new legislation where the need had been demonstrated. (The Artisans Dwellings Act and acts regulating Charities and Hire-Purchase are good examples.)

Not least among the Association's contributions to the social services was its scrupulous recording and filing of information. In the early days it prided itself on the fact that its methods of case-recording, etc., were studied and followed by at least one statutory authority and by other charitable bodies. The long-standing work of the Information Department, particularly the publication of the *Charities Digest* and the *Guide to the Social Services*, continues to be widely welcomed. Although it has done far less detective work than in its early days this remains a subsidiary activity and it still gives useful service in exposing fraudulent practices or bogus charities. The Association's great concern has always been to offer a ready source of information on the effect of social policy on ordinary families. Long before the Citizens Advice Bureaux were set up the C.O.S. had acted as interpreter, bringing anomalies and deficiencies to the notice of the statutory authorities and explaining social enactments to bewildered clients. It frequently sent memoranda and reports, based on its experience of work among families, to statutory Committees of Enquiry.[*]

In the past its secretaries, both at 'Central' and in the Districts, served on numerous statutory committees. The outstanding example came from the pioneer period when C. S. Loch served on three Royal Commissions: in particular, with the full approval of the Society, he gave a great part of his time for several years to the Royal Commission on the Poor Laws. The Society believed that the Majority Report was largely inspired, if not actually written, by Loch. Certainly the following quotation has the authentic C.O.S. quality: 'The many subtle problems' (of human need), 'especially when it is a family rather than an individual that requires rehabilitation, cannot be solved by the simple process of sending off each unit to a separate authority for maintenance and

[*] In the early days the C.O.S. often took the initiative. Later the F.W.A. or its C.A.B.x usually contributed, as did other societies, by invitation.

treatment. What is needed is a disinterested authority, practised in looking at all sides of a question and able to call in skilled assistance.'[6] This, written in the first decade of the twentieth century, is concerned with problems only now being resolved.* The Association foretold, and continued to fight against, 'the fragmentation of the social services'.

C.O.S. hostility to 'mass social action' was based on the fear that it would fail to recognise the uniqueness of the individual with his personal needs, as it would fail to recognise the responsibility of the individual and his family for his own 'betterment'. Later generations have heard with something akin to horror that the C.O.S. opposed the feeding of schoolchildren and the granting of old age pensions. They have seldom understood that the Society did this, not only under the influence of a misguided Individualism, but in the belief that hungry schoolchildren and poverty stricken old people were a glaring example of the inadequacy and the fragmentation of the public services.

Today the F.W.A. fully supports the view that responsible action is helped, not hindered, by national schemes for social security. While we may regret the early obstructionist policy of the Society, we can at the same time recognise some of the values inherent in its beliefs. An American historian has recorded his view that 'The supreme contribution of the Society grew out of its conviction that the indispensable condition for social progress was steady, self-reliant individuals and families. . .'.† Workers within both the statutory and voluntary agencies are still asking, as in Loch's day, how best to help—particularly when long-term 'supportive help' is needed—without discouraging personal effort or diminishing the self-respect of the individual. One of the skills of the trained caseworker is to help the client at the earliest moment to accept responsibility for his own actions.

One of the striking characteristics of the Association's history has been its willingness to keep its methods under review. It has

* The Seebohm Report (Report of the Committee on Local Authority and Allied Personal Services, July 1968) showed that the arguments for administrative unification were accepted. The Local Authority Social Services Act which followed in 1970 ensured that by April, 1971, a single statutory committee would replace the Children's and Welfare committees and take over some of the work of the Health Committee.

† It should be added that Professor Owen was critical of other aspects of the Association's record.

never been afraid of self-criticism. Indeed, the 'problem cases' published in its journals were deliberately selected to provoke discussion. Over the years there have been many changes in its methods and approaches, but one thing has not changed: its underlying purpose. Despite its faults, the F.W.A. has shown an unwavering concern for individuals and families and an unflagging determination 'to provide a family casework service in order to assist persons in distress towards a solution of family difficulties'.

As new needs arise the Association must, if it is to survive, follow its long-established tradition of pioneering; it must continue to examine its function and methods in the light of changing conditions. To carry out this policy it must not be too harassed by shortage of funds.* In the last resort a voluntary body depends upon the goodwill and support of the public which, in modern terms, means financial help from local authorities and charitable trusts.

As we look back on the Association's one hundred years of family social work it is not difficult to see why, at times, it provoked hostility. But, equally clearly, we recognise how valuable was the pioneer work done by devoted men and women, some eminent, some obscure, who contributed to the development of family welfare and pointed the way to the provision of services which are now an integral part of our community life. The history of the F.W.A. is not merely the history of an experiment in voluntary charitable work; it is a case-study of the developing sensitivity of the nation to social and personal problems. It is in this that its wider sociological significance lies.

Tail-Piece

It is interesting to set side by side the following statements:

1. 1971. *Kay Richards, Director of Social Work, County Council of Clackmannon*

Over the past few years there has been . . . a failure to recognise that management, casework and community work are all concerned with relationships, with mobilising capacities and resources within the individual, the organisation and the community to enable

---

* This chapter was in draft before the severe financial crsis of 1970–71. See foreword by the chairman, 1971, to the F.W.A. *Annual Report*, 1969–70.

them to function more effectively in all their relationships. (Article based on paper delivered to Directors of Social Services, November, 1970, reported in *Social Work To-day*, 8th April, 1971, Vol. 2, No. 1.)

2. 1893. *Helen Dendy (later Bosanquet), C.O.S. Family Social Worker and Author*

Now this thoroughness of knowledge at which we aim . . . will involve, first a careful study of the individual men and women with whom we come in contact . . . and it will involve, further, a full acquaintance with the wider social conditions and tendencies within the limits of which we work . . . the man, with his character such as his temperament and surroundings have made it, can only act within the community of which he is a fraction. His every movement is influenced by relations of innumerable kinds. (Paper on *Thorough Charity*, published in 1893 by the Charity Organisation Society.)

Notes on Primary Sources

1. *Family Welfare Association Archives* (now on permanent loan to the Goldsmiths Library, University of London and to the Library of the National Institute for Social Work Training).

The Early Period

The publication of reports and pamphlets was an outstanding activity of the Charity Organisation Society; these, together with the papers given in the years preceding the Society's foundation were zealously preserved. The *Annual Reports* (the first, 1870) were large volumes bound together with detailed reports from the Districts and kept year by year in the Council's library. Minute books were also kept, often bound in heavy calf. There were miscellaneous collections of Forms and Notices and in particular *Books and Forms* and *Visitors' Handy-book*. *Complaints, Criticisms and Abuse* were also filed.

Charity Organisation Papers and *C.O.S. Occasional Papers* on subjects of special concern to family social workers were published at frequent intervals and listed in the Annual Reports. In addition, *Special Reports*, the result of Committees of Enquiry set up by the Society, were widely publicised (see a useful list in C. L. Mowat, *The Charity Organisation Society, 1869–1913*, p. 179). The Society also ran a weekly journal, *The Reporter*, 1872–84, which was replaced by a monthly, *The Charity Organisation Review*, in 1885. More important, an annual *Charities Register and Digest* (1st pub. 1882), was increasingly in demand. Similarly, a handbook, *How to Help Cases of Distress*, appearing separately from the Digest in 1883, continued to find wide acceptance (later as *The Prevention and Relief of Distress* and, more recently, as *Guide to the Social Services*).

Letters to the Press (especially those of C. S. Loch to *The Times*) and contributions to periodicals were collected and bound. The *Encyclopaedia Britannica* carried a long article on Charity by C.S.L. (the 11th ed. is most often quoted). Loch's more substantial contributions were collected and published in book form on behalf of the Society (see text Chapter 2). A copy of Loch's Diary (unpublished) was added later. Other prominent members of the Society, notably Helen (Dendy) Bosanquet and Octavia Hill were influential writers for the C.O.S. in the early period.

The Modern Period

In the years between the two World Wars and in the post-war period primary source material was less prolific. *Annual Reports* continued to be the main source of information on Council and District activities; they diminished appreciably in size over the years. *Occasional Papers* were published intermittently, ceasing altogether after Astbury. *Social Work*, which replaced the Charity Organisation Review in 1939, was, till recently, the main vehicle for the Association's discussion of family social work and related questions. A *Pringle Memorial* study by Marjorie Smith and the *Loch Memorial Lectures* by various speakers (see especially that by Una Cormack) were published by the F.W.A., indicating what subjects were of interest at different periods. A series of *Special Projects* sponsored by Charitable Trusts led to the publication of some useful reports by the F.W.A. (see Text, Chapter 10).

Events have led to the hiving off of some of the publications of the Association, including *Social Work*, *The Charities Digest* and, more recently, *Guide to the Social Services*. The F.W.A. library has been dispersed and future enquirers must look to the collection in the Goldsmiths Library (University of London) and to the Library of the National Institute for Social Work Training.

2. *Collections of Documents*, etc. (see Source Notes for details).

> The *Solly Collection*.
> *Alfred Marshall: Official Papers*.
> The *London County Council Archives* (later G.L.C.)
> The *Fabian Tracts*.

3. *Biographies* and *Autobiographies* and *The Dictionary of National Biography*.

These have thrown considerable light on the Association and its influential members (many of them were written by critics of their methods or of their philosophy); outstanding among them were:

> Beatrice Webb, *My Apprenticeship*; George Lansbury, *My Life*; Clement Attlee, *The Social Worker*; Henry Snell, *Men, Movements and Myself*; Henrietta Barnett, *Canon Barnett, His Life, Work and Friends*; Violet Markham, *Return Passage*; E. Moberley Bell, *Octavia Hill* (see also her *The Story of Hospital Almoners*); Barbara Wootton, In *A World I Never Made*; Mary Stocks, *My Commonplace Book*.

4. *Parliamentary Papers*

Reports of Royal Commissions and other 'Blue Books' collected by the Society formed the nucleus of a valuable reference library on social questions. Outstanding among them were the Reports of Royal Commissions of which C. S. Loch was himself a member (see text Ch. 2). These gave source material for the early period. In the modern period a long series of official reports were valuable primary sources from that of the *Curtis Committee* in 1946, to the *Younghusband Report* in 1959, culminating in the *Seebohm Report* of 1968. The official *History of the*

Second World War, Problems of Social Policy, Richard Titmuss, 1950, gave important documentation of the work of family social workers. All these were widely discussed in professional journals of which the following in the field of family social work are a selection:

Professional Journals, etc.
   Social Work, originally an F.W.A. quarterly
   Social Service, National Council of Social Service; *Case Conference*, a journal for the Social Worker and the Social Administrator.;
   The Almoner, a journal of Medical Social Work; *The British Journal of Psychiatric Social Work*; *Mental Health*, National Association for Mental Health; *Crucible* (earlier, Moral Welfare), C. of E. Board for Social Responsibility.

Some of these were amalgamated, after the formation of the British Association of Social Workers, in the production of *Social Work Today*, and in April 1971, a quarterly, *The British Journal of Social Work*.

To the above should be added *Public Administration* (Institute of Public Administration), *The British Journal of Sociology*, and *The Lancet*.

American Journals are not listed here, but special note should be taken of *Some Impressions of Social Services in Great Britain by an American Social Work Team*, the Report of the U.S. Educational Commission on the U.K., 1956.

Periodicals
Since the Second World War articles on family social work and related questions have appeared frequently in periodicals, e.g. *The New Statesman, New Society, The Spectator, The Listener*.

Histories of the Society
Helen Bosanquet wrote the first history of the Society under the title *Social Work in London, 1869–1912*. There was also a short study by W. A. Bailward, *The Charity Organisation Society: an Historical Sketch, 1869–1906*. The most recent study, *The Charity Organisation Society, 1869–1913*, Charles Loch Mowat, 1965, was also concerned with the early period. Other writers have dealt with particular aspects, notably a comparative study (England and the United States) by Kathleen Woodroofe, *From Charity to Social Work*, 1962, and a Cambridge dissertation (unpublished) by Calvin Woodard, *The Charity Organisation Society and the Rise of the Welfare State*.

The Society also figures in a group of studies on voluntary organisations and on philanthropy and in some more general studies, e.g. Constance Braithwaite, *The Voluntary Citizen*, 1938; A. F. C. Bourdillon, *Voluntary Social Services*, 1945; H. A. Mess, *Voluntary Social Services since 1918*, 1947; William Beveridge, *Voluntary Action*, 1948, Madeline Rooff, *Voluntary Societies and Social Policy*, 1957; B. Kirkman Gray, *A History of English Philanthropy*, 1905; David Owen, *English Philanthropy*, 1965; Gertrude Williams, *The State and the Standard of Living*, 1936; A. F. Young and E. T. Ashton, *British Social Work in the Nineteenth Century*,

1956. The Society also takes its place in studies of casework, e.g. *Social Casework in Great Britain*, ed. Cherry Morris, and a series of studies in particular fields by Noel Timms (see Source Notes).

Note

The list of other sources is too long for inclusion here, but I would like to acknowledge my great debt to both English and American social historians.

Source Notes

Chapter One

1. Friedrich Engels, *The Condition of the Working Class in England* (German ed. 1845), Blackwell, 1958.
2. *Royal Commission on the Aged Poor*, 1893–95, Qu. 10,356, Alfred Marshall; quoted J. H. Clapham, *An Economic History of Modern Britain*, Vol. 3, p. 416, C.U.P., 1951.
3. *C.O.S. Pamphlets* C86, quoted H.B., p. 53.
4. C. L. Mowat, *The Charity Organisation Society, 1869–1913*, p. 5, Methuen, 1961.
5. J. H. Clapham, *opus cit.* Vol. 3, p. 419. See also Mary Stocks, F.W.A. *Loch Memorial Lecture*, 1966: *Social Work Now and Yesterday*.
6. C. S. Loch. *Three Thousand Years of Social Service*, F.W.A., 1938, reprint of *Encyc. Brit.* 10th ed., *Charity*, C.S.L.
7. *The Solly Collection*, In the possession of the London School of Economics and Political Science, University of London.
8. M. Simey, *Charitable Effort in Liverpool in the Nineteenth Century*, Liverpool University Press, 1951.
9. V. Lipman, *A Century of Social Service*, Routledge, 1959.
10. J. C. Pringle, *Social Work of the London Churches*: A study of the Metropolitan Visiting and Relief Association, O.U.P., 1937.
11. K. Woodroofe, *From Charity to Social Work*, p. 9, Routledge & Kegan Paul, 1962.
12. K. Heasman, *Evangelicals in Action*, p. 196, Bles, 1962.
13. *C.O. Review*, Oct.–Nov., 1892, Lord Lichfield, in a *Letter to Dr Hawksley*, 1874, quoted H.B., p. 28.
14. Susan Tweedsmuir (Buchan), *The Lilac and the Rose*, pp. 87 ff., Duckworth, 1952; and E. M. Goldberg, *Welfare in the Community*, N.I.S.W.T., 1966.

Chapter Two

1. *Times*, 25th Jan. 1923, quoted C. L. Mowat, *The Charity Organisation Society*, 1869–1913, p. 172, Methuen, 1961.
2. *C.O. Quarterly*, April, 1923, E. C. Price.
3. *Diary*, 30th April, 1877.

4. *C.O. Quarterly*, 1934, Ilse van Arlt, *3rd Loch Memorial Lecture.*
5. C. L. Mowat, *Opus cit.*, p. 64.
6. *Diary*, 19th Sept., 1881.
7. *New Statesman*, 16th June, 1961, Richard Titmuss, Review of C. L. Mowat, *The Charity Organisation Society.*
8. *Social Work*, Jan. 1954, note by Mrs Mowat, and *C.O. Review*, Sept. 1912, C. S. Loch, *In Memoriam, Octavia Hill.*
9. C. L. Mowat, *Opus cit.*, p. 66.
10. *D.N.B.*, 1922–1930, *C. S. Loch*, R. B. Mowat.
11. *C.O. Review*, Oct. 1912, p. 222, C. S. Loch, *In Memoriam, Octavia Hill.*
12. *Diary*, 30th April, 1877.
13. Henrietta Barnett, *Canon Barnett, His Life, Work and Friends*, p. 659, John Murray, 1921.
14. *Diary*, 15th April, 1877.
15. *Diary*, 19th July, 1879.
16. *Diary*, 15th April, 1877.
17. N. Masterman, ed., *A Selection of passages and scenes*, Chalmers on Charity, Constable, 1900.
18. C. S. Loch, *Three Thousand Years of Social Service*, F.W.A., 1938, p. 345, reprint of *Encyc. Brit., Charity*, C.S.L. (11th ed. p. 885).
19. *Ibid.*, p. 346.
20. *C.O. Review*, Feb. 1913.
21. *D.N.B.*, 1922–30, *C. S. Loch*, R. B. Mowat.
22. E. Barker, *Political Thought from 1848–1914*, p. 31, Thornton Butterworth, 2nd ed., 1928.
23. *C.O. Review*, Feb. 1904, p. 67 (given as a paper to the C.O.S. Council, June, 1903).
24. *Diary*, 26th June, 1879.
25. *C.O. Review*, Feb. 1904, *Development of Charity Organisation.*
26. *Diary*, 14th Sept., 1876.
27. *Ibid.*
28. B. Bosanquet, *Philosophical Theory of the State*, p. 169 (4th ed., Macmillan, 1923), quoted C. L. Mowat, *Opus cit.*, p. 72.
29. *New Society*, 15th April, 1965, Donald MacRae, Review of *English Philanthropy*, D. Owen.
30. C. S. Loch, *Opus cit.*, p. 368.
31. *Diary*, 17th April, 1877.
32. *C.O. Review*, March 1913.
33. C. S. Loch, *Charity Organisation*, p. 4, Swan Sonnenschein, 3rd ed., 1905.
34. C. S. Loch, *Three Thousand Years of Social Service*, p. 400.
35. *Fabian Tract*, No. 54, 1894, J. F. Oakeshott. *The Human Urgency of the Poor Law*; see also *Tract* No. 158, 1911.
36. *Diary*, 23rd Sept., 1888.
37. *Diary*, 17th Sept., 1877.
38. Beatrice Webb, *My Apprenticeship*, Pelican, p. 335, Penguin Books, 1938.

39. C. S. Loch, *Opus cit.*, p. 396.
40. Beatrice Webb, *Opus cit.*, p. 222.
41. Beatrice Webb. *Opus cit.*, p. 223.
42. Beatrice Webb, *Opus cit.*, 223–4.
43. *Diary*, 30th Oct., 1877.
44. *Proceedings of Council*, 12th Oct., 1914, inset *The Reporter*, 1914, p. 348, C.O.S.
45. J. C. Pringle, *Fragments of the Case for Voluntary Social Service in a Planned Community*, C.O.S., 1935.
46. *Diary*, 17th Sept., 1877.
47. *D.N.B.*, 1923–30, *Charles Stewart Loch*, R. B. Mowat.
48. *Diary*, 14th April, 1883.

Chapter Three

1. *C.O.S. Provisional Rule*, 1869, quoted H.B., p. 53.
2. Goschen Minute, *Relief to the Poor in the Metropolis*, 20th Nov., 1869. George J. Goschen, President, Poor Law Board.
3. *O.P.*, No. 24.
4. Kensington and Lambeth, *An. Rpt.*, 1871.
5. C. S. Loch, *Report on Islington* made to C.O.S. Council, 6th Feb., 1882.
6. Marylebone, *An. Rpt.*, 1872.
7. Chelsea *An. Rpts.* 1901 to 1906.
8. Islington *An. Rpt.*, 1882–83.
9. Islington *An. Rpt.*, 1872.
10. *C.O.S. Pamphlets*, 1870–82.
11. Report of the *C.O.S. Committee on the Position of the District Committees*, 1872.
12. *Diary*, entry undated—inserted between entries for Nov. 1885 and Aug. 1886.
13. C.O.S. *An. Rpt.*, 1880, p.13.
14. *Ibid.*, 1880, p. 15.
15. *An. Rpts.* of the Council and District Committees: The example is taken from the year 1883–84, page 19.
16. C.O.S. *An. Rpt.*, 1877.
17. C. L. Mowat, *The Charity Organisation Society*, 1869–1913, p. 41, Methuen, 1961.
18. George Lansbury, Preface, *My Life*, Constable, 1928.
19. Lord Snell, *Men, Movements and Myself*, pp. 66 ff., Dent, 1936.
20. Poplar *An. Rpt.*, 1913.
21. *C.O. Review*, Feb. 1904, paper by C. S. Loch.
22. Islington *An. Rpt.*, 1882–83.
23. Islington 1st *An. Rpt.*, Jan. 1871–Sept. 1872.
24. *C.O. Review*, March 1904, p. 113.

Chapter Four

1. *Report of the Poor Law Board, 1869–70*, quoted Sidney and Beatrice Webb, *English Poor Law History*, Part II, Vol. I, p. 323, Longmans Green, 1929.
2. Fulham and Hammersmith *An. Rpt.*, 1883–84.
3. E. Moberly Bell, *The Story of the Hospital Almoner*, Faber, 1961.
4. C.O.S. *An. Rpt.*, 1912.
5. Chelsea *An. Rpt.*, 1907–8.
6. Chelsea *An. Rpt.*, 1908–9.
7. *O.P.* No. 58, 1st Series, 1896, by the Hon. Secretary of the Paddington Committee; *O.P.* No. 16, 3rd Series 1903, a reprint from a report by the Hackney Committee.
8. Margery J. Smith, *Professional Education for Social Work in Britain*, p. 38, published for the Pringle Memorial Fund by the F.W.A., 1952.
9. *C.O. Review*, New Series, Vol. XXXV, Jan. 1914, *What we mean by Inquiry*.
10. Chelsea *An. Rpt.*, 1909–10.
11. South-West Ham 1st *An. Rpt.*, 1907.
12. South-West Ham *An. Rpt.*, 1909.
13. St Marylebone *Skilled Employment Committee* 5th *An. Rpt.*, Oct. 1909, bound together with the *District Report* of that year.
14. Lewisham *An. Rpt.*, 1912.
15. *O.P.* 4th Series No. 28, 1912. See also *C.O. Review*, Dec. 1912.
16. *O.P.* 4th Series, No. 29, 1913, report by H. L. Woollcombe.

Chapter Five

1. C. B. P. Bosanquet, *The Charity Organisation Society*, p. 11, 1874.
2. *C.O.S. Pamphlets* 1870–82, W. H. Wilkinson, Feb. 1875, *A Contribution towards the History of the Origin of the C.O.S.*
3. C. L. Mowat, *The Charity Organisation Society*, 1869–1913, p. 56, Methuen, 1961.
4. H. Bosanquet, *Social Work in London*, p. 334, John Murray, 1914.
5. C.O.S. *An. Rpts.*, 1886 and 1887.
6. C.O.S. *An. Rpts.*, 1891.
7. C.O.S. *An. Rpt.*, 1924.
8. Hampstead *An. Rpt.*, 1925.
9. Young and Ashton, *British Social Work*, Chapter 10, Routledge & Kegan Paul, 1956, and M. Rooff, *Voluntary Societies and Social Policy*, Part IV, Routledge & Kegan Paul, 1957.
10. C.O.S. *An. Rpt.*, 1876, quoted H.B., p. 190.
11. C.O.S. *An. Rpt.*, 1877, and *The Reporter*, Vol. VI, pp. 57 and 62, C.O.S.
12. C.O.S. *An. Rpts.* for 1878 and 1879.
13. Report of the *C.O.S. Committee on The Education and Care of Idiots, Imbeciles and Harmless Lunatics*, 1877.

14. *Letter to C.O.S. from Lord Shaftesbury*, 1873, quoted H.B., p. 197 fn.
15. C.O.S. *An. Rpt.*, 1888.
16. *Letter from A. D. Graham to Loch*, C.O.S., June 1888, quoted H.B., p. 248.
17. *Ibid.*, p. 255.
18. *Resolution of the C.O.S. Council*, 17th March, 1871.
19. C.O.S. *An. Rpt.*, 1884–85.
20. H. Bosanquet, *Opus cit.*, p. 223.
21. U. M. Cormack, *The Welfare State, F. W. A. Loch Memorial Lecture*, 1953.
22. Elizabeth Macadam, *The Social Servant in the Making*, p. 23, Allen and Unwin, 1945.
23. C.O.S. *An. Rpt.*, 1873.
24. C.O.S. *An. Rpt.*, 1874.
25. C.O.S. *An. Rpt.*, 1875.
26. C.O.S. *An. Rpt.*, 1880.
27. C.O.S. *An. Rpt.*, 1881.

Chapter Six

1. C.O.S. *An. Rpt.*, 1917–18, p. 5.
2. North Lambeth *An. Rpt.*, p. 4.
3. C.O.S. *An. Rpt.*, 1920, p. 3.
4. C.O.S. *An. Rpt.*, 1919, p. 8.
5. Minutes of *C.O.S. Administrative Committee*, April 1918.
6. C.O.S. *An. Rpt.*, 1919, p. 4.
7. *O.P. V.* 15, W. A. Bailward, 1916.
8. *O.P. V.* 11, 1916.
9. *O.P. V.* 19, 1917.
10. *Ibid.*
11. *O.P. V.* 22, H. D. Oakeley, 1918.
12. C.O.S. *An. Rpt.*, 1918–19.
13. E. Lipson, *A Short Economic History*, p. 420, Black, 4th ed., 1959.

Chapter Seven

1. *C.O. Quarterly*, Vol. 12, July 1938, T. E. Lloyd, *Memoir on J. C. Pringle*, p. 121–24.
2. T. E. Lloyd, *Opus cit.*
3. C.O.S. *An. Rpts.*, 1926–30.
4. C.O.S. *An. Rpt.*, 1927.
5. J. C. Pringle, *Social Work of the London Churches*, p. 211 ff. A study of the Metropolitan Visiting and Relief Association, O.U.P., 1937.
6. *Opus cit.*, p. 214.
7. *C.O. Quarterly*, Vol. 5, 1931, pp. 176–77, R. V. Seymour, *Case-work*.
8. J. C. Pringle, *British Social Services: The Nation's Appeal to the Housewife and her Response* (Chapter 1). Longmans Green, 1933.

9. C.O.S. *An. Rpts.*, 1933–37.
10. *C.O. Quarterly*, Oct. 1931, p. 157.
11. Islington *An. Rpt.*, 1937–38, p. 4.
12. *Social Service Quarterly*, Summer 1963—Social Pioneers, Series No. 35, National Council of Social Service.

Chapter Eight

1. C. L. Mowat, *Britain Between the Wars*, Chapter IX, Methuen, 1955.
2. C.O.S. *An. Rpt.*, 1925–26, article by Pringle.
3. C.O.S. *An. Rpt.*, 1922–23, pp. 8 ff.
4. C.O.S. *An. Rpt.*, 1920–21.
5. C.O.S. *An. Rpt.*, 1919–20, p. 7.
6. C.O.S. *An Rpt.*, 1921–22.
7. Helen Bosanquet, *Strength of the People* p. 320, Macmillan, 1902.
8. L.C.C. Minutes *Public Assistance (General Purposes) Sub-Committee*, Vol. 2, 9th Nov., 1932, L.C.C. (later G.L.C.) Archives.
9. L.C.C. Rpt., of *General Purposes Sub-Committee*, 24th Oct., 1934, L.C.C. (later G.L.C.) Archives.
10. C.O.S. *An. Rpt.*, 1921–22, pp. 1–3.
11. C.O.S. *An. Rpt.*, 1920–21.
12. Islington *An. Rpt.*, 1922–23.
13. C. L. Mowat, *Opus cit.*, Chapter IV.
14. C.O.S. *An. Rpt.*, 1937, p. 14.
15. Islington *An. Rpt.*, 1931.
16. Fulham *An. Rpt.*, 1924–25.
17. C.O.S. *An. Rpts.*, 1924, 1925 and 1929.
18. C.O.S. *An. Rpt.*, 1929.
19. C.O.S. *An. Rpt.*, 1932.
20. C.O.S. *An. Rpt.*, 1935, p. 28.
21. Islington *An. Rpt.*, 1928–29.
22. Islington *An. Rpt.*, 1932–33.
23. East Lewisham *An. Rpt.*, 1937.
24. Lewisham *An. Rpt.*, 1931–32.
25. East Lewisham *An. Rpt.*, 1937.
26. *O.P.* No. 45, 5th Series, B. Astbury.
27. Islington *An. Rpt.*, 1937–38.
28. C.O.S. *An. Rpt.*, 1938.
29. *The Study of Society*, ed. F. C. Bartlett *et al.*, Ch. XV, p. 380, S. Clement Brown, *The Method of Social Case Workers*, Kegan Paul, Trench, Trubner, 1939.
30. *O.P.* No. 28, 5th Series, 1927, p. 5, *Lessons from Jung About Casework*, J. C. Pringle.
31. *C.O. Quarterly*, 1930, Olive Crosse, *American Experiences*.
32. E. J. Urwick, *The Principle of Reciprocity in Social Life and Action*, The Second Sir Charles Loch Memorial Lecture, C.O.S., 1930.
33. *C.O. Quarterly*, 1931, Vol. 5, *Ideals of Social Service*.

34. *C.O. Quarterly*, April 1931, G. A. Bompar, *Social Insurance and Social Work in the Home*.
35. C.O.S. *An. Rpt.*, 1938.
36. C.O.S. *An. Rpt.*, 1929–30.
37. *O.P.* No. 36, 5th Series, *A Re-statement of Case Work*.
38. Lambeth *An. Rpt.*, 1927–28, pp. 2–3.
39. *British Refugees from Spain Fund*, Report July, 1937, p. 41.

Chapter Nine

1. Elizabeth Macadam, *The Equipment of the Social Worker*, Allen and Unwin, 1925, *The New Philanthropy*, Allen and Unwin, 1934, and *The Social Servant in the Making*, Allen and Unwin, 1945.
2. *O.P.* No. 36, 5th Series, 1931.
3. *C.O.S. Pamphlet, The Homeless Man* (no date, probably 1935).
4. *Social Work*, April 1950, pp. 408–18.
5. C.O.S. *An. Rpt.*, 1939.
6. R. H. Titmuss, *Problems of Social Policy*, pp. 261–62, *History of the Second World War*, H.M.S.O. and Longmans, 1950.
7. C.O.S. *An. Rpt.*, 1939–40.
8. R. H. Titmuss, *Opus cit.*, p. 262, fn. 2.
9. C.O.S. *An. Rpt.*, 1942–43.
10. C.O.S. *An. Rpt.*, 1943–44.
11. R. H. Tuitmuss, *Opus cit.*, p. 262.
12. Wm. Beveridge, *Social Insurance and Allied Services*, Cmd. 6404, H.M.S.O., 1942.
13. Minutes of *F.W.A. Administrative Committee*, 10th May, 1956.
14. *Social Work*, Oct. 1946 and July 1948.
15. F.W.A. *An. Rpt.*, 1954–55.
16. Mary Stocks, *My Commonplace Book*, p. 187, Peter Davies, 1970.
17. F.W.A. *An. Rpt.*, 1956–57, p. 25.
18. U. M. Cormack, *Social Work*, 1941: reprinted as a pamphlet, April, 1941.

Chapter Ten

1. Wm. Beveridge, *Voluntary Action*, p. 277, Allen & Unwin, 1948.
2. *Silver Jubilee Report of the C.A.B.x in Central London*, 1963–64, p. 7, F.W.A.
3. R. M. Titmuss, *Problems of Social Policy*, p. 292, *History of the Second World War*, H.M.S.O. and Longmans, 1950.
4. C.O.S. Leaflet, *The Work of the Charity Organisation Society and Citizens Advice Bureaux*. 1st Oct., 1939–30th Sept., 1940.
5. *Ministry of Health* Circular to Local Authorities, Nov. 1945, and Beveridge, *Opus cit.*, p. 278.

6. *Report of the Committee on Legal Aid and Legal Advice*, Cmd. 6641, H.M.S.O., 1945.
7. Wm. Beveridge, *Opus cit.*, pp. 284–85.
8. *Social Work*, Vol. 2, No. 5, April 1943, *Function of interpretation in C.A.B. work.*
9. F.W.A. *An. Rpt.*, 1955–56, p. 11.
10. *Municipal Review*, May 1962, quoted F.W.A. *An. Rpt.*, 1964–65, p. 17.
11. *C.A.B.x in Central London*, 1960–61, F.W.A.
12. *Report of the Committee on Procedure in Matrimonial Causes*, Cmd. 7024, H.M.S.O., 1947.
13. *Report of the Departmental Committee on Grants for the Development of Marriage Guidance*, Cmd. 7566, H.M.S.O., 1948.
14. *Social Work*, Jan. 1951; E. Eichholz, *The Development of Family Discussion Bureaux.*
15. *Social Casework in Marital Problems*, Tavistock Publications Ltd., 1956, with a foreword by B. E. Astbury, F.W.A.
16. F.W.A. *An. Rpt.*, 1953–54.
17. F.W.A. *An. Rpt.*, 1956–57, p. 9.
18. *The Family: Patients or Clients*, p. 15, published for the F.W.A. by the Faith Press, 1961.
19. *Ibid.*, p. 16.
20. *Ibid.*, p. 68.
21. F.W.A. *An. Rpt.*, 1961–62.
22. *The Family: Patients or Clients*, Appendix III, pp. 77–132.
23. ed. S. K. Ruck, *The West Indian Comes to England*, a report prepared for the Trustees of the London Parochial Charities by F.W.A., Routledge & Kegan Paul, 1960.
24. ed. S. K. Ruck, *Opus cit.*, Pt. III.
25. ed. S. K. Ruck, *Opus cit.*, pp. 67–68.
26. *Ministry of Health* Circular 27/54, H.M.S.O., 1954.
27. F.W.A. *General Minutes Book*, pp. 248 and 249, Oct. 1951.
28. *Ibid.*, Nov. 1951.
29. *Guide to the Social Services*, p. 13, F.W.A., 1967.
30. F.W.A. *An. Rpt.*, 1962–63, p. 8.
31. *Social Work*, Oct. 1960, article by K. Wells, F.W.A.
32. *New Society*, 27th Oct., 1966.

Chapter Eleven

1. C.O.S. *An. Rpt.*, 1901–02, quoted H.B., p. 86.
2. M. Cunliffe, *Review of the Family Welfare Association*, p. 48, F.W.A. (unpublished) report, 1960.
3. C.O.S. *An. Rpt.*, 1912–13, p. 2.
4. *St George's* C.O.S. *Letter to Central*, 26th March, 1870, quoted H.B., pp. 37–38.
5. C.O.S. *An. Rpt.*, 1897–98, quoted H.B., p. 85.
6. C.O.S. *Council Minutes* with Minutes of the *Administrative Committee* and Minutes of the *Districts Sub-Committee*, 1916.

7. C.O.S. *Report of Secretaries' Meetings*, June 5th, 1916–December 17th, 1920.
8. F.W.A. *An. Rpt.*, 1959–60.
9. *Case Conference*, Vol. 14, No. 1, May, 1967, article by Patricia Daniel, ed. Kay McDougall.

Chapter Twelve

1. *O.P.* 1st Series, No. 46, reprinted from the *C.O. Review*, Jan. 1895.
2. C.O.S. *An. Rpt.*, 1895–96 (pub. 1897).
3. Marjorie J. Smith, *Professional Education for Social Work in Britain*, p. 16, published by F.W.A., 1952, for *Pringle Memorial Fund*.
4. *O.P.* second series, No. 11.
5. *O.P.* third series, No. 3.
6. Elizabeth Macadam, *The Social Servant in the Making*, p. 23, Allen and Unwin, 1945.
7. C.O.S. *Minutes of Council*, 20th July, 1903, M. Smith, *Opus cit.*, p. 30.
8. *C.O.S. Pamphlets*, 1895, 1907.
9. M. Smith, *Opus cit.*, p. 36.
10. Helena Reid, *The Application of C.O.S. Principles to Present Conditions*, *C.O.S. Pamphlet*, 1923.
11. M. Ashdown and S. C. Brown, *Social Service and Mental Health*, Routledge, 1953, and N. Timms, *Psychiatric Social Work in Great Britain*, Routledge, 1964.
12. Eileen L. Younghusband, *Report on the Employment and Training of Social Workers*, Carnegie United Kingdom Trust, 1947.
13. Eileen Younghusband, *Social Work in Britain*, Carnegie United Kingdom Trust, 1951, and *Report of the Working Party on Social Workers in the Local Authority Health and Welfare Services*, H.M.S.O., 1959.
14. J. E. Mayer and N. Timms, *The Client Speaks*, Routledge, 1970.
15. H. F. Philp and N. Timms, *The Problem of the Problem Families*, Family Service Units, 1957.
16. *The Study of Society*, ed. F. C. Bartlett, M. Ginsberg, E. J. Lindgren and R. H. Thouless, Part IV, Chapter XV, S. Clement Brown, Kegan Paul, Trench, Trubner, 1939.
17. *The West Indian Comes to England*, ed. S. K. Ruck, Routledge & Kegan Paul, 1960.
18. *The Family: Patients or Clients*, published for the F.W.A. by the Faith Press, 1961.
19. *Family Casework and the Country Dweller*, ed. A. V. Lochhead, published for the Carnegie United Kingdom Trust by the F.W.A., 1951.
20. Marjorie J. Smith, *Opus cit.*
21. *Case Conference*, Vol. 1, No. 1, May 1954, ed. Kay McDougall (later published jointly by the Association of Social Workers and Case Conference Ltd.).

22. Noel Timms, *Psychiatric Social Work in Great Britain*, 1939–62, Routledge & Kegan Paul, 1964, and *Social Casework, Principles and Practice*, Routledge & Kegan Paul, 1964.
23. *Nuffield College Report*, 1946, *Training for Social Work*.
24. *Case Conference*, April 1964, E. H. Davison, *The Contribution of the Case Work Agencies*.

Chapter Thirteen

1. C. Ribton-Turner, *Suggestions for Systematic Enquiry into Cases of Distress*. C.O.S. (no date), before May 1872).
2. C.O.S. *Pamphlets* C.86, 1870, quoted H. Bosanquet, *Social Work in London*, p. 53–4, John Murray, 1914.
3. C.O.S. *Council*, Discussion, Feb. 1877, *Personal Work among the Poor*, etc., quoted H.B., p. 55.
4. C.O.S. *Report of Committee*, 1877, *A Re-consideration of Pamphlet C. 86*, quoted H.B., p. 56.
5. O.P. No. 46, Mrs Dunn Gardner, 1894.
6. O.P. No. 11 second series, 1898, and M. J. Smith, *Professional Education for Social Work in Britain*, published by F.W.A., 1952, for *Pringle Memorial Fund*.
7. O.P. No. 25, 4th Series, K. Lawrance, *The Importance of Good Casework*.
8. C.O.S. *An. Rpt.*, 1912–13.
9. C.O.S. *Records of Secretaries' Meetings*, 1919.
10. C.O. *Quarterly*, July 1922, Miss E. F. Bolton.
11. O.P. 36, 5th Series.
12. *The Family Welfare Association*, pamphlet issued 1956–57, by the F.W.A.
13. H. Dendy (Bosanquet), *Thorough Charity*, p. 4, C.O.S. *Pamphlet*, 1893.
14. *The Long View*, Russell Sage Foundation, p. 574, quoted Patricia H. Todd, *Case Conference*, Vol. 5, No. 4, Sept. 1958.
15. O.P. No. 28, paper originally read in 1876 on *District Visiting*.
16. Quoted Noel Timms *Social Casework*, p. 18, Routledge & Kegan Paul, 1964, from H. Bosanquet, *The Standard of Life*, 1898.
17. E. M. Goldberg, *Welfare in the Community*, p. 22, N.I.S.W.T., 1966.
18. Octavia Hill, O.P. No. 15, 1st Series, 1889.
19. C.O.S. *An. Rpt.*, 1905, p. 33.
20. *The Prevention and Relief of Distress*, C. S. Loch, *Principles and Methods of Charity* (Handbooks), P. S. King and C.O.S.
21. H. Dendy (Bosanquet), *Opus cit.*, p. 4
22. C.O. *Review*, Vol. XXXV, pp. 14–15, *What we mean by Enquiry*.
23. *British Journal of Psychiatric Social Work*, Vol. VI, 1962, No. 4.
24. O.P. No. 46, 1st Series, 1894.
25. C.O.S. *Administrative Committee Minutes*, Vol. 59, 13th Dec., 1928.
26. C.O. *Quarterly*, July 1932, *Some Observations of a C.O.S. Worker*.

27. *C.O. Quarterly*, 1928, G. E. Elliott, *Who shall 'scape Whipping?*
28. Noel Timms, *Social Casework*, p. 32, Routledge & Kegan Paul, 1964, and *Casework in the Child Care Service*, Butterworth, 1962.
29. Noel Timms, *Social Casework*, p. 44, quoting Perlman, *Social Casework—a Problem-Solving Process.*
30. *C.O. Review*, Vol. XLIII, New Series, Jan.–June 1918, p. 5.
31. *Social Work*, April 1946, letter from Una Cormack.
32. Barbara Wootton, *Social Science and Social Pathology*, p. 291, Allen & Unwin, 1959, and *In a World I Never Made*, Allen & Unwin, 1967.
33. Una Cormack, *Opus cit.*
34. *Social Work*, Oct. 1958 and Jan.–April 1959.
35. *The Family: Patients or Clients*, published for the F.W.A. by the Faith Press, 1961, and *Social Work*, Jan. 1967, p. 21, Malcolm Ford.
36. David Donnison, *Social Policy and Social Administration*, Ch. 11, Allen & Unwin, 1965.
37. F.W.A. *An. Rpt.*, 1953–54, p. 9.
38. *Social Work*, Oct. 1953 (Report of F.W.A. Reorganisation).
39. Muriel A. Cuncliffe, *Review of the Family Welfare Association*, F.W.A. (unpublished) Report, 1960.
40. *Case Conference*, Vol. 13, No. 1, May 1966, *An Adventure in Staff Development and Administration*, M. P. Daniel.

Chapter Fourteen

1. *Case Conference*, Vol. 14, No. 4, p. 133.
2. Strand *An. Rpt.*, 1880, p. 10.
3. C.O.S. *An. Rpt.*, 1905, p. 19.
4. Helen Bosanquet, *Social Work in London*, pp. 79–80, John Murray, 1914.
5. Stepney and Mile End with St Georges-in-the-East *An. Rpt.*, 1925, p. 4.
6. *C.O. Review*, April 1913.
7. Hammersmith District *An. Rpt.*, 1941–42.
8. *Social Work*, July 1962, Obituary notice by U. Malleson.
9. C.O.S. *Administrative Committee*, 29th May, 1919, p. 261.
10. *C.O. Quarterly*, Vol. 6, 1932, pp. 98.
11. *C.O.S. Council*, Nov. 1879, quoted H.B., p. 65
12. C.O.S. *An. Rpt.*, 1895, p. 43.
13. St Saviour's (Southwark) *An. Rpt.*. 1900, p. 10.
14. Hammersmith *An. Rpt.*, 1900, p. 8.
15. C.O.S. *An. Rpt.*, 1900, p. 2.
16. *Ibid.*, p. 6.
17. *O.P.* Second Series, No. 11.
18. *C.O. Review*, Feb. 1904, p. 64.
19. C.O.S. *Administrative Council Minutes*, 7th April, 1919, and *Minutes of Secretaries' Meetings.*

20. Violet Markham, *Return Passage*, p. 60, Oxford University Press, 1953.
21. C.O.S. *An. Rpt.*, 1918–19.
22. C.O.S. *An. Rpt.*, 1911, p. 24.
23. C.O.S. *An. Rpt.*, 1920–21, p. 3.
24. *C.O. Quarterly*, Vol. 6, April 1932, article by Miss Kellaney.
25. *C.O.S. Reporter*, 1905, p. 33, *Death of Mr Mocatta*.
26. *Letters from Mocatta to Loch* written in the 1880s and '90s, quoted D. Owen, *English Philanthropy*, p. 427, London, O.U.P., 1965 (Cambridge, Massachusetts, Harvard University Press).
27. *C.O. Review*, Feb. 1905, p. 106.
28. E. Moberley Bell, *Octavia Hill*, pp. 107–15, Constable, 1942.
29. *C.O. Review*, Sept. and Oct. 1912. C. S. Loch, *In Memoriam*.
30. *C.O. Review*, Jan. 1895, *The Training of Volunteers*, later published as *O.P.* No. 46.
31. *Social Work*, Oct. 1953, Chap. 14, p. 853, E. F. Bolton, *Pioneers of Family Casework*, Sophia Lonsdale.
32. *O.P.* No. 27, 5th Series, 1924. *What does the C.O.S. Do? Come and See.*
33. *Social Work*, *Opus cit.*, p. 857.
34. *Social Work*, July 1953, p. 832.
35. F.W.A. Area III *An. Rpt.*, 1949–50, p. 11.
36. *Ibid.*
37. *Social Work*, April 1951, pp. 543–44.
38. *O.P.* No. 22, Fourth Series.
39. *O.P.* No. 14, Fifth Series.
40. *Social Work*, Jan. 1955, *In Memoriam*.
41. *O.P.* No. 25, Fourth Series.
42. *Indianopolis C.O.S., 1891*, Octavia Hill, *A Plea for Justice*.
43. H. Morris, *Notes on the Misses Barber*, Manuscript, 1967.
44. Chelsea and Fulham *An. Rpt.*, 1946–47.
45. *O.P.* No. 3, Third Series, Helen (Dendy) Bosanquet, *Methods of Training*.
46. *C.O. Quarterly*, July 1925.
47. *C.O. Quarterly*, April 1923.
48. *The Spectator*, 13th March, 1922, B. Bosanquet, *A Necessary Social Function*.
49. Islington *An. Rpt.*, 1917 and 1921.
50. Whitechapel *An. Rpt.*, 1925.
51. Hampstead *An. Rpt.*, 1925.
52. C.O.S. *An. Rpt.*, 1925.
53. Area I *An. Rpt.*, 1950, p. 5.
54. Kensington *An. Rpt.*, 1915, p. 9.
55. Chelsea and Fulham *An. Rpt.*, 1945, p. 4.
56. *Cunliffe Report*, p. 79, 1960, F.W.A. (unpublished).
57. *Crucible*, Oct. 1963, The Lady Norman, *The Lay Committees and the Professional Worker*.
58. E. J. Urwick, *Loch Memorial Lecture*, 1930, p. 11.
59. Cunliffe, *Opus cit.*, pp. 79–80.

Chapter Fifteen

1. *C.O.S.* Minutes of the *First Meeting of the Executive Council*, 22nd April, 1869, F.W.A. Archives.
2. *C.O.S.* Minutes, 20th Jan., 1869, quoted H.B., p. 22.
3. *C.O.S. Sub-Committee Report*, Dec. 1869, quoted H.B., p. 22.
4. C.O.S. *An. Rpt.* 1887, quoted C. L. Mowat, *The Charity Organisation Society, 1869–1913*, pp. 86 and 87, Methuen, 1961.
5. *Ibid.*
6. C.O.S. *An. Rpt.*, 1913–14, p. xxix.
7. H. Bosanquet, *Opus cit.*, pp. 78–9.
8. F.W.A. *An. Rpt.*, 1966–67, p. 13.

Chapter Sixteen

1. H. Bosanquet, *Social Work in London*, p. 116, John Murray, 1914.
2. C.O.S. Annual Meeting, March 1876, quoted H.B., p. 124.
3. *The New Age*, 1888, *An Exposure of the Charity Organisation Society*, quoted H.B., p. 137 and pp. 123–31 *passim*.
4. G. Lansbury, *My Life*, pp. 129 ff., Constable, 1928.
5. North West Ham *An. Rpt.*, 1909.
6. Clement R. Attlee, *The Social Worker*, p. 64. G. Bell and Sons, 1920. See also reply in *C.O. Quarterly* (New Series, Vol. XLVII, Jan.–June, 1920).
7. Henry Snell, *Men, Movements and Myself*, pp. 80 ff., Dent, 1936.
8. Beatrice Webb, *My Apprenticeship*, p. 222, Pelican ed., Penguin Books, 1938.
9. *C.O. Review*, May 1904, pp. 236 ff.
10. *Quarterly Review*, 1907, W. A. Bailward, published as pamphlet, *The Charity Organisation Society*, 1907.
11. *Fabian Tract* No. 158, 1911, *The Case Against the C.O.S.*
12. Violet Markham, *Return Passage*, pp. 66 ff., O.U.P., 1953.
13. *C.O. Review* 1912, 30th Jan. and letters 7th, Feb., 10th Feb. and 14th Feb.; Violet Markham's letter to *The Spectator* was dated 20th Jan., quoted C. L. Mowat, *The Charity Organisation Society, 1869–1913*, p. 167, Methuen, 1961.
14. *Royal Commission on the Aged Poor*, 1893–95, Minutes of Evidence, qu. 10, 210, J. M. Keynes, ed. *Alfred Marshall, Official Papers*, p. 203, 1926.
15. Henrietta Barnett, *Canon Barnett, His Life, Work and Friends*, pp. 658–61, John Murray, 1921.
16. *Ibid.*, p. 657.
17. Review in the *Daily News*, 20th April, 1894.
18. L. Marson, *Charity Organisation and Jesus Christ*, p. 33, quoted D. Owen, *English Philanthropy*, p. 215, O.U.P., 1965.
19. Barbara Wootton, *In A World I Never Made*, p. 189, Allen & Unwin, 1967.

20. E. Macadam, *The Social Servant in the Making*, p. 62, Allen & Unwin, 1945.
21. *C.O. Quarterly*, July 1923, Mrs H. Reid.
22. C.O.S. *Minutes Administrative Committee*, Vol. 64, 18th Dec., 1941.

Appendix

1. *O.P.*, 1927, Vol. 29.
2. *C.O. Quarterly*, Oct. 1927, *Who Should 'scape Whipping*, Gilbert Elliott.
3. *C.O. Quarterly*, Jan. 1928, Letter from E. O. Legatt of the Western Group of C.O. Committees.
4. *Social Work*, Oct. 1949, *Two Sides of the Picture*.
5. Holborn, Finsbury and City *An. Rpt.*, 1937–38, p. 5.
6. East Lewisham *An. Rpt.*, 1936–37. Hon. Organising Sec. Miss W. Locket.
7. Islington *An. Rpt.*, 1932–33, p. 6.
8. *Social Work*, Oct. 1948.
9. *Ibid.*, Jan. and July, 1949.
10. Area VI *An. Rpt.*, Oct. 1951–March 1953.
11. *Ibid.* Introduction to the record of the Kirk Family.
12. *Social Work*, July 1954. *A Case History from a Family Agency*.
13. *The Family: Patients or Clients*, preface by Mrs Godfrey, published for the F.W.A. by the Faith Press, 1961.
14. *Opus cit.*, Appendix III, pp. 77–9.
15. F.W.A. *An. Rpt.*, 1966–67, pp. 5–6.
16. J. E. Mayer and Noel Timms, *The Client Speaks*, Routledge, 1970.

Conclusion

1. Barbara Wootton, *Social Science and Social Pathology*, 1959, Ch. 9, Contemporary Attitudes in Social Work, Allen & Unwin, 1959.
2. *Social Work*, Vol. 25, No. 2, April 1968, p. 2.
3. David Hobman, *You and your Job*, The Observer, 21st March, 1971.
4. Martin Shaw, *Scarce Resources and the Social Worker*, Casework, Oct. 1967.
5. William Beveridge, *Unemployment a Problem of Industry*, Longmans, 1909, and *Voluntary Action*, p. 146, Allen & Unwin, 1948.
6. *British Journal of Psychiatric Social Work*, Vol. VIII, 1966, No. 4, p. 4, D. V. Donnison, *Social Work and Social Change*.
7. David Owen, *English Philanthropy*, p. 236, O.U.P., 1965.

Abbreviations

C.O.S.	Charity Organisation Society
F.W.A.	Family Welfare Association
C.O. Review	*Charity Organisation Review*
C.O. Quarterly	*Charity Organisation Quarterly*
O.P.	C.O.S. *Occasional Paper*
Diary	*Diary* kept by C. S. Loch, 1876–88
An. Rpt.	*Annual Report* (of District or of C.O.S./F.W.A.)
D.N.B.	*Dictionary of National Biography*
Encyc. Brit.	*Encyclopaedia Britannica*
N.I.S.W.T.	National Institute for Social Work Training
H.B.	Helen Bosanquet, *Social Work in London,* John Murray, 1914.

Index

Mental Health—*cont.*
  examples, *see* Appendix
  mentioned, 241
  see also Medical Aid
Metropolitan Visiting and Relief
  Association, 29, 124, 131
Middlesex County Council, 199
Mill, J. S., 27
Milnes, Mrs, 132, 262, 327
Mocatta, F. D., 256, 286
Montefiore, Colonel, 106, 275
Moral Welfare Workers, 268
Morris, Cherry, 243
Morris, Sir Francis, 140
Morris, Honor, 284, 293
Morris, Sir Parker, 191, 192
Morton, Miss T. M., 87, 103, 148
Mowat, Charles Loch, 36, 37, 49,
  215, 309

Napier and Ettrick, Lord, 109
National Association for Mental
  Health, 207, 209
National Association for the Care
  of the Feeble-minded, 100
National Council of Social Service,
  117, 118, 183, 186, 229
National Health Insurance, 144,
  148
National Health Service, 104, 179,
  198, 266, 361
National Institute for Social Work
  Training, 49, 230, 244, 248
National Union of Women
  Workers, 236, 237
Neville, Edith, 289–91; *mentioned*,
  280
New Society, 212, 232
New Statesman, 324, 328
Norman, R. C., 186
North America, *see* America and
  Canada
Nottingham, 206
Nursing Associations, *see* Medical
  Aid

Owen, David, 41, 42, 302, 364

Paget, Dr Luke, 169
Peckham Health Centre, 195
Peek Enquiry, 274
Perlman, H., 261
Personal Service Association, 280
Personal Service League, 72
Peters, Frank, 37, 41
Peters, Sophia (Loch), 41
Pincus, Mrs Lily, 195
Political and Economic Planning
  (P.E.P.) Reports, 83
Poor Law
  C.O.S., 53–6 *passim*
  Goschen Minute, 47, 53–4, 131,
    141
  Royal Commission on the Poor
    Laws, 38, 108, 141, 296, 321,
    363
  mentioned, 24, 26, 61, 70, 71, 143,
    219
  see also Family Welfare Associa-
    tion
Poor Man's Valuer Service, 175,
  188
Poverty, 24–28 *passim*, 46, 47, 56,
  70, 73, 93, 96, 135, 143, 250,
  252, 286, 326, 356, 357
Price, E. C., 296
Pringle, J. Christian, Chapter 7
  admirer of Loch, 36, 50, 125
  conservatism, 322, 357
  E. Neville, 289
  ideas
    on casework, 254
    on fragmentation, 127, 134
    on psychology, 156
  L.C.C., 141, 152
  Memorial fund for, 133 244
  on Denison, 28
  publications, 124
  support for Astbury, 170
  mentioned, 120, 148, 228, 253
Probation Officers
  C.O.S./F.W.A. cooperation, 149,
    268, 357
  F.D.B., 196, 198
  Home Office courses, 248
  mentioned, 208, 241